Christian Music

Christian Music
A Global History

Tim Dowley

FORTRESS PRESS
Minneapolis

CHRISTIAN MUSIC
A Global History

Fortress Press Edition: 2011

Cover image: *Choir Performing* © O'Brien Productions/Brand X Pictures/Getty Images; Angels' Concert, Isenheim Altar, Erich Lessing / Art Resource, NY; Thomaskirche, Leipzig, Germany, Vanni / Art Resource, NY
Cover design: Joe Vaughan

Library of Congress Cataloging-in-Publication Data available

ISBN 978-0-8006-9841-6

Manufactured in China

16   15   14   13   12   11   1   2   3   4   5   6   7   8   9   10

Contributors

Revd Sugu J. M. Chandy is presbyter of the Church of South India at Kottayam, India.

Dr J. Nathan Corbitt is Professor of Cross-Cultural Studies at Eastern University, Pennsylvania, USA, and President and co-founder of BuildaBridge International. His research into African Christian music began in 1979 in Malawi, and he served as a music consultant in eastern and southern Africa from 1982 to 1992.

Dr Mark Evans is Associate Professor and Head of Department of Media, Music, and Cultural Studies at Macquarie University, New South Wales, Australia.

Dr Ivan Moody is a composer, conductor, and priest of the Greek Orthodox Church, and researcher at CESEM (*Centro de Estudos de Sociologia e Estética Musical*), Universidade Nova, Lisbon, Portugal.

Revd Dr Michael Nai-Chiu Poon is Director and Asian Christianity Co-ordinator at the Centre for the Study of Christianity in Asia, Trinity Theological College, Singapore.

Pablo Sosa, of the Protestant Institute for Higher Theological Studies (ISEDET), is Professor of Choral Conducting at Carlos Lopez Buchardo National Conservatory of Music, Buenos Aires, Brazil.

Dr Angela C. C. Tam is Professor of Church Music, Alliance Bible Seminary, Hong Kong, and editor of the bilingual hymnal *Hymns of Universal Praise*.

Mike Wheeler is an adult education tutor from Derby, England.

♫ **For Juliet, David, and William**

Contents

Foreword

The prospect of writing a new popular history of Christian music of all eras, all regions, and all varieties appeared very alluring when I was first invited to undertake this project. It seems no less attractive at the finish of the assignment; but I am now even more conscious of the huge gaps in my knowledge. Fortunately I have been able to call upon the expertise of a team of scholars and musicians worldwide who have been able to shed light on continents outside Europe and traditions outside the Western. I am most grateful to them: the old adage applies to them – if you want to get a job done professionally and rapidly, go to the busy person!

Nevertheless I am all too aware there remain omissions in this book. Within a relatively short account, it has been possible only to sketch in the extraordinary breadth of musical expressions of Christians of different centuries, classes, colours, and traditions. I have done all I can to avoid the text becoming a mere listing of names and compositions, but have on occasion had to summarize information in order to cover a particular topic adequately. I am also aware that, despite rigorous checking and recourse to a number of scholars, there remain unintended and probably embarrassing errors and misstatements: I apologize for these and would hope to regularize them in future editions.

The reader will soon become aware of continuing themes in Christians' experience of music. Again and again believers have debated how to define "Christian music". Is it solely music used in Christian worship? Music by Christian composers? Music using Christian themes or Christian texts and lyrics? Or music which moves the listener and expresses spirituality? Are there, conversely, forms of music that are essentially unchristian and therefore to be shunned by believers? Is rock "of the devil"? Should Christians sing the blues? Within the area of Christian worship: should hymns and psalms be sung unaccompanied – or is organ/piano/band accompaniment permissible and/or scriptural? Such questions recur and are currently still debated.

My thanks to four commissioning editors at Lion Publishing: Morag Reeve, who originally commissioned this book; Stephanie Heald, who encouraged it on its way; and Kate Kirkpatrick and Ali Hull who finally took it from typescript to published book.

My first major task in publishing, more than thirty years ago, was to commission and edit the *Lion Handbook to the History of Christianity*, something I look back on with some pride but also with astonishment at the audacity of youth. Now, further on in my career, I have enjoyed writing another survey volume, and hope it may find wide acceptance.

Tim Dowley
Dulwich, London
December 2010

The mosaic-decorated domes of the Basilica of San Marco (St Mark's), Venice, Italy, where, particularly during the seventeenth and eighteenth centuries, distinguished and distinctive music was created.

CHAPTER 1

Before the Church: The Jewish Musical Tradition

Jubal… was the father of all such as handle the harp and organ.

Genesis 4:21, KJV

Left: Detail of King David playing his harp, from *The Adoration of the Holy Trinity* (1511), also known as the Landauer Altarpiece, by German artist Albrecht Dürer (1471–1528), now in the Kunsthistorisches Museum, Vienna, Austria. David's harp is, of course, not depicted with historical accuracy.
Below: A nineteenth-century Bible illustrator's conception of the silver trumpets (*khatsotsrah*) blown by Jewish priests in biblical times.

We cannot start seriously to discuss the music of the Christian church without first looking at what is known of the music of the ancient world, and particularly the music of ancient Israel. Just as, for Christians, the New Testament cannot fully be understood without a knowledge of the Old Testament, in the same way the music of Christianity and the church cannot properly be understood without at least some knowledge of the music of the ancient Jewish people.

We start with a major disadvantage. For obvious reasons, we possess no recorded music from two millennia ago; nor do we have any contemporary notated music that might give some indication of how ancient music sounded. The nineteenth-century German musicologist Ambros bewailed the fact that "we did not have the opportunity of listening to [ancient music] for even one minute in order to be able to judge its sound". There are a few written records concerning music, but apart from these we are reliant on interpreting the evidence derived from stone, clay, metal, and bone artefacts discovered by archaeologists.

Until very recently, most historians have based their researches into the music of ancient Israel almost solely upon the written evidence available in the Jewish Scriptures. However, modern scholarship has widened this methodology, by first investigating and interrogating the evidence of archaeology and then allowing the fruits of that research to

qualify and interpret the evidence of the Old Testament (and the New).

Despite the researches of seekers after "authentic" performance, even for relatively recent composers such as Bach and Beethoven we are still far from confident in understanding exactly how their musical compositions were originally performed and how they might have sounded to, and been experienced by, contemporary listeners. How much more shaky is our knowledge of, for instance, the harmonies made by King David on his "harp" or the sound of the musicians in King Solomon's famed Temple.

While musicologists generally agree that the ancient Jewish musical tradition lies somewhere at the roots of modern Jewish synagogue music, some ethnomusicologists have ventured to suggest that modern Jewish communities in Iraq (ancient Babylon) and Yemen may have preserved something of the actual ancient Jewish

Above: The Idolatry of Solomon by the Italian artist Sebastiano Conca (1676/80–1764) illustrates music-making at the decadent court of Solomon's later years, though with little historical verisimilitude.
Right: Relief from Sennacherib's palace, Nineveh c. 700 BC, depicting prisoners from Israel/Palestine playing the lyre (British Museum).

sounds, since they were relatively insulated both from non-Jewish communities and from the Western musical tradition. However, this seems unlikely, as these Jewish communities can hardly have failed to have been influenced over many succeeding centuries, for instance by Islamic music – not least by the all-pervasive voice of the *muezzin*, calling the faithful to prayer from the minaret of the mosque.

In any event, since much of the musical experience of the ancient world was never entrusted to writing but passed on solely by word of mouth, we must resign ourselves to the fact that our knowledge of ancient music will almost certainly remain fragmentary and incomplete. As one musicologist has pointed out, the problem is that not only do we have no means of reproducing acoustically the music of ancient Israel, but nor can we recreate with any accuracy the social and psychological situations of ancient times. In our world of aural contamination and abuse, where even in the depths of the countryside we can be assaulted by the roar of helicopters and jet planes and the dull rumble of road traffic, it is difficult to imagine a tranquil past where the blasting of a goat's horn or the soft rustling of ornaments worn on a woman's ankles could exert a significant musical impact on listeners.

As we have mentioned, until recently most scholars writing on the music of ancient Israel relied almost exclusively on the biblical texts. However, even at early stages, linguistic misunderstandings and misinterpretations were introduced – for example in the third or second century BC, when the Hebrew of the Jewish Scriptures was translated into Greek in the version we know as the Septuagint (LXX). In this translation, and in later biblical translations such as the Syriac *Peshitta*, translators often confused the names of musical instruments. By contrast the later Latin translation of the Hebrew Bible, overseen by the Christian writer Jerome (c. 347–420) in the early fifth century and known as the Vulgate, is considerably more consistent in its naming of ancient musical instruments.

In addition to the biblical texts, a few Roman writers shed some light on Jewish music of the Roman period, while the Jewish holy writings known as the Mishnah and the Talmud, dating to the second to sixth centuries AD, offer several descriptions relevant to this music, though not always of great historical accuracy. (For instance, they mention an instrument found in Jerusalem called the *magrephah*, which was allegedly capable of producing a thousand tones and of being heard more than ten miles away in the city of Jericho.)

The early translators of the Bible into English made similar anachronistic and linguistic errors. John Wycliffe's translation imported a "hurdy-gurdy" into Luke 15:25 (c. 1385); William Tyndale (1526) introduced the "fiddle"; the Geneva Bible (1560) mentions the "dulcimer"; and the Authorized (King James) Version (1611) names the "organ", the "viol", and other seventeenth-century musical instruments.

Two Renaissance writers were the first in more modern times systematically to survey ancient Jewish music. A Jewish doctor, Avraham Portaleone (1547–1612), from Mantua in Italy, attempted to research the music of the ancient Jewish Temple in Jerusalem. However, like many of the early Old Testament translators, he introduced a chronological fallacy by translating a number of the ancient Hebrew words for instruments with the names of instruments from his own time. For instance, the Hebrew *minnîm* Portaleone translated anachronistically as "clavichord", and the *'ûgab* as the "viola da gamba". Unfortunately his flawed precedent was followed by most other writers on the subject for the next three centuries.

The second early modern writer on Jewish music, the German Protestant musician Michael Praetorius (c. 1571–1621), provided more accurate descriptions of musical instruments of Bible times, but reinforced the prevailing misplaced sole reliance on written sources by asserting that "in Palestine, Asia Minor and Greece, no more vestiges of older instruments exist" – a statement modern archaeologists have refuted.

However, despite these problems of translating obscure Hebrew words for musical instruments (the Greek Septuagint, for instance, translates the single Hebrew word *kinnôr* variously as *kithára*, *kin´yra*, *psaltérion*, and *órganon*), the Old Testament in its original Hebrew remains the single most important written source for music in ancient Israel. It provides, for example, vivid descriptions of the 288 musicians

whom the chronicler mentions as leading King David's procession to conduct the sacred Ark of the Covenant into the city of Jerusalem (1 Chronicles 15:16–28), and of the musicians – most importantly trumpeters – who performed at the dedication of King Solomon's Temple (2 Chronicles 5:12–14). Other useful textual sources, interpreted carefully, include Jewish and Christian apocryphal texts and some writings of the early Church Fathers. Scholars have also been able usefully to compare evidence about music from parallel cultures such as Sumeria and Ugarit to throw light on the music of ancient Israel and have utilized archaeological evidence gained from the numerous excavations in the Near East.

♫ Musical Instruments of the Bible

There remain many difficulties in understanding the Hebrew terms for musical instruments mentioned in the Bible. For instance, it is still today unclear how to translate the word for the Hebrew instrument known as the *'ûgab*, while the *nebel* is another instrument much argued over. Bearing in mind these difficulties, we will look at the main musical instruments mentioned in the Jewish Scriptures – the Christian "Old Testament".

Khalil[1]

The Hebrew word *khalil* means a type of pipe – not a laterally held flute-like instrument – and appears in the Old Testament in connection with celebrations surrounding the anointing of a new king and following a military victory. The *khalil* is also linked with prophetic ecstasy, was used during Jewish ritual lament, and featured both in the Jerusalem Temple "orchestra" – which was supposed to include between two and twelve of these instruments – and also at some animal sacrifices, on pilgrimages, and at burials. The *khalil* seems to have been an oboe-like instrument, made of reed or bone, or sometimes of bronze or copper, with a single or double reed (like the modern clarinet or oboe respectively). Some musicologists believe double-pipe, double-reed instruments were the most common wind instruments of the ancient Near East.

Khatsotsrah

This instrument is mentioned thirty-one times in the Old Testament, including Numbers 10:2–10,[2] where God instructs the great Jewish leader Moses to "make two trumpets of hammered silver, and use them for calling the community together…" (v. 2, NIV). From this time the *khatsotsrah* was reserved for the sole use of priests

and blown to summon the Jewish people at religious festivals, during the transport of the sacred Ark of the Covenant, and in time of war. This trumpet-like instrument could produce a strong, sustained sound and also shorter, staccato blasts. The apocalyptic *War Scroll*, one of the Dead Sea Scrolls discovered at Qumran, originating between the last two centuries BC and the first century AD, gives detailed rules "for the trumpets of summons and the trumpets of alarm… ".[3]

The description in Numbers 10 renders it indisputable that the *khatsotsrah* is a trumpet made of beaten or hammered silver, probably about 40 centimetres (1 cubit/15 inches) long, with a thin body and wide bell-like end. Its design may have been borrowed from the Egyptians, and it may have sounded similar to the celebrated trumpets discovered in the tomb of Tutankhamun (ruled c. 1333–1324 BC).[4] It is important to

Left: Relief from the Arch of Titus, Rome, celebrating Titus's victories, including the sack of Jerusalem. Roman soldiers are depicted carrying off loot from Herod's Temple, including the *menorah* (left) and *khatsotsrah* trumpets (right).
Below: Cave IV at Qumran, Israel, site of discovery of the Dead Sea Scrolls.

distinguish the *khatsotsrah* from the *shophar*, the ram's-horn trumpet discussed below.

Kinnôr

One of the most significant musical instruments of the ancient Jews, the *kinnôr* – a type of lyre – is mentioned forty-two times in the Old Testament. There is archaeological evidence for this instrument from as early as the mid-third millennium BC, and it is also mentioned in a letter dating to the eighteenth century BC found at Mari in Syria. The lyre soon became the dominant instrument of the ancient Near East in general, and of Israel/Palestine in particular, and retained this pre-eminence during the Iron Age and the period of the Jewish monarchy, from King David onwards. The word *kinnôr* is thought to be related to the place-name "Kinnereth" (Joshua 19:35).[5]

The *kinnôr* is first mentioned early in Genesis to stand for the craft of musicians (Genesis 4:21), and is known from the Old Testament to have been played during family celebrations, in mourning, and in religious praise, as well as by prostitutes and during ecstatic prophesying (Genesis 31:27; Job 30:31; 2 Samuel 6:5; Isaiah 23:16; 1 Samuel 10:5[6]). The young David is famously mentioned as playing the *kinnôr* to the melancholy King Saul for its therapeutic effect (1 Samuel 16:16). Although *kinnôr* has been variously translated in the Septuagint and the Vulgate, and has commonly been known as "the harp of David", it is generally agreed today to have been a form of lyre.[7]

From the time of King Solomon the Jewish *kinnôr* was usually made of almug timber (red sandalwood, or possibly juniper) imported from Lebanon (2 Chronicles 2:8). With somewhere between six and ten strings (fewer than the *nebel*), it could be played either with a plectrum or by the hand alone.

Archaeologists have discovered more than thirty visual representations of the lyre in ancient Israel/Palestine, some symmetrical, others asymmetrical, some with diverging arms, others with parallel arms. One well-known representation of a lyre-player appears on a jar dating to 1150–1000 BC excavated at Megiddo in Israel, and a lyre-player is also pictured on the famous fresco from a nineteenth-century BC tomb at Beni Hasan in Egypt. This "Beni Hasan mural" depicts a relatively small instrument (around 50 x 30 centimetres) held horizontally by the performer so it could be played while simultaneously walking and singing. A seventh-century BC relief from Nineveh, showing prisoners taken from Lachish in Israel by the Assyrian king Sennacherib, depicts three captive Hebrew lyre-players. Sennacherib boasted that among the 200,150 people he expelled from Judah, he captured King Hezekiah's "male and female musicians".[8]

Msiltayim (or Zelzelim)

This Hebrew word, translated *kymbalon* and *cymbala* in the Septuagint and Vulgate respectively, is generally agreed to mean "cymbals". These instruments were used (along with others) by the Levites officiating at the Jewish Temple (Ezra 3:10) – at the transfer of the Ark of the Covenant, at the dedication of King Solomon's Temple, and

at the burnt- and sin-offerings made at the Temple (1 Chronicles 15:28; 2 Chronicles 5:13; 29:25). The *msiltayim* are described in 1 Chronicles 15:19 as bronze cymbals (NIV and other modern translations), with which the ancient Jewish historian Josephus agrees, stating that "the cymbals were broad and large instruments, and were made of bronze".[9]

The New Revised Standard Version (NRSV) translates Psalm 150:5: "Praise him with clanging cymbals; praise him with loud clashing cymbals!", suggesting that the psalmist is referring here to both types of cymbal common in the region – cymbals held horizontally with a handle and struck lightly, and cymbals held vertically and struck forcibly. Archaeologists have discovered many ancient cymbals in ancient Israel/Palestine, in two sizes: between 7 and 12 centimetres in diameter, and between 3 and 6 centimetres in diameter. It is suggested these two sizes represent the two types mentioned in Psalm 150. Some of the excavated cymbals which have survived intact have been tested and produce a broad, resonant sound.

Nebel

The precise meaning of the word *nebel* has still not been soundly established. Suggestions have varied as widely as the lyre, the lute, and the bagpipe! The Hebrew term *nebel* occurs twenty-eight times in the Old Testament (for example in Isaiah 5:12, Psalm 33:2, and 2 Chronicles 5:12),

---

Left: This Palestinian lyre-player, part of a painting from a tomb at Beni Hasan, Egypt, dating back to 1920–1900 BC, affords rare visual evidence of musical practice in ancient Israel/Palestine.
Above: A Jewish coin minted during the Bar Kokhba (or Second Jewish) Revolt against the Romans (AD 132–36), depicting a four-stringed broad lyre.

twenty-two of which are also associated with the *kinnôr*. Like the *kinnôr*, the *nebel* was constructed from almug-wood and plucked by hand (1 Kings 10:12; Amos 6:5). It was played by the Levites (assistants to the priests) and featured at the transfer of the Ark of the Covenant, the dedication of the rebuilt walls of Jerusalem following the Jewish Exile, Israelite victory celebrations, and in ecstatic prophesying (1 Chronicles 15:16; 2 Samuel 6:5; Nehemiah 12:27; 2 Chronicles 20:28; 1 Samuel 10:5).

Ancient sources offer little help in defining this instrument, though Josephus usefully distinguishes between the *nebel*, which had twelve strings and was played with the fingers, and the *kinnôr*, with six to ten strings plucked with a plectrum. Although most scholars favour translating *nebel* as "harp", archaeologists have as yet discovered no harps in this region dating to earlier than the Hellenistic period. For this reason it has been suggested the *nebel* is a form of lyre peculiar to the Near East, with more and thicker strings than the *kinnôr* – giving it a louder sound – yet still played without a plectrum. With its thicker strings and deeper

tone, the *nebel* was possibly deployed as a tenor or bass instrument in the Second Temple orchestra, from the late sixth century BC onwards.[10]

Pamonim

This Hebrew term is found in only Exodus 28:33–34 and 39:25–26 and refers to the gold bells fastened to the bottom of the Temple high priest's robe. Although the sound of these bells was said to be pleasant, their main purpose was as a warning:

> *Aaron* [the first high priest] *will wear this robe whenever he enters the Holy Place to minister to the* LORD, *and the bells will tinkle as he goes in and out of the* LORD's *presence. If he wears it, he will not die.*

(Exodus 28:35, NLT)

Such functional warning bells were not unique to the Jews: a depiction of a fifteenth-century BC Assyrian ambassador and a statue of an ancient high priest from Syria both depict similar bells worn near the hem.

A man blows a ram's-horn trumpet (*shophar*) to inaugurate the restored synagogue at Masada, Israel, in 2005.

Shophar

Mentioned as many as seventy-four times, the *shophar* is by far the most frequently referenced musical instrument in the Hebrew Scriptures. It is also the sole instrument from ancient Israel to have survived little changed in its usage in modern Jewish liturgy.

The *shophar* is the natural horn of a goat or ram (never a cow), though the generally more reliable Vulgate translators led many succeeding scholars astray by dubbing it a *"tuba"* (Latin for military trumpet). The Hebrew Scriptures give little further information about the *shophar*; however, the Jewish Talmud and some writings from Qumran provide fuller descriptions. Apparently two types of *shophar* were in use: a curved horn covered in silver at *Yom Kippur* (the annual Jewish day of atonement fast), and at New Year a straight horn, apparently untwisted after immersion in hot water. Such horns have been found in eighteenth-century BC images excavated at Mari in Syria and in depictions from ninth-century BC Carchemish (in modern eastern Turkey). The *shophar* is also unique among the instruments of ancient Israel as it was played as a solo instrument. It can produce only two or three tones – a "voice", a "trumpet blast", a "shout", and even "moaning" – evidently used to give different signals in religious and military contexts.

The *shophar* featured at the Jewish observance of *Yom Kippur* (Leviticus 25:9), as well as at the transfer of the Ark of the Covenant, in wartime, after military victories, and even at political coups (2 Samuel 6:15; Judges 6:34; 1 Samuel 13:3; 2 Samuel 15:10). The *shophar* was also blown on the feast of *Rosh Hashanah* (New Year), while every fifty years it announced the jubilee year. The sound of the *shophar* was so powerful that it could be experienced by its hearers as supernatural (Exodus 19:13). After the destruction of Herod's Temple by the Romans in AD 70, the blowing of the *shophar* on the Sabbath was restricted to wherever the Sanhedrin – the Jewish legislature and court between 191 BC and AD 358 – was located. In later times, its religious use increased because the Jews banned the playing of all other musical instruments as a sign of mourning for the destruction of the Jerusalem Temple.

Today the *shophar* is still blown in synagogues to announce the New Year and New Moon, to introduce the Sabbath, at four particular occasions during the prayers on *Rosh Hashanah*, and at *Yom Kippur* to mark the end of the day of fasting.

Toph

The ancient instrument known in Hebrew as the *toph* – a type of drum – is mentioned sixteen times in the Old Testament, in five of which the player is a woman. Best known of these references is to Miriam, sister of Moses, following the Hebrews' successful traversing of the Red Sea after the Exodus from Egypt (Exodus 15:20). Though not exclusively a woman's instrument, only women seem to have played the *toph* as a solo instrument, and it does not appear to have featured in the Temple music (Judges 11:34). The *toph* was widely used in ancient Israel/Palestine.

Most modern scholars agree the *toph* was a drum with a circular wooden frame about 25 to 30 centimetres in diameter, similar to the tambourine but without the metal jingles. The membrane, probably made of leather or ram's hide, was struck with the hand.

'ûgab

As with the *nebel*, there is considerable controversy about the precise meaning of the word *'ûgab*. It occurs only four times in the Old Testament, and the Septuagint translates it as the *kithara*, the *organon*, and the *psalmos*. Even today interpretations vary from the pan-pipe or bagpipe to the lute or harp, while others regard the *'ûgab* as a purely symbolic instrument. The best supported suggestion is that the *'ûgab* was a type of long, transverse flute, such as was also found in ancient Egypt and Sumeria.

♫ Instruments in Babylon

The fourth chapter of the Old Testament book of Daniel describes a much-discussed group of musical instruments from a non-Israelite musical culture, often referred to as the "orchestra of Nebuchadnezzar": "… when you hear the sound of the horn, pipe, lyre, trigon, harp, drum, and entire musical ensemble, you are to fall down and worship the golden statue… " (Daniel 3:5, NRSV).[11] The "horn" is probably a clay or metal trumpet, and the "pipe" a reed instrument. The "lyre" would have been a small, symmetrically shaped instrument, about 50 by 25 centimetres in size, and the "trigon" a small, angular harp, held vertically, with its sound-box resting on the player's shoulder. This contrasts with the "harp" of Daniel 3:5, which was probably a larger, angular harp, held horizontally and possibly beaten with sticks.[12]

♫ Jewish Music in the Old Testament

The first book of Chronicles offers a rich account of the musicians deployed when King David transported the holy Ark of the Covenant to Jerusalem (1 Chronicles 15:16–28). Particularly fully described in the Old Testament are the music of David's last years, the music at the

Artist's impression of the bronze laver and main sanctuary of Solomon's Temple, Jerusalem, focus of Jewish worship before the Babylonian Captivity. Artwork by Alan Parry.

coming of the Ark of the Covenant to King Solomon's Temple (2 Chronicles 5:11–14), and that performed at Temple sacrifices during the later reign of King Hezekiah of Judah (1 Chronicles 23–25; 2 Chronicles 29:25). King Hezekiah apparently reformed the ritual of the Jerusalem Temple and its music, reorganizing the Levite musicians and incorporating instrumental – particularly stringed-instrument – music into the sung liturgy (2 Kings 18:4–5; 2 Chronicles 29:25–26; 30:21).

Following the Exile of the Jews in Babylon in 586 BC and the subsequent return to Judah of many deportees under the relatively benevolent rule of Cyrus II of Persia around 537 BC, the Second Temple was built and Temple worship recommenced. The lists of returning Jews in the books of Ezra and Nehemiah include huge choirs of singers and grand orchestras (Ezra 2:41, 65; Nehemiah 7:44, 67; 12:27–43).

♩ Singing

Until now we have discussed almost exclusively instrumental music. However, singing is also frequently mentioned in the Old Testament, particularly of course in the Psalms. In the Hebrew vocabulary of the Old Testament, there are more than twelve terms for vocal music, outnumbering the terms for instrumental music. The Mishnah reports that the choir of the Jewish Temple consisted of a minimum of twelve male singers (women were excluded) aged between thirty and fifty, together with some Levite boys "to add sweetness to the song". The singers evidently underwent a five-year training apprenticeship before being admitted to the choir.

One scholar has usefully summarized our knowledge of the Temple musicians:

Temple musicians served in groups not as individuals; there seemed to be a balance between instruments and voices in the music of the Temple; most of the accompanying instruments were string instruments; the musicians were ordinarily male, adults, well-trained and (at least in post-exilic times) Levites; the number 12 was an idealized quorum of Temple musicians.[13]

In the Jewish Mishnah we have an account of the musical routine at the Jerusalem Temple in the first century BC. Temple musicians stood on a platform that divided the Court of the Priests from the Court of Israel (*Middoth*, 2.6). After the day's designated sacrifices, a priest sounded the mysterious *magrephah* (see p. 13), after which the priests entered the Temple sanctuary itself and prostrated themselves, while the Levites commenced their musical performance. Two priests stood at the altar and blew the *shophar* trumpets, a Levite cymbal-player sounded his instrument, and the Levites started to sing part of the day's allotted psalm or a section from the Pentateuch (the Books of Moses). At the end of each section, a trumpet sounded and the assembled congregation prostrated themselves.[14]

One scholar has concluded that the canticles of the Old Testament provide evidence of the different ways in which songs were performed, broadly divided into responsorial and corporate singing. Such canticles include the "Song of the Sea" or "Song of Moses and Miriam".[15] Among other Old Testament canticles are the "Song of Deborah and Barak" (Judges), "David's Lament" and "David's Song of Thanksgiving" (2 Samuel), and Isaiah's "Hymn of Praise" (Isaiah), as well as the Psalms themselves.

The call-and-response form was, of course, particularly suited to a context where the congregation had no written prayer-books from which to sing. It is suggested that in the Second Temple period there were five possible ways of performing responsorial canticles:

1. The congregation repeats each unit after the leader.
2. The congregation repeats a standard refrain after each verse by the leader. Psalm 136 gives evidence of this form:

   O give thanks to the LORD, for he is good,
   For his steadfast love endures for ever.
   O give thanks to the God of gods,
   For his steadfast love endures for ever… etc.
   (Psalm 136:1–3, NRSV)

3. The congregation completes the second half of the unit started by the leader.
4. The leader sings the incipit (opening words) of each unit; the congregation repeats the incipit and completes the unit.
5. The leader sings the whole song and the congregation then repeats it.

The same scholar also found evidence of two ways of performing corporately:
1. The whole congregation sings the song.
2. A leader of one gender sings the incipit; the congregation of the same gender sings the following part of the song.[16]

Rabbi Akiba (c. AD 50–135), who would have observed services in the Second Temple (later known as Herod's Temple) before it was razed to the ground by the Romans in AD 70, similarly reported three forms of responsive public singing:
1. The leader intones the first half-verse; the congregation repeats this; the leader intones each succeeding half-line, but the congregation always repeats the initial half-verse, as a refrain. This method was adopted to sing Psalms 113–118 (known as the *Hallel* – hence "alleluia").
2. The leader sings a half-line at a time, following which the congregation repeats what the leader has just sung.
3. The leader sings the entire first line, the congregation responds with the entire second line, and so on.

♩ The Psalms

The Psalms were probably the main "lyric" of Jewish worship – and incidentally provide us with rich literary evidence about ancient Jewish music. The second half of Psalm 150, for instance, offers an evocative description of the "Temple orchestra" and of other contemporary musical instruments (Psalm 150:3–6, NRSV). The nineteenth-century Christian commentator Alexander Maclaren went as far as to suggest that this psalm embodies a form of "stage directions", enumerating the order in which instruments entered the musical performance in the Temple, culminating with the entry of the human voice.[17]

The Mishnah records that certain psalms were sung on particular days in the Temple:

This was the singing which the Levites used to sing in the Temple. On the first day they sang "The earth is the Lord's and all that therein is, the round world and they that dwell therein" [Psalm 24]; on the second day they sang, "Great is the Lord and highly to be praised in the city of our God, even upon his holy hill" [Psalm 48] … On the Sabbath they sang "A Psalm: A Song for the Sabbath Day" [Psalm 92].[18]

A number of Old Testament psalms commence with a title or description, such as "According to Alamoth" (Psalm 46), "According to The Gittith" (Psalm 8), "According to Lilies" [*shoshannim*] (Psalm 45), "According to Mahalath" (Psalm 53), and "A Song of Ascents" (Psalms 120–134). In many instances these subtitles are instructions as to how to perform the respective psalm: which tune or instrument(s) to use, the musical tempo and emotional context (praise or lament), as well as breathing instructions, pauses, and the like. For example, "According to Alamoth" (Psalm 46) probably indicates the psalm was to be accompanied by a flute in its upper register or by a high-pitched voice ("soprano voices", NLT). Other psalm subtitles seem to indicate popular tunes to be used (just as today it might be suggested "The Lord's My Shepherd" be sung to the tune "Crimond"). Titles such as "The Deer of the Dawn" (Psalm 22, NRSV; "Doe of the Dawn", NLT), "The Dove on Far-off Terebinths" (Psalm 56, NRSV; "Dove on Distant Oaks", NLT), and "Lily of the Covenant" (Psalms 60, 80, NRSV) seem to be the names of contemporary popular or "folk" tunes (now sadly unknown) to which the respective psalms should be sung. The subtitle "Do Not Destroy" (Psalms 57–59, 75) has been linked with a wine-harvesting song quoted in Isaiah 65:8. So it appears likely that a number of psalms were intended to be sung using tunes or melodic formulae already familiar to the performers. The adoption of local popular tunes to liturgical texts is common throughout world cultures and (as we will see) throughout the history of Christian music.[19]

The ubiquitous – and puzzling – Hebrew word *selah*, which appears seventy-one times in the text of thirty-nine psalms, possibly indicates an "interlude" where the performers were to pause, or is perhaps a cue for the choir or a specific instrumentalist, such as the drummer, to stress the rhythm of, or a particular word in, the text: "… when they reached a break in the singing they blew upon the trumpet".[20]

The Psalms of Ascent (Psalms 120–134) may have been sung to accompany the Jewish high priest's ritual ascent of the Temple Mount, or may have been chanted by pilgrims "going up" to Jerusalem (Zion) for the great Jewish festivals of Unleavened Bread, Harvest, and Ingathering (Exodus 23:14–17).

The "tunes" of this period and region differed from the melodies of modern Western music. Ancient "tunes" consisted of thematic ideas or kernels made up of a few notes and known as *makam*. These themes were tetrachordal (four tones filling an interval of a perfect musical fourth) rather than pentatonic, and each theme had a range of less than a musical fifth, but included a leap of a third. The melodic theme was strictly observed, but freely embellished and ornamented. The interpretation and elaboration of the musician performing the piece was seen to be of paramount importance. Some of the psalm subtitles or instructions referred to earlier may have been intended to indicate the *makam* to be used in performance. Harmony was unknown to musicians of this period.

♫ Instruments of the New Testament

In contrast to the Old Testament, which as we have seen boasts numerous references to a wide variety of musical instruments, the Christian New Testament includes only twenty-nine references to instruments, of which twelve are virtually repetitions in the book of Revelation, and only four distinct musical instruments are discernible. However, since these texts are relatively more recent, deriving from the first and second centuries AD, and were originally written in Greek, the Latin renderings in the Vulgate translation are generally consistent, so we can be much more confident in our interpretation of them than in the case of the instruments of the Old Testament.

Four specific musical instruments are mentioned in the New Testament texts:

Aulos
This refers to a single- or double-reeded pipe similar to the *khalil* of the Old Testament. Archaeologists in Israel have found many such pipes dating to Roman times. A fine mosaic depiction of an *aulos* was discovered at a fifth-century AD synagogue excavated at the Hellenistic city of Sepphoris, near Lake Galilee. Such pipes were played at weddings and wakes (Matthew 9:23; 11:17).

Lyre

The lyre (Greek *kithara*) is mentioned eight times in the New Testament, and in the book of Revelation is referred to as "God's harp" (Revelation 15:2). A lyre is depicted in a mosaic at a synagogue dating to AD 244 at Dura-Europos in modern Syria. The lyre was considered by both Jews and Christians to symbolize spiritual and physical harmony.

Trumpet

In the main the trumpet (Greek *salpinx*) is also referred to symbolically in the New Testament, usually apocalyptically as "God's trumpet" (1 Thessalonians 4:16,

NRSV), and is the signal for the resurrection and last judgment (1 Corinthians 15:52b; 1 Thessalonians 4:16). It is from such passages that the *tuba mirum* of the Latin text of the Christian requiem mass derives. The Arch of Titus in the ancient forum of Rome, dating to AD 72 and celebrating Rome's triumph over the Jewish Revolt, depicts two long trumpets next to the Jewish seven-branched lamp-stand (*menorah*) plundered from Herod's Temple, but it is unclear whether this accurately represents the trumpets from the actual Temple or is simply a representation of typical Roman trumpets (see p. 15).

Cymbal

The "clanging cymbal" (Greek *kymbalon*) of 1 Corinthians 13:1, in the apostle Paul's celebrated love/charity chapter, is now thought to be a resonating brass vase – used in Greek theatre to amplify voices – rather than a musical instrument in the strict sense.

Left: First century AD Roman copy of a Hellenistic statue of the god Apollo holding his characteristic lyre, from the Palazzo Altemps, Rome.
Right: Relief from court of the Assyrian king Ashurbanipal, Nineveh, 645 BC, showing musicians playing the tambourine, lyre, cymbals, and dulcimer.

♪ Jewish Music in the New Testament Period

Archaeologists have discovered many pictorial representations of musical instruments and musicians from this period. Greek and Roman figurative representations reveal close connections between music and the Dionysus cult, the god Pan, and erotic performances. The Hellenistic Dionysus cult was particularly strong in the first centuries BC and AD, and in Israel/Palestine centred on the city of Scythopolis (modern Beth Shan), just south of Galilee. Such links with pagan cults reinforced the frequent condemnation of instrumental music by both orthodox Jewish rabbis and early Christians.

The almost total destruction of the Second Temple (Herod's Temple) by the Romans in AD 70 during the savage suppression of the Jewish Revolt marked a nadir in Jewish history. It meant the end of Temple worship. To mourn the loss of the Temple, the rabbis banned musical performances, whether instrumental or vocal, and prohibited all music during synagogue worship. As noted previously, only the *shophar* escaped this ban. (Though even before AD 70 there is little evidence that any instruments – except possibly the *shophar* – were used in the synagogue.)

However, music was not so easily suppressed. Almost inevitably a musical tradition survived – which rabbis were soon forced to acknowledge – as local synagogue rituals began to take the place of the central Temple liturgy. As early as the Babylonian Exile of the Jews (586–537 BC), the Jewish leader Ezra had pioneered the public chanting of the Torah (the five Books of Moses, or Books of the Law – Genesis, Exodus, Leviticus, Numbers, and Deuteronomy). The Talmud seems to indicate that reading the Torah "without chant" was considered a minor sacrilege.[21] By the second century AD, Rabbi Akiba, who laid the foundations of Rabbinic Judaism and was devoted to the practice of the Torah, required its daily chanting as a means of study.

By the third century AD chanting – or "cantillation" – to the required melody was *de rigueur*. The choral singing of the Temple was often subsumed in the solo chanting of a cantor, a layperson with a good voice. Although the text of the Torah was available in written form, on papyrus scrolls, the accompanying music was transmitted by oral tradition, with a system of hand and finger signals ("chironomy") to preserve and communicate the correct musical rendition. In the sixth century AD the Masoretes – groups of Jewish scribes and scriptural scholars based in Tiberias and Jerusalem – developed the existing written system of twenty-eight symbols (*neumes*) that represented the missing vowels and punctuation of the Hebrew text so it also included melodic indications. It appears that from an early stage (as today) the chanting of different books of the Bible (say, Ruth and Ecclesiastes) sounded distinctive, with different and appropriate-sounding *neumes* assigned to them.

CHAPTER 2

Psalms and Hymns and Spiritual Songs: Music and the Early Church

… Be filled with the Spirit, as you sing psalms and hymns and spiritual songs among yourselves, singing and making melody to the Lord in your hearts…

Ephesians 5:18–19, NRSV

♫ The Temple and the Synagogue

The first Christians in the Jewish holy city of Jerusalem, still dominated by the impressive Herod's Temple, met as a group within their inherited Jewish faith. Outsiders regarded them as a Jewish sect, the "Nazarenes" (referring to their devotion to Jesus "of Nazareth", Acts 24:5), and, as the new faith grew and spread outside Jerusalem, many of the early believers remained Jews whose religious background had been strongly shaped by synagogue worship. In this way, Christianity inherited traditions from Jewish Temple ritual and synagogue worship. Like Jesus, the apostles and the earliest Christian disciples valued the Jewish Temple and continued to go there at times of prayer. Similarly, like their founder Jesus, the first Christians valued the synagogue (Acts 13:5; 14:1; 18:26).

There is some doubt as to how far singing was practised in the synagogues of Judea/Palestine in the time of Christ, although the Talmud laid down that, in the synagogue, "Man should always first utter praises, and then pray".[1] In any event Christian recourse to singing was not simply a continuation of synagogue patterns of worship. Accounts

Below: Nineteenth-century French artist James Tissot's visualisation of Jerusalem and Herod's Temple in the time of Christ.

of the earliest Christian believers in the book of Acts highlight their joy in their new experience of faith and belief in the risen Christ (Acts 2:1–13; 3:8; 5:41–42 etc.), and exultant psalm- and hymn-singing was not confined to worship in services. The travelling missionaries Paul and Silas comforted themselves by singing when imprisoned in Philippi (Acts 16:24–25) and believers elsewhere were encouraged to express their joy in "songs of praise" (James 5:13 , NRSV). As one twentieth-century scholar commented, "we should expect that a movement which released so much emotion, and loyalty, and enthusiasm, would find expression in song… ", concluding colourfully: "… it would have been strange indeed if the Church had remained songless in the first glorious dawn when the light from Christ came breaking across the horizons, making all things new."[2]

However, the church remained unrecognized, prohibited, and sometimes persecuted for its first three centuries. Christians did not meet in special buildings – there were as yet no local church structures, cathedrals, or abbeys. Instead believers met in homes, sometimes in secret caves, in forests, and in Roman cellars and catacombs. Such venues were not conducive to elaborate music-making and secrecy must often have dictated quiet if not silent worship.

🎵 Other Worship Traditions

While the first Christians undoubtedly inherited many worship traditions from the Jewish Temple and synagogue – including probably responsive and antiphonal singing

Above: Detail from a panel depicting Paul of Tarsus, part of an altarpiece by Masaccio (1401–28) commissioned in 1426. This panel is now in the Museo Nazionale di Pisa, Italy.
Below: A section of the Catacombs of Priscilla, on the *Via Salaria*, Rome, Italy.

of psalms and canticles, as described in the previous chapter – they also drew on other traditions which fostered the singing of hymns.

In his work *On Ascetics* (*De Vita Contemplativa*), the Hellenized Jewish author Philo (c. 20 BC – AD 50) describes the worship practices of a group of pre-Christian ascetics in Egypt. He stated that at their meetings, one worshipper got up and sang a hymn to God, either a new one he had composed, or an old one by an earlier composer. The others followed one by one in appropriate order, while everyone listened in complete silence,

except they sang the refrains and responses.[3] At their night-time services, the men and women of this community first met as segregated gender groups, singing hymns – sometimes antiphonally – and making rhythmic body movements. After this, the men and women joined to form a single choir singing "hymns of thanks to the Saviour God".

Like the group in Alexandria, it seems the much-debated Jewish ascetic community at Qumran around the same period featured music in their worship. The Essene scribe of the community wrote:

> *I will sing with knowledge and for the glory of God shall all my music be, the strumming of my harp for his holy order, and the whistle of my lips I shall adjust to its correct scale…*[4]

♫ Hellenistic Influences

The first Christians must have been to some extent influenced by the Hellenistic culture pervasive in the Mediterranean world of

Below: An Attic (Greek) *kylix*, or ceramic drinking cup, made by the painter Makron c. 490–480 BC, depicting Dionysus and the Maenads, who are dancing and playing musical instruments including the pipes.
Right: The Greek thinkers Plato (left) and Aristotle depicted by Raphael (1483–1520) in the *Scuola di Atene* (School of Athens) fresco in the Apostolic Palace, the Vatican, Rome, Italy.

the first century AD. Greek thinkers believed music represented a cathartic and creative – even mystical – force that could help people attain access to metaphysical knowledge and constitute a moral influence for good or ill, and the Greeks utilized music both in theatrical presentations and in worship.

Employing mathematics to understand music, the sixth-century BC Greek thinker Pythagoras divided taut strings into equal parts to create sound intervals and hence scales. For Pythagoras and his followers, the musical system, ordered by numbers, represented the order of the cosmos. The Lydian, Dorian, and Aeolian modes, discovered by early Greek musicians, were still known by these names when Christians started to use them a millennium later. The Greeks distinguished two types of music: that linked with the god Apollo and performed on the lyre, which they believed helped to uplift and calm the listener; and that linked with Dionysus, played on the *aulos*, which they believed created excitement and ecstasy.

The ancient Greek philosopher Aristotle (c. 384–322 BC) introduced an ethical dimension to musical theory. He taught that music can imitate the human passions and temperaments – anger, courage, gentleness, temperance, excess, and the like. When the listener hears music that imitates a particular passion, he or she imbibes that passion or temperament. So, according to Aristotle, over time a particular type of music – noble or ignoble – exerts a moral influence on its audience. Both Aristotle and his teacher Plato (c. 427 – c. 347 BC) believed that, for this reason, care should be taken to listen to the right sort of music, in moderate amounts. (Such thinking is not absent today: older church-goers often

deplore the playing in church of rock music or electric guitars and drums for their alleged malign impact on listeners.) Similarly, the Greek thinker Diogenes of Babylon (c. 230 – c. 150 BC) believed there is an insoluble bond between music and piety, and Plotinus (AD 204/05–70), founder of Neoplatonism, affirmed that the perception and knowledge of beauty – for example in music or other arts – serves to purify the soul.

The Greeks even invented a form of music notation, placing little words or symbols over the lyrics to indicate the pitch the performer was supposed to use. Sadly, we possess no key to these symbols, so are no nearer to being able to hear their music. However, as in Jewish culture, text and music were closely linked. The rhythm and melody of the music were constructed around and upon the poetry of the text, whether Hebrew Scripture or Greek drama. Ancient Greek music, like ancient Jewish music, knew nothing of harmony or polyphony (where two or more independent lines sound together), but frequently called for improvisation by the performer (who was often also the composer); such improvisatory freedom may have influenced early Christian music.

Greek religion sometimes featured hymns offered to cult divinities. Like their Christian equivalents, such hymns contained elevated thoughts and often invoked the deity. While Greek hymns often invoked many gods, in the hope that one at least would respond, Christian hymns addressed a single God who was approached with confidence. As we will see below, many early Christian hymns doubled as confessions of faith.

♫ Psalm-Singing

At the time of Jesus, psalm- and hymn-singing appears to have been more prevalent in the synagogues established by Jews dispersed outside the Holy Land than among the more conservative Jews remaining in Palestine and in Jerusalem itself. However, Mark's Gospel recounts that at the end of the Passover meal at which Jesus instituted the Lord's Supper, Jesus and the apostles sang a "hymn" before going out to the Mount of Olives. This would almost certainly have been the traditional Jewish *Hallel*-hymn drawn from Psalms 113–18 (see p. 22).

The first Christians widely appropriated the Jewish psalms, as is evidenced by their frequent quotation within prayers found in the books of Acts and Hebrews. Similarly, a hymn quoted in Revelation consists largely of excerpts from the Old Testament psalms (Revelation 15:3–4[5]); while the pioneer Christian missionary Paul also alludes to singing psalms in Ephesians 5:19 and Colossians 3:16, though in the latter instance he is probably referring to new Christian compositions, as these are "Spirit-inspired" – and possibly spontaneous – psalms. Certainly Paul's instructions seem to imply churches in which the congregation was strongly involved in making the music and where spontaneity was both experienced and expected. However, the first explicit literary evidence for the use of Old Testament psalms in Christian worship is not until c. AD 190, in the apocryphal *Acts of Paul*, which refers to "singing of David's psalms and hymns".[6]

In early Christian gatherings psalms were probably both spoken and sung, as they were in Jewish synagogue worship; and the first Christians probably chanted and intoned ("cantillated") the psalms and hymns in a similar way to the Jews. One scholar suggests this was a sung recitation "on a single pitch, with melodic figures (cadences) attached to the middle and end of the verse… ".[7] It is important to emphasize that in Christian worship both men and women sang: there was no discrimination against women.

Almost certainly singing was unaccompanied: Christian writers argued forcibly against instrumental accompaniment, which they regarded as associated with secular entertainment. There are repeated attacks in early Christian writings on the playing of instruments, and specifically on the use of the pipes, flute, harp, cithara, and Eastern sambuca (a four-

stringed triangular guitar), which believers felt to be polluted by usage in the theatre, and in the drunken wedding feasts and licentious banquets of Greco-Roman society. For similar reasons, sacred dance was almost universally condemned by the first Christians.[8] Christian worship seems to have concentrated on the word, excluding instruments as they might have distracted from, or clouded the clear expression of, the text.

♫ New Testament Canticles

The Christian New Testament reveals lyric-writing that exhibits continuity with the Old Testament tradition. The opening chapters of the Gospel of Luke feature four canticles that can be set out in strophes, or stanzas, and all of which retain a strong carry-over of Old Testament wording. The first of these New Testament canticles is the *Magnificat* (Luke 1:46–55), Mary's hymn of exultation following the angel's annunciation that Mary is to bear the promised Messiah. The familiar Latin name derives from the first word of the Vulgate translation of verse 46: "My soul *magnifies* the Lord… ". As we will see, these same words have been set by innumerable composers down through the Christian centuries.

The *Benedictus* (Luke 1:68–79), similarly named after its opening word in the Vulgate translation, is the old Jewish priest Zechariah's hymn of rejoicing that God had responded to Jewish prayers for deliverance by sending him a son, John the Baptist, to prepare the way for the coming Messiah. This, too, has found a secure place in Christian liturgies over the centuries, with numerous different musical settings.

As early as the fourth century AD we have evidence that the *Gloria in excelsis* ("Glory to God on high… " – the angels' chorus to the shepherds outside Bethlehem in Luke 2:14) had become a regular feature of the church's morning worship, according to the

Apostolic Constitutions, eight books of early Christian worship and doctrine. The same source confirms that the *Nunc dimittis* (Luke 2:29–32) – the aged Simeon's song of praise that he had lived to see the coming of God's Messiah – was incorporated early on into the church's liturgy as an evening hymn.

Christians also appear to have taken over certain hymn strophes or stanzas directly from the liturgy of some Greek-speaking Jewish synagogues. An example is found in Revelation 4:8, quoting from Isaiah 6:3, often referred to as the *Ter sanctus* from its opening words in Latin: "Holy, holy, holy…". In composing this text, it seems likely that John the Divine, the writer of Revelation, was using parts of the church's liturgy as he knew them to create a picture of worship in heaven: by this means we probably have access to a passage from one of the liturgical texts of the earliest Christians. Other similar fragments of hymn-like praise from the New Testament include Romans 11:33–36 and 1 Timothy 1:17: "To the King of the ages, immortal, invisible, the only God, be honour and glory for ever and ever. Amen." The opening description of God here ("the King of the ages", NRSV) is the same as is used in Jewish domestic and synagogue prayer; while the phrase "for ever and ever" is a Greek expression that would have been familiar to Greek-speaking believers.

♫ The First Christian Hymns

However, the New Testament seems to indicate that, in addition to Jewish psalms, from the earliest times the church also used distinctively *Christian* hymns. The apostle Paul describes worship practice in Corinth: "When you come together, each one has a hymn… " (1 Corinthians 14:26, NRSV). Some have argued that this implies that hymn-singing opened Christian worship, as it did in the synagogue, according to the Talmud; but this verse alone is insufficient to prove this.

Paul also instructs the church at Colossae to "… sing psalms, hymns and spiritual songs to God" (Colossians 3:16, NRSV; see also Ephesians 5:19–20). Scholars find it difficult to differentiate the three terms Paul uses here: the "psalms" may have been Old Testament psalms, whereas the "hymns" may have been longer compositions and the "spiritual songs" (Greek *odai pneumatikai*) spontaneous, ecstatic praise. One scholar has suggested these "spiritual songs" were melismatic "Alleluias and other chants of a jubilant or ecstatic character, richly ornamented."[9] ("Alleluia" derives from the Hebrew *halelu-yah*: praise to *Jahweh*, or Jehovah.) Another scholar has claimed that the entire biblical evidence of song in apostolic times indicates spontaneous – sometimes ecstatic – praise. Whether or not this is so, over time any such spontaneous utterances seem to have evolved into more formal, stylized patterns of worship. Such was this progression that by its second century the church already possessed worship manuals and service books.

♫ Primitive Hymns

Scholars have discovered the vestiges of what they believe to be very early Christian hymns in a number of the apostle Paul's writings. The clearest example of verbal fragments from an early Christian hymn comes in a verse from Paul's letter to the Ephesian church, which he himself states to be a quotation:

Sleeper, awake!
Rise from the dead,
and Christ will shine on you.

(Ephesians 5:14b, NRSV)

Paul implies this invocation would be well known to his Christian readers, strengthening the argument that it comes from a contemporary hymn. This passage, in its original Greek, naturally falls into three lines, with the first two lines ending in the same rhyming sound. Possibly these were the first lines of a responsorial song, led by the president and answered by the church;

or perhaps this was the chorus that the congregation chanted in response to verses sung solo by the worship leader, retelling the story of Jesus' resurrection. With its imagery of sleep, death, and light, some scholars have suggested this is a fragment from a chant used at Christian baptism, where emergence from the baptismal water represented spiritual awakening from death.

Other passages where scholars have detected fragments of primitive Christian hymns include 1 Timothy 3:16, again both a hymn and a creed.[10] With its contrast between two worlds – the divine and the human – it has been suggested this hymn is essentially Greek in thought-form, and originated in a Hellenistic Jewish-Christian community, such as the group associated with the first Christian martyr, Stephen, a leader of the church in Jerusalem.[11] Further primitive hymn fragments occur in Philippians 2:6–11, which can be organized as a three-stanza (or even a six-verse) Greek hymn;[12] Colossians 1:15–20, which has been considered as two Greek stanzas concerning respectively Christ and creation (verses 15–18a) and Christ and the church (verses 18b–20); and Hebrews 1:3, with its "elevated, ceremonial style".[13]

There is no clear evidence within the New Testament that the earliest churches observed a set order of service, and scant information has been found about their worship practices. Although musical instruments such as the harp and/or lyre, the pipe, cymbal, and trumpet are mentioned in the New Testament writings, there is no evidence they were used in worship – indeed specialists believe they definitely were not.[14] We have noticed the distaste for instrumental music among the first Christians. The musicologist Gerald Abraham sums up Christian music of this time as "essentially an Eastern, Judaic, dialect of Hellenistic-Roman" music.[15]

♪ Music of the Second-Century Church

The Roman official Pliny[16] (c. AD 61 – c. 112), governor of the Black Sea Roman province of Pontus and Bithynia (in modern Turkey) between AD 111 and 112, in a report to the Emperor Trajan mentioned that Christians "… were in the habit of meeting before dawn on a stated day and singing alternately a hymn to Christ as to a god… ", permitting us a unique and valuable glimpse of early Christian worship, as we have little other written evidence for another fifty years. The "stated" day Pliny mentions was probably Sunday, and a pre-dawn timing was necessary before believers commenced their day's work. Although scholars have debated the precise meaning of Pliny's Latin phrase, "*carmenque Christo quasi deo dicere secum invicem*", normal Latin usage and most Christian commentators support a translation that (the Christians) "chant verses alternately among themselves in honour of Christ as if to a god".[17] So Pliny's evidence suggests strongly that Christians were singing not just psalms, but hymns specifically naming Christ.

A little later, the Christian martyr Ignatius of Antioch (c. AD 35–110) uses a metaphor drawn from music when writing to encourage his fellow Christians, underlining their familiarity with singing in worship – and the prevalent use in the church of monophonic rather than polyphonic or harmonic music:

Therefore by your concord and harmonious love Jesus Christ is being sung. Now all of you together become a choir so that being harmoniously in concord and receiving the key note from God in unison you may sing with one voice through Jesus Christ to the Father.

Worship Patterns
In time, the Christian community began to observe a daily pattern of worship, often known as the daily "office", involving prayer, Bible-reading, and singing psalms together with hymns naming Christ. By the third century in both the Christian East and West there had evolved a regular pattern of daily prayer, either threefold (9 a.m., 12 noon, and 3 p.m.) or fivefold (these three plus morning and evening prayer).

Although by the third century there is evidence of various differentiated roles within the church, such as deacon, subdeacon, reader, acolyte, exorcist, doorkeeper, deaconess, and widow, there is no mention of a cantor, psalmist, or solo singer. However, the Christian writer Tertullian reveals that psalm-singing formed a regular element in Sunday worship: "the Scriptures are read, psalms are sung, sermons are delivered, and petitions offered". He also describes with fascinating detail worship in his own community in North Africa:

After manual ablution, and the bringing in of lights, each is asked to stand forth and sing, as he can, a hymn to God, either one from the holy Scriptures or one of his own composing…[18]

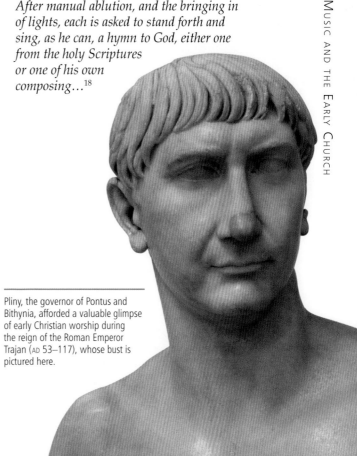

Pliny, the governor of Pontus and Bithynia, afforded a valuable glimpse of early Christian worship during the reign of the Roman Emperor Trajan (AD 53–117), whose bust is pictured here.

Hymns

In 1909 a complete collection of forty-two hymns was discovered that probably originated among Jewish Christians in Palestine in the late first century. Known as the *Odes of Solomon*, these celebratory and mystical hymns were originally written in Syriac or Greek, and exhibit striking connections with non-orthodox Gnostic thought, though they were probably created by orthodox Christians. The hymns speak of Christ as the Word and as the Wisdom of God incarnate, and startlingly depict the Holy Spirit as a feminine divine personification.

Top: Tertullian (c. 160 – c. 220) left a rare description of worship practices in his Christian community in Carthage, North Africa.
Above left: The English composer Gustav Holst (1874–1934) set part of the apocryphal "Hymn of Jesus" in 1917.
Opposite: The Orthodox Holy Fire ceremony at the Church of the Holy Sepulchre, Jerusalem. One of the oldest hymns still in use in the church is the Greek *Phos Hilaron* ("Gladdening Light").

From a less orthodox source comes a much-debated composition known as the "Hymn of Jesus", for which the English composer Gustav Holst (1874–1934) wrote a setting. This "hymn" is found in the apocryphal *Acts of St John*, a Gnostic document which the Christian leader Augustine of Hippo (354–430) attempted to suppress, and which gives an alternative description to Mark and Matthew of the hymn-singing that ended the Last Supper. However, the nineteenth-century theosophical writer G. R. S. Mead cast doubt on whether this was ever a "hymn" in any accepted sense, still less an orthodox Christian text.

Apart from this, we have few traces of early hymns. The *Paedagogos* ("Tutor") of Clement of Alexandria (Titus Flavius Clemens, c. AD 150 – c. 220) includes a hymn of praise to Christ, written in classical metre, though it is unclear whether it was intended for singing during worship.[19] Often known as "Clement's Hymn", or *Hymnos tou Soteros Christou* ("A Hymn of the Saviour"), it has been paraphrased by Henry Dexter (1821–90): "Shepherd of tender youth/Guiding in love and truth… ".

Early Musical Notation

More important is a third-century hymn to the Holy Trinity discovered in 1918 on a scrap of papyrus (No. 1786) found at Oxyrhynchus in Middle Egypt, which appears to include rudimentary Greek musical notation. This has been translated as:

While we hymn Father, Son and Holy Spirit,
Let all creation sing Amen, Amen, Amen.
Praise, power to the sole giver of all good
things. Amen. Amen.

The music for the last part of this hymn – both its pitch and rhythm – has been reconstructed and transcribed, and is the earliest fragment of written Christian church music yet discovered.[20] The Austrian-born musicologist Egon Wellesz (1885–1974) concluded that the melody is built up from a group of "formulas" characteristic of Semitic melody formation. It has been claimed this discovery shows "that the music of the Byzantine Church, so rich in hymns, developed in an unbroken tradition from the music of the primitive Church". However, since only this single scrap survives, we have no idea how typical it was of contemporary Christian music practice. This apart, we possess no further fragment of written music until the eighth century and no complete Christian manuscript with recognizable musical notation until as late as the ninth century.

Though we have no notion of its tune, we do possess the text of a more extensive Greek hymn, recorded in the fourth century but already then described as "old" and probably dating from as early as the second Christian century. Known in Greek as *Phos Hilaron* ("Gladdening Light"), this hymn is still today sung as part of the liturgy of the Eastern Orthodox Church when the evening lamp is lit:

Having come to the setting of the sun
and seeing the evening light,
we hymn the Father, the Son and the Holy
*   Spirit of God.*

This hymn has been translated a number of times, the English hymn-writers John Keble (1792–1866) and Robert Bridges (1844–1930) creating versions entitled respectively "Hail! Gladdening Light" and "O Gladsome Light, O Grace".

There is little other written evidence about second- or third-century hymns, yet it is certain Christians continued to use verse and song in worship, since pagan critics singled out singing as a distinguishing Christian characteristic. Celsus, a second-century opponent of Christianity, even argued that the emotional power of Christian chants threatened to deaden believers' senses and weaken their reason!

3

The Church Goes Public: Christian Music After Constantine

I wept at the beauty of your hymns and canticles, and was powerfully moved at the sweet sound of your church's singing. These sounds flowed into my ears, and the truth streamed into my heart, so that my feeling of devotion overflowed, and the tears ran from my eyes...

Augustine, *Confessions*, **IX.vi.14**

With the official recognition of the church within the Roman Empire in the fourth century, the pattern of prayer and worship that had developed privately over the preceding centuries could now become public. Instead of house churches, Christians now constructed dedicated buildings for worship. In the larger cities which had already become Christian hubs, such as Jerusalem, Antioch, Rome, and Alexandria, great basilicas were built which provided a catalyst for the development of music for the church. The church's liturgy, music, and architecture now grew together.

♩ Sacred or Secular?

But acceptance of the church by the state brought new and unforeseen problems. Early Christian leaders felt they had not only to combat the infiltration of pagan thought patterns into the church, as the many new converts brought with them alien cultural and philosophical traditions, but also to decide whether music itself, with its powerful pagan associations, was suitable for true Christian worship. Not surprisingly, they were still reluctant to admit instrumental music into the church: such music had for centuries formed an essential component of Greek and Roman secular entertainment, and the Romans in particular had come to associate music with debauched entertainment and behaviour.

The Christian writer Clement of Alexandria (c. AD 150 – c. 215) pulled few punches in attacking such music: "...we must abominate extravagant music, which enervates men's souls, and leads to changefulness – now mournful, and then licentious and

Left: Sixteenth- or seventeenth-century icon of John Chrysostom, Archbishop of Constantinople, who believed that music liberated the soul.
Right: Following the official recognition of Christianity, great church structures began to be built. One such is the Church of the Holy Sepulchre, Jerusalem, whose vast dome is pictured here.

voluptuous, and then frenzied and frantic."[1] By contrast, the preacher John Chrysostom (c. 347–407) recognized the utility of music in daily life and was second to none in his praise for Christian chant: "Nothing elevates the soul [of the believer], nor gives it wings, nor liberates it from earthly things as much as divine chant, in which rhythm and melody form a real symphony…". Yet even he agreed that "everything must be banished which recalls the cult of pagan gods and the songs of actors".

♫ Instruments with Voices?

Vigorous argument ensued. Some Christian writers believed all musical instruments should be excluded from Christian worship. Clement wrote: "We have need of only one instrument, the word of peace, and not the psaltery nor the trumpet, the cymbals, the flute beloved of those who go to battle." Others proposed the use solely of instruments named in the Bible. The increasingly virulent clerical attacks on the use of instruments in worship are probably evidence of widespread popular pressure to use them. Preaching in the Christian centre of Antioch in 386/87, Chrysostom tried to dissuade believers attracted by instrumental performances from attending the prosperous local synagogue, which apparently had a full orchestra: "Do you wish to see that God hates the worship paid with kettledrums, with the lyre, with harps and other instruments?… do you run to listen to [the synagogue's] trumpets?"[2]

The views of the purists eventually won the day, with the result that for virtually the entire first millennium most vocal music in the church was unaccompanied. Yet even the most puritanical allowed singing – indeed regarded it as positively good. Basil of Caesarea (c. 330–79), a prominent leader of the Eastern church, wrote: "God blended

the delight of melody with doctrines in order that through the pleasantness and softness of the sound we might unawares receive what was useful in words…".[3] But for some even singing offered temptations, and ascetic Christians deplored the use of florid melodies. The fourth-century Egyptian Christian monastic leader Pambo (d. c. 375), a follower of the pioneering monk Antony of Egypt, disciplined his monks for singing too melodiously, since such singing could not "produce contrition and [made] the church and their cells resound with their voices as if they were a herd of bulls".

♫ Singing Psalms

Despite these controversies, the psalms continued to play a central role in the worship of the church:

> The command to sing psalms is in force in all churches which exist among the nations, not only for the Greeks but also for the Barbarians, throughout the whole world, in towns and villages and in the fields too, in short, in the whole Church the people of Christ, who are gathered from all nations sing hymns and psalms with a loud voice, so that the voice of the psalm singers is heard by those standing outside.

So wrote Eusebius, Bishop of Caesarea (c. 263 – c. 339), in his *Commentary on the Psalms*. Even allowing for rhetorical exaggeration, psalm-singing was clearly both widespread and popular. In his commentary on the book of Psalms, Ambrose of Milan gives a remarkable apologia for their singing by Christians:

> Psalms are sung by emperors; the common people rejoice in them. Each man does his utmost in singing what will be a blessing to all. Psalms are sung in the home and rehearsed on the streets. A psalm is learned without labour and remembered with delight. Psalmody unites those who disagree, makes friends of those at odds, and brings together those who are out of charity with one another. Who could retain a grievance against the man whom he had joined in singing before God? The singing of praise is the very bond of unity, when the whole people join in a single act of song.[4]

🎵 The Cathedral Office

The threefold or fivefold prayer cycle that had evolved previously[5] was now observed by most Christians, not as previously in private in the home or in secrecy elsewhere, but openly as part of the church's daily liturgy. Morning and evening prayer in church now became communal observances, led by clergymen offering praise and intercession for the church. This "cathedral office", as it is often called, became a broad pattern for church worship across the world and down the centuries. In the morning, Psalms 51 and 63 and, especially, Psalms 148–50 were extensively used. In the evening, the Eastern church utilized Psalm 141 together with the ancient Greek hymn *Phos hilaron* as the lamps were lit (see p. 35); in the West, Psalm 105 was in frequent use.

In addition to the psalms, the litany (derived from *litaneia*, Greek for supplication) – a series of petitions said or sung by a priest or deacon – was widely used as a form of prayer. The congregation would respond – again in speech or song – with the Greek words *Kyrie eleeson* ("Lord, have mercy", usually spelt *Kyrie eleison*). For the first few centuries, worship was largely in Greek; then, with official recognition of the church, Latin became more widely used and soon became the official language of the Western church. By the fifth century the Eastern litany had been incorporated into Latin liturgies of the eucharist, with the Greek words *Kyrie eleison* left untranslated. On her pilgrimage to Jerusalem in the 380s, the Spanish abbess Etheria (or Egeria) wrote an account of her experiences,[6] reporting that a boys' choir in

Left: Basil of Caesarea, Bishop of Caesarea Mazaca, Cappadocia, Turkey – "Basil the Great" (AD 330–379).
Above: "St Augustine in his Cell", a panel painted around 1490–94 by Sandro Botticelli (c. 1445–1510), now in the Uffizi Gallery, Florence, Italy. The torn paper on the floor is thought to reflect the saint's intense effort to express truth in his writing.

the Holy City responded to the litany with the words *Kyrie eleison* – not, as she expected, with an "amen". Pope Gregory the Great (ruled 590–604), who revised the Roman liturgy of the eucharist, made the *Kyrie eleison* part of the official text, and confirmed that the petition *Christe eleison* was also normal in Rome, though not in the Eastern church. In later centuries these two petitions were arranged into various patterns, for example a ninefold repetition of the *Kyrie eleison* and threefold repetition of the *Christe eleison*, which were then set to music of more or less elaborate styles.

At first developing separately from the urban churches, Christian monasteries evolved their own patterns of daily prayer. However, in time monastic prayer patterns came to influence the "cathedral" liturgy, as members of the clergy were attracted to the ascetic life and drew on the monastic experience. Etheria reported that the Church of the Holy Sepulchre in Jerusalem celebrated the daily "offices" of matins, sext, none, and vespers, as well as the annual festivals of Nativity, Epiphany, Holy Week, Easter, Ascension, and Whitsun, each featuring psalms, antiphons (short sentences in song), and hymns "proper" (distinctive) to the day. It was around this time too that the Latin word for the mass – *missa* – was first recorded, derived from the Latin words of dismissal at the close of the service – *Ite missa est*.

🎵 Christian Canticles

Psalms remained a staple of Christian praise, while other texts with a strong biblical content became increasingly important. The *Gloria in excelsis* ("Glory to God on high") – essentially a Christianized form of words of praise found in the Psalms – was sung in Greek as a hymn, featuring in the morning office of the Eastern church, and in the eucharist of the Western church from the early sixth century. A briefer form of words of praise to the three persons of the Trinity, the *Gloria Patri* ("Glory to the Father... "), also came into use in the fourth century. The monk Cassian (360–450) reports from Gaul around the year 420 that the whole congregation joined in what he terms the "small doxology" – the *Gloria Patri*.

From the fourth century, too, the churches both East and West began to sing near the beginning of the eucharist the hymn known

in Latin as the *Sanctus* ("holy"), based on the seraphs' cry in Isaiah 6:3, "Holy, holy, holy" (the "*Ter sanctus*"). A further hymn was added to the eucharist service in the sixth century, the *Benedictus qui venit* ("Blessed is he who comes in the name of the Lord", Matthew 21:9).

The "canticles" described earlier also remained popular. The *Magnificat* and *Benedictus* were sung in morning and evening liturgies in both East and West, while the *Nunc dimittis* was widely used, particularly during evening prayer. The Eastern church in particular also used Old Testament canticles such as the Song of Moses (Exodus 15:1–18; Deuteronomy 32:1–43), Hannah's Prayer (1 Samuel 2:1–10), and Judah's Song of Victory (Isaiah 26:1–21); and the *Benedicite*, based on part of the apocryphal Song of the Three Children (the Hebrew exiles Shadrach, Meshach, and Abednego), was popular in both East and West.

All these canticles were probably chanted in a way similar to that in contemporary Jewish synagogues. The centuries-old Jewish melodic formulas used as the basis for singing psalms and canticles in the synagogue would have been adaptable to the new Christian canticles. One authority goes as far as to suggest:

In the early days of Christianity the readers may have preserved the rules of Jewish cantillation [chanting], which permitted a certain amount of improvisation as long as the traditional formulas and cadences were kept.[7]

But this is speculation.

🎵 Christian Hymns

In addition to these scriptural texts, existing and new Christian hymns became more commonly used. During the fourth century furious debates raged within the church concerning such vital questions as

A Medieval depiction of the "three holy children" – Shadrach, Meshach, and Abednego – in Belshazzar's burning fiery furnace. Part of their "Song" has continued as the canticle known as the *Benedicite*. German School, fifteenth century.

Ephrem (c. 306–73), the most famous writer in the Syriac church and a gifted Christian poet, is chiefly remembered for his hymns and his influence on Byzantine (Eastern) liturgy. Drawing upon Syriac poetry and music, he wrote in a regular pattern of syllables, allowing every stanza of a hymn – and more than one hymn – to be sung to the same popular melody. Ephrem's hymns were intended to teach orthodox theology, for which he often used powerful and distinctive feminine imagery to describe God. Ephrem's many hymns (he wrote hundreds) became of central importance in the eastern and western Syrian church and were translated into Armenian, Greek, Latin, and other languages, and widely imitated. Other Greek hymn-writers of this period include the Eastern theologian Gregory of Nazianzus (329–89), while the preacher John Chrysostom ("golden-tongued") promoted congregational hymn-singing in the churches of Constantinople.

The earliest known author of Latin hymns is Hilary of Poitiers (c. 315–66), recorded by Jerome as having written a "book of hymns and mysteries". Only fragments of his compositions survive, but enough to show that he too used his songs to teach his congregation Christian truth.

the nature of the incarnation and of the Trinity. Both sides in these arguments – the heterodox Arians and orthodox Nicenes – used hymns and songs as one method of promoting their positions.

♫ Ambrose of Milan

Ambrose (c. 339–97), the gifted hymn-writer who became the bishop of Milan in 374, introduced to this strategic city in the Roman West the Greek tradition of congregational singing. At Easter 386, Ambrose led his congregation in a protest sit-in at one of Milan's main churches, which was surrounded by threatening Arian troops, during which he is supposed to have introduced his flock to the practice of antiphonal singing.

Although Ambrose preferred women to keep quiet in church, he declared he would rather have them sing psalms than chatter. Like others, Bishop Ambrose believed hymns provided a valuable method of instructing Christians in theology, and taught his congregation simple but moving compositions to help reinforce orthodox Christian belief. Ambrose's doctrinal foes, the Arians, clearly believed his approach worked, since they claimed he had "bewitched" his flock. He responded: "Some claim that I have ensnared the people by the melodies of my hymns: I do not deny it!"[8] Only a few of Ambrose's hymns survive, but his compositions vitally influenced the development of the liturgy of the Western church.

Ambrose of Milan (c. 339–66), a gifted hymn-writer, is supposed to have introduced the practice of antiphonal singing. Portrait by Matthias Stom (c. 1600–after 1652).

Ambrose's hymns were so highly valued in the West that many compositions were falsely attributed to him. Augustine of Hippo (354–430) attributed to his mentor Ambrose the text of four well-known hymns: *Deus Creator omnium, Jam surgit hora tertia, Aeterna rerum conditor,* and *Veni, Redemptor gentium,*[9] all of which are found in the Catholic liturgy book known as the *Roman Breviary* and later appeared in translation in *The English Hymnal.* A number of tunes have long been linked with Ambrose's texts, but it is unclear whether these date from his time, let alone were composed by Ambrose. The musicologist Alec Robertson has argued that, if later melismata (changes of pitch of a syllable of text while it is being sung) are stripped out of these tunes, authentic fourth-century melodies are revealed.

♫ Other Hymn-writers

Another significant hymn-writer in the Western church was the Spanish poet Prudentius (Aurelius Prudentius Clemens, c. 348–410), a government administrator who in retirement turned to Christian devotion and writing. From Prudentius's many lyrical poems in classical metre excerpts were later taken for use as hymns. Following a classical convention, although the poems were written in Latin, they were given Greek titles. Collections by Prudentius include the *Cathemerinon* ("The Daily Round"), a cycle of twelve hymns for daily use, together with hymns for Christmas, Epiphany, and the burial of the dead; and the *Peristephanon* ("On Martyrs' Crowns"), fourteen poems praising Spanish and Italian Christian martyrs. Of Prudentius's hymns, still in use are *Corde natus ex parentis* (translated into English by John Mason Neale [1818–66] and Henry Williams Baker [1821–77] as "Of the Father's Love Begotten"); *O sola magnarum urbium* (literally, "O chief of cities, Bethlehem", paraphrased as "Earth Has Many

a Noble City" and "Bethlehem, of Noblest Cities… "), a hymn for Epiphany – both from the *Cathemerinon* – as well as *Salvete, flores martyrum* (translated by H. T. Henry [1862–1946] and J. M. Neale as "All Hail! Ye Infant Martyr Flowers… ") and *Quicumque Christum* ("Lift Up Your Eyes, Whoe'er Ye Be", translated by R. Martin Pope).

Only two Christian hymns survive from the output of the fifth-century Latin poet Caelius Sedulius, probably from Italy: *A solis ortus cardine* ("From East and West") and *Hostis Herodes impie,* from his longer poem *Paean alphabeticus de Christo* (translated by Neale as "When Christ's Appearing Was Made Known"). Both more gifted and more prolific was Venantius Fortunatus (c. 540–601) from northern Italy, who settled at Poitiers, in Aquitaine. Venantius's most famous hymns celebrate the cross of Christ and were written to mark the presentation of a supposed relic of the true cross, a gift from the Byzantine Emperor Justin II, at a new convent in Poitiers in 569. *Pange, lingua, gloriosi proelium certaminis* ("Sing, My Tongue, the Glorious Battle") seven centuries later inspired Thomas Aquinas's *Pange, lingua, gloriosi Corporis mysterium,* and also *Vexilla Regis prodeunt* ("The Royal Banners Forward Go"), adopted as a marching song by the crusading armies and still sung at vespers during Holy Week; *Quem terra, pontus aethera* ("The God Whom Earth and Sea and Sky… "); and *Salve festa dies* ("Hail, Festal Day"), used in the Middle Ages as a processional hymn.

The origins of the best-known early Latin hymn – the *Te Deum* – are unclear. Written in rhythmic prose rather than verse, it praises God the Father and Son. Various authors have been suggested, but we have no idea who its true author was. By the sixth century the *Te Deum* was already widely in use and over time it was incorporated into the office of matins, and subsequently set to music by countless composers.

♫ Choirs and Soloists

Almost everywhere church music was still performed unaccompanied. In churches, the psalms were often led by a singer – a young man, sometimes even a boy – who intoned the text as a solo or led the congregation in a responsive format. As we have seen, the responsorial form of psalm singing was possibly imported from the Jewish service of the synagogue, where the whole congregation would respond with a refrain such as "for his steadfast love endures for ever" (Psalm 136, NRSV).

From the later fourth century, church choirs became more common, and in the great city churches they sometimes became quite large. Yet there remained a body of opinion in the church which felt music possessed such emotional power that it needed strict control – even proscription. Some Christians in North Africa believed chanting was more acceptable than singing, though many others believed that music positively enhanced rather than damaged worship.

The Ecumenical Church Council of Laodicea (c. 363–64) prohibited all except trained and designated singers from participating in services – but this was apparently in an effort to ensure the highest standards prevailed, not to prevent singing. The same council condemned the use of all non-biblical texts as "*psalmi idioci*", but with little effect, since Christian hymns continued to be composed and sung, with increasing popularity, while the Fourth Council of Carthage (419) dedicated a special blessing to liturgical singers: "Take heed that what you sing with your mouths you believe in your hearts…".

♫ Christian Thinkers and Music

Greek philosophers had long seen the science of *musica* as one of the liberal arts. In ancient Greece, the word *mousike* (from the Greek form of the word "muse") meant any of the arts or sciences presided over by the Muses, a convention that Christian thinkers continued. Those who believed a good secular education was useful for spiritual learning included *musica* in their recommended syllabus. But *musica* was not "musical theory" as we understand it today, but rather the theoretical study of the mathematical relationship between sounds.

Augustine, the great medieval Christian apologist, attempted to synthesize Christian and neo-Platonist theories of rhythm and metre. Desperately conflicted about music (as about much else), Augustine recognized its powerful and positive influence, yet constantly feared its sensual pull.

> [I am] inclined… to approve of the use of singing in the church, that so by the delights of the ear the weaker minds may be stimulated to a devotional frame. Yet when it happens to me to be more moved by the singing than by what is sung, I confess myself to have sinned criminally…

(*Confessions*, X.xxxiii)[10]

Though Augustine wrote a six-volume work *On Music*, such was his later fear of overindulging the senses he also spoke approvingly of the practice of Athanasius of Alexandria (c. 296–373), chanting the psalms with such limited modulation that it sounded nearer to speech than song.

♫ Music in Christian Education

In the educational regime of the Middle Ages, *musica* was regarded as part of the mathematical *quadrivium*: arithmetic, geometry, astronomy, and *musica*. The Christian philosopher Boethius (c. 480–524/25) subdivided *musica* itself into three topics: *musica universalis*, *musica humana*, and *musica instrumentalis*. Of these, only *musica instrumentalis* referred to performed sound, or music as we know it – sung or played on instruments. *Musica universalis* referred to the relationship and proportions of the spheres of the planets and stars – seen as a form of music, but with no sound necessarily being heard. (From this grew the later concept of "music of the spheres".) Although mainly a synthesizer of ancient Greek thought, Boethius's musical writings were regarded as authoritative in medieval Europe, and with his parallel stress on the ethical influence of music, the subject became an important component of moral and philosophical education.

Detail from a fourteenth-century depiction of "*musica mundana*" or "*musica universalis*", showing the harmony between the stars and planets that was believed to produce inaudible music.

♫ Decline and Fall

In AD 395 the Roman Empire broke into two, with an Eastern Empire centred on Byzantium (Constantinople) and a Western Empire with its capital in Rome. After constant civil wars, barbarian invasions, and attrition, the last Western emperor finally abandoned his throne in 476, leaving the papacy with increased responsibility and – potentially – power. The political collapse of the Western Empire meant that for the next several centuries – until around the tenth century – the Christian church served as the principal vehicle of culture and unity for the West. The church preserved and created much of the musical inheritance of the West.

Although medieval musicians knew nothing of Greek or Roman music – partly because Christians had avoided it – the medieval West inherited from antiquity several vital *ideas* about music, such as music as a single, melodic line; the interlinking of words and melody, using rhythm and metre; a tradition of improvised performance, within conventional formulas; music's potential to affect its hearers positively or negatively; and a system of scales based on tetrachords.

Music in the Orthodox Church

🎵 The Orthodox Liturgy

The principal rite of the Orthodox Church is the Byzantine, resembling the Western rite in terms of organization, in that it includes a celebration of the eucharist (the divine liturgy, usually according to the order attributed to St John Chrysostom, and on certain days according to that attributed to St Basil the Great), and a divine office, including *Orthros* (roughly equivalent to Western matins and lauds) and *Hesperinos* (vespers), *Apodeipnon* (the after-supper service, compline), *Mesonyktikon* (midnight service), and the four hours: first, third, sixth, and ninth.

The liturgical year is structured according to two cycles, one centred on *Pascha* (including the cycles for Lent, Pascha, and Pentecost), and the other a yearly series of commemorations, including Christmas, Epiphany, the *Dormition* (called the Assumption in the West), and commemorations of the saints. In addition, the *Octoechos* organizes the liturgical sequence into a cycle of eight weeks, one week per mode.

🎵 Music and Hymnography in the Orthodox Church

Music is inseparable from liturgy in Orthodox worship and is traditionally exclusively vocal: instruments are not used in worship.

Byzantine music, in the strictest sense, is the sacred chant of churches of the Greek-speaking world, following the Byzantine rite, between the construction of the capital, Constantinople, in 330 and its fall in 1453. But the continuation of this liturgical tradition throughout the remains of the Byzantine Empire and its spread to non-Greek-speaking countries means the term is frequently used, inaccurately, to describe such liturgical chant up to the present day. The origins of this chant lie in the classical Greek world and in whatever music was sung by the early Christians of Alexandria, Antioch, and Ephesus.

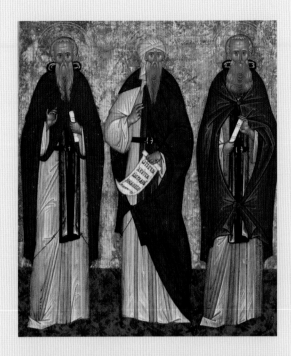

Left: Ceiling frescoes in the eleventh-century Karanlik Kilise (or Dark Church), carved into the soft rock at Göreme, Cappadocia, Turkey. A fine example of Byzantine Christian art, the images include Christ Pantocrator (All-powerful), the Nativity, the Adoration of the Magi, and the Crucifixion.
Above: St John Climacus ("of the ladder"), St John of Damascus, and St Arsenius (left to right) on an icon of the Novgorod School, now in the Novgorod Museum, Russia.

♫ Byzantium and the Byzantine Legacy

Byzantine chant is organized according to the *Octoechos;* that is, a series of eight *echoi* (modes). The origins of this system remain obscure, though tradition attributes it to St John of Damascus (c. 676–749), who lived at the monastery of St Sabas, near Jerusalem. While his work may have formed part of a move toward systemization in contemporary Palestine, it is clear the eight-mode system was firmly in place by the eighth century.[1]

The development of Byzantine chant inevitably went hand in hand with that of hymnography. The earliest and simplest genre is the *troparion,* a single-strophe hymn for which early musical sources are lacking precisely because of their melodic familiarity. Both the vespers hymn *Phos hilaron* and the liturgical antiphon *O Monogenes Huios,* attributed to Justinian I (ruled 527–65), fall into this category.

Large-scale hymnography first appeared in the fifth century, in the form of the *kontakion,* a lengthy metrical sermon, probably Syriac in origin, whose greatest exponent was the sixth-century St Romanos the Melodist, who, though born in Syria, worked in Constantinople. Syllabic settings of the *kontakia* were sung during the course of *Orthros* (matins) as part of the now obsolete cathedral rite. To Romanos is attributed the best-known *kontakion,* the "*Akathistos* Hymn", comprising twenty-four stanzas and still in liturgical use. By the ninth century, however, musical treatment of the *kontakion* had become melismatic and the text reduced from some twenty or thirty *oikoi* (stanzas) to the opening *prooimion* and the first *oikos.*

From the seventh century, the *kontakion* was superseded in importance by the *canon,* whose greatest exponent was St Andrew of Crete (c. 650 – c. 740). The canon is a series of nine odes or canticles, interspersed with the nine biblical canticles. Each ode comprises an opening *troparion,* the *heirmos,* followed by three, four, or more *troparia* which follow exactly the metre of the *heirmos.* *Heirmoi* were collected in books called *Heirmologia,* though few have survived. Music for the *sticheron,* on the other hand, is plentiful, in collections called *Sticheraria.* Musically more elaborate and varied than the *heirmoi, stichera* are intercalated with psalm verses for vespers and matins, and were written for the yearly festal cycle, Great Lent, and the eight-week *Octoechos* cycle.

Though liturgical poetry was still being written in southern Italy up to the mid-twelfth century, the completion of the greater part of the hymnography for the services meant that, in its later period, Byzantine chant was concerned principally with the creation of more elaborate settings for the traditional texts, either by variations of earlier melodies, or new, richly ornamented compositions, whose style was called "kalophonic", or "beautiful-sounding". The exponents of this new style were the *Maistores,* the "masters", of whom the most celebrated was St John Koukouzeles (c. 1280 – c. 1360). These new compositions were recorded in special manuscripts, and Koukouzeles initiated the compilation of large collections known as *akolouthiae,* containing virtually all the music necessary for the divine liturgy and office.

In the early nineteenth century, the notation for Byzantine chant was reformed: the repertory codified by this "New Method" is the basis of what is sung in Greek churches today, as well as in churches in countries that came within the Byzantine sphere of influence, such as Romania and Bulgaria. Arab Orthodox Christians also use Byzantine chant. In each case, however, not only had the chants composed in these countries already acquired a national character, but the music had been adapted to the language of the country. The liturgical language in Bulgaria, as in other Slavic countries, is Slavonic – the missionary work initiated by Saints Cyril and Methodius had encouraged Tsar Boris I to instruct Bulgarian clergy to serve in Slavonic, and it became the country's official liturgical language in 893, when the Greek clergy were expelled.

Serbia's history, like that of Bulgaria, is closely connected with that of Byzantium, and is musically part of the history of the legacy of Byzantine chant, though original hymnody in Slavonic was initiated early, with the work of St Sabas (c. 1173/76 – c. 1235/37). A number of highly original Serbian compositions survive in fifteenth-century sources, including the famous *Polyeleos Servikos* by Isaiah the Serb. Greek influence continued, and the work of the Greek-taught chanters Dimitrije Krestić and Dionisije Čupić at the Karlovci Seminary in the late eighteenth century gave rise to what would later become known as "Karlovci chant". This repertoire was recorded in Western notation by the composer Kornelije Stanković (1831–65), and today forms the basis of most Serbian church singing.

Below: Saints Cyril and Methodius were Byzantine Greek brothers who brought Christianity to the Slavic peoples, and are credited with devising the Glagolitic alphabet used to transcribe Old Church Slavonic. This monument to them stands in St Michael's Square, Kiev, Ukraine.
Right: Mar Saba (St Sabas) Monastery stands isolated in the Judean hills, a little east of Bethlehem, where the Georgian liturgical tradition originated in the seventh century.

♫ The Balkan Countries and Polyphony

Polyphony is used only in a few places in Greece, though the Greek Orthodox Church in the USA still has many parishes with polyphonic choirs, whose repertoire is largely based on the work of the controversial reformer Ioannis Sakellarides (c. 1853–1938), who radically simplified the extant corpus of monophonic chant. Although this style of chant has almost entirely disappeared elsewhere, it was taken to North America by Greek immigrants. Notable composers of polyphony who have contributed to this tradition include Frank Desby (1922–92), Tikey Zes (b. 1927), and Peter Michaelides (b. 1930). In Greece itself, polyphony was cultivated only by Themistokles Polykratis (1863–1926) and the brilliantly idiosyncratic Emilios Riadis (1880/88–1935).

Polyphony had appeared in Romania in the mid-eighteenth century through Russian influence, but only later did it become popular, with the work of such composers as Gavriil Musicescu (1847–1903), Gheorghe Cucu (1882–1932), and Ioan Chirescu (1889–1980). In Bulgaria, polyphonic choirs appeared in the late nineteenth century; the most important figures providing choral music were Petar Dinev (1889–1980), unique in reconciling Western harmony and Byzantine melody, and Russian-influenced composers such as Atanas Badev (1860–1908), and especially Dobri Hristov (1875–1941). Contemporary Bulgarian composers writing liturgical music include Philip Kutev (1903–82), Alexander Tekeliev (b. 1942), Velislav Zaimov (b. 1951), and particularly Ivan Spassov (1934–96), whose *Holy Bulgarian Liturgy* is a landmark in contemporary liturgical settings.

In Serbia, the corpus of Karlovci (rather than Byzantine) melodies formed the basis for the work of the first composers of harmonized church music: principally Stanković himself and the renowned Stevan Stojanović Mokranjac (1856–1914), but also other outstanding composers such as Petar Konjović (1883–1970), Miloje Milojević (1884–1946), Stevan Hristić (1885–1958), and Kosta Manojlović (1890–1949).

♫ Music of the Orthodox Church in Georgia

Unique among the traditions of Orthodox liturgical singing, Georgian hymnody begins with the official adoption of Christianity in Georgia in the fourth century. The Georgian liturgical tradition began at St Sabas Monastery in Palestine in the seventh century, with translations of Greek texts collected in lectionaries. Subsequently, the first independent collection of hymns was created, the *Iadgari*, comprising the hymns for the entire year. Though Georgian chant was probably initially monophonic, its polyphonic character was established early, though its modal organization owes nothing to the West. The chant is divided into two main stylistic branches, East (Kartli-Kakhetian) and West (Imeretian-Gurian), extant in plain and ornamented versions, and is, like other Orthodox traditions, based upon an eight-mode system.

Georgian hymnody developed in the tenth century in the South Georgian monastic schools, notably through the efforts of Grigol Khandzteli, who devised the *Satselitsdo ladgari*, a complete set of chants for the year. This sparked the development of new Georgian hymnody, informed by developments in Byzantium. Outside Georgia, other centres of importance in the development of Georgian liturgy and chant included Iviron, on Mount Athos, and Petritsoni (Bachkovo), in Bulgaria, founded in 1083 by the Georgian Grigol Bakuriani. John Petritsi, who resided at the monastery, is the earliest informant about Georgian three-part polyphony. He subsequently went to the Monastery of Gelati, in western Georgia, which remained an important centre of chant until the beginning of the twentieth century.

The subsequent history of Georgian chant (transmitted entirely orally until the late nineteenth century) consists of a series of declines and revivals, on account of political disputes, wars, and finally the domination of the Soviet Union. Towards the end of the twentieth century, however, a movement for the restoration of Georgian chant began, and it is currently the only authorized music in the Georgian church.

♫ Expansion

The so-called "Diaspora" (countries that have received Orthodox *emigrés* who have usually established their own communities) has often reflected the tensions between monophony and polyphony of the countries from which the *emigrés* originally came. However, the prolific production of Greek-American composers such as Zes and Michaelides, and of English composers Sir John Tavener (b. 1944), James Chater (b. 1951), and Ivan Moody (b. 1964), has created a tradition whose roots are both Eastern and Western. The Estonian Arvo Pärt (b. 1935: currently resident in Germany) and the Greek-Canadian Christos Hatzis (b. 1953) have tended to work more in the paraliturgical realm.

One remarkable instance of a genuinely Western Orthodox phenomenon is to be found in Finland, where an originally Russian-informed tradition was developed into something distinctively Finnish by composers such as Pekka Attinen (1885–1956) and Boris Jakubov (1894–1923). Subsequent composers of importance have included Peter Mirolybov (1918–2004), Leonid Bashmakov (b. 1927), and Timo Ruottinen (b. 1948), and younger composers such as Pasi Torhamo (b. 1968) and Mikko Sidoroff (b. 1985).

Ivan Moody

CHAPTER 4

Christian Chant: The Core of Medieval Worship

Let the chant be full of gravity; let it be neither worldly, nor too rude and poor… Let it be sweet, yet without levity, and, while it pleases the ear, let it move the heart… It should not contradict the sense of the words, but rather enhance it.

Bernard of Clairvaux (1090–1153)

After years of neglect, in the late twentieth century Christian chant made an unexpected commercial come-back, linked to the burgeoning interest in "New Age" phenomena, selling millions of CDs with such unlikely titles as *Gregorian Chillout* and *The Best Gregorian Chant Album in the World… Ever!*

Chant featured in both Jewish and Christian worship from the early years, and in succeeding Christian centuries inspired numerous compositions, remarkable in surviving so long unmediated and relatively unchanged. Christian chant is essentially a simple art: a Latin text sung in unison to a single melody. It can often take the form of a repeated "arch shape", starting on a lower tone and rising before falling back to the original lower tone. Pure chant – often also helpfully described as "plainsong" (*cantus planus*) to distinguish it from later medieval polyphonic music (*cantus mensuratus* or *cantus figuralis*, "measured" or "figured" song) – has no harmony, no instrumental accompaniment, no pronounced rhythm, and no accents. Its tunes cover only a narrow span of notes; its rhythm is the rhythm of the words chanted. Yet heard in a vast cathedral it resonates magnificently. It is transparent and straightforward and often strikes the listener as pure and innocent. In chant at its best, text and melody become as one – neither dominates.

Fragment of a colourfully illuminated sixteenth-century Gregorian chant manuscript from Venice, Italy.

♪ The Beginnings of Chant

Chanting – or "cantillation" – was practised both in the Jewish Temple and in the synagogues that began to appear after the destruction of Solomon's Temple (586 BC) and the geographical dispersal of the Jewish people. Central to Jewish worship was the recitation of the Hebrew Scriptures; the reading and remembering of the text was often aided by chanting it rather than speaking it. The Talmud stipulated that the Bible should be read in public and made understandable to its hearers in a "sweet, musical tone".

Jewish chant was built up from a succession of melodic formulas indicated by a sign or accent (*ta'amin*) written above or below the Hebrew text of the Scripture. Each sign indicated a melisma, or melodic block – a group of notes that was to be applied to the text being read and that constituted a *neume*. The rhythm of the chanting was dictated by the words of the particular passage being chanted. In Jewish cantillation, the scale modes to which the accents were sung were normally based on tetrachords (groups of four musical notes, the first and last of which form a perfect fourth), each book of the Bible having its particular musical mode. One musicologist has pointed out similarities between Jewish cantillation and the reading tone (*tonus lectionis*) set for chanting the Christian Scripture. Similarly, resemblances can be heard between Oriental Jewish psalmody and the psalm tones in "Gregorian" chant.

So-called "Gregorian" chant was not far removed from Jewish chant, with its emphasis on syllabic recitation and step-wise motion. A leading Jewish scholar has affirmed the debt of Gregorian chant to Jewish cantillation, though he qualifies this by adding that

> by establishing for [Christian] *'Plain Chant'* the rule of equal time-value for all notes of the chant, [it] robbed the song, which it had borrowed from the Synagogue, of its distinctive features: the unrhythmical, free character of improvisation, and the embellishment, which is the very colour of Oriental life.[1]

The same scholar believes the church adopted part of its traditional song from the Jewish synagogue, as witnessed by the seventh-century Spanish archbishop of Seville, Isidore (c. 560–636): "The tune of the *Laudes* – that is sung Alleluias – is of Hebrew origin."[2]

From the early fourth century, chant was developed to be sung in the great buildings of the newly legitimate and official Christian faith – the basilicas of the episcopal sees and the great churches of Rome and other Christian centres. With no electrical sound-systems available, Scripture readings (lessons) would have been inaudible if delivered with the normal speaking voice in the spacious new stone-built basilicas; partly for this reason the lessons were chanted, a method that also lent them solemnity. Carefully marked-up punctuation also helped the listening worshippers understand what they heard.

♪ Christian Worship

When the first Christians came together for worship they read from the Scripture, chanted psalms, and offered prayers – often set rather than extempore. Gradually a formal pattern of worship emerged, the first surviving description of which is given by Justin Martyr (AD 100–165).

Justin set out the following order of service for the *Synaxis*, the non-eucharistic Christian service:

a. Opening greeting by the leader and response by the congregation[3]

b. Reading (lesson)

c. Psalmody

d. Lesson

e. Sermon

f. Those in the congregation who are not yet members of the church dismissed[4]

g. Prayers

h. The church is dismissed.

Distinct from and additional to this was the eucharist, or communion service, which initially consisted of the following:

a. Offertory: the bread and wine taken and placed together on a table

b. Prayer: The officiant/ president gives thanks to God over the bread and wine

c. Fraction: The bread is broken

d. Communion: The bread and wine are distributed to believers.

Gradually these two services – the *Synaxis* and the eucharist – merged, so that by the fourth century they were regarded as inseparable, forming the single rite known as the "mass".

♫ The Daily Office

Following state recognition of the Christian faith in the early fourth century, and the rapid growth of the church and development of its structures, the bishops of Rome – the popes – tried increasingly to legislate for and organize every aspect of church life in the West – including its music. Whereas liturgy and music previously varied and were often spontaneous and ecstatic, now the church hierarchy made them more and more structured, ordered, and organized. The church's daily and annual worship patterns were firmly established, with readings and hence music fixed for each ritual, each festival, each day of the week, and each fixed time of day.

By around the end of the fifth century, Rome had devised a system whereby every biblical psalm (150 in all) was read in church over the course of a week. Around the sixth century, this was formally set out in the Rule of Benedict – the foundation document of Western monasticism – as part of the divine office (the *opus Dei*) that was to be observed in all Benedictine monasteries. Elsewhere and in other churches, simpler patterns were observed, with fewer psalms. But whether more or fewer, a cycle of chanted or sung psalms and canticles now became the norm in the church.

With the gradual interpenetration of the monastic and the cathedral worship traditions, by the Middle Ages in many places all or most of the following series of daily offices were regularly observed in both institutions:

Two offices in the early morning (*Orthros* – Greek for "dawn"):

• Mattins (or "matins" – from the Latin *matitinus*, "of the morning"), the long night office before daybreak, hence originally called "vigils". Except in the monasteries, the *Te Deum* was sung.

• Lauds (from the Latin *laudate*, "praise"); Psalms 148–50, originally sung at dawn. Except in the monastic office, the *Benedictus* was sung.

• Prime (from the Latin *primus*, "first"), the first of the daytime offices, at the first hour – 6 a.m.

• Terce (from the Latin *tertius*, "third") at the third hour – i.e. 9 a.m.

• Sext (from the Latin *sextus*, "sixth") at the sixth hour – 12 noon.

Except in the monastic office, the *Nunc dimittis* was sung.

This pattern varied from place to place and from time to time. In many places and on many occasions, part of the service was sung. For each office, specific Scriptures – especially psalms – and chants were designated. Vespers featured the *Magnificat*, for which superb musical settings were written long after the golden age of chant had passed – for example by Mozart in the eighteenth century.

Eventually the text and the music of the office took fixed shape. The texts were collected into the Breviary (meaning "abridged") and the music into the *antiphonale*. The *Antiphonale Romanum* includes more than 2,000 antiphons, or responses to psalms and other texts in the service. The psalms were chanted antiphonally – first by one side of the choir

- Nones (from the Latin *nonus*, "ninth") at the ninth hour – 3 p.m.
  (Terce, sext, and nones are sometimes known collectively as the "little hours".)

- Vespers (from the Latin *vesper*, "evening"), the oldest of the "hours", in the evening between 4 p.m. and 6 p.m. Vespers was originally called "*Lucernarium*", the lighting of the lamps. Except in the monastic office, the *Magnificat* was sung.

Also commonly observed was:

- Compline (Latin *completorium*, "completion" = Greek *Apodeipnon*, "after supper"), an eighth "hour" at the end of the day, before retiring for the night.

Opposite: Justin Martyr (AD 100–65) left an important summary of the order of service in the early church.
Above: A robed male choir sings at the celebration of mass, and (below) an organist plays while a helper operates the bellows. From a fifteenth-century Spanish psalter of Alfonso V of Aragon.
Right: W. A. Mozart (1756–91) was only one among many composers to provide a setting of the *Magnificat;* portrait by Johann Tischbein (1751–1829).

then by the other – after the cantor intoned the antiphon from the *antiphonale* at the centre of the church sanctuary. The antiphon became very popular in the medieval church, consisting of short, freely-composed refrains interpolated between psalm verses to comment on, or emphasize the meaning of, the Scripture text.

The Mass

The mass is the central worship service of the Roman Catholic and Lutheran churches, and is followed by that of the Church of England. Originally chanted, parts of it have been set to numerous different musical arrangements by countless composers across the centuries. Some parts of the mass remain unchanged throughout the year and are known as the "ordinary" of the mass; other parts change to fit the different seasons, feasts, and saints' days of the year, and are known as "proper" (as in the French *propre*), appropriate and specific to that day or season. For instance, there are parts "proper" to Advent, Easter, and so forth. It is mainly the sections forming the ordinary of the mass that have been set to music as separate movements. Many of the texts of the mass have been discussed earlier, and are classic statements of Christian belief, worship, and praise, such as the *Benedictus*.

The ordinary of the mass consists of:

- *Kyrie* (*Kyrie eleison*, "Lord, have mercy")

- *Gloria* (*Gloria in excelsis Deo*, "Glory to God in the highest")

- *Qui tollis* (*Qui tollis peccata mundi*, "Who takes away the sin of the world")

- *Quoniam* (*Quoniam tu solus Sanctus*, "For you alone are holy")

- *Cum Sancto Spiritu* ("Together with the Holy Spirit")

- *Credo* ("I believe" – the Creed)

- *Et incarnatus* ("And was made flesh")

- *Et resurrexit* ("And he rose again")

  Amen

- *Sanctus* ("Holy") and *Benedictus* (*Benedictus qui venit in nomine Domini*, "Blessed is he who comes in the name of the Lord")

- *Agnus Dei* ("Lamb of God") and *Dona nobis pacem* ("Grant us peace").

The *Credo* was first included in the mass in the East, and later sung in Spain, Gaul, and Germany, but was not formally added to the Roman mass until the eleventh century, by which time well-endowed churches celebrated this service with great elaboration.

The chants of the proper of the mass, often sung by a trained choir or *schola cantorum*, consist of:

- Introit

- Gradual or Alleluia

- Alleluia or Tract

- Offertory

- Communion.

The Requiem Mass

The requiem mass, a special mass intended to remember the departed and pray for their eternal rest, became of particular musical significance as a number of composers from the eighteenth century onwards, such as Mozart, Verdi, and Berlioz, wrote especially moving or memorable settings for it. The requiem mass text omits the *Credo* and the *Gloria*, but adds three new movements:

• *Requiem aeternam* ("Eternal rest")

• *Dies irae* ("Day of wrath")

• *Lux aeternam* ("Eternal light").

Medieval monks would have chanted psalms, hymns, and especially antiphons, as well as the required passages of Scripture, at all the offices mentioned above. They would also have sung the movements of the ordinary of the mass listed above, and often also parts of the proper of the mass, such as the gradual, the alleluia, the tract, the offertory, the preface, the *Pater Noster* (Lord's Prayer), and the communion.

♫ The Chant Repertory

At first the chants and liturgies of the West varied from place to place, though they shared certain fundamental characteristics inherited from the Eastern church. They were elaborated and developed in some of the great monastic and church centres of north-west Europe, such as the Benedictine abbeys of St Gall and Einsiedeln in modern Switzerland, and Metz, Chartres, Laon, and Montpellier in modern France, as well as in Rome itself.

Between the fifth and eighth centuries Celtic chant flourished in Britain and Ireland; Hispanic/Visigothic chant (known as "Mozarabic" following the eighth-century Moorish conquest of Spain) in Spain; Gallican chant in Gaul (France); Beneventan chant in southern Italy; Old Roman in Rome; and Ambrosian (named after Ambrose, the local bishop, though it is unlikely that the music was written by him), or Milanese, chant in northern Italy.[5] Each local chant had its characteristic sound and peculiarities.

From the ninth century until the sixteenth century, the liturgy was increasingly Romanized. The Gallican liturgy, used by the Franks in Gaul, drew on both the Celtic and the Byzantine Christian heritage. However, Pepin the Short, king of the Franks from 751 to 768, and his son Charlemagne imposed Roman chant in this region so successfully that we know little about the original Gallican rite. Similarly the Roman liturgy officially replaced the Hispanic in 1071, though traces of the original

Left: In medieval Europe, female choirs sang only in nunneries and convents. Here nuns are singing in the choir stalls in an illumination from a psalter of Henry IV of France dating to the early fifteenth century.
Right: Montpellier Cathedral (Catédrale Saint-Pierre de Montpellier), Languedoc-Roussillon, France, one of several significant places where chant developed in early medieval Europe.

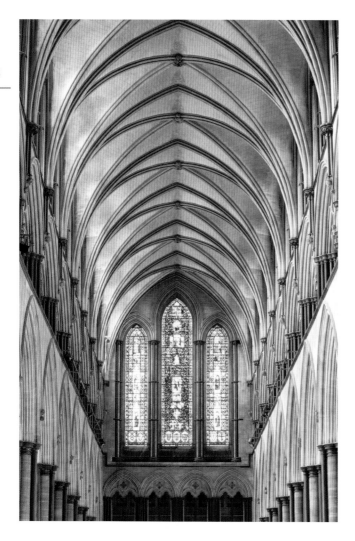

Above: The nave, Salisbury Cathedral, Wiltshire, England, where the "Sarum rite" emerged in the late medieval period.
Right: Pope Gregory the Great, supposed originator of Gregorian chant, characteristically portrayed with a dove representing the Holy Spirit inspiring him. Detail from an altar frontal, Downside Abbey, Somerset, England.

as the thirteenth, continuing in use even after Romanized "Gregorian" chant had spread into the Frankish kingdom.

Eventually, with the exception of Ambrosian chant, all these local variants disappeared or coalesced into a centralized, uniform liturgical practice authorized and controlled by Rome, and generally known as Gregorian chant. Ambrosian chant survives to some extent in the cathedral and diocese of Milan, and is not too dissimilar to Gregorian chant: it tends to have smaller intervals, and "roughness… sudden changes and peculiar exuberance".

One other survival was in England, where a "dialect" of Gregorian chant developed known as the "Sarum liturgy", or "Sarum (Salisbury) rite", used from the late medieval period until the English Reformation. Salisbury was celebrated for its music, the quality of which was safeguarded by a statute of Bishop Giles of Bridport (d. 1262): "… we ordain that hereafter none shall be presented to the office of vicar in this church unless he has a good and musical voice and skill in plainsong…". By 1427 the Sarum liturgy was in use virtually throughout England, and was formally reimposed after the Reformation by Mary Tudor in 1553.

can still be heard in a handful of churches in Valladolid, Salamanca, and Toledo. We still possess written records of the local Hispanic (also known as Visigothic, Old Hispanic, Old Spanish, or Mozarabic) liturgy, but cannot now decipher the notation of the melodies. Old Roman chant dates back to at least the eighth century and survived as late

Gregorian Chant

The Roman chant, generally known as Gregorian, is regarded as particularly successful in marrying word and tone. The name "Gregorian" derives from Pope Gregory the Great, though there is much debate about how much – if anything – Gregory contributed to either the creation or the development of this style of chanting, notwithstanding that popular legend had it he single-handedly composed the hundreds of chants codified around this time.[6] An anonymous eighth-century Frankish monk claimed that Pope Leo I (ruled 440–61) drew up a cycle of chants for the church's liturgical year, as did Gelasius I (ruled 492–96) and other popes in the sixth century. The monk completed his list of contributing popes with Gregory I ("the Great") and Martin I (ruled 649–53).

We do not know what the Roman music that Pepin and Charlemagne prescribed for the Frankish lands actually sounded like. Undoubtedly some of it dated back to the earliest years, and around thirty to forty antiphon melodies may indeed have originated from the time of Gregory the Great. Some may have formed part of the Old Roman chant, or have been tracts, graduals, offertories, alleluias, and other pieces used in Rome. Modern scholarship now tends to believe that the corpus of Gregorian chant owes much to the Old Roman rite, reorganized by Gregory

and by the later Pope Vitalian (ruled 657–72), and was only slightly modified in Gaul. It is this fund of chant, which we now know as Gregorian, that has been transmitted to us through the surviving Frankish manuscripts.

Chant remained the music of Western monasteries for centuries. The two great collections of Gregorian music for the mass and divine office contain in total some 3,000 melodies covering every aspect of the church's worship. This corpus of music is entirely monophonic, with a single, unaccompanied melodic line, yet its singing demands skilled musicianship. The melodies are remarkable in their variety and their ability to express a broad range of emotions. The absence of any regularly recurring strong accent gives the chant a characteristic flexibility.

The collected melodies of Gregorian chant include three different types:
1. Syllabic – with a note for each syllable.
2. Neumatic (from *neume*) – with groups of notes for each syllable.
3. Melismatic – with florid and often lengthy musical passages for each syllable – though the text can still be clearly discerned.

The texts chanted were mostly from the Bible, and mostly in Latin (although there are some Greek texts such as *Kyrie eleison* and *Hagios Theos* ["Holy God"]).

Most cathedrals in the West had their own specially trained choir, led by a choirmaster and later an organist too, who was often also a composer. Performing standards gradually improved and the music became increasingly elaborate. In the great churches, performances at the major festivals sometimes became more like concerts than services, with the result that one pope attempted to ban performances by exhibitionist musicians.

Roman, or Gregorian, chant forms a remarkable musical heritage, comparable in grandeur, scope, and inspiration with the visual inheritance of Romanesque church architecture. It formed the basis of the Western church's liturgy for centuries and, with its stress on the importance of the words, held a vital role in teaching and evangelizing the people of medieval Europe. Missionary monks took the chants with them when they ventured into unchurched areas, and by this means proclaimed and taught the basics of Christian belief in a memorable and dramatic way.

Tropes and Sequences

During the ninth century, elaborations were introduced to chant. Monks added to the antiphonal chants in the proper of the mass, creating new melodies known as "tropes". In "troping", words were added to an existing chant melody – one syllable per note. In this way the original melismatic melody was transformed into a syllabic melody. So, by adding words to an existing chant, or by extending the melisma on the last vowel of an alleluia, monks found they could extend and vary the chant repertoire. For instance, we have a trope from Salisbury cathedral where the text *Christe eleison* ("Christ, have mercy") is elaborated to become *Christe, rex unice, Patris almi nate co-aeterne, eleison* ("Christ, the only king, eternally begotten of the beloved Father, have mercy"). When the monks realized that tropes were not prohibited in the monasteries of tenth- and eleventh-century Western Europe, troping became widespread and popular,[7] though it is unclear exactly where it began – or who started it.

Sequencing (nothing to do with MIDI computer-generated music!) also became popular in chant music. Long melodies, apparently popular tunes of the time, were inserted into chant settings. Sequences sometimes consisted of extended melisma passages – very long and fast melodies in one voice – but contained lengthy texts. The introduction of tropes and sequences imported into church music popular folk-song-like melodies, such as the *Dies irae* and *Veni Sancte Spiritus*, and later laid open the way for the development of liturgical drama.

For sequencing – as for other innovations in medieval music – there is a traditional "inventor": Notker *Balbulus* ("the Stammerer", c. 840–912), a monk from the Abbey of St Gall in Switzerland. Notker made an early collection of sequences, known as the *Liber hymnorum* ("Book of Hymns"), consisting of mnemonic poems written to remind the reader of the series of pitches sung during a melisma in chant, particularly in the alleluia, though it is unclear how many "hymns" in this collection are actually by Notker. It is doubtful whether Notker did actually "invent" the sequence, but he probably introduced the form to Germany, possibly based on sequences rescued by a monk fleeing from the sacked Abbey of Jumièges, near Rouen in France, in 862. Many other abbeys also participated in sequence-writing, and the practice of performing them spread throughout Western Europe. The twelfth-century monk Adam of St Victor (d. 1146) – an abbey near Paris – composed many Latin hymns and sequences, developing the genre by writing rhythmic, metrical verses.

Some celebrated sequences were composed at this time, not least by Hildegard of Bingen (see pp. 62–63). The Easter sequence *Victimae paschali laudes* ("To the Victim of Easter Praise"), attributed to Wipo of Burgundy (c. 995 – c. 1048), had an unrhymed text. The well-known *Veni Sancte Spiritus* ("Come, Holy Spirit"), sometimes known as the "golden sequence", was intended for the Mass of Pentecost and has a rhyming text. Its author is unknown, though it has been attributed to both Pope Innocent III and Archbishop Stephen Langton of Canterbury. The *Veni Sancte Spiritus* has since been set many times, particularly by composers of the European Renaissance such as Dufay, Palestrina, and Byrd. Another well-known sequence is Thomas Aquinas's *Lauda Sion Salvatorem* ("Sion, Praise the Saviour"), originally commissioned by Pope Urban IV (ruled 1261–64) for the novel Mass of the Feast of Corpus Christi (along with Aquinas's other celebrated sequence, *Pange, lingua*). *Lauda Sion* describes the institution of the eucharist, and teaches the Catholic doctrine of transubstantiation, the miraculous changing of the bread and wine to the body and blood of Christ at their consecration during the eucharist. Another great sequence is the terrifying *Dies irae* ("Day of wrath"), purportedly by Francis of Assisi's hagiographer, Thomas of Celano (c. 1200–60/70), again written in rhymed verse. Mozart is reputed to have claimed he would have given all his works to have

written the Gregorian *Dies irae*. The last well-known and enduring sequence dating from the Middle Ages is the *Stabat Mater dolorosa* ("The Sorrowful Mother [Mary] Was Standing"), attributed both to Pope Innocent III and to the Franciscan Jacopone da Todi (1228–1306).

Later, as part of the Catholic church's efforts to reform liturgical practice, the Council of Trent stipulated that only four of the many sequences in use at that date would henceforth be permitted: the *Victimae paschali laudes*, *Veni Sancte Spiritus*, *Lauda Sion Salvatorem*, and *Dies irae*. A fifth, the *Stabat Mater*, was allowed again for liturgical use in only 1727, but was subsequently memorably set by many composers, notably Pergolesi, Haydn, and Rossini.

Left: The east end of Pisa Cathedral, Italy, built between 1063 and 1350.
Below: Notker *Balbulus*, from the Abbey of St Gall, Switzerland, made an early collection of sequences. Most of the present monastery dates from between 1755 and 1768 and is in the late Baroque style.

Liturgical Drama

With the elaboration of tropes, we encounter early examples of dramatized presentations of parts of the Gospel narrative. From the Easter Mass trope, *Quem quaeretis* ("Whom seek ye?" – the angel's dramatic question to the three Marys at the tomb of Christ), developed a dramatized version of the resurrection narrative, with the clerics dressing appropriately for their roles. As early as 980 we have records of this trope being enacted at Winchester in England, and the "Visit to the Sepulchre" became popular all over Europe in succeeding centuries. From these small beginnings, medieval producers used plainsong, antiphons, hymns, sequences, and folk-melodies to create musical dramas based on a growing number of Scripture-themed presentations. As the drama became less reverent and more secular, it moved by stages from the church sanctuary to the church porch and finally outside the church to the marketplace. From the little trope *Quem quaeretis*, we can trace the rebirth of theatre – even musical theatre – in Western Europe.

New Editions of the Chant

Around the middle of the twelfth century, Cistercian monks began to edit the Gregorian chant they inherited from the Benedictines, purging extended melismas from some chants and suppressing accidentals in others, believing such music exceeded the range of the ten-stringed harp set out in Psalm 143:9 (144:9 in Protestant versions), and thereby violated Scripture. These Cistercian reforms resulted in distortions to the chant.

Between the Catholic Reformation's Council of Trent in the sixteenth century and the nineteenth century, the chant was re-edited several times and notation began to show a new kind of measured rhythm. In France Gregorian chants were often replaced by modern imitations, known as "neo-Gallican" chants, and both Gregorian and neo-Gallican chants were now frequently accompanied by musical instruments, especially the serpent. However, during the nineteenth century there was a return to the Gregorian melodies, initially by resurrecting the seventeenth-century style, in the "Mechlin" (Malines) and "Ratisbon" (Regensburg) editions.

Solesmes

Toward the end of the nineteenth century, the French Benedictine monks of Solesmes, having studied the early sources, attempted to restore the chant melodies to their pre-seventeenth-century form. Dom Pothier (1835–1923) prepared a revised edition of the gradual and antiphonary which was intended to conform to ancient traditions of the chant, and in 1883 published the *Liber usualis*, a liturgical book containing the most frequently used Gregorian chants. In Pothier's "equalist" system, all notes were sung at more or less the same speed/length. Dom André Mocquereau (1849–1930), a disciple of Pothier, then published the initial volume of his *Paléographie musicale* (1889), comparing manuscript versions from different periods and places. These were given papal approval in 1903 by Pius X, which helped revive Gregorian chant in churches, while forbidding its accompaniment by piano and "all noisy or irreverent instruments such as drums, kettledrums, cymbals, triangles, and so on…". Pius also encouraged the use of "more modern music", though warning against the use of anything "profane" or "reminiscent of theatrical pieces" (shades of Verdi's *Requiem*).

The encouragement of new church music in Pius X's pronouncement contributed to a renaissance of church music in France. Charles Bordes had already founded the Schola Cantorum in Paris in 1896, to teach liturgical chant and church music. The French composer Louis Vierne (1870–1937), associated with this school, wrote organ music for both the concert hall virtuoso and the village church harmonium-player.

A number of other French organist/ composers thrived in this period. Charles Marie Widor (1844–1937), organist at St Sulpice, Paris – France's most coveted post for organists – is celebrated for the *Toccata* from his *Symphony for Organ No. 5*, often played as a recessional at wedding ceremonies. Charles Tournemire (1870–1939) wrote *L'Orgue mystique*, a cycle of organ compositions based on the Gregorian chant for each Sunday in the church year, and Jehan Alain (1911–40) wrote *Litanies*, also for organ. Marcel Dupré (1886–1971) too wrote primarily for organ rather than the voice, and was also a noted recitalist. The blind Jean Langlais (1907–91) composed for both choir and organ, his *Missa Salve Regina* (1954) using elements from the medieval plainsong of the same name. Maurice Duruflé (1902–86), organist and composer, was commissioned by the wartime French Vichy government to write a liturgical *Requiem*, completed in 1947, which expressed plainsong melodies in the most lavish romanticism.

The Solesmes version of Gregorian chant supplanted what was regarded as the faulty Ratisbon version and remained the official Catholic edition until Vatican II, but was itself subsequently criticized for ignoring some of the early manuscripts' rhythmic indications, and inserting others not in the manuscripts. However, many of the most popular chant records, including those of Solesmes under Dom Joseph Gajard and of the monks of Santo Domingo de Silos, used the Solesmes system. In the 1960s, the Solesmes monk Dom Eugène Cardine studied the earliest notation, and interpreted the longer and shorter notes as rhythmic "nuances". His versions form the basis for some modern performances of great rhythmic complexity, for example by the Ensemble Gilles Binchois, where there is great contrast between longer and shorter sounds.

Gelineau and Taizé

Another attempt to breathe new life into the psalmody of the Roman Catholic church was made by the French Jesuit Joseph Gelineau (1920–2008). Inspired by the new French translation of the Psalms in the *Jerusalem Bible*, he started setting this more rhythmic translation to music. Working at a time when the mass still had to be sung in Latin, his French settings could not be used in the church's main liturgy, but were soon being extensively utilized in other services. Gelineau claimed his music was inspired both by the ancient rites and by folk-song, and aimed to write simply enough for all to participate.

Gelineau went on to write chants for the ecumenical Taizé community in eastern France, which has become renowned for the beauty of its chanted worship. This community of Protestant, Roman Catholic, and Orthodox monks was founded in the early 1940s by Brother Roger Schütz, a Swiss Reformed pastor, and settled at the village of Taizé in Burgundy.

The promotion of mass in the vernacular following the Second Vatican Council (1962–65) led to the rapid disappearance of Latin chant. In response, the Cambridge scholar Mary Berry (1917–2008) attempted to revive and conserve Gregorian chant. Through the Schola Gregoriana she promoted the study and performance of Gregorian liturgical music, and her singers were the first to record a festal service based on the tropes and organa of the Winchester Troper, two-part pieces compiled in the tenth/eleventh centuries at Winchester Cathedral, England.

"Sybil of the Rhine": Hildegard of Bingen (1098–1179)

Among the almost exclusively male and anonymous chant composers of medieval Europe, the only composer we know definitely by name is the extraordinary German nun, Hildegard of Bingen. At a time when few women wrote, she produced both theology and visionary writings, practised healing, advised bishops, popes, and kings, and founded a convent; yet until the 1990s she would not have received a mention in most histories of music.

Although Hildegard has excitedly been claimed as a "first" in so many fields, at the heart of her creativity were

---

Below: Illustration from the *Liber Scivias* showing Hildegard receiving a vision and dictating to her scribe and secretary, c. 1151.
Background: The neo-Romanesque Benedictine Abbey of St Hildegard, Rüdesheim am Rhein, Eibingen, Germany, successor to the abbeys of Rupertsberg and Eibingen founded by Hildegard, here viewed from a nearby vineyard.

her accomplishments in music. A breakthrough recording in 1982, alluringly titled *A Feather on the Breath of God* (Hildegard's own self-description), was the catalyst for intensive interest in, and a number of recordings of, the so-called "Sybil of the Rhine". Following the rediscovery of Hildegard's music, she was initially hijacked by the New Age movement, attracted by her supposed proto-feminism, mystical writings, and ethereal music.

Hildegard was born at Bemersheim and dedicated to the church at birth. Aged eight, Hildegard was sent to an anchoress named Jutta, near Bingen, Rheinland-Pfalz, where she absorbed the music of the divine office at the neighbouring Benedictine monastery of Disibodenberg, took the veil, and joined an embryonic Benedictine convent, after Jutta's death becoming its abbess. From 1141, Hildegard experienced a series of visions that changed her life.[1] She recorded her visions in *Scivias* ("Know the ways of the Lord") and her fame spread. Between 1147 and 1150 Hildegard relocated the growing convent to Rupertsberg, near Bingen, and subsequently founded another convent at Eibingen, on the opposite bank of the Rhine.

"I composed and chanted plainsong in praise of God and the saints even though I had never studied either musical notation or singing," Hildegard wrote. Her music resembles

plainsong – sometimes also drawing on folk-music – yet, in contrast to the narrow tonal range of most contemporary chant, Hildegard's music features a wide range and extremes of register, as well as florid ornamentation. Plainchant conventionally did not use intervals larger than a third, yet Hildegard's music leaps up and down in fourths and fifths, and can encompass more than two and a half octaves. She also expands and contracts melodic phrases to create the "soaring arches" characteristic of her music. Since Hildegard's music dates from a time when musical notation was still underdeveloped, while the pitch of her music is normally clear, the rhythms are not, so modern interpretations can vary hugely in their sound and effect.

In the 1150s, Hildegard combined her music in a monumental collection, *Symphonia armonie celestium revelationum* ("Symphony of the Harmony of Heavenly Revelations"), which includes more than seventy hymns, sequences, antiphons, versicles, and responsaries, set to her own texts, creating a cycle of music for the main festivals of the liturgical year. Paradoxically a woman – the sex frequently regarded by medieval monks as an ancillary to the devil – created this unparalleled outpouring of Christian music.

In singing and playing music, Hildegard believed that Christians integrate mind, heart, and body, heal discord, and celebrate heavenly harmony in the *opus Dei* – the service of God. Hildegard theorized that music represents the symphony of angels praising God, the balanced proportions of the revolving celestial spheres, the weaving together of body and soul, and the concealed designs of nature. According to her, in Eden Adam had a pure voice and joined the angels in singing praises to God; after the Fall, music and musical instruments were invented to worship God. Hildegard regarded music as a means of recapturing the beauty of Paradise.

5

Medieval Polyphony: The Church Discovers Harmony

We approve of such harmony as follows the melody at the intervals, for example, of the octave, fifth, and fourth, and such harmony that may be supported by the simple chant of the church.

Pope John XXII (1325)

The eleventh century marked a turning-point in Europe. It saw the rise of the modern city, the beginnings of European trade, the founding of the first universities, and a rebirth of culture. In music, the momentous change was the introduction of polyphony, a technical-sounding Latin term for a simple concept: instead of music consisting solely of one note sounded at a time, with no harmony and no accompaniment, composers now began to write for two or more differently sounding parts. Without polyphony, chant is really the only option for voices; with polyphony, endless choices, variations, and opportunities open up.

♫ Musical Notation

As mentioned earlier, we have no surviving early manuscripts with musical notation, so no real idea of the *sound* of chanting in the first Christian centuries. Even the earliest surviving examples of musical notation date to only the ninth century, and these give no indication of the musical intervals required.

Guido of Arezzo (991/92 – after 1033) is often regarded as the inventor of modern musical notation. Three centuries earlier, Isidore of Seville (c. 560–636) lamented: "… unless sounds are held in the memory by man, they perish, because they cannot be written down." While a Benedictine monk at Pomposa, Italy, Guido noticed that singers found great difficulty in memorizing Gregorian chants and came up with a method to help them learn more quickly. He was also concerned that Gregorian chant be accurately preserved and handed on. The most

Left: Guido of Arezzo (991/2 – after 1033), the inventor of modern musical staff notation and author of a musical treatise called *Micrologus*. *Right:* The French Pope John XXII (ruled 1316–34), an outspoken opponent of polyphonic music.

primitive musical notation consisted of symbols above the written text to show how high or low the note should be sung. Moving to Arezzo, Guido developed new methods for teaching music, such as staff notation and solmization or *solfeggio* (progenitor of the *do-re-mi* scale), where the initial syllable is taken from each of the first six musical phrases of the first stanza of the popular hymn *Ut queant laxis*.[1] Guido put symbols on parallel lines, each of which represented a tone of the mode, and thus each symbol a note – though its duration was still not indicated. Next to the influential writings of Boethius, Guido's *Micrologus* (1025/26) became the most widely distributed medieval treatise on music.

♫ The Beginnings of Polyphony

We do not know – and it is almost impossible that we could know – when and where the practice of polyphony began. There are hints of it as early as the seventh century – and it is difficult to imagine that a number of people had not experimented with the concept from time to time. The first written evidence of the practice is in the anonymous ninth-century treatise *Musica enchiriadis* ("A Handbook of Music"),[2] which attempted to formulate rules for polyphony in Western music. Early experiments with polyphony seem to have centred on the schools of St Martial at Limoges in France, and Santiago de Compostela in Galicia, north-western Spain, but probably culminated in the great Paris school of Notre Dame.

The advent of polyphony necessitated other major musical changes. Because of its increased complexity, polyphony could not be sung by untrained and illiterate worshippers, but called for a body of practised and literate singers, and its introduction coincided with an increased differentiation between clergy and laity. As polyphony became more complex, it became increasingly difficult for the listener to comprehend the text being sung, since the words were sung in several different voice parts simultaneously. Later use of "imitation" in polyphony could sometimes make the sung text almost impossible to follow, an obvious cause for concern to more perspicacious clergy. Music – no longer merely the servant of the liturgy – was assuming a place of its own. In fact, as polyphonic experimentation became increasingly elaborate, there was a danger that the text might become subservient to the music.

Polyphony was not universally welcomed. The Avignon Pope John XXII rejected it in a strongly worded decree, while John of Salisbury, a twelfth-century bishop of Chartres, objected:

One sings low, another higher, a third higher still, while a fourth puts in every now and then some supplemental notes… When they see the lascivious gesticulations of the singers, and hear the meretricious alternations and shakings of the voices, the people cannot restrain their laughter, and you would think they had come not to prayer, but to a spectacle, not to an oratory, but to a theatre.[3]

Organum

The earliest form of polyphony in the church was also the simplest: two lines of melody tracking each other in parallel motion ("parallel organum"), perhaps in fourths or fifths, or even octaves. (In a sense, this is not true polyphony but enhanced melody.) We know that the abbey choir of St Martial, Limoges, practised this regularly. When men and boys sang together, each with parallel melodic lines, four-part parallel motion was introduced.

The interval between F and B, a "tritone", was considered restless and dissonant – even "dangerous" – and at some point was styled the *diabolus in musica* ("the devil in music") for its scary sound. To avoid it, strict parallel motion was dispensed with and other intervals used. Although the intervals of a third and a sixth were also regarded as dissonant, they were permitted in the course of time.

With this relaxation of the rules on dissonance, by the eleventh century more interesting variations in polyphony could be introduced. In addition to parallel motion, there also appeared contrary motion and oblique motion – that is, convergent and divergent motion. In this way, the independence of each line – "Western polyphony" – was introduced, although for a long time the melody itself still derived from Gregorian chant. We have evidence of early organum in an anonymous twelfth-century treatise from Milan entitled *Ad organum faciendum* ("How to Make Organum").

In the eleventh century too another type of organum appeared: usually known as "florid organum", it consisted of one singer chanting slowly, while simultaneously a second sang a more ornamented part.[4] This offered the opportunity for virtuosic performance by a talented soloist while a less skilled singer – or sometimes the congregation – sang the slower chant. The slow chant melody came to be known as the *cantus firmus* ("fixed chant/song") as opposed to the more elaborate fast-moving part. Later still, the singer of the *cantus firmus* became known as the tenor (from the Latin *tenere*, "to hold", as he "held down" the long, lower chant tone).

As long as the two singers were singing the same rhythm, non-rhythmic musical notation was adequate. However, as soon as the *cantus firmus* parted with the melodic voice, a new form of notation was needed to indicate when the two lines were to finish together. For this reason, notation known as "rhythmic modes" was introduced, without which it would have been impossible to transcribe and pass on complex music.

Until the fourteenth century, all organum music was transcribed in three-time – whether 3/4 or 6/8 – called "perfect time". Here theology overrode musical theory: it was felt important that music reflect the Trinitarian nature of the godhead. Despite this predilection for triple time, in the fourteenth century the "imperfect" mode of duple time (2/4) was introduced.

More New Forms

With the introduction of primitive notation, the way was open for the creation of increasingly complex forms of music. Composers – from now on normally known by name – were able to show clearly by their notation what they wanted the performers to do – the pitch, later the rhythm, and in due course the speed and the dynamics. Innovation was the order of the day. In the first half of the twelfth century came the new form known as the *conductus* (from the Latin *conducere*, "to lead") – a song that "led" the reader to the lectern to read the lesson. The *conductus* used as its lyric a Latin poem instead of a text from the Bible or the mass, and in place of the previous long chant tones, the composer set the words syllabically to an original melody, in two, three, or four parts.

Later in the same century came the "motet", another development of the organum. In this form, a second text – sometimes a Latin hymn that paraphrased, or elaborated on, the main text – was added to the liturgical text sung by the tenor. The motet developed out of *clausula*, polyphonic compositions performed as an alternative to the original plainchant passages they were intended to replace. The motet was a three-part structure in which the lowest part – normally a plainsong theme – was sung, or more likely played on an instrument such as a viol or organ. Often the three lines of a motet had different texts (polytextual) or even different languages (polylingual): for instance the treble (*triplum*) line might be "*O Maria Virgo Davidica*", the *motetus* line "*Ave maris stella*", and the tenor the related plainsong source. These sophisticated medieval motets should not be confused with the very different type of "motet" written during the Renaissance by Palestrina, Byrd, and their contemporaries.

Probably the most influential musical theorist of the later Middle Ages, Franco of Cologne (c. 1240 – c. 1280) collected his ideas in *Ars cantus mensurabilis* ("The Art of Measuring Music"), where he set out notation for four note values: the "double-long", the long, the breve, and the semibreve. Franco's division of time remains the basis of modern Western musical notation, with its semibreves, minims, and crotchets.

The First Polyphonists?

The earliest known named composers of polyphonic music are the shadowy figures *Magister* Leoninus *optimus organisator* (Master Léonin, c. 1159–1201, "greatest composer of *organum*") and *Magister* Perotinus Magnus (Master Pérotin the Great, c. 1170 – c. 1236), both of whom may have had connections with Notre Dame de Paris. Léonin was possibly choirmaster at Notre Dame in the first half of the twelfth century and wrote a major book of two-part compositions for the church year, *Magnus Liber Organum* ("The Great Book of Organum"), much of which has been lost.[5] He has been credited with adding to the chant a second line (*duplum*), sung fast, with up to forty notes against a single note of the original chant.

The early polyphonists Master Léonin and Master Pérotin both seem to have had connections with Notre Dame de Paris, seen here in a painting by the French artist Félix Benoist (1818–96).

Pérotin seems to have further improved organum, making it more lively by adding a third and sometimes a fourth part. This created much more complex music, in contrapuntal style – and also inevitably introduced three- and four-part "chords" which we would recognize as akin to the major and minor triads of later composers. He also added a triple pulse to the prevalent duple time, giving a pleasing lilting effect – and, as we have mentioned, a deliberate consonance with Trinitarian theology.

Pérotin's most important pieces are usually considered to be his four-part compositions, *Viderunt omnes* ("All the Ends of the Earth Have Seen the Salvation of Our God") and *Sederunt principes* ("For Princes Sat and Spoke Against Me", Psalm 119:23; the Gradual for the Feast of St Stephen), both with startling dance-like rhythms in the higher parts, and possibly the first four-part music in the West. A third contemporary, Pierre de la Croix (Petrus de Cruce, c. 1250 – after 1300), from Amiens in France, is important for having freed the treble part from a set number of semibreves, allowing greater melodic and rhythmic independence.

Below: The magnificent south portal of the west façade of Rheims Cathedral, France, where Guillaume de Machaut was both priest and composer.
Opposite: Composers Guillaume Dufay (left) and Gilles Binchois pictured with an organ and harp respectively on a vellum illuminated manuscript of *l e Champion des Dames* ("The Champion of Women") by Martin le Franc (c. 1410–61).

🎵 A New Art

Composers of the fourteenth century saw themselves as musically innovative, proudly contrasting their "new art" in music (*Ars nova*) with the Old Art (*Ars antiqua*) of Léonin and Pérotin in the previous century. *Ars nova* accepted more fully "imperfect" rhythmic modes such as duple time. Toward the end of the century a further novelty was introduced: "isorhythm" – periodically repeated rhythmic patterns in the upper voices, not just in the tenor. Other musicians now introduced *musica ficta* ("false" or "feigned" music), where chromatic notes outside the diatonic system selected for a particular piece were introduced, particularly to avoid harsh intervals, such as the infamous *diabolus in musica*, the tritone. Around this time, too, the introduction of the *faulx bourdon* ("false bass") began to emphasize the vertical sound of chords, rather than chords simply happening to result from notes in melodies combining horizontally. Such music, with its greater reliance on precise mensuration, could develop only alongside the increasingly sophisticated system of notation.

Guillaume de Machaut (c. 1300–77), based in France, was by far the most important fourteenth-century composer and the pre-eminent exponent of the *Ars nova*, with isorhythm among his innovations. Troubadour and poet, secretary to the king of Bohemia, and priest and composer at Rheims Cathedral in France, Machaut wrote much secular music, but only one surviving setting of the mass, the masterly four-part *Messe de No(s)tre Dame* ("Mass of Our Lady"), composed in the 1360s for the Feast of the Purification of the Virgin Mary, and almost certainly performed unaccompanied. Machaut's austere mass is the earliest we have that is in its entirety by an identified composer, and the first major work to exhibit structural integrity throughout its

movements (*Kyrie, Gloria, Credo, Sanctus, Agnus Dei*, and a final *Ite, missa est* – a pattern followed after him by numerous composers), with a short chant motif found in each section.

The English composer John Dunstable (or Dunstaple, c. 1385–1453), "astronomer, musician, mathematician and what not", wrote hymns, songs, and motets for which he was lavishly praised by the Flemish composer Johannes Tinctoris (c. 1435–1511): "[music] in our time took such a wonderful flight because it seems to be a new art which originated with the English under the leadership of Dunstable". Dunstable, who, the contemporary poet Martin le Franc claimed, influenced the eminent Burgundian composers Dufay and Binchois, wrote a fine motet, *Quam pulchra est,* for solo voice and two instruments, but is best known for his *Veni Sancte Spiritus.*

Dunstable's fellow Englishman Lionel (Leonel) Power (1375/80–1445) was equally able and wrote the mass cycle *Alma Redemptoris Mater*, where the movements are, as in Machaut's mass, unified by the use in each of the same plainsong theme. On such foundations Dufay and Ockeghem built in the following century. Also at work was

Richard Davy (d. c. 1521), whose *Passion for Palm Sunday* survives partially in the Eton Choirbook, one of a handful of collections of Latin liturgical music to survive the English Reformation. The outstanding English composer during the reigns of the first Tudor monarchs, Henry VII and Henry VIII, was Robert Fayrfax (1464–1521). His mass, *O bone Jesu*, is considered to be the earliest "parody mass" (a mass based on a pre-existing melody), and his music influenced Taverner and Tallis later in the sixteenth century.

Burgundy

Its frontiers now long forgotten, the duchy of Burgundy exerted huge political and cultural influence in this period in the region now covered by the Netherlands, Belgium, and north-eastern France. The musical centre of Burgundy was the cathedral of Cambrai and, under the patronage of Burgundy's dukes, leading musicians composed magnificent secular and sacred music.

Outstanding among these composers was Guillaume Dufay (c. 1400–74), described by Piero de' Medici as "the greatest ornament of our age". Dufay became chief musician at Cambrai, after having spent time in Rome, Savoy, Flanders, Florence, and Ferrara. He composed fine motets and masses, including a three-part *Magnificat*, an outstanding *Missa Ecce ancilla Domine* ("Behold the Handmaid of the Lord"), and a parody mass using the theme of the well-known folk-song *"L'Homme armé"* ("The Armed Man"),[6] as well as a mass using his own love song *"Se la face ay pale"*. A Catholic musicologist commented:

Possibly the oldest organ in the world still in use, this instrument at the basilica of Notre Dame de Valère, Sion, Switzerland, was probably built around 1430 (though previously dated to 1390).

A great deal of unnecessary fuss has been made about the use of secular themes as the cantus prius factus in a Mass setting. Only a very sharp and trained ear would have been able to recognize the tune… but in any case, no irreverence was intended. On the contrary, it would have been held that the secular melody had been sanctified by its use in church music.[7]

Dufay, who set the ordinary of the mass at least eight times, was instrumental in helping to establish the sung mass as a coherent, unified entity and in preparing the way for its development by the polyphonic composers of the following century. In some of his later works, Dufay placed the tune in the top part rather than in the conventional tenor voice. Gradually the rather austere and mathematical music of the medieval centuries was evolving into the more personal expressiveness of the Renaissance.

The Organ
During the Middle Ages, the organ was introduced and developed, and in some places pedals were added. The blind Italian organist Francesco Landini (or *degli Organi*, c. 1325–97), though not as far as we know a composer of church music, introduced triadic chords and the "Landini cadence" (where the sixth degree of the scale is inserted between the leading tone and the octave). Both innovations were quickly adopted by other church composers.

"Ave Verum Corpus"

"Ave verum corpus natum" is a piece of medieval religious poetry attributed to Pope Innocent VI (ruled 1352–62). Although only five lines long, it covers the incarnation, the passion, the eucharist, and the last judgment. During the Middle Ages it was sung at the elevation of the host during the consecration, being a meditation on the Catholic belief in Jesus' real presence in the sacrament at the eucharist.

> **A**ve verum corpus natum de Maria Virgine.
> V**e**re passum immolatu in cruce pro homine:
> cu**i**us latum perforatum fluxit aqua et
>   sanguine:
> est**o** nobis praegustatum mortis in examine.
> O Ies**u** dulcis! O Iesu pie! O Iesu fili Mariae.

Medieval writers enjoyed acrostics; the first letter of the first line, the second letter of the second line, and so on, spell A-E-I-O-U.

CHAPTER **6**

The Music of the Renaissance: The Peaks of Polyphony

He alone mastered the notes whereas the others were mastered by them.

Martin Luther on Josquin des Prez

In the European Renaissance, visual artists rediscovered and re-used themes and styles from classical Greece and Rome. The painting *Primavera* (or "Allegory of Spring", c. 1482) by Sandro Botticelli (c. 1445–1510) portrays mythological figures in a fertile garden and refers to poems by the Roman authors Ovid and Lucretius.

While the Renaissance in Europe saw the rebirth of classical learning and visual arts, musicians had no means of referring back to Greek and Roman music. Instead of using classical models as their example, Renaissance musicians and composers had creatively to innovate. Although it has become commonplace to cite a conflict of secular and sacred during the Renaissance, music again appears to present an exception, since many more composers than in earlier centuries wrote both secular and religious music. There was even a "cross-over" effect, whereby composers frequently used a popular contemporary melody as the basis for a church mass; the popular French song "*L'Homme armé*" was often deployed as the *cantus firmus* for setting the ordinary of the mass; more than forty different examples have survived, including Josquin's *Missa L'Homme armé super voces musicales*.

The mid-sixteenth-century Roman Catholic reform movement, until recently often known as the "Counter-Reformation", which

attempted among other things to promote more orthodox and biblical expression in the arts, discouraged this usage of secular melodies. To elude such criticism, composers sometimes continued to build a mass on a secular tune, but labelled it *Missa sine nomine* ("Mass with No Name") to disguise the melody's origin.

As we have noticed, with the exception of organ accompaniment in some places for the previous few centuries, most church music until this period was solely vocal. However, during the Renaissance other instruments began to be employed alongside the choir – strings, brass, and small ensembles. The Renaissance choir was typically a four-part ensemble, with each voice given equal importance, producing a smooth, homogeneous tone. The voices were generally the soprano, alto, tenor, bass (SATB) familiar in the modern choir – though the upper parts were sung by boys with unbroken voices.

Sacred music still came mainly in the form of the mass and the motet. The polyphonic mass would consist of the five or six movements of the ordinary of the mass – the *Kyrie, Gloria, Credo, Sanctus* (with or without a separate *Benedictus*), and *Agnus Dei*. Although we have become accustomed to hearing this music performed in concert halls with no significant gap between movements, it was of course originally intended to function within a church as the liturgy of the mass, with considerable time lapses between some movements. The Renaissance motet was a single piece, set to words of Scripture – often drawn from the Psalms – or from the liturgy, and primarily intended for use during the divine office, but also often sung during the mass.

The Printing Revolution

Normally considered for its massive impact on literacy and book publishing, the invention of the printing press in 1450 by Johannes Gutenberg (c. 1398–1468) also had a huge effect on music. The earliest known example of printing from movable type was a Roman missal, with the lozenge-shaped

The Printing Press by John White Alexander (1856–1915), a mural in the Library of Congress, Washington, DC, shows Johannes Gutenberg examining a proof from his newly-invented printing press. Printing was important to the dissemination of music as well as the word.

notes for plainsong printed in black and the music staves in red. The breakthrough came in 1501 when the Venetian printer Ottaviano dei' Petrucci (1466–1539) found a way of printing polyphonic music using movable musical type. He went on to publish the works of such leading composers as Josquin des Prez and Antoine Brumel. The publication of some works by Flemish composers rapidly brought their style and influence to bear in Italy, where much new music was written in this period. As with the printed book, the introduction of printed music also ensured much greater textual accuracy and uniformity, and the rapid and widespread circulation of compositions, with a resultant increase in the early influence of composers upon one another.

♫ New Forms

At the time of the Renaissance, new forms began to be employed by musicians. Often initially introduced into secular compositions, these forms were subsequently adopted by composers of sacred and liturgical music. Instrumental compositions appeared in such new forms as the *canzone*, the *ricercar*, and theme and variation. There was also the *frottola* (a simple chorus form with many verses), the *lauda* (a popular type of devotional song), and sacred madrigals (*madrigali spirituali*). The *laude* were sacred songs in the vernacular based on popular melodies and took the place of the Latin liturgical hymns, which for the most part people could not understand. *Laude* from Tuscany and Umbria tended respectively to be lyrical or dramatic. Jacopone da Todi (1228–1306), supposed author of the devotional work *Stabat Mater*, toured Umbria singing such songs of sorrow and repentance. By the sixteenth century the *lauda* had evolved from an outdoor unison melody to a three- or four-part song performed inside churches or private houses.

♫ The Burgundian Composers

While Dufay was the single outstanding fifteenth-century composer, by the end of that century the field was much richer. Johannes Ockeghem (c. 1410/30–97), another Burgundian, and possibly a pupil of Dufay, is generally considered the most influential Western composer between Dufay and Josquin. While a singer at the cathedral of Notre Dame, Antwerp, between 1443 and 1444, he probably encountered the English compositional style that had a potent influence on European music in the second half of the fifteenth century. In 1452 Ockeghem moved to Paris, where he held a post at the cathedral of Notre Dame.

Like many of his contemporaries, Ockeghem wrote a number of motets and *chansons*, and his fifteen surviving masses are notable for their protracted melodies. Ockeghem and his Burgundian contemporaries finally established four- instead of three-part writing. A distinguished bass singer, Ockeghem's compositions are distinctive for their wide-ranging and rhythmically active bass lines. Sometimes criticized for excessive complexity, Ockeghem's *Missa Ecce ancilla Domine* is actually a model of simplicity, while his *Requiem* is the earliest surviving polyphonic setting of this service. Josquin des Prés described Ockeghem as "music's very treasure and true master".

Antoine Brumel (c. 1460 – c. 1520), born near Chartres in France, was a respected musician – but a difficult employee, which possibly explains his frequent moves from post to post in Europe. We know of six mass settings by Brumel, of which his *Missa de Beata Virgine* is considered the most impressive, with its assured counterpoint and daring dissonances. But the most famous – and productive – Renaissance composer of masses before Josquin was Jacob Obrecht (1457/58–1505), only son of the city trumpeter of Ghent, who held posts in both Italy and northern Europe. Obrecht apparently enjoyed complexity in his work: his *Missa Sub presidium tuum* uses three voice parts in the *Kyrie*, but increases this movement by movement, culminating with seven voice parts in the final *Agnus Dei*.

Probably born in Hainault, Josquin des Prez (or Desprès, c. 1445–1521) – often referred to simply as Josquin – was regarded as the greatest composer of his age and compared to his contemporary, the gifted sculptor and painter Michelangelo. With Josquin, polyphony reached maturity; at least 347 works have been attributed to him, though many of these were anonymous pieces to which his name was attached to improve sales. Before leaving Italy for France around the turn of the century, Josquin wrote *In te Domine speravi* (a setting of Psalm 30 [31 in Protestant versions], "I have placed my hope in you, O Lord"), probably as a memorial to the Italian reformer Girolamo Savonarola, who was burnt at the stake in Florence in 1498 and whom Josquin admired. Josquin returned briefly to the service of Ercole, Duke of Ferrara, in 1503, writing some of his best-known works, including a sombre *Miserere*, again influenced by Savonarola. He also wrote *Missa Hercules dux Ferrariae*, based not on a plainsong theme but on the vowels of the duke's name: the epitome of Renaissance artistic patronage. The same year Josquin returned to his home region, where he spent the remainder of his life.

Josquin lived at a transitional period in musical history, and his travels enabled him to absorb styles from different regions – Ockeghem's sinuous musical lines, the complex counterpoint of Obrecht and his contemporaries,[1] and the homophonic textures of the Italian *lauda* – unifying and synthesizing all these into a new and international musical language later deployed by Palestrina and Lassus. Emotional expressiveness is key to much of Josquin's music: he sought to move his listeners. In his sacred music, he used the technique of "suspension", in which a note is held by one voice while the other voices move on to a new chord, setting up a tension resolved only when the held note also moves to the correct new note. Josquin also practised imitation, where one voice repeats part of what another voice has just sung. He ultimately developed a simplified style where each voice in a polyphonic composition moved freely and smoothly, yet the text was clearly heard. Josquin frequently used *cel motis* – short, easily recognizable melodic fragments that passed from voice to voice, endowing the piece with internal unity: an organizing principle characteristic of much Western music ever since.

Mass Forms

By the fifteenth century, the mass had evolved into a long, multi-section musical form, offering possibilities for complex structure and organization. Josquin and his successors employed a number of structural techniques, including:

1611 woodcut of Josquin des Prez based on a lost portrait of the Burgundian composer made during his lifetime.

- *Cantus firmus mass* – where a pre-existing tune appears, mainly unchanged, in one voice, while the other voices sing freely composed music;

- *Paraphrase mass* – where a pre-existing tune appears in all voices, with many different variations;

- *Parody mass* – where a pre-existing multi-voice song appears whole or in part, with material from all voices in use, not just the tune;

- *Soggetto cavato* – where a tune is derived from the syllables of a name or phrase;

- *Canon* – where the whole mass is based on canon, and no pre-existing material is used.

A significant contemporary of Josquin was Heinrich Isaac (also known as "Arrigo il Tedesco", 1450/55–1517), another Flemish-speaking composer from the southern Netherlands. Isaac was prolific and diverse in his output, which includes thirty-six surviving masses. His greatest claim to fame is his *Choralis Constantinus*, a collection of 450 chant-based polyphonic motets for the proper of the mass for every Sunday in the year plus some saints' days, commissioned in 1508 by the cathedral at Konstanz (Constance) in Germany.

A pupil of Josquin, Nicolas Gombert (c. 1495 – c. 1560), also from Flanders, worked for, and travelled with, the Emperor Charles V and helped carry the new musical style into the Iberian peninsula. Gombert took polyphony to a further stage of development, often writing for five or six voice parts. He also used dissonance to expressive effect, as in his six-part motet on the death of Josquin, *Musae Jovis*, and is remembered for his motets and eight surviving settings of the *Magnificat.* Another significant Flemish composer of sacred music in this period, Jacobus Clemens non Papa[2] (also known as Jacques Clément, c. 1510/15–55/56), worked mainly in Flanders, and is remembered for

his *Souterliedekens* – polyphonic settings of all the psalms in Dutch, designed to be sung in the home, and the only surviving Protestant part-music of the Renaissance.[3] His settings used contemporary popular songs as their *cantus firmus.*

Among the most prolific Burgundian composers of the late Renaissance, Orlando (or Roland de) Lassus (c. 1532–94), born at Mons in modern Belgium, spent much of his career attached to the chapel of Duke Albrecht V at Munich in Bavaria. Lassus took the writing of Flemish polyphony to its highest development in the Renaissance. Among his works written for the Catholic Reformation, Lassus's motets stand out, especially his collection *Magnum opus musicum* ("Great Work of Music", published in 1604), consisting of 516 pieces. Most celebrated are some of Lassus's earlier works, especially his seven *Psalmi Davidis poenitentiales* ("Penitential Psalms of David", written around 1560 but published in 1584), of which the *De profundis* ("Out of the depths… ", Psalm 129/130) is often regarded as one of the high points of Renaissance polyphony. Lassus completed his *Lagrime di San Pietro* ("Tears of St Peter"), a powerful cycle of sacred madrigals dedicated to Pope Clement VIII, just three weeks before his own death.

♪ The Italian Renaissance

Another Fleming, Adrian Willaert (1490–1562), was appointed *maestro di cappella* (choirmaster) of San Marco (St Mark's), Venice, in 1527, and helped transplant the polyphonic style of Burgundy to Italy and found the Venetian school of music. Venice, with its independent republican tradition and wealth, had an old liturgy of its own and in San Marco a unique architectural jewel. Not conventionally cross-shaped, San Marco was a circular church, with musicians seated around the walls and in raised galleries, encouraging antiphonal singing. Also, unlike elsewhere, the Venetians liked instruments as well as voices in church, and their "choirs" often included instrumentalists as well as singers. Willaert's pupil Andrea Gabrieli (c. 1510–86), subsequently made organist and director of music at San Marco, like his teacher utilized the galleries to create "conversations"

Left: Lassus's *Lagrime di San Pietro* was dedicated to Pope Clement VIII (ruled 1592–1605), portrayed here blessing Carmelite nuns in a painting by Fabrizio Santafede.
Below: San Marco, Venice, was the crucible for a rich strand of distinctive polyphonic church music, starting with the works of Adrian Willaert. The unusual architecture of the building, whose ceilings and walls are richly decorated with mosaics, encouraged aural experimentation.

between facing choirs. His polychoral works – when later published – were called *concerti*.

Andrea's nephew Giovanni Gabrieli (c. 1554/57–1612) – another in the line of great composers from Venice – was appointed director of music at the city's Scuola Grande di San Rocco. Not content with writing for a single chorus, he often composed for double, triple – even quintuple – chorus singing antiphonally ("polychoralism"), also using large instrumental ensembles. With such forces at his disposal, it is not surprising that Gabrieli exploited contrast in his music, and was one of the earliest composers to indicate loud (*forte* or *f*) and soft (*piano* or *p*) in his scores. Gabrieli's music was harmonic rather than polyphonic, consisting of great blocks of chords with sonorous textures, played on a variety of instruments. He also explored the contrast between low and high voices, and later became interested in vocal and instrumental colouring, as in his motet *Exaudi Deus* ("Hear, O Lord", 1597), which boasted seven separate lines for basses and

baritones. In time the Venetian approach – its use of instruments and the harmonic style – was copied in France and elsewhere in Italy, though the Spanish clung on longer to polyphony.

Born into an aristocratic family in Mantua, Italy, Alessandro Striggio (c. 1536/37–92) entered the service of the Medici family in Florence in 1559, rapidly becoming their principal composer. Few of Striggio's sacred works survive; his mass *Ecco sì beato giorno* ("Behold the Blessed Light"), in forty parts (five eight-part choirs), rising to sixty at the end, was only rediscovered in 2005 by the American musician Davitt Moroney. It is fully as magnificent as any contemporary Florentine art or architecture.

Giovanni Pierluigi da Palestrina (1526–94) was born in the town of the same name and spent most of his career in Rome, where in 1551 Pope Julius III appointed him *maestro di cappella* of the *Cappella Giulia* at St Peter's. Palestrina's first published work was the earliest book of masses by a native Italian at a time when most sacred music emanated from the Netherlands, France, and Spain.

"Palestrina: saviour of church music" is a frequently repeated myth that was even used as the plot for the opera *Palestrina* (first staged in 1917) by the German composer Hans Pfitzner (1869–1949). According to this legend, the Council of Trent was about to ban polyphonic music completely, and only relented after hearing a piece by Palestrina – often said to be the *Missa Papae Marcelli* ("Pope Marcellus Mass"), published with six other mass settings in 1567, with Palestrina's explanation that he was attempting to "adorn the holy sacrifice of the Mass in a new manner". The Council of Trent aimed to reform the Catholic church, and as part of this policy a strong impetus built up to reject polyphony and return to the sole use of the chant. In 1562 the council ordered the authorities to "banish from church all music that contains, whether in singing or in organ-playing, things that are lascivious or impure" and to reject the trend for complex vocal pieces: the text had henceforth to be clearly intelligible to all (or at least, all who knew Latin).

While baseless – the mass in question was actually written ten years before the cardinals' instruction – the myth does reflect Palestrina's commitment to sacred music and his desire to please the leaders of the church; and it is no coincidence that his *Missa Papae Marcelli* features in the legend, as it is regarded as a perfect example of Counter-Reformation style. Palestrina's music was recognized as a model of clarity, with up to six well-balanced and beautifully harmonized voice parts. The melodies he creates within his counterpoint (dubbed by Claude Debussy "divine arabesques") are both beautiful and comfortable for the singer,

the text easy to discern, and the syllables of the words are given proper stress and length. Palestrina also devoted energy to "purging, correcting, and reforming" Gregorian chant, resulting in a new "Medicean" edition published in 1614. Many chants that used tropes – additional texts – were removed, leaving few of the hundreds of sequences that had accumulated over time.

Famous in his day, Palestrina's reputation only increased after his death. His students Ruggiero Giovannelli, Arcangelo Crivelli, Teofilo Gargari, Francesco Soriano, and Gregorio Allegri continued to write in his style (*prima practica*). This "Palestrina Style" – codified by the Austrian author of the influential counterpoint manual, *Gradus ad Parnassum*, Johann Joseph Fux (1660–1741) – continues to be taught as "Renaissance polyphony".[4]

The composer Carlo Gesualdo (c. 1560/66–1613) is best remembered for having murdered his wife and her lover. His music, which included many madrigals, is extraordinary, with its bizarre, neurotic sound – Stravinsky described him as "the crank of chromaticism". Gesualdo set extravagantly words expressing extreme emotion – love, ecstasy, death, and the like – while he also memorably set gloomy penitential motets. His greatest religious work is his set of responses for Holy Week, *Tenebrae responsoria*, in effect madrigals on sacred texts (*madrigali spirituali*), published in 1611.

Meanwhile the organ, so often and vainly proscribed by popes and church edicts, was becoming an increasingly common feature in larger churches. The organist of St Peter's, Rome, Girolamo Frescobaldi (1583–1643), attracted crowds numbering thousands to hear him perform.

Opposite: Giovanni Pierluigi da Palestrina, so-called "saviour of church music", holding his *Missa Papae Marcelli*, in a portrait by an unknown artist, from San Pietro Maiella Conservatoire, Naples, Italy.
Left: The nave of St Peter's Basilica, Vatican City, Rome, where Frescobaldi attracted crowds to hear his organ recitals in the early seventeenth century.

♪ Spanish Music of the Renaissance

The Spanish Habsburg monarchs, Charles V (1516–56) and his son Philip II (1556–98), were both generous patrons of the arts who ensured that Spain's creative excellence – including both musicians and composers – was known throughout Europe. As the Habsburg realms extended in this period to the Netherlands and Germany as well as the Iberian Peninsula, musical influences travelled far and fast.

Cristóbal de Morales (c. 1500–53) became one of Spain's best-regarded church musicians. Pope Paul III invited him to join the Spanish singers of the Sistine Chapel choir and, under the pope's patronage, Morales travelled around Western Europe, introducing his music to many of the great cathedrals. In 1545 he returned to Spain to become *maestro de capilla* (choirmaster) of the cathedral of Toledo, though that cathedral's tradition focused on organ music whereas Morales' strength lay in writing unaccompanied music for mass, using Gregorian melodies. Morales' pupils, Francisco Guerrero and Juan Navarro, became the finest Spanish church composers of their own generation.

Francisco Guerrero (1528–99), nicknamed "Mary's singer", wrote many masses, motets, and Passions which remained popular, especially in the cathedrals of Latin America. A letter of his to the chapter of Seville Cathedral shows that by this time it was common for instruments such as the shawm, cornet, sackbut, bassoon, and recorder to be used in cathedral worship, and even for their players to practise improvisation – though some churchmen remained fiercely opposed to both practices, citing the authority of Thomas Aquinas. Like Guerrero, Juan Navarro (c. 1530–80) wrote psalms, hymns, and *Magnificats* that long remained the most popular settings in Spain, Portugal, and Mexico. Antonio de Cabezón (1510–66), a blind keyboard-player and expressive composer, was Philip II's favourite personal musician, and made a considerable contribution to organ music with some works of great contrapuntal complexity, many published by his son as *Obras de música para tecla, arpa, y vihuela*.

Tomás Luis de Victoria (1548–1611) started his career as a singer to the Jesuit *Collegium Germanicum* in Rome, where he composed many a cappella choral pieces, influenced by Palestrina. In 1587 he returned to Madrid to serve as chaplain to the dowager Empress María, Charles V's daughter. Victoria's last work, published in 1603, was a *Requiem*

Left: An allegorical painting by the Italian Mannerist Parmigianino (1503–40) of the Habsburg Emperor Charles V receiving the world, c. 1529.
Right: Primate Cathedral of St Mary of Toledo (1226–1493), Spain, where Cristóbal de Morales was appointed *maestro de capilla* in 1545.

Mass composed in memory of the empress, but a joyful rather than gloomy work. Like Morales, Victoria was primarily a composer of vocal music for the liturgy and wrote at least twenty settings of the ordinary of the mass in a direct style, expressing the ideals of the Catholic Reformation. One of the most powerful sixteenth-century polyphonic composers, he expresses musically something of the intense mysticism of Teresa of Avila in her writings. Particularly celebrated are his *Lamentations*, *Crucifixion of Jesus*, and his motets, especially *O magnum mysterium*, depicting the creatures present at the Nativity.

Villancicos

In Spain, the intentions of the musical instructions issued by the Council of Trent were ignored when church composers introduced the *villancico* secular folk-song form into worship, especially on feast days. Later, well-known tunes were given new texts, or wholly new songs were created, which the old guard found uncomfortable, and ultimately the form was banned.

🎵 The English Renaissance

The English composer John Taverner (c. 1490 – c. 1548), probably from Lincolnshire, began his known career as "master of the children" (that is, choirboys) of Wolsey's Cardinal College (later King's College, now Christ Church), Oxford. Brilliantly deploying the rich English polyphonic tradition, and combining it with the continental device of imitation – where a phrase sung in one voice was repeated in another – Taverner's works have greater shape and structure than those of his English predecessors. Taverner is particularly remembered for his *Western Wind Mass*, based on the song of that name, and his *Missa Gloria tibi Trinitas*.[5]

Equally at home writing traditional polyphonic music and the simpler polyphony required by the reformed Church of England, Thomas Tallis (c. 1505–85) had to navigate the politically treacherous waters of Tudor England, where the rapid succession of Edward VI and Mary Tudor after Henry VIII meant equally rapid changes in official religion. During the brief reign of the young Protestant Edward VI, Tallis was required to write simple settings to vernacular texts, and responded with such memorable

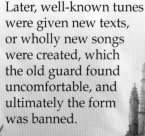

settings as the anthem "If Ye Love Me" (John 14:15–17). In contrast to Taverner and earlier polyphonic composers, Tallis possessed a talent for setting words sensitively. With the accession of the Catholic Mary I, he reverted to writing music for the Latin rite, much of it for the queen's own chapel, combining contemporary European style with more conservative English polyphonic practice, as in his impressive six-voiced responsory *Videte miraculum* ("Behold the Miracle of the Mother of the Lord"), part of the liturgy of the Virgin Mary.

Tallis is remembered above all for his contrapuntal masterpiece for five eight-part overlapping choirs, the forty-part motet *Spem in alium*, regarded as one of the peaks of Renaissance polyphony.[6] Possibly written to celebrate Queen Elizabeth's fortieth birthday in 1573, a later Cambridge Professor of Music, Thomas Tudway (c. 1650–1726), considered it so complex as never to have been intended for performance. It has been suggested Tallis wrote this piece after having been challenged by the duke of Norfolk to "sett as good a songe" as that brought to England by the Italians – possibly a reference to Striggio's mass *Ecco sì beato giorno* or his motet *Ecce beatam lucem*. Tallis also set the *Lamentations of the Prophet Jeremiah*, for use in Holy Week, which includes an unforgettable *Jerusalem convertere ad Dominum Deum tuum.*[7] More widely known is Tallis's canonic hymn-tune, adapted by Thomas Ravenscroft in the early seventeenth century and later set to Bishop Thomas Ken's evening hymn, "Glory to Thee, My God, This Night".

William Byrd (1542/43–1623), "*Britanniae musicae parens*" ("father of British music") according to his peers, was a Roman Catholic in Protestant England, part of an oppressed minority, and probably the last significant Catholic composer in England until Edward Elgar. Writing protest music on behalf of his co-religionists and composing, publishing, and circulating music for their undercover masses, Byrd achieved a prominent position which allowed him relatively freely to contribute to the Catholic cause. Despite his Catholic faith, Byrd seems to have had no

scruples about writing for the Anglican church. In 1575, in collaboration with Tallis, Byrd published a book of thirty-four Latin motets entitled *Cantiones sacrae* ("Sacred Songs"). Probably in the 1580s, Byrd produced his *Great Service* for the Anglican liturgy, for a double six-part choir. Byrd often used imitative counterpoint as practised in Europe, adding occasional sharp dissonances in an idiosyncratic fashion. He described the effect on him of the Bible texts:

I have found that there is such a power hidden away and stored up in those words that… all the most fitting melodies come as it were of themselves, and freely present themselves when the mind is alert and eager.

Byrd was living a double life, and after 1575 clear signs emerge of his recusancy (refusal to attend the Church of England when it was compulsory to do so). He set Latin texts lamenting the oppression of his fellow Catholics, using Scriptures that could easily be interpreted metaphorically. For instance part of his motet *Domine tu iurasti* translates: "O Lord… deliver us from the hand of Pharaoh, king of Egypt, and from the servitude of Egypt" – which could be understood as a plea for release from servitude to Protestantism.

Byrd's published output of music reached a climax between 1588 and 1591, with two English songbooks and two more books of Latin motets – dedicated to Catholic patrons and understood by contemporaries to be covert Catholic pieces – establishing him as the leading English composer. Byrd now retired from London and started to write music for clandestine Catholic services. He published three masses – for three, four, and five voices – with no title page indicating where and by whom they were printed, though the name "Byrd" appeared above the music. They were probably intended for use in the domestic chapel of his Catholic patron, and are more expressive than his austere Anglican music. There followed Byrd's two-volume magnum opus, the *Gradualia* (1605 and 1607), a comprehensive collection of liturgical propers for Catholic services, including anthems to the Virgin Mary. Byrd's pupil Thomas Morley declared that his master was "never without reverence to be named of the musicians".

Left: Title page of Tallis and Byrd's *Cantiones, Quae Ab Argumento Sacrae Vocantur*, released by the composers in London 1575 using their twenty-one-year monopoly on publishing polyphonic music granted by Elizabeth I.
Above: Engraving of William Byrd by the Dutch artist Gerard van der Gucht, c. 1700. "For Motets and musick of piety and devotion… I prefer above all… William Byrd… " (Thomas Morley).

The Organ

*Whence hath the church so many organs and musical
instruments? To what purpose, I pray you, is that terrible
blowing of bellows, expressing rather the cracks of
thunder, than the sweetness of a voice?*

Aelred of Rievaulx (1160)

Organs spread to the West from Byzantium during the Middle
Ages; by the end of the tenth century several monasteries
had installed them. They varied hugely in size, from the
portable, single-keyboard instruments of the Middle Ages and
Renaissance to the vast creations of the early twentieth century.

Until the sixteenth century, organs were most commonly
used along with voices. A regular practice in the Catholic
liturgy was for alternate phrases or verses of a text to be
sung to unaccompanied chant, the intervening passages
represented by the organ playing *versets*, based on the
relevant plainsong melody. The texts were generally
regarded not as the primary focus of attention but more as a
background presence to the actions of the liturgy.

One effect of the Protestant Reformation and Roman
Catholic response to it was to bring words to the fore in
worship. They were to be readily heard and understood, and
the organ's role changed to that of *supporting* the singing.
The German Lutheran church also developed the chorale
prelude, in which the organist played a more or less elaborate
version of a chorale (hymn) tune before it was sung by the
congregation. This practice has left us some of J. S. Bach's
best-loved organ pieces, and continues to this day.

Some of the more radical Reformers wanted to ban organs
from churches altogether, along with other forms of elaborate
music. There are many contemporary accounts of organs
being destroyed by Puritan soldiers during the English Civil
War (1642–49). During the eighteenth and first half of the
nineteenth centuries, English rural parish churches mostly
lacked organs, and some cultivated "West Gallery" music,
with bands of singers and instrumentalists encouraging
congregational singing, usually from a gallery at the church's
west end. Under the influence of the Oxford Movement,
organs and robed choirs began to replace these gallery
bands, a process reflected in Thomas Hardy's novel *Under
the Greenwood Tree* (1872). Gallery music has undergone a
revival since the early 1990s.

The Eastern Orthodox Church has traditionally excluded
organs – along with all other instruments – regarding the
human voice as the most perfect vehicle for worship.

As well as accompanying choirs and congregations, organ
music has evolved its own autonomous role in Western
church services. This includes music played before and
after the service – the so-called "voluntary", which can be
improvised or an existing composition. During the service
itself, organists often improvise at points where no words
are being said or sung, usually taking a hymn or other
appropriate tune as a basis.

♫ Repertoire

The earliest known source of organ music is the
Robertsbridge Codex, with six pieces dating from about
1360. Although written in England, some of the music it
contains is French. About a century later the *Buxheimer
Orgelbuch* ("Buxheim Organ Book"), the most comprehensive
fifteenth-century source of keyboard music, was compiled
in Munich, Germany, probably under the leadership of the

blind German organist Conrad Paumann (c. 1410–73). Over half of the 250 pieces it includes are based on vocal music from France, England, Italy, and Germany from the previous five centuries.

As yet, there was little distinction in style between music for the organ and for other keyboard instruments, such as the virginals. Organ music began to evolve a distinctive idiom in the hands of organists and composers such as Antonio de Cabezón, Jan Sweelinck, Girolamo Frescobaldi, and the expatriate Englishman John Bull (1562/63–1628).

Organ composition flourished particularly in the Baroque period (roughly 1600–1750). Important French composers included Jean Titelouze (c. 1562/63–1633), Nicolas de Grigny (1672–1703), and François Couperin, while the North German school, stemming from Sweelinck, included Johann Pachelbel (1653–1706), Dietrich Buxtehude (c. 1637–1707), and Johann Sebastian Bach.

Interest in composing for the organ declined during the later eighteenth and early nineteenth centuries (Mendelssohn's six *Sonatas* are a notable exception), and the next important wave of organ music came from France. Alexandre Guilmant (1837–1911) may be regarded as the first of a long line that continues unbroken to the present day, including César Franck, Charles-Marie Widor, Marcel Dupré, Olivier Messiaen, and Naji Hakim (b. 1955).

In England, a tradition was maintained through the nineteenth century by organist-composers such as Samuel

Sebastian Wesley, followed by Sir Charles Stanford and Sir Hubert Parry. Important twentieth-century figures included Herbert Howells, Kenneth Leighton (1929–88), and William Mathias (1934–92), and cathedral organists such as Francis Jackson (b. 1917) and Arthur Wills (b. 1926).

In the German tradition there are major works by Franz Liszt, with a number of shorter pieces by Johannes Brahms. The symphonist Anton Bruckner, although an organist himself, left no important music for the instrument. The late Romantic style is represented by Max Reger (1873–1916), Franz Schmidt (1874–1939), and Sigfrid Karg-Elert (1877–1933), while the three sonatas by Paul Hindemith reflect the leaner sound-world of the 1930s. More recently, the Czech composer Petr Eben (1929–2007) produced a number of large-scale organ works.

Among leading avant-garde composers of the later twentieth century, the Hungarian-born György Ligeti (1923–2006) wrote *Volumina* (1961/62), not in conventional notation but as a sequence of graphic shapes, giving the player only general indications of pitch and volume. The English composer Jonathan Harvey combined organ and pre-recorded tape in his *Toccata*.

MIKE WHEELER

Opposite: The organ of St Stephen's Cathedral, Passau, Germany, the largest outside the United States, and the largest cathedral organ in the world, with 17,774 pipes, 233 registers, and five manuals.
Above: 1884 portrait of Franz Liszt by Franz von Lenbach (1836–1904), from the Kunsthalle, Hamburg, Germany.
Below: Portrait of a man, generally believed to be François Couperin *"le grand"* (1668–1733) , by an unknown artist, in the Château de Versailles, France.

CHAPTER 7

A Safe Stronghold: The Music of the Lutheran Reformation

Music is one of the greatest gifts that God has given us: it is divine and therefore Satan is its enemy… The devil does not stay where music is.

Martin Luther

The German Reformer Martin Luther was born in Eisleben in Thuringia, a province noted for its musicians, most notably Johann Sebastian Bach. As a child, Luther sang in the village *Kurrende* – a choir that performed at weddings and funerals – and heard the music of the Burgundian composers Ockeghem, Isaac, Obrecht, and Josquin. Luther loved the old Latin hymns and later revised many for use in reformed worship; although he attacked corruption in the Roman church, he never lost his regard for its musical traditions.

Long before Luther began to reform the mass, the German church had already started to develop its own musical tradition. For centuries German Christians had sung the little hymns known as tropes and sequences in services, together with folk-tunes and semi-religious songs called *Leisen*, mostly in unison and in the style of Gregorian chants. (Luther was not, as has sometimes been claimed, the originator of congregational singing.) Often German churches also already used the German language rather than Latin for parts of the service.

♫ The Lutheran Mass

In 1523, Kaspar Kantz, prior of the Carmelite monks of Nördlingen in Bavaria, published the first musical setting of the mass in German. Later the same year, the radical reformer Thomas Mün(t)zer (c. 1488–1525) published the first completely German liturgy, while other German masses appeared in 1524 in Reutlingen, Wertheim, Königsberg, and Strasbourg. With the appearance of a number of different vernacular masses, many turned to Luther to restore uniformity to liturgical practice – though Luther

Above: Martin Luther translating the Bible, Wartburg Castle, 1521, by Eugene Siberdt (1851–1931).
Right: The doors of the Castle Church (*Schlosskirche*), Wittenberg (Lutherstadt), Sachsen-Anhalt, Germany, on which Martin Luther is said to have posted his famous 95 Theses. The tower of the church is inscribed with the words, *Ein feste Burg ist unser Gott.*

believed the different parts of the newly reformed church should each feel free to create their own liturgy, borrow from others, or retain the Latin mass.[1] Luther held that the mass should be celebrated in both Latin and vernacular German: in Latin in cathedrals and abbeys, where most of the participants could understand that language, and in German in parish churches. In practice, often a single service would be conducted in both languages, sometimes with readings or hymn verses first in one language then in the other.

In his *Formula missae et communionis* ("Order of Mass and Communion") of July 1523, Luther proposed an order for the mass in Latin, but added: "I also wish we had as many songs as possible in the vernacular which the people could sing during mass, immediately after the gradual and also after the *Sanctus* and *Agnus Dei*." The Latin Lutheran mass was not terribly different from the old Roman Catholic mass: the main distinction was that the bread and wine were now freely available to all Christians. Luther similarly encouraged full congregational participation in the church's music, but also the continuing practice of the daily office – especially vespers, compline, and matins – and the regular singing of the entire psalmody. He was loath to impose a rigid, uniform liturgical settlement.

Faithful to his principles, Luther also wrote his own *Deutsche Messe* ("German Mass", 1526), to be used where most of the congregation did not understand Latin. Created with the aid of Conrad Rupsch, kapellmeister (choirmaster) to the elector of Saxony, and Johann Walther, it was designed not as a choral masterwork for performance by priest and choir, but for use by congregation, priest, and choir. Luther wanted to include all believers in corporate worship, not just trained musicians and their *musica reservata*, as had become common practice before the

Reformation. (Not that he opposed elaborate musical settings: Luther also believed in refined music in the church.) The *Deutsche Messe* used idiomatic German and gave great impetus to congregational singing.

♫ Chorales

Martin Luther insisted that German hymns, or "chorales", be used in all services, in order that the congregation should participate intelligently in worship. His own most lasting and important musical contribution lay in the composition and adaptation of these chorales. Unlike chant melodies, which often used many notes for a single syllable of text, Luther's chorales applied just one note to each syllable, making them simple to learn, sing, and remember; in them we find one of the origins of the modern hymn.

But even chorale singing was not new; some fifty years before Luther, Jan Hus and his Bohemian Brethren (Moravians, or Hussites) had practised the congregational singing of hymns adapted from Gregorian melodies or popular airs. In 1504 the Moravians published the first collection of eighty-nine hymns in the Czech language[2] – some by Hus himself – including battle hymns such as "Oh, Ye Warriors of the Lord" and hymns for communion. (The Moravians believed that all believers, not just the clergy – as in the Roman Catholic church – should receive the wine as well as the bread.) Hus's communion hymn, "Jesus Christ, Our Blessed Saviour", still appears in some Lutheran hymnals.

Luther's first hymn-book, the *Achtliederbuch* ("Hymnal of Eight"),[3] also created with the help of Walther, was published in 1524, and included eight metrical chorales and four hymns by Luther himself. By 1545, the Reformer had compiled a total of nine hymnals. The melodies in these chorale books consisted of a mixture of Latin hymns, popular religious songs, and

secular tunes – medieval melodies of the Minnesingers, the Meistersingers, and tunes from outside Germany. Among them is *In dulci jubilo* ("Good Christian Men, Rejoice"), originally a lullaby from one of the medieval mystery plays and still popular as a Christmas carol. The *Erfurt Enchiridion* (also published in 1524) includes three chorales adapted from chant: *Nun komm, der Heiden Heiland* ("Saviour of the Nations, Come"), *Christum wir sollen loben schon* ("Now Praise We Christ, the Holy One"), and *Komm, Gott Schöpfer heiliger Geist* ("Come Holy Ghost, Our Souls Inspire") – translations, respectively, of the Latin hymns *Veni, Redemptor genitum* (ascribed to Ambrose), *A solis ortus cardine* (by Sedulius), and *Veni, Creator Spiritus* (probably by Rhabanus Maurus [c. 780–856], archbishop of Mainz).

The first secular melody in the chorale books, *Mein Freud' möcht sich wohl mehren*, was adapted by Luther to become *Herr Christ, der einig Gotts Sohn* ("Christ, the Only Son from Heaven"). He similarly transmuted the popular ballad *Innsbruck ich muss dich lassen* ("I Must Leave You, Innsbruck") into "I Must Leave You, O World"!

Few new melodies were written in the early years of the Reformation. Although there were competent Protestant composers, the Reformers generally preferred to use melodies already familiar to congregations. Among the trickle of new melodies are two of the finest Renaissance chorales: *Vom Himmel hoch da komm' ich her* ("From Heaven Above to Earth I Come") and *Allein Gott in der Höh' sei Ehr* ("All Glory Be to God on High").

When compiling his *Wittenberg Gesangbuch* of 1524, Luther chose the melodies and texts, while Walther composed simple polyphonic settings for four voices. Walther's own *Gesangbüchlein* ("Little Book of Songs", also 1524) used two types of polyphony – first simple settings, and secondly more elaborate, contrapuntal settings, employing imitation and canon, to create chorale motets and chorale anthems for performance by the choir. An example of this new genre of Protestant music is Walther's *Nun bitten wir den heiligen Geist* ("Now We Implore God the Holy Ghost"), in five-part polyphony.

It is unclear how many chorales Luther himself composed. Thirty-eight are generally attributed to him, but not all of these are original compositions, and Luther borrowed freely both the texts and the melodies for many of his chorales – as did other contemporary composers. The best-known chorale attributed to Luther is *Ein' feste Burg ist unser Gott* ("A Safe Stronghold Our God is Still" or "A Mighty Fortress is Our God"), a paraphrase of Psalm 46, "God is our refuge and strength… ", the tune of which is woven from Gregorian and other sources. A draft of *Ein' feste Burg*, sometimes dubbed "the Reformation Hymn" (the German poet Heinrich Heine called it "the *Marseillaise* of the Reformation") survives in Luther's own hand. Three centuries later it was memorably (and archaically) translated into English by the Scots historian Thomas Carlyle (1795–1881) with such lines as:

> With force of arms we nothing can
> Full soon were we down-ridden.
> But for us fights the proper Man
> Whom God himself hath bidden…

🎵 Lutheran Liturgy

The main Lutheran Sunday service – which could last as long as five hours – consisted musically of a motet, the Lutheran mass, several chorales, and a cantata. During Luther's time, congregational chorales or hymns were mostly sung without instrumental accompaniment, by the congregation in unison, or occasionally by the choir with simple polyphonic harmonization. The organ was never used to accompany chorales, and only cathedrals and larger city churches could normally afford a choir. In both Catholic and Lutheran churches, the polyphonic choir would be positioned in a west-end gallery and have instrumental support, though during major church festivals, singers and players might be positioned at other significant parts of the church.

Luther was not enthusiastic about using the organ. It was utilized to play preludes, to give the pitch to the priest and choir, and in chorales alternating with the choir – one verse on the organ, the next sung unaccompanied by choir and congregation. However, Luther did encourage the use of

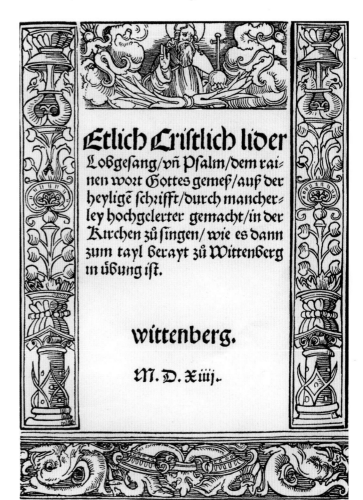

Decorative title page of the first edition of the first Lutheran hymn book, *Etlich cristlich lider Lobgesang und Psalm* (or *Achtliederbuch*), published in 1524, purportedly in Wittenberg, Germany.

wind instruments in the performance of chorale motets in the larger churches with trained choirs.

Martin Luther did not claim to be a great composer; his greatness lies in his establishment of the new Lutheran liturgy and in the importance he placed on music. Unlike some other Protestant Reformers, he did not reject the composers of the Roman Catholic church and borrowed freely from them. When a collection of burial hymns appeared in 1542, he explained: "… we have made some selections from the beautiful music and hymns used in the papacy, in vigils, masses of the dead, and at burials… However, we have changed the texts… ".

The Second Generation

Luther's hymns were followed by Protestant hymns written by the next generation of composers such as Nicolas Decius (1458–1546), Hans Leo Hassler (1562–1612), and Lucas Osiander (1534–1604). Osiander's 1586 hymnal included chorale melodies with a basic harmonic accompaniment. Like Luther, he felt the entire church should sing, as indicated in the collection's title: *Fifty Sacred Songs and Psalms Arranged So That an Entire Christian Congregation Can Sing*.

The sophisticated tradition of the Renaissance Catholic church offered little music for the people to sing, while the Calvinists excluded instrumental music entirely from corporate worship. By contrast, the Lutheran Reformation encouraged both art music and simple congregational songs, resulting in a flourishing tradition of Protestant music. Music in the German Protestant church continued to prosper after

Luther, with composers such as Johann Walther, Michael Praetorius, Heinrich Schütz, and Dietrich Buxtehude putting musical flesh on Luther's belief that music was a gift of God.

On Luther's commendation, Johann Walther (1496–1570) became the first Lutheran cantor, when appointed musical director of the Latin school and church at Torgau. Setting many texts from Luther's German Bible, he put into practice Luther's goal of encouraging worshippers actively to participate in the service by singing the new German chorales. Walther also wrote a poem, "In Praise of the Noble Art of Music" (1538), in which he quoted almost every passage of Scripture about music.

For centuries, priests had chanted the Passion story during Holy Week, with one singing the Gospel narrative, another the words of Jesus, and a third those of other *dramatis personae*. Walther now created new Passion settings, still featuring solos for the Gospel-writer (or "Evangelist") and Jesus, but allocating the words of the other characters and of the crowd to the choir. This pattern was followed by later Protestant composers, notably Schütz and J. S. Bach.

Michael Praetorius (1571–1621) was a pivotal figure in Lutheran church music, respecting the old tradition of music performed by trained choirs, but also creating new chorales for the people to sing. A former colleague of Johann Walther, he served as kapellmeister at Dresden and Magdeburg, achieving recognition as both a performer and composer. Praetorius set many traditional liturgical texts to music, often adopting the new Venetian polychoral technique of employing two, three, or four choirs singing from various positions in the church to produce an impressive "stereophonic" effect. He composed in all 1,200 chorale settings and harmonizations for voices and instruments. In many of Praetorius's settings, for one stanza the choir, accompanied by wind and string instruments, sang an elaborate arrangement of the hymn, while the congregation responded by singing the next stanza in unison, thus creating a conversation between choir and congregation. Praetorius also wrote an illustrated multi-volume encyclopedia of music history and church music, *Syntagma musicum* (1615–20), and the nine-volume *Musae Sionae* ("Muses of Zion", 1605–10), which included more than 1,000 German psalms and hymns for the entire church year and for almost every conceivable combination of voices, based mainly on chorales.

After Luther

The seventeenth-century Lutheran church in Germany was dogged by theological debates. Some believers, such as Philipp Jakob Spener (1635–1705), advocated the revival of a more practical, devotional Christianity, with greater emphasis on practical Christian living and with sermons that nourished the soul and resulted in changed lives. The resulting "Pietist" movement strongly influenced a number of Lutheran poets and composers, who soon began to write hymns that were paraphrases not only of biblical psalms and canticles but also of Bible stories, in order to instruct the people. The Pietists also began to reject much of the liturgical ceremony of Lutheran worship, though their hymns were

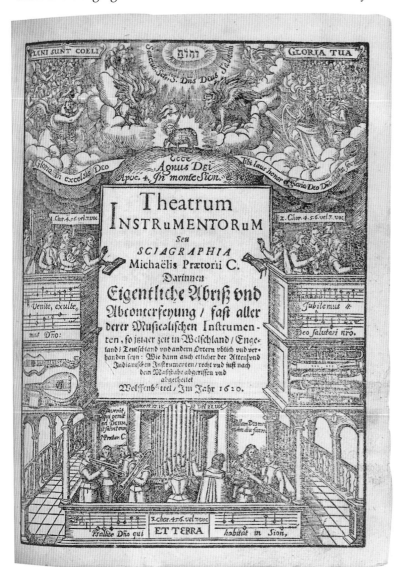

Opposite: Contemporary portrait of Michael Praetorius, composer, organist, and writer about music.
Left: The illustrated title page of Praetorius's three-volume magnum opus, *Syntagma musicum*, which covered the history and theory of music, affords some insight into contemporary musical practice.

probably initially sung in domestic devotions rather than in church.

Possibly the best-known German chorale after Luther's hymn is Martin Rinkart's *Nun danket alle Gott* ("Now Thank We All Our God"), based on the apocryphal book of Sirach (Ecclesiasticus) 50:22–24, and written around 1636, amid the devastations of the Thirty Years War. Sung in thanksgiving at the end of that war, it has become a sort of German *Te Deum*, heard at national occasions. Rinkart was Lutheran minister in Eilenburg in Saxony. The tune "*Nun danket*" is first found in the 1656 hymnody *Praxis pietatis melica* by the Pietist composer Johann Crüger (1598–1662), and reached Britain in the nineteenth century, thanks to a memorable translation by Catherine

Winkworth (1827–78), supported by a fine harmonization by Mendelssohn.

Winkworth's collected chorale translations, *Lyra Germanica* (c. 1853/54, 1858), *The Chorale Book for England* (1863), and *Christian Singers of Germany* (1869), were the main vehicles for introducing the German chorale tradition – and Pietist hymns – to English-speaking worship. Among other enduring translations by Winkworth are "Praise to the Lord, the Almighty" (originally by Joachim Neander [d. 1680]), "All My Heart This Night

Below: The Relief of Constance, 1633, during the Thirty Years War, by Vicente Carducci (1568–1638). The figure on the left is probably the Spanish general Gómez Suárez de Figueroa, Duke of Feria.
Right: Paul Gerhardt, the great Pietist German hymn-writer.

Rejoices", and "Jesu, Priceless Treasure" (both by Johann Franck [1618–77]).

The so-called "Passion chorale", *Herzliebster Jesu, was hast du verbrochen* ("Ah, Holy Jesu, How Hast Thou Offended?") by Johann Heerman (1585–1647), also dates from this period. Other enduring chorales include "Wake, for the Night is Flying" and "How Brightly Shines the Morning Star" from *Mirror of Joy* by Philipp Nicolai of Westphalia (1556–1608), written when the advent of plague was feared.

There was an expanding market for hymns in Germany, and from the mid-seventeenth century the actual size of hymnals grew rapidly. While the *Dresden Hymnal* of 1622 contained 276 hymns, the 1673 edition boasted 1,505. Similarly the *Lüneburg Hymnal* of 1635 had 355 hymns, and the 1694 version 2,055. Hymns were particularly popular within the Pietist movement, whose most popular hymnals, the *Geistliches Gesangbuch* (1704) and *Neues geistreiches Gesangbuch* (1714), both by Johann Anastasii Freylinghausen, were combined in 1741 to form the *Halle Hymnal* – also known as the *Freylinghausen Gesangbuch* – containing 1,581 hymns and 597 tunes. This collection was carried to North America by German immigrants for use there. The Dutch Reformed mystic Gerhard Tersteegen (1697–1769) also wrote many hymns, and relaunched the hymnal *Bundes-Lieder*, originally by Neander, tripling it in size.

Paul Gerhardt (1607–76), born at Gräfenhainichen, situated between Handel's Halle and Luther's Wittenberg, is often considered Germany's greatest hymn-writer. Bringing a new subjectivity to hymn-writing, his work expressed both Pietistic devotion and personal sadness – unsurprising in one who suffered the depredations of the Thirty Years War. Among his hymns are "Jesus, Your Boundless Love to Me" and "O Lord, How Shall I Meet You?", as well as a new version of the hymn attributed to Bernard of Clairvaux, "O Sacred Head, Now [or "Sore"] Wounded", translated into English by the poet laureate Robert Bridges (1844–1930). Many of Gerhardt's best-known hymns were originally published in church hymnals, such as that for Brandenburg (1658); others appeared in Johann Crüger's *Geistliche Kirchenmelodien* (1649) and *Praxis pietatis melica*. The first complete collection of Gerhardt's hymns appears in *Geistliche Andachten*, published in 1666–67 by Johann Georg Ebeling (1620/37–76), Crüger's successor as cantor of St Nicholas's Church, Berlin, where Gerhardt had been minister.

Gerhardt left a detailed description of Christmas morning service at St Nicholas's (the *Nikolaikirche*), listing the impressive musical forces employed: a choir of schoolboys, another of mixed voices, a band (*collegium musicum*) of violinists and woodwind-players (including shawms and bombards – a kind of soprano shawm), a chamber organ as well as the large main organ, a male-voice quartet, and finally a military band of trumpets, kettledrums, and drums.

Schein, Scheidt, and Schütz

An important development in Lutheran music was the *chorale concertato*, created by such composers as Johann Hermann Schein (1586–1630) and Samuel Scheidt (1587–1654). Schein was appointed to the influential post of Thomas Cantor at Leipzig (a position later famously held by J. S. Bach) in 1616. Primarily a vocal composer, Schein was one of the first German composers to absorb the novelties of Italian Baroque and introduced figured bass, the *concertato* style, and monody to Lutheran music. Scheidt, a fine organist from Halle (Handel's birthplace), studied under the Dutch composer Jan Pieterszoon Sweelinck (1562–1621) in Amsterdam, and became the first significant German Baroque composer of organ music. Sweelinck is remembered largely for his organ music, but also wrote psalms and *cantiones sacrae* (sacred songs). During his time, the Dutch were pioneering the organ recital, performed in church but without any liturgical significance.

As a boy, the soprano voice of Heinrich Schütz (1585–1672) was noticed by Count Moritz of Hesse-Kassel, who invited him to join his court choir, and later sent him to Venice (1609–19) to learn from Giovanni Gabrieli, giving him the opportunity to absorb the innovations of early Italian Baroque. When Schütz returned, the elector Johann Georg I of Saxony lured him to his own court at Dresden, the foremost German musical establishment of the time, where he became kapellmeister in 1618. Schütz stayed there most of his remaining life, applying the fruits of his period in Italy to Lutheran texts, returning to Venice in 1628 to study the new operatic style with Claudio Monteverdi.

Schütz wrote twenty-seven fine settings of the psalms of David in German (*Psalmen Davids*, 1619) in the grand style of Gabrieli, for multiple choirs (sometimes four separate vocal groups) and instruments – performance of which was possible only because of the wealth of the Dresden court. Between 1629 and 1650 Schütz also published three volumes of *Symphoniae sacrae*, Latin and German religious songs with instrumental accompaniment. Schütz wrote the *Musikalische Exequien* (1636), a Lutheran requiem, and his *Die sieben Worte Jesu Christi am Kreuz* ("Seven Last Words from the Cross", 1657) and *Christmas Oratorio* (1660) utilized Lutheran chorale tunes in a way that Bach emulated in his own compositions.

During the latter part of the Thirty Years War in Germany, the exigencies made the grand performances of his earlier years impractical, and Schütz's later works often used much sparser forces – sometimes just one or two voices accompanied by organ and a bass instrument. In his eighties, Schütz wrote three masterpieces of sacred choral music: the *St Matthew* (c. 1665), *St Luke*, and *St John Passions*, in a pared-down, more austere and archaic style than his earlier works, using no instruments and with no commentary on the biblical narrative. The narrator, or "Evangelist", retells the story in what Schütz called "German recitative" – not far removed from plainchant – while the crowd have more active harmony and rhythm. In his *St Matthew Passion* the Evangelist is sung by a tenor, Jesus by a "manly" baritone, Judas by a counter-tenor. These settings by Schütz are still used by Lutheran churches during Holy Week.

Dietrich Buxtehude (c. 1637–1707), the greatest organist of the generation before Bach, was the son of a Danish Lutheran organist. At thirty-one he took the influential post of organist at St Mary's Church, Lübeck, which had a magnificent organ with fifty-two stops, and he remained there until his death. Many of Buxtehude's compositions feature a chorale melody set simply or highly ornamented. His musical introductions were sometimes so complex that the congregation was unclear which hymn was to be sung – a predicament said to have led to the practice of listing the

German Hymn-writers

The eighteenth-century German poet Christian Fürchtegott Gellert (1715–69) wrote a number of "spiritual songs" acceptable to both German Catholics and Protestants. Known for his piety and philanthropy, his Easter hymn *"Jesus lebt, mit ihm auch ich"* was translated into English as "Jesus Lives! Thy Terrors Now… " by Frances E. Cox in her collection, *Sacred Hymns from the German* (1841). Matthias Claudius (1740–1815), a German newspaper editor and poet who adopted Pietist views in later life, wrote the German harvest-festival hymn *"Wir pflügen und wir streuen"*, translated into English by

Left: Heinrich Schütz, the German composer who pioneered choral Passion music.
Below: Interior of St Mary's Church, Lübeck (*Lübecker Marienkirche*), northern Germany, where Dietrich Buxtehude served as organist and composer between 1668 and 1707.

numbers of the chosen hymns on a board. Buxtehude wrote many choral works in Latin and German (later called "cantatas") which, with his organ performances, formed part of his famous *Abendmusiken* ("evening music") at the church. The cantata is a short work, not unlike an oratorio, which normally employs chorus, orchestra, and soloists, and has several contrasting movements. It is a form J. S. Bach was to bring to its classic expression. Buxtehude's concerts famously attracted the attention of the twenty-one-year-old Bach, who in 1705 travelled 280 miles to attend the *Abendmusiken*.

Georg Philipp Telemann (1681–1767) was regarded in his day as the greatest German composer, and if judged on output – forty operas, forty-six Passions, five complete cycles of cantatas for the Lutheran liturgical year – he would still be a strong contender. However, over the succeeding centuries Bach has eclipsed him, and Telemann has often been dismissed as relatively superficial, with a facility to write in almost any style except one distinctive to himself. This rather facile judgment has recently come under question.

Jane M. Campbell (1817–78) as "We Plough the Fields and Scatter". In both German and English the preferred tune is called "*Wir pflügen*", attributed to Johann A. P. Schulz (1747–1800).

🎵 Lutheran Hymns in Scandinavia

Sweden

Following the Lutheran Reformation, Laurentius Petri Nericius (born Lars Persson, 1499–1573), the first Protestant Swedish archbishop, required that parts of the liturgy still be sung in Latin, with the result that congregational hymn-singing developed quite slowly. Jesper Swedberg (1653–1735), father of the mystic Emanuel Swedenborg, published the first Swedish hymnal, known as *Swedberg's Book of Hymns*, as late as 1694. However, this

was rapidly withdrawn as theologically "unsound", and republished in acceptable form, with around 500 hymns, a year later. Other Swedish hymn-writers include the poet Bishop Haquin (Håkan) Spegel (1645–1714) and Johan Olof Wallin (1779–1839). Wallin, who became archbishop of Uppsala, and made a new authorized collection of Swedish hymns first published in 1819, is remembered for such hymns as the Christmas classic "*Var hälsad, sköna morgonstund*" ("All Hail to You, O Blessed Morn") and "*Vi lovar Dig, O Store Gud*" ("We Worship You, O God of Might").

Known as the "Fanny Crosby of Sweden", Lina Sandell (1832–1903) wrote some 650 hymns in Swedish, all of which were set to music by the Pietist guitarist Oskar Ahnfelt (1813–82), the "spiritual troubadour" of Sweden. Sandell wrote gratefully: "Ahnfelt sang my songs into the hearts of the people."

Finland

Michael Agricola (c. 1510–57), bishop of Turku in Finland, who studied under Luther, published his Finnish translation of the New Testament in 1543; yet Lutheranism spread relatively slowly in his country, with the Orthodox part of Karelia (the province of Käkisalmi) and the Lapps not converting until the following century. The first Finnish hymn-book was published in 1583 by Jacobus Finno (Jakko Suomalainen, c. 1540–88), headmaster of Turku Cathedral school.

In 1582 Theodoricus Petri (Rutha) Nylandensi (Theodoric Petri of Nyland, c. 1560 – c. 1630) published in Greifswald (in Pomerania, on the Baltic coast of Germany) *Piae Cantiones Ecclesiasticae et Scholasticae Veterum Episcoporum* ("Devout Ecclesiastical and School Songs of the Old Bishops"), a collection of seventy-four medieval Latin sacred songs compiled by Finno.[4] These largely monophonic songs were set to popular melodies, some several centuries old, many originating from central Europe and some from Scandinavia.[5] Several numbers from *Piae Cantiones* are still sung as Christmas carols, including "*Gaudete*", "*Corde natus*", "*Personent hodie*", "*In dulci jubilo*" – so closely linked with J. S. Bach that it is sometimes attributed to him – and the spring carol "*Tempus adest floridum*" – the melody to "Good King Wenceslas".

A Finnish translation of *Piae Cantiones* by Hemming Henriksson (Hemminki Maskulainen, 1550–1619) of Masku, entitled *Vanhaim Suomen maan Pijspain ja kircon Esimiesten Latinan kielised laulud*,[6] was printed in Stockholm in 1616, and is regarded as

the first Finnish anthem book. Many of Henriksson's translations are still found in the anthem book of the Evangelical Lutheran Church of Finland. A second musical edition of the Latin version of *Piae Cantiones* appeared in 1625, edited by Henricus Fattbuur and Matthias Tolja, the music

Left: Georg Philipp Telemann, the self-taught German composer and musical director of Hamburg's five largest churches from 1721 until his death in 1767.
Below: The altar of Turku Cathedral, mother church of the Lutheran Church of Finland. Jacobus Finno, compiler of the first Finnish hymn book, was also headmaster of the Turku Cathedral school.

edited by Daniel Friderici, cantor of St Mary's Church, Rostock.

The songs of *Piae Cantiones* remained popular in Finland until the nineteenth century, but then fell into disuse. However, renewed interest has restored their popularity and they form part of the standard repertory of Finnish and Swedish choirs. Outside Scandinavia, interest in *Piae Cantiones* appeared earliest in Britain, where J. M. Neale and T. Helmore drew on them for their *Carols for Christmas and Eastertide* (1853).

Denmark

Between 1387 and 1814, Norway and Denmark were united as a single kingdom, with broadly the same church and written language. Lutheranism arrived early: invited by Christian III, the German Reformer Johannes Bugenhagen (1485–1558) drew up a Lutheran church order in 1537. A Lutheran hymn-book containing just ten hymns, *Det kristelige Messeembede* ("The Christian Mass-Book"), had been published in 1528 by Hans Mortensen in Malmø, and was revised and expanded by Bishop Hans Tausen in 1544. But it was *Den danske Psalmebog* ("The Danish Psalm-Book"), containing 268 hymns, published by Hans Thomissøn in 1569, that was for 150 years the authorized hymn-book of Denmark and Norway. These Danish hymn-books still included a few pre-Reformation hymns such as "O Mary, Virgin Undefiled" and "O Day Full of Grace" alongside translations of Latin hymns and German Lutheran chorales.

Christian V's revision of church order in 1685, in his *Danmark og Norgis Kirke-Ritual,* finally rejected Gregorian chant from the Danish church. To meet the need for a revised hymn-book *Den forordnede Salmebog* (usually known as Kingo's *Salmebog*) was published in 1699, with about 300 hymns, 85 by Thomas Hansen Kingo (1634–1703). This book contained all the hymns and chants required for the church year, and was used in Denmark, Norway, and the Faeroe Islands until the mid-nineteenth century. Kingo, "Poet of Easter", and "Singer of Orthodoxy", built on Thomissøn's foundations, and added new hymns, such as some by Hans Christenson ("Lord Jesus Christ, My Saviour Blest"). Other Danish hymn-writers followed: Hans Brorson (1694–1764), "poet of Christmas", with "I Walk in Danger All the Way" and "Behold a Host"; and Birgitte Boye (1742–1824) with "He is Arisen! Glorious Word!", "Rejoice, Rejoice This Happy Morn", and "O Light of God's Most Wondrous Love".

Nikolai Frederik Severin Grundtvig (1783–1872), "poet of Whitsun", was the last and greatest of this triumvirate of Danish hymn-writers,[7] his hymns so popular it was said, "Kingo's harp has been strung afresh." Grundtvig wrote about 1,500 hymns, mostly between 1837 and 1860, typically treating the church and the sacraments or emphasizing the Bible as the guide for the Christian believer, publishing *Sang-Værk til den Dansk Kirke* ("Song Work for the Danish Church") in 1837–41. Among his better-known hymns are "Built on a Rock, the Church Doth Stand", "Peace to Soothe Our Bitter Woes", and "God's Word is Our Great Heritage". Grundtvig also produced a body of Christmas music, including "*Dejlig er den himmel blå*" ("Bright and Glorious is the Sky"), "*Der kimer nu til julefest*" ("The Bells of Christmas"), and "*Et barn er født i Bethlehem*" ("A Child is Born in Bethlehem"); his hymns and other writings have profoundly influenced Danish culture.

Norway

The earliest significant Norwegian hymn-writers were contemporaries of Kingo: Petter Dass (1647–1707), son of a Scottish merchant, best known in English for his hymn "*Herre Gud dit dyre navn og ære*" ("Mighty God, to Thy Dear Name be Given Highest Praise"), and Dorothe Engelbretsdotter (1634–1716), "poetess of the North". Subsequent Norwegian hymn-writers included Bishop

Johan Nordahl Brun (1745–1816), the champion of Lutheran orthodoxy against rationalism, who wrote "How Blest are They Who Hear God's Word", and Wilhelm Wexels (1797–1866), who wrote "O Happy Day When We Shall Stand".

Further Norwegian hymn-books appeared, notably Guldberg's hymn-book (1778), Brun's *Evangelical Hymns* (1786), and Balle's evangelical Christian hymn-book (1798). As elsewhere, the hymnals usually contained only words; the music was printed in a separate chorale-book (*Koralbog*) for use by trained church musicians. Without printed music, differences arose in several regions over how hymns should be sung, and church leaders sang them in various ways, as they remembered them or in line with their own musical preference. In some cases, Norwegian folk-tunes were employed for hymns, as with "Behold a Host", "In Heaven Above", and "The Sun Has Gone Down".

Magnus Landstad produced a new Norwegian hymn-book in 1869, which included some of his own hymns, such as "When Sinners See Their Lost Condition" and "I Know of a Sleep in Jesus' Name", and quickly gained acceptance in Norway and with Norwegian

immigrants in America. To accompany it, Ludvig Lindeman published a new chorale-book (1871), which comprised old chorale tunes, Scandinavian folk hymns, and some of his own compositions.

Iceland

At the time of the Reformation, Iceland formed part of the Danish-Norwegian kingdom. The earliest Icelandic hymn-books were published in 1555 and 1558 and contained hymns translated from German and Danish. Hallgrímur Pétursson (1614–74), the most important poet of early modern Iceland, wrote fifty "Passion hymns" in various metres. By tradition, during Lent these classic hymns are sung or read for devotional use, and even today broadcast on radio. "*Allt eins og blómstrið eina*" ("Just as a Single Flower"), a reflection on death, is customarily used at Icelandic funerals. Pétursson's lasting popularity partly results from his romantic personal life, but his religious verse continues to move.

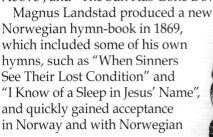

Above: Title page of Petter Dass's *Den Nordske Dale-Viise*, written in Danish and published in Copenhagen, 1683.
Right: Nikolai Grundtvig, a formative figure in Danish cultural history, in an engraving by Christoffer Eckersberg (1783–1853).

Sermons in Song: The Moravians and Their Music

The Moravian church can be traced back to fifteenth-century Bohemia and Moravia, to the followers of the Czech religious Reformer Jan Hus, executed as a heretic in 1415. Later, the Moravian *Unitas fratrum* ("Unity of Brethren") developed from a Protestant community that in 1722 sheltered from Catholic persecution on the estate of Count Nikolaus Ludwig von Zinzendorf in Bohemia, creating the town of Herrnhut, the first of many Moravian settlements formed throughout the world. Moravians had simple ideals of community life and worship: the entire community was regarded as a family unit, and organized by marital status, gender, and age – with a widows' house, a widowers' house, an unmarried brothers' house, and an unmarried sisters' house.

The Moravians also developed unique musical practices. Zinzendorf believed the truest language of devotional Christianity was song, and that Christian truth is best communicated in hymns, not in theology or polemics. The Moravian church's distinctive worship service was the *Singstunde*, consisting almost entirely of hymns, with stanzas from different hymns woven together to express the day's theme – a "sermon in song". Zinzendorf wrote many hymns for the *Singstunden*, often composing them extempore.

Initially their music was choral, but in 1764 the use of the trombone was approved by the Synod of the Moravian church, and as communities were set up elsewhere in Germany, trombone ensembles (*Posaunenchor*) were formed.

Right: The tower of the Old Moravian Church, Bethlehem, Pennsylvania, USA, showing the platform from which the *Posaunenchor* played.
Below: Tenor and bass trombonists of the Moravian *Posaunenchor* of Bethlehem, Pennsylvania, Easter morning, c. 1948.
Opposite: The Moravian Church, Nain, Labrador, Newfoundland, Canada.

Moravians who settled at Zeist in the Netherlands and Christiansfeld in Denmark also soon boasted trombone choirs.

The Moravians claim to be the longest-established musical institution in the USA, with trombone ensembles formed in the early Moravian communities at Winston-Salem, North Carolina, and Nazareth and Bethlehem (1745), Pennsylvania. Although the *Posaunenchor* tradition gradually died out in Europe, in the USA Moravians still maintain a tradition of amateur brass-playing.

The *Posaunenchor* usually consisted of four instruments, matching soprano, alto, tenor, and bass voices. It substituted for the church bell, playing from the church tower to summon the congregation or announce the death of a church member, and played at the graveside and on holy days. The trombone choirs mainly performed chorales from the Moravian version of the Lutheran hymn-book, some seasonal and others that gave recognized signals to the community. There were specific chorales to announce the death of a church member and for a funeral, and for different groups in the community: for example, in Bethlehem, Pennsylvania, *O Haupt voll Blut und Wunden* ("O Sacred Head, Sore Wounded" – the "Passion Chorale") announced that a death had occurred, and another chorale indicated the status of the deceased – married, widowed, single, or child. Christian Gregor (1723–1801), a Moravian bishop, was a prolific composer, more than 1,100 of whose works are found in American collections. His much-loved *Hosanna* is performed during Advent and on Palm Sunday, sung in antiphonal call-and-response across the congregation or between men and women.

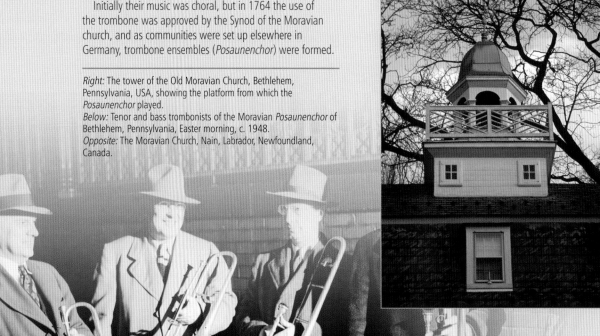

In some parts of the USA, trombone ensembles remained till modern times. Individual trombone groups sometimes displayed remarkable longevity: one at Bethlehem started in 1818 and stayed together for almost fifty years. Though today trombone-only groups are rare, nearly every Moravian church has an ensemble of some kind, some including anyone who can blow an instrument or some meeting just annually to play for the Easter sunrise service. The Moravian Trombone Choir of Downey, California, founded in 1965 and led for many years by Jeffrey Reynolds, bass trombone of the Los Angeles Philharmonic, brought this genre to a wider audience with well-received recordings.

In mid-nineteenth-century Germany, leaders of the Protestant revival often replaced the organ with brass instruments. As the revival spread, congregations outgrew their buildings, and services were held outdoors, where brass instruments were ideal. The *Posaunenchor* tradition survives in modern Germany, though today it normally consists of a church brass band rather than a trombone group. They are often heard at village festivals and in Protestant churches on Sunday morning.

The *Psalmodikon*: another way of accompanying Hymns

The *psalmodikon* – a single-stringed musical instrument – was developed in Scandinavia to play simple music in churches and schools. In 1835 Lars Roverud received permission from the King of Norway for it to be played in church. After this, some hymn-books were published with *Sifferskrift* (numerical notation), with numbers corresponding to numbers painted on the fret-board of the *psalmodikon*, allowing players who could not read music to accompany hymns. The instrument became much used throughout Norway and Sweden.

When the first wave of emigration to America began, many migrants took *psalmodikons* with them, or made them when they arrived, playing them at home, at school, and in church. Many congregations could not afford an organ, and the violin was banned as it was used for dancing and so deemed unfit. The *psalmodikon* was inexpensive to make, took up little space, could be played with little musical training, and had a slow, melodic sound which worked well with the hymns. However, as churches became able to afford organs, the *psalmodikon* became rarer, and by the late twentieth century it was seldom seen outside museums.

CHAPTER 8

"In Quires and Places Where They Sing...": The Making of the Anglican Tradition

God is truely worship'd, as of old, in the beauty of Holines... [sic]

Thomas Tudway (1716)

Below: The *Armada Portrait* of Elizabeth I of England, by George Gower, possibly painted in the year of the Armada, 1588, celebrates the defeat of the Spanish Armada and the attempt to re-establish Roman Catholicism in England. Queen Elizabeth imposed a moderate Protestantism.
Opposite: Illustration of Old St Paul's Cathedral, London, destroyed in the Great Fire of 1666.

The Church of England has historically encompassed a wide range of musical styles – as it has doctrinal positions. During the reign of the young Protestant monarch Edward VI (1537–53), a royal visitation of English cathedrals, undertaken in an attempt to ensure all elements of Catholic worship had been purged, typically prescribed to Lincoln Cathedral:

[The choir] shall from henceforth sing or say no anthems of our Lady or other Saints, but only of our Lord, and them not in Latin; but choosing out the best and most sounding to Christian religion, they shall turn the same into English, setting thereunto a plain and distinct note for every syllable one; they shall sing them and none other.[1]

♫ A New Prayer Book

In 1549 the vernacular *Book of Common Prayer* was published, with a simplified form of the mass, renamed "holy communion", omitting the gradual. Just three years later, a revised and more strongly Protestant edition deleted further sections from the proper of the Roman Catholic mass, leaving few of the texts composers had regularly set until this time. The old Latin daily office was rewritten and compressed to create just two daily vernacular services – matins and evensong. Matins, based on the Sarum rite used at Salisbury Cathedral, included the canticles the *Venite* (Psalm 95) and *Te Deum*, the *Benedictus* (from lauds) and on occasion the *Quicumque vult* (or Athanasian Creed, from prime). Evensong combined vespers, with its psalms and *Magnificat*, and compline, with its *Nunc dimittis*. Nothing remained of terce, sext, and nones from the daily office.

In his *The Booke of Common Praier Noted* (1550), John Merbeck(e)[2] (c. 1510 – c. 1585), a Yorkshireman and organist at St George's Chapel, Windsor, from 1541, wrote a setting of the liturgy of the newly reformed Church of England to semi-rhythmical melodies, in part adapted from Gregorian chant. When the prayer book was revised in 1552, Merbeck's settings became redundant. However, nineteenth-century scholars rediscovered his music and adapted some of it for use with the 1662 *Book of Common Prayer*. The publication of this new edition in 1843 helped launch the Oxford Movement and revive the daily singing of matins and evensong in Anglican cathedrals.

Christopher Tye (c. 1505 – c. 1572), possibly Edward VI's music teacher, was another early Protestant composer, who wrote services and anthems for the young Anglican church but had previously composed Latin church masses, including one based on the song "The Western Wynde" (as did John Taverner and John Sheppard/Shepherd [c. 1512–63]).

♫ The Elizabethan Church

Queen Elizabeth I issued another revision of the 1552 prayer book, following her accession in 1558, as part of her policy to establish a moderately Protestant Church of England, after Mary Tudor's brief attempt to reinstate Roman Catholicism. In the injunctions issued by Elizabeth in 1559, she set out her requirements for Anglican church music:

> *… a modest distinct song, so used in all parts of the common prayers in the Church, that the same may be plainly understood, as if it were read without singing, and yet nevertheless, for the comforting of such as delight in music, it may be permitted that in the beginning, or in the end of common prayers either at morning or evening, there may be sung a Hymn, or such like song…* [3]

Most psalm settings used in collegiate churches and cathedrals from the time of the first English Prayer Book until the English Civil War, and the temporary suppression of the Anglican liturgy, were harmonized plainchant. Although this period is regarded as a golden age for English composers, the increasingly vocal Puritan movement within the church

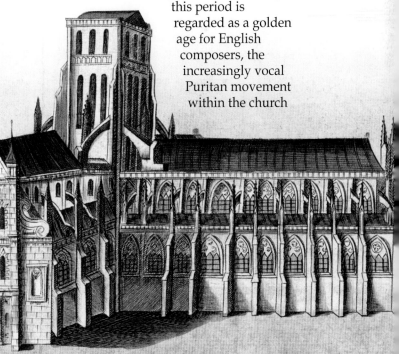

discouraged the use of the organ and of choral music, and the unaccompanied singing of metrical psalms became particularly popular (see chapter 9). In 1560 the bishop of Salisbury reported that it was common to find a crowd of 6,000 singing psalms outside St Paul's Cathedral in London after the service.

♫ Anglican Anthems

The reformed Church of England required music not only for the new services of holy communion and morning and evening prayer, but also for the anthem (possibly derived from the word "antiphon") that officially replaced the motet in the Anglican liturgy in 1559. Apart from Byrd, Orlando Gibbons (1583–1625), well known for his madrigals, is the outstanding English church music composer of his generation, writing such fine anthems as "Behold, Thou Hast Made My Days" and "Hosanna to the Son of David", as well as a number of enduring hymn-tunes.

Although at parish level music was kept simple, the historic Chapel Royal enjoyed richer fare, even after the Reformation. It appears that by the turn of the seventeenth century anthems were regularly sung there, as they were more rarely in the cathedrals. The poet and composer Sir William Leighton (c. 1560 – c. 1617) published a collection of fifty-four devotional verses, *The Teares or Lamentations of a Sorrowfull Soule*, while in jail for debt, and enlisted John Bull (1562/63–1628), William Byrd, Thomas Wilbye (1574–1638), Thomas Weelkes (1576–1623), and Gibbons among others to set them. Some of the resulting anthems have become staples of Anglican cathedral music, as have canticle settings by the great Elizabethan composers

Byrd, Gibbons, Thomas Tomkins (1572–1656), and Weelkes.

An invaluable source for seventeenth-century English cathedral music is a compilation published by John Barnard of St Paul's Cathedral: the *First Book of Selected Church Music* (1641), which demonstrates that Anglican chant was successfully supplanting plainsong. Similarly some "directions" for music at St Paul's, published in 1633, outline the cathedral's liturgy: at matins an organ voluntary was played after the psalms; the *Te Deum* sung after the first lesson; the *Benedictus* or *Jubilate* after the second lesson; an anthem and the litany after the third collect; and another organ voluntary followed the blessing. At the evening service (evensong) again an organ voluntary succeeded the psalms; the *Magnificat* followed the first lesson; the *Nunc dimittis* or *Deus miseratur* the second lesson; an anthem came after

Right: The English composers Thomas Tallis (top) and William Byrd (below) from an engraving by Niccolo Francesco Haym (1688/9–c. 1729).
Opposite: Portrait of Henry Purcell, creator of "English Baroque", by or after John Closterman (1660–1711).

the third collect and another anthem after the sermon. It was during this period that a group of "High-Churchmen" began to emphasize the solemnity and beauty of the performance of the liturgy and its music – a cause revived by the nineteenth-century Oxford Movement.

In 1645, following the victory of the parliamentary forces in the Civil War, use of *The Book of Common Prayer* was prohibited and all church music except metrical psalm-singing banned. During the English Republic, the Chapel Royal was disbanded and instruments were banned for use in worship under parliamentary ordinances of 1644 "for the speedy demolishing of all organs…" in cathedrals and parish churches.

♩ Restoration

With the restoration of the English monarchy in 1660, the Anglican choral tradition was revivified and began to prosper again, though the depredations of the Civil War period broke the continuity in development of English church music. An Act of Uniformity (1662) reinstated *The Book of Common Prayer* in revised form.

The restored monarch, Charles II, sent the young Pelham Humfrey (1647/48–74) to France and Italy aged only seventeen to learn from continental composers, knowledge he used to good effect in the anthems he wrote for the newly re-established Chapel Royal, most of which called for a string orchestra. King Charles introduced violins to the

Chapel Royal, a French (and thus Catholic) innovation which the diarist John Evelyn complained was "better suited to a Tavern or Play-house than a church". And while vernacular English was ubiquitous in the church at large, the Chapel Royal also heard some Latin anthems – in effect accompanied motets – such as John Blow's *Salvator mundi* ("Saviour of the World").

The 1662 *Book of Common Prayer* famously stated: "In quires and places where they sing, here followeth the anthem." After the Restoration, composers began to write new Anglican chants and anthems, while English cathedrals started to develop trained choirs, whose prerogative it became to sing anthems in the larger churches and cathedrals. Congregations were mainly silent. Sophisticated Protestant composers did not disdain to use Latin – setting the *Benedictus, Jubilate, Te Deum laudamus*, and *Nunc dimittis* – and voluntaries by composers such as William Byrd also came into fashion.

The sacred works of the greatest English Protestant composer of his age, and creator of "English Baroque", Henry Purcell (1659–95), combining voice and instruments in anthems, were later to influence Handel. Purcell became one of the "children of the Chapel Royal" aged only five, and in 1682 was made organist of the Chapel Royal. He wrote the anthems "I Was Glad" and "My Heart is Inditing" (1685) for the coronation of James II; a magnificent *Te Deum and Jubilate* (1693); and for Queen Mary's funeral (1694) two anthems, "Blessed is the Man That Feareth the Lord" and "Thou Knowest, Lord, the Secrets of Our Hearts", the latter having been sung at every choral funeral service since at both Westminster Abbey and St Paul's Cathedral. Purcell died aged only thirty-six and, fittingly, was buried near the organ at Westminster Abbey.[4] Having studied and performed Tudor music, his compositions often exhibit an exquisite melancholy.

William Croft (1678–1727), another child of the Chapel Royal, later provided anthems and services for that chapel (his setting of the Anglican burial service is still in use) and wrote a number of hymn-tunes, notably "St Anne" – "O God Our Help in Ages Past". His *Te Deum in D Major* (1709) was probably written for a thanksgiving service for the Duke of Marlborough's victory at Malplaquet.

A contemporary of Handel, William Boyce (1711–79) has suffered from standing in the German's shadow. He composed around sixty anthems, five services, and an oratorio entitled *David's Lamentation over Saul and Jonathan* (1736), but is more important for taking over from Maurice Greene on the latter's death in 1755 the Herculean task of compiling and editing three volumes of Anglican church music, *Cathedral Music* (1760–73),[5] which included services by Byrd, Gibbons, Purcell, and others.

Left: Sir John Stainer, Victorian composer and pioneer of early music, described by Sir Arthur Sullivan as "a genius".
Right: "The Village Choir" c. 1847, by Thomas Webster (1800–86), now in the Victoria and Albert Museum, London, painted to illustrate a comic and sentimental essay by Washington Irving entitled "Christmas Day". It is often used to exemplify the West Gallery choirs of rural England.

Chiefly remembered today as composer of *Rule Britannia*, the Catholic Thomas Arne (1710–78) wrote no music for the Anglican service, but produced two oratorios, *The Death of Abel* (1744) and *Judith* (1761), which an early critic compared disadvantageously with Purcell and Handel. A performance of *Judith* in London in 1773 is believed to have been the first time an oratorio had female chorus members – though they sang only the soprano line. Until this time, both upper parts were sung by boys, as they were (exclusively until the late twentieth century) in English cathedral choirs.

Samuel Wesley (1766–1837), younger son of the hymn-writer Charles Wesley, entered the Roman Catholic church in 1784, possibly attracted by Gregorian chant, and wrote much of his choral music for that church, including five masses, as well as motets such as *Exultate Deo* and *Tu es sacerdos* ("Thou Art the Priest") and the eight-part *In exitu Israel* ("When Israel Went Forth"). He also attempted to make J. S. Bach known in England. His son, Samuel Sebastian Wesley (1810–76), with a more individual style than his father, wrote almost exclusively for the Anglican church, with five services and twenty-six anthems, many of which continue to be performed, such as *The Wilderness*, *O Lord Thou Art My God*, *Thou Wilt Keep Him in Perfect Peace*, and *Cast Me Not Away*.[6]

Thomas Attwood (1765–1838), a favourite pupil of Mozart, became organist of St Paul's Cathedral and composer to the Chapel Royal in 1796, but apart from some short "hymn-anthems" such as *Turn Thy Face from My Sins* and *Come, Holy Ghost*, his work has largely been forgotten. His pupil and godson, Thomas Attwood Walmisley (1814–56), also contributed to the Anglican canon, for instance with his *Magnificat* and *Nunc Dimittis in D Minor*.

Sir John Stainer (1840–1901) helped revive English cathedral musical life, inspired by his research into what is now known as "early music". He wrote a standard work on the music of the Bible and published the first pointed psalter to achieve wide acceptance, while his *Cathedral Prayer Book* provided music for every ecclesiastical occasion. Stainer also made arrangements of chant and of Merbeck's music for the eucharist. Yet few composers have undergone such posthumous vilification as Stainer, criticized for his "sentimentality", and now known almost solely for his Passiontide cantata *The Crucifixion*, composed for St Marylebone Church in London, where it has been performed every Good Friday since 1887. Like the German Passions, *The Crucifixion* includes narrative recitatives to recount the events of Easter, ariosos to meditate on those events, and hymns for the congregation. At its heart is the simple unaccompanied quartet "God So Loved the World". *Olivet to Calvary* by J. H. Maunder (1858–1920) enjoyed similar popularity for many years.

During the nineteenth century, the Oxford Movement helped revive the belief that the eucharist should be the main focus of Christian worship, which led to the

introduction into the Church of England of singing at the eucharist for the first time since the Reformation. This in turn paved the way for the revival in some Anglican churches of Gregorian chants for the mass as well as the divine office. In some parts of the church it now became customary to use an English translation of the Roman Missal (*Missale Romanum*) rather than *The Book of Common Prayer*. In the late nineteenth century, a Gregorian Association was founded to promote the use in the Anglican church of chant books in English, especially Thomas Helmore's *The Psalter Noted* and *The Hymnal Noted*. By the turn of the century, English chant adaptations began to be informed by the scholarship of the Solesmes monks, and measured values were abandoned in favour of equal rhythm, which eventually altered the performance style of Anglican chant.

The Irishman Sir Charles Villiers Stanford (1852–1924) contributed fine new works to Anglican service music, especially his *Morning*, *Evening*, and *Communion Services in G* (1904) and in *C* (1909). With such works and his academic teaching he helped bring about something of a renaissance in Anglican music.

The British symphonist (and clergyman's son) Ralph Vaughan Williams (1872–1958), though an agnostic, also wrote liturgical music, including a *Te Deum*, a Christmas cantata called *Hodie* ("Today"), two motets, and an unaccompanied *Mass in G Minor* (1923), with characteristic reference to medieval music, Byrd, and folk-song.

Herbert Howells (1892–1983), born in Gloucestershire, studied with Stanford, but the death of his nine-year-old son in 1936 so affected him that he ceased composing for a time. When he restarted, he committed himself to writing for the Anglican church. Howells' austere yet affecting *Hymnus Paradisi* (1938, first performed in 1950) for chorus and orchestra is based on a requiem-like eclectic text, drawn from the Latin *Vulgate* Bible, the *Missa pro defunctis*,

Salisbury plainchant, and *The Book of Common Prayer*, and includes sections from an unaccompanied *Requiem* written soon after his son's death. Howells also wrote settings of psalms and canticles for Anglican matins and evensong, and an unaccompanied motet, *Take Him, Earth, for Cherishing* (1964), dedicated to the memory of President John F. Kennedy. His sacred music employs unusual chords, and draws on Tudor music, Gregorian chant, plainsong, and pentatonic, whole-tone, and exotic scales.

Jonathan Harvey (b. 1939) was commissioned by Winchester Cathedral to set the *Magnificat and Nunc Dimittis* (1978), and in the resulting work instructs the choir not only to sing but also to speak, shout, and whisper. Harvey went on to write a *Passion and Resurrection* (1981) for dramatic presentation in large church spaces such as cathedrals.

The English composer John Rutter (b. 1945) has written and arranged many Christmas carols, while his larger-scale works – particularly his *Gloria* (1974), *Requiem* (1985), and *Magnificat* (1990) – were quickly established in the choral repertoire. His *Carols for Choirs* collections, edited jointly with Sir David Willcocks (b. 1919), have become standard texts. In 2002 Rutter's setting of *Psalm 150* was commissioned for Elizabeth II's Golden Jubilee and his *Mass of the Children* had its première in New York's Carnegie Hall in 2003. Perhaps slightly defensively, Rutter states, "I write music that people will enjoy singing."

Oranges and Lemons: The Story of Church Bells

Bells have become part of the Western Christian tradition, awakening, summoning, reminding, celebrating, mourning, and sometimes warning. The bells of Christmas, the peal of the wedding, and the toll of the cortège all possess their own resonance.

The earliest use of bells in the church probably dates back to the first centuries, when as a carry-over from pre-Christian times handbells were sometimes used in an attempt to fend off evil spirits. Small bells, possibly intended to protect the souls of the departed – or the souls of the living – have been discovered in Roman catacombs. Similar handbells were used by hermits in the desert to chase away tempting spirits.

The use of bells is mentioned in the Rule of St Benedict (c. 540), and Benedictine monks of Italy are credited with casting the first bells in the West around the end of the sixth century, taking this skill with them as they travelled through Western Europe. Benedictine bells were used to signal the divine office, mass, the angelus (for the *Angelus* prayer, in the morning, at midday, and in the evening), death knells, and other services. Pope Stephen II (ruled 752–57) ordered three bells of different sizes to be installed in a campanile at St Peter's Basilica in Rome, and by the eighth century bells and bell towers had been installed in numerous chapels and oratories. Significant bell collections dating to the twelfth to fourteenth centuries include campaniles at Pisa, Florence, and St Mark's, Venice.

During the Middle Ages, a bell called the *Sanctus* fixed outside the church was rung from within to announce the approach of the canon of the mass.[1] After the thirteenth-century introduction into the liturgy of the mass of the elevation of the Host (when the consecrated bread and wine are displayed to the people), a handbell was rung to signal this point, since the laity's view of the altar was often blocked by a rood screen. This practice continues in the Roman Catholic church and in some High Anglican and Lutheran churches.

The first set of cast bells in British North America, a peal of eight, was installed in Christ Church, Boston, in 1744, while the mission of San Luis Rey, on the west coast, boasted a peal of eight bells cast in Castile, Spain. As different denominations became established in nineteenth-century USA, churches competed for church-goers with the best chimes, some playing complete hymn-tunes.

Below: St Peter's Basilica and the Ponte Sant'Angelo, Rome, Italy.

🎵 Carillons

Carillons originally developed as an accessory to church-tower clocks. The bells sounding the hour were augmented with smaller bells that played just before the hour (*voorslags* in Flemish/Dutch) to forewarn people, so they did not miscount the number of strikes when they started. Further bells were added, allowing more interesting tunes to be played. The first carillon keyboard, for a nine-bell instrument, was installed in Oudenaarde (modern Belgium) in 1510, followed by one at Antwerp Cathedral in 1541.

Carillons reached the height of their development in the seventeenth century in the founding of the Hemony brothers, Pieter van den Gheyn and his family, and the Dumery family in the Low Countries. The Hemonys cast more than fifty carillons, including a legendary instrument at St Rombout's Cathedral, Mechelen (1558), and others at the New Church, Delft; the Domkerk, Utrecht; and St Jans Cathedral, 's-Hertogenbosch. Andreas Josef van den Gheyn (1727–93) later improved tuning techniques and created twenty-three carillons, while his brother, Matthias (1721–85), bell master of Louvain, wrote the most important carillon repertoire of the time. However, by the mid-nineteenth century the carillon had been largely relegated to a folk instrument.

The Belgian performer and composer Jef Denyn, who played at Mechelen from 1881 to 1941, revived the art of building and performing the carillon, making technical and artistic advances in the mechanism, and organizing concerts that raised its profile. In 1922 the carillon was introduced to the United States, where later the world's two largest, each with seventy-two bells, were built for the Riverside Church in New York City and for the Rockefeller Chapel at the University of Chicago. Since the Second World War the number of carillons in the Low Countries has mushroomed from 100 to nearly 500, many controlled electronically, enabling composers to write regardless of the stamina of a human performer. Modern composers include Staf Nees (1901–65), Frank Percival Price (1901–85), Leen 't Hart (1920–92), Emilien Allard (1915–76), Ronald Barnes (b. 1927), Johan Franco (1908–88), Albert Gerken (b. 1937), Roy Hamlin Johnson (b. 1929), Milford Myhre (b. 1931), and Gary White (b. 1937).

The clock-chime tune most often heard in English-speaking countries is the "Westminster Quarters" (originally known as "Cambridge Quarters") – the four notes E-D-C-G in various combinations every quarter-hour. Composed in 1793 by an organ student, William Crotch, for use with the new clock at Great St Mary's Church, Cambridge, its use from 1859 in the clock tower of the Houses of Parliament in London resulted in its present name and fame. Also frequently heard is the "ting-tang" repeated alternation of two notes, as used at St Paul's Cathedral, London.

♫ Change-ringing

Bell-ringing took a different direction from Europe in England, where it evolved into change-ringing – an intricate series of changes (different orderings in the ringing sequence) effected by pulling ropes attached to bell wheels. The earliest known guild of English bell-ringers was established at Westminster in the thirteenth century. Many English parish churches possessed a peal of two or three bells, while larger churches and monastic establishments boasted as many as eight. Early in the Reformation the "whole-wheel" apparatus, which allowed a bell to be fully rotated, was introduced, permitting complex change-ringing. By 1990 more than 5,000 English parish churches had bells capable of change-ringing ("campanology").

Left: Bells of the carillon in the tower of the Oude Kerk (Old Church), the oldest parish church in Amsterdam, where Jan Sweelinck was organist.
Below: With possibly the world's most famous clock chime, Big Ben is the Great Bell of the clock on the tower at the end of the Palace of Westminster, London.

♫ Tuned Handbells

The history of handbells began more than 400 years ago with small bells cast to test the quality of bell metal, and for change-ringers to practise on before ringing the heavy tower bells. By the eighteenth century, handbells boasted improved tuning and a wider range – up to five octaves – and they became popular in nineteenth-century Britain. The legendary showman P. T. Barnum introduced handbell ringing to the USA in 1844, touring the Lancashire Ringers from northern England dressed colourfully as "Swiss bell-ringers". During the twentieth century the American Guild of English Handbell Ringers developed the art, using chromatically tuned handbells, and there are now more than 500 bell choirs in the USA.

9

Psalms, Canticles, and Hymns: The Genesis of Christian Hymns

The first and chief Use of Musick is for the Service and Praise of God, whose gift it is.

John Playford (1623–86)

Following the Reformation, while Lutheranism soon developed its rich tradition of chorales in the vernacular, the Reformed and Anglican churches largely felt that the Bible in general, and the Psalms in particular, provided the only legitimate texts for singing in church, and that singing should be performed without instrumental accompaniment.

♫ The Genevan Example

Huldrych Zwingli (1484–1531), the reformer of Zurich, though himself an enthusiastic and talented musician, at first banned all music from his Reformed church, believing it might present an idolatrous snare to worshippers. This ban was not lifted until 1598. In his "model" Reformed church in Geneva, John Calvin (1509–64) as early as 1537 proposed congregational singing of psalms: "When we have looked thoroughly everywhere and searched high and low, we shall find no better songs nor more appropriate to the purpose than the Psalms of David…".[1] But Calvin prohibited the use of harmony or of accompanying instruments: "Instrumental music was only tolerated in the time of the Law

Left: Fresco from Stein am Rhein, Switzerland, of the Swiss Reformer Ulrich Zwingli preaching in Zurich.
Above: Relief of the Reformer John Calvin, part of the Reformation Wall in Geneva, Switzerland.

[that is, in Old Testament times] because of the people's infancy."

Exiled in Strasbourg from 1538 to 1541, Calvin was moved by the psalm-singing he heard there, and so collected some of the French paraphrases by the Paris court poet Clément Marot (1496–1544). Returning to Geneva, Calvin published the *Genevan Psalter* (1542),[2] which included thirty of Marot's metrical psalms, set by Louis (or Loys) Bourgeois (c. 1510/15–61), probably the composer of the tune now known as the "Old Hundredth".[3] In the preface to his 1545 *Psalter*, Calvin wrote:

> Care must always be taken that the song be neither light nor frivolous; but that it have weight and majesty (as St Augustine says), and also that there be a great difference between music which one makes to entertain men at the table and in their houses, and the psalms which are sung in the church in the presence of God and his angels.

Bourgeois seems to have enlisted tunes from various sources – Lutheran, folk, and even Gregorian chant – of which his co-religionists would have disapproved, producing many polyphonic settings of the psalms. Other composers to set Marot's metrical psalms included Claude Goudimel (c. 1514–72), who converted from Roman Catholicism in 1560 and was killed in Lyons during the St Bartholomew's Day massacre of French Huguenots, and Claude Le Jeune (c. 1528–1600). The Genevan psalms are written in more than one hundred regular and irregular metres and the tunes have a pronounced rhythmic intensity and modal flavour, sometimes making them sound more like Renaissance madrigals than hymns. Elizabeth I is said to have dismissed them as "Genevan jigs" for their dance-like nature. Goudimel circumspectly warned, in the introduction to his 1565 collection, that these arrangements, with their harmonies and instrumental accompaniments, were not for church use but "for glorifying God specifically in the home".

As more psalms were paraphrased, Calvin's *Psalter* increased in length, and the work was completed in 1562 by Calvin's successor, Theodore Beza (1519–1605). These Genevan psalms continue to be sung in the Netherlands, Hungary, South Africa, and elsewhere, but soon fell out of use in the English-speaking world, apart from a few tunes.

♫ The Anglican Example

With the establishment of the reformed Church of England, the first edition of *The Book of Common Prayer* (1549) set out the biblical psalms to be read each Sunday and feast day. Even the paraphrasing of psalms was initially discouraged: instead a form of unison chanting was developed where the worshippers sang the first part of a line from the selected psalm on a sustained pitch, with harmonic support, resolving this harmony in a series of chords beneath the final syllables. Such chanting demanded some musical skill, making it better suited to choirs than to the congregation; this tradition continued within Anglican churches until the twentieth century.

However, a desire for congregational participation in singing soon led to the creation of basic paraphrases of the psalms which could more easily be sung by church-goers to simple, repeated tunes. A metrical psalter entitled *The Whole Book of Psalms*, collected by Thomas Sternhold (1500–49, Groom of the Robes to Henry VIII) and John Hopkins (d. 1570), was published in 1562.[4] This psalter translated the Hebrew psalms as accurately as possible – but often awkwardly – into English rhyme and metre. Most paraphrases were made into verse with a simple metre – predominantly common, short, and long metres[5] – which itself strongly influenced the development of English hymnody. The editors used a letter to signify the pitch required for each psalm.

Sternhold and Hopkins set out their aims on the title page, underlining that their psalms were intended for private as much as public use:

> Very meet to be used of all sorts of people privately for their solace & comfort, laying apart all ungodly songs and ballads, which tend only to the nourishing of vice and corrupting of youth…

Although Hopkins (with sixty-one psalms) and Sternhold (with forty-one) were the main authors, others included, with twenty-four, William Kethe (d. 1594), a Scots refugee in Calvin's Geneva and author of, among others, the well-known paraphrase of Psalm 100, "All People That on Earth Do Dwell"; and, with twenty-five, Thomas

"Rackmaster"[6] Norton (1532–84). Tunes came from a number of different sources, including English folk songs and ballads, German hymns, and French metrical psalmody, while some were original. Of the Genevan and German tunes, by far the most popular was the "Old Hundredth", from the *Genevan Psalter* of 1551. Some tunes from "Sternhold and Hopkins" have endured and are still widely used, such as that for Psalm 132 in the 1562 edition, which survives as "St Flavian", and "Cheshire" (Psalm 146), "Southwell" (Psalm 45), and "Winchester Old" (Psalm 84), which first appeared in editions published between 1563 and 1599.

An important new musical edition of Sternhold and Hopkins was published by Thomas Ravenscroft (c. 1590 – c. 1633) in 1621, with fifty-one settings by Ravenscroft himself, together with tunes by many other English composers, including John Dowland, Giles Farnaby, John Farmer, George Kirbye, Thomas Morley, Martin Peerson, Thomas Tallis, and Thomas Tomkins. Among enduring tunes from Ravenscroft's edition are "Bristol" (Psalms 16 and 64), "Durham" (Psalms 28 and 76), "Lincoln" (Psalms 7 and 56), and "St David" (Psalms 42 and 95). By 1700, more than 500 separate editions of the monophonic version of this psalm book had been printed. The hymnologist Robin Leaver regards the Sternhold and Hopkins collection, which became popularly known as the "Old Version", as "the foundation stone on which the English tradition of metrical psalmody and hymnody has built".

In 1650 the Church of Scotland published its own metrical *Scottish Psalter*, containing paraphrases of all 150 psalms, of which the most enduringly popular is its version of Psalm 23, "The Lord's My Shepherd… ". Since it is written in common metre, there was no shortage of suitable tunes: not until 1872 did the familiar tune, "Crimond", by the Scottish composer Jessie Seymour Irvine, first appear. The Scots metrical psalm was typically sung by "lining out": the minister appointed poet laureate in 1692) and Nicholas Brady (1659–1726) published *A New Version of the Psalms of David* (London, 1696, revised 1698). These new versions were intended to be sung to tunes already familiar to congregations, but represented a marked literary improvement on those in the "Old Version", and included familiar "hymns" still sung today, such as "Through All the Changing Scenes of Life" (a version of Psalm 34) and "While Shepherds Watched Their Flocks by Night".[8] With his version of Psalm 136, "Let Us with a Gladsome Mind", allegedly written when he was only twelve years old, the English epic poet John Milton (1608–74) also showed it was possible to write a metrical psalm without sacrificing either meaning or poetry.

Isaac Watts

Isaac Watts (1674–1748), a dissenting clergyman sometimes (erroneously) called the "Father of English hymnody",[9] like many of his contemporaries objected to the poor poetry of Sternhold and Hopkins. (John Wesley later spoke of the "Old Version" as "wretched, scandalous doggerel".[10]) Watts also criticized its performance:

> To see the dull indifference, the negligent and thoughtless air, that sits upon the faces of the whole assembly while the psalm is on their lips, might tempt even a charitable observer to suspect the fervour of inward religion.

In an attempt to remedy this dire situation, Watts wrote new hymns and metrical versions of the psalms, better utilizing the poetic possibilities of English. As his weekly sermon took shape, Watts would write a hymn to provide his congregation with a sung response to it. In 1707 Watts published *Hymns and Spiritual Songs*, a collection of 365 pieces, followed by *The Psalms of David* (1719). In these collections he attempted to interpret Old Testament psalms with New Testament theology in contemporary language and with poetic

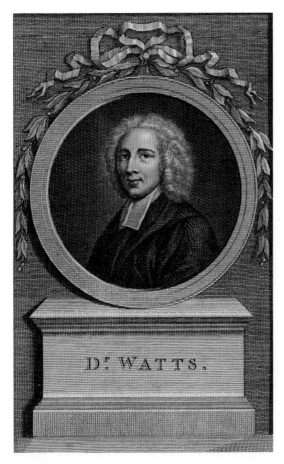

Isaac Watts, writer of such famous hymns as "When I Survey the Wondrous Cross".

or precentor introduced each line, which was then repeated by the congregation. Gradually ornamentation was added and the melodies grew in complexity, becoming known as "long tunes". The singing of these long tunes or "long metres" survives today among the Gaelic-speaking populations of the Western Isles, such as the Isle of Lewis.[7]

A century after its first publication, there were many critics of the paraphrases of the "Old Version", some arguing that on occasion "their piety is better than their poetry". In an attempt to improve the literary quality of paraphrased psalms, the Irish-born clergymen Nahum Tate (1652–1715;

fluency, also adding some freely composed hymns on biblical themes. Watts did not confine himself to paraphrases, nor were his hymns literally biblical; they were rather independent compositions, written in order to be sung, to be memorable, and above all to be spiritually effective. Watts also pioneered in publishing a collection of thirty-six hymns specifically for children, *Divine Songs Attempted in Easy Language for the Use of Children*, dating from later in his life.[11]

Although Watts wrote in the first instance for his own Congregational churches, his psalms and hymns marked a new start for English hymns, and some of them still form the foundation of English hymnody interdenominationally and internationally. Enduring favourites (many of them written before Watts was twenty-one) include: "When I Survey the Wondrous Cross",[12] "Jesus Shall Reign Where'er the Sun" (based on Psalm 72), "Our God, Our Help in Ages Past" (written upon the death of Queen Anne in 1714, and based on Psalm 90),[13] "Joy to the World" (Psalm 98), and "I'll Praise My Maker While I've Breath"

(Psalm 146). By producing such memorable hymns (around 750 in all), Watts prepared the way for succeeding hymn-writers such as the Wesley brothers, John Newton, and Philip Doddridge.

The new hymns of Isaac Watts also had significant musical implications. "Lining out" was still widely practised: the clerk would read or sing a line of the psalm, that was then repeated by the congregation, which meant singing a long psalm could become extremely tedious. Watts felt that lining out could not "presently be reformed", and so wrote his hymns to accommodate it by ensuring each line contained a completed thought, with nothing hanging over to the next. And Watts still wrote only in the handful of metres used by the old English metrical psalms, so his hymns could easily be sung by congregations familiar with the old tunes.

As yet, there was not necessarily one set tune for a particular hymn text. Watts's "Joy to the World" provides an example of how hymns could develop. Today this hymn is often sung to a melody by Handel, chosen and arranged by the American musician Lowell Mason (1792–1872), who recognized that the text and melody would work well together – as usage has proved. Mason

Below: The Radcliffe Camera, Oxford, England. The Methodist movement had its roots in a group of Oxford students who gathered to nurture their spiritual life.
Right: Medallion portrait of the Wesley brothers, Charles (left) and John.

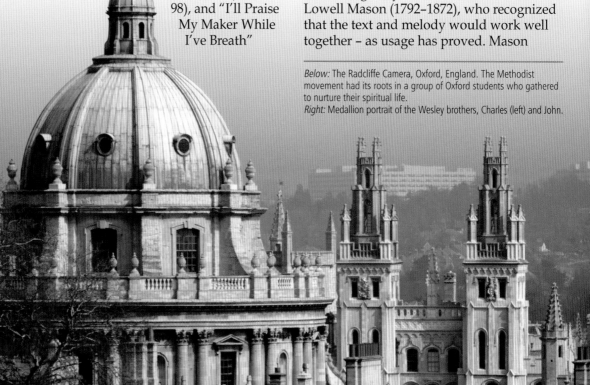

and others similarly brought together and arranged a number of other hymn texts and melodies, such as "Hark, the Herald Angels Sing" (text by Charles Wesley, melody by Felix Mendelssohn, arrangement by William Cummings).

Philip Doddridge (1702–51), another English dissenting minister, wrote many Scripture-based hymns, though they were not collected and published until 1755, four years after his death. Some of his hymns remain popular, such as: "O Happy Day, That Fixed My Choice", "O God of Bethel, by Whose Hand", and "Grace, 'tis a Charming Sound". Like Watts, Doddridge wrote mainly in short, common, or long metre, aiming for the simplicity necessary when the words were still taught by "lining out".

♫ The Wesley Brothers

The eighteenth-century Evangelical Revival began in part at the "Holy Club" at Oxford University – a group of students who aimed to organize their spirituality with a "method" (hence the initially derisive nickname "Methodists"). Linked with this group were the brothers John and Charles Wesley, who were to create the vast Methodist hymnody; James Hutton and John Gambold, who were to edit and publish Moravian hymnals; and George Whitefield, who also edited an important hymn collection. From its beginnings in the early 1730s, Holy Club members used hymns – for the most part Watts's – in their meetings and private devotions.

After leaving Oxford, the Wesleys spent part of the mid-1730s in North America, where John edited a small hymnal, *A Collection of Psalms and Hymns*, consisting mainly of pieces by Isaac Watts. On their return from America, John Wesley famously had a "heart-warming" religious experience in the spring of 1738, closely followed by his brother, as a result of which Charles wrote his celebrated hymn "And Can it Be That I Should Gain… ". A year later Charles wrote another poem, "O, for a Thousand Tongues to Sing… ", which subsequently became the first hymn in John's 1780 *Collection*. The Wesley brothers soon recognized that hymns – with their appeal to both heart and mind – provided an ideal popular vehicle for Christian devotion, renewal, evangelism, and theological teaching. Their conviction is borne out when we recognize how frequently simple phrases from hymns are used in Christian devotion (and public discourse): for instance "change and decay" from "Abide with Me"; "the rich man in his castle" from "All Things Bright and Beautiful"; "meek and mild" from "Once in Royal David's City"; and "God moves in mysterious ways", paraphrased from the first line of Cowper's hymn "Light Shining Out of Darkness".

Charles Wesley (1707–88),[14] the "sweet singer of Methodism", produced a flood of personal, scriptural verse, including such fine hymns as: "Jesu, Lover of My Soul", "Soldiers of Christ, Arise", "O Thou Who Camest from Above" (for which his grandson Samuel Sebastian Wesley later wrote the associated tune), and "Rejoice!

The Lord is King" – probably more than anyone else except perhaps the nineteenth-century American Fanny Crosby. Charles Wesley wrote in total around 8,990 hymns, verses, and religious poems. As the English hymn-writer Timothy Dudley-Smith asked pertinently: "Where would we be at Christmas without 'Hark! The Herald Angels Sing'?[15] [and] at Easter without… 'Christ the Lord is Risen Today'?"

In all the Wesley brothers published some fifty-six hymn collections, of which at least thirty-six included their own hymns alone. The slim *Hymns for Times of Trouble and Persecution* (1744) reflected the opposition the nascent Methodist movement faced, while other special collections included *Funeral Hymns* and *Children's Hymns*. Most enduring was John's *A Collection of Hymns for the Use of the People Called Methodists* (1780), designed for the Methodist societies (later churches) he had formed throughout Britain, and used unchanged by them until 1904. Wesley's hymnal was intended to provide both a primer in theology and a guide for public worship and private devotion. Many Methodist converts were virtual newcomers to Christianity, unfamiliar with the Bible or basic Christian doctrine; the Wesleys' hymns often simply versify Christian teaching and, like their preaching, aim at converting sinners. John's *Collection* included 525 hymns, made up largely of hymns by the Wesley brothers, but also by other writers, including Watts, and nineteen translations from Moravian or Pietist originals.

The tunes for the Wesleys' hymns were usually simple and catchy. The brothers borrowed melodies from folk-tunes, German songs, and popular plays, such as John Gay's *The Beggar's Opera*.[16] Charles Wesley – not constrained by the need to write in common metres for Anglican worship – used more than forty different iambic metres, allowing his hymns a new freedom. For some of them, new tunes had to be composed or existing tunes adapted, often with refrains.

Charles Wesley sometimes wrote with specific tunes in mind, notably "Love Divine, All Loves Excelling", a parody of the poet John Dryden's "Fairest Isle, All Isles Excelling", from Purcell's opera *King Arthur*; so Methodists sang Wesley's new Christian text to an adaptation of Purcell's theatre music. At open-air meetings, John Wesley may sometimes have used an oboe to aid the singing, presumably to give the note. But the young Methodist Conference was wary of any other instruments except the organ or bass viol, while John Wesley warned that Anglican anthems contained too much "vain repetition" and carried the threat of introducing "dead formality".

New Collections

After 1750 many other new hymnals were published, mostly anthologies containing hymns by several authors. Notable collections were those by George Whitefield (1753), Martin Madan (1726–90) – *A Collection of Psalm and Hymn Tunes* "to be used at the Lock Hospital", a charity for women with venereal diseases (1763) – Joseph Hart (1759), and Augustus Toplady (1776), the last including "Rock of Ages". There is a much-repeated story that Toplady (1740–78) wrote this hymn on a playing-card while sheltering from a storm in a spectacular rock-cleft at Burrington Combe, near Blagdon, Somerset: however, sadly, this picturesque legend has no basis in fact. Toplady likely had in mind a passage from a book on communion: "O Rock of Israel, Rock struck and cleft for me, let those two streams of blood and water which once gushed out of thy side bring down pardon and holiness into my soul… ". A fervent Calvinist, Toplady also wrote the hymns "A Debtor to Mercy Alone" and "A Sovereign Protector I Have".

Hymnals of this period did not print tunes alongside the texts, a practice which started only late in the nineteenth century. Instead the lyrics were printed with a note specifying the metre; a suitable tune filling that metre was then chosen. The tunes might be printed in another section of the book, in a separate tune-book, or be found in another collection. Although some hymns were from the outset linked with a particular tune, this was certainly not invariably the case. The congregation would often sing a new lyric to a tune they knew and with which they felt comfortable.

Olney Hymns

In 1764, following ordination in the Church of England, John Newton (1725–1807) moved to the village of Olney, Buckinghamshire, where he started a prayer service, for which he often wrote a hymn to be sung to a familiar tune. William Cowper (1731–1800), a fellow Olney resident and nationally recognized poet, also wrote hymns for these meetings. (Hymns were at this date still prohibited in Anglican church services.) Newton collected 280 of his hymns and 68 of Cowper's in *Olney Hymns*, published in 1779, which – like Watts's collection – relied largely on three metres: common, short, and long. Among well-known hymns in the Olney collection are Newton's "Amazing Grace!", "Glorious Things of Thee Are Spoken", and "How Sweet the Name of Jesus Sounds", and Cowper's "Oh! For a Closer Walk with God" and "There is a Fountain Filled with Blood". Cowper's celebrated hymn "God Moves in a Mysterious Way… " (entitled "Light Shining Out of Darkness")[17] dates from 1773, when the author feared the return of the depression that periodically afflicted him.

Not for nothing has the eighteenth century been seen as a golden age of hymnody. Other enduring hymns by contemporary authors include "The God of Abraham Praise" by Thomas Olivers (1725–99); "All Hail the Power of Jesus' Name" by Edward Perronet (1726–92); and "Guide Me, O Thou Great Jehovah [or "Redeemer"]" written in Welsh by the itinerant preacher William Williams of Pantycelyn (1717–91), "sweet singer of Wales" and founder member of the Calvinistic Methodist movement, and translated into English by the Welsh preacher Peter Williams (1722–96). Not until the twentieth century did the tune "*Cwm Rhondda*" (by John Hughes) appear, now inseparable from this hymn and a virtual second Welsh national anthem.[18]

Baptists

The European Anabaptists started out, in the mid-1520s, with a complete ban on singing: "We find nothing taught in the New Testament about singing, no example of it… Paul very clearly forbids singing in Ephesians 5:19 and Colossians 3:16…". But this prohibition did not endure long. An early leader, Felix Manz, composed at least one hymn before his martyrdom in 1527, its opening line, "*Mit Lust so will ich singen*" ("I will sing heartily"), and after this Anabaptists produced a stream of verse, often set to the tunes of secular songs. The resultant collection of Anabaptist hymnody, *Ausbund* (1564), is the oldest Protestant hymnal still in use.

However, seventeenth-century English Baptist churches still prohibited singing: the General Baptist Assembly of 1689 condemned the "carnal formalities" involved (such as rhyme and metre) and the risk that saved and unsaved might sinfully join together in praise. One Baptist leader, Benjamin Keach (1640–1704), challenged the Particular (Calvinistic) Baptists on this question, persuaded that his congregation at Southwark, in south London, should follow the pattern of the Last Supper and sing a hymn after the Lord's Supper. His views were divisive, but regardless in 1691 he published his own collection of around 300 hymns, *Spiritual Melody*, together with a defence of hymn-singing in worship, *The Breach Repaired in God's Worship; or Singing of Psalms, Hymns and Spiritual Songs Proved to Be a Holy Ordinance of Jesus Christ.*

By the second half of the eighteenth century, English Baptists' opposition to hymn-singing had largely ended, and Baptist hymn-writers emerged, such as Anne Steele (1717–78), writing under the pen-name "Theodosia" and best remembered for her hymn on Scripture, "Father of Mercies, in Thy Word". Other Baptist hymn-writers included Benjamin Beddome (1717–95), Samuel Stennett (1727–95), and John Rippon (1751–1836), pastor of the Baptist church at Carter Lane (later the first London chapel of the celebrated Victorian preacher C. H. Spurgeon), whose *A Selection of Hymns from the Best Authors* (1787) included many by fellow-Baptists.

♫ Hymns in North America

While in exile in Holland, the English Puritan Henry Ainsworth published his own 342-page *Psalter* (1612), with psalms in both poetry and prose, utilizing thirty-nine tunes from England, France, and the Netherlands, again including the "Old Hundredth". The Pilgrim Fathers took copies of this *Psalter* with them to America in 1620. Early colonial America followed the English pattern, with congregational singing consisting almost solely of metrical psalms. Most congregations sang from the "Old Version", though in some

Puritan churches there may have been no singing at all, since it was regarded as sinful for believers and unbelievers to praise God together. The Puritans also banned antiphonal singing ("We allow… not of tossing the psalm from one side to the other"[19]), singing in harmony or with accompaniment (they dubbed the organ the "Devil's bagpipes") – all such practices being too reminiscent of "popery".

Deciding they required a more faithful translation from the Hebrew, thirty "pious and learned ministers", including John Eliot and Richard Mather, produced *The Whole Booke of Psalmes, Faithfully Translated into English Metre* (1640), the first book printed in the English North American colonies. From the mid-seventeenth century on, almost all the Puritan churches in the Massachusetts Bay Colony employed this new "Bay Psalm Book", whose editors explained their intentions in their preface: "… we have respected rather a plain translation, than to smooth our verses with the sweetness of any paraphrase, and so have attended… fidelity rather than poetry… ". Like the

Below: The First Thanksgiving, a romanticized depiction of the first harvest festival celebrated in New England by the Pilgrim Fathers in 1621, by Jennie A. Brownscombe (1850–1936), now in the Pilgrim Hall Museum, Plymouth, Massachusetts.
Right: George Whitefield, the fiery preacher who championed the use of Watts's hymns in North America.

"Old Version", the "Bay Psalm Book" prioritized literal translation over poetic quality, using only six metres – mainly common metre, the simplest rhythmic pattern. The book included no music; the translators recommended the use of tunes from Ravenscroft's *Psalter*.

Since New England congregations knew few tunes and only two or three simple metres, they too adopted the practice of lining out. However, the ninth edition of the "Bay Psalm Book" (1698) added a simple system of notation – notes headed with squares, triangles, and circles – to indicate pitch. These "shape notes" were thought to be easier to read than traditional musical notation and later became widely used in southern and rural parts of North America.

The Puritan Cotton Mather (1663–1728), better known for his part in the infamous Salem witch trials, wrote a number of hymns and published a collection in 1697. His efforts were sometimes risible:

Ye monsters of the bubbling deep
Your Maker's praises spout;
Up from the sands ye codlings peep
And wag your tails about.

But, like his fellow New England ministers, Mather continued to oppose the use of hymns in church services, preferring metrical psalms. So, while Isaac Watts's new hymns were already being sung enthusiastically across Britain, most North American churches and ministers argued against them, preferring to stay with the "divinely inspired" words of their psalters, confining hymns to private devotions.

Yet it was Cotton Mather who made the earliest attempts to import English hymns into North America, publishing a few hymns by Isaac Watts as early as 1712, and in 1715 a further twenty-two in a collection entitled *Honey Out of the Rock*, probably still for devotional rather than church use. Watts's complete *Hymns and Spiritual Songs* was finally printed in Boston, Massachusetts, between 1720 and 1723, while the polymath Benjamin Franklin published an edition of Watts's *Psalms of David* in 1729. On his visit to the North American colonies in 1737 young John Wesley published *A Collection of Psalms and Hymns*, including hymns by Watts and other British authors. But this was a false dawn: Franklin sold few of his hymnals, Wesley's collection made little impression, and Watts's was poorly received.

In 1738 the celebrated English preacher of the Great Awakening, George Whitefield (1714–70), made his first tour of the North American colonies, finally marking a turning-point for the new hymns. Whitefield's championing and effective use of Watts's hymns led to at least six American reprints of the latter's hymn collections within five years. Whitefield also introduced to North America the Wesley brothers' *Hymns and Sacred Poems* (first published in London in 1739), and other British hymnals now also appeared there.

Some New England congregations now started to sing Isaac Watts's hymns in their meeting houses. In 1742, Jonathan Edwards

(1703–58), minister at Northampton, Massachusetts, and a supporter of hymn-singing, reported that his congregation had adopted these hymns "and sang nothing else". Amid growing dissatisfaction with both the "Bay Psalm Book" and the "Old Version", by the mid-eighteenth century American churches finally started to turn to Tate and Brady's *New Version of the Psalms*, although the days of metrical psalms were numbered. Finally, in the 1760s and 1770s churches began to abandon the diet of "psalms alone" and adopted Watts's hymns – and some hymns by other authors. In 1766 the Baptist *Hymns and Spiritual Songs* (the "Newport Collection") was published, the first Baptist hymnal in North America, and one of the first that was not merely a reprint of a British version.

By the beginning of the nineteenth century, Watts's hymns were being used so widely that they enjoyed the same status in North American churches as metrical psalms had a century earlier. American Presbyterians and Congregationalists were singing almost solely Watts's psalms and hymns, and his influence was so strong that editors of American hymnals often attributed any anonymous hymn to him.

Soon American hymn-writers started to appear. A pioneer was Samuel Davies (1723–61), a Presbyterian minister, fourth president of Princeton, and champion of Watts. Among other hymns, Davies wrote "Great God of Wonders!". The first Lutheran pastor ordained in America, Justus Falckner (1672–1723), wrote "Rise, Ye Children of Salvation" in German (*"Auf, ihr Christen, Christi Glieder"*). However, no American writer arose during the eighteenth century to rival the English hymn-writers of the Evangelical Revival. In the following century C. F. W. Walther (1811–87) of the Lutheran Missouri Synod wrote such hymns as "He's Risen, He's Risen"; and U. V. Koren (1826–1910) of the Norwegian Synod "Ye Lands, to the Lord".

Singing Schools

By 1707, no pipe organ had as yet been installed in any church in New England. Despairing of the musical illiteracy in New England, a clergyman in Newbury, Massachusetts, John Tufts (1689–1750), published the first North American music primer, *An Introduction to the Singing of Psalm-Tunes, in a Plain and Easy Method, with a Collection of Tunes in Three Parts* (c. 1721), using letters instead of notes to delineate the tunes. In another response to pleas for better psalm-singing in church, singing schools were established from the early eighteenth century. One minister had complained: "… no two men in the congregation quaver alike or together. It sounds in the ears of a good judge like five hundred different tunes roared out at the same time… ". Singing schools taught mainly sacred music and were usually held in church buildings. They were soon emulated in some English rural parishes.

One of the earliest books for teaching music, *The Grounds and Rules of Music Explained* (1721), by Thomas Walter of Roxbury, Massachusetts, used shaped notes and bar lines. From the 1760s, American tune-books began to include more complex "fuguing" tunes[20] and anthems for trained singers in addition to the ordinary psalm- and hymn-tunes for congregational use. It was in such tune-books that many North American Christians first encountered the hymns that were to become part of their standard repertory. Rehearsing them in singing school meant people felt better prepared to sing them in church services.

Best known of the eighteenth-century North American music educators and hymnal compilers was William Billings of Boston (1746–1800), a tanner, blind in one eye and disabled in one arm and leg, often regarded as the "father" of American church and choral music. His first tune-book, *The New-England Psalm-Singer* (Boston, 1770), was the earliest to contain solely music by a single North American composer. Billings published six major collections, containing more than 250 original psalm- and hymn-tunes, with sixty-five texts by Isaac Watts. Some hymns Billings arranged in simple four-part harmony and others in basic imitative counterpoint – a style he called "fuguing tunes": "Notes flying after each other, altho' not always the same sound…". Billings was also responsible for teaching singing and organizing choirs, and set up singing schools in several East Coast towns.

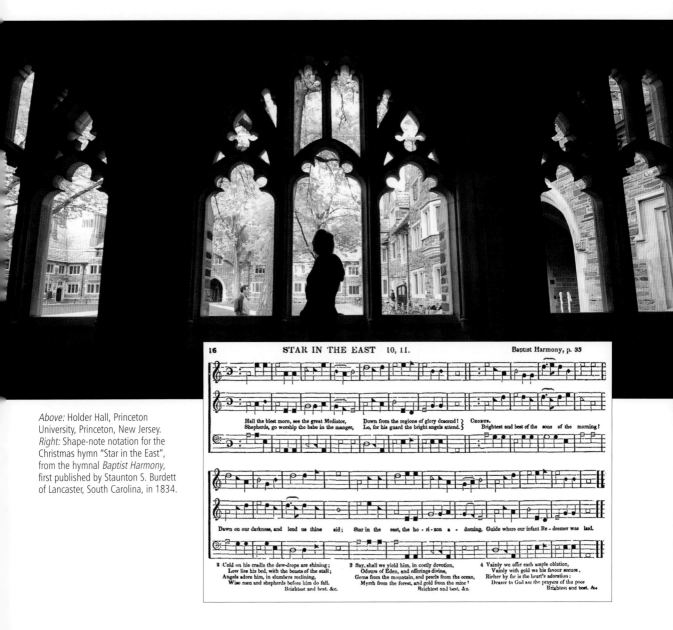

Above: Holder Hall, Princeton University, Princeton, New Jersey.
Right: Shape-note notation for the Christmas hymn "Star in the East", from the hymnal *Baptist Harmony*, first published by Staunton S. Burdett of Lancaster, South Carolina, in 1834.

"Amazing Grace"

Featuring in 2006 as the title of a film about the abolition of the slave trade, the hymn "Amazing Grace" has pursued a remarkable path since it was originally written to accompany a sermon delivered in an obscure rural parish church in the English Midlands in the late eighteenth century, to become one of the best-known hymns, with a remarkable capacity to move the listener.

John Newton (1725–1807), author of "Amazing Grace", was born in Wapping in London. Pursuing a career in the slave trade, during a violent storm at sea in 1748 Newton concluded only God's grace could save him. Ordained in 1764, and appointed curate of Olney, Buckinghamshire, he probably wrote "Amazing Grace" while composing his sermon for New Year's Day, 1773; it first appeared in print in *Olney Hymns* (1779). Newton's lyrics became a favourite for many Christians, because they sum up the doctrine of divine grace, and for supporters of freedom and human rights, who assumed it reflected the author's testimony about his slave-trading past.

In her novel *Uncle Tom's Cabin* (1852), the American novelist Harriet Beecher Stowe quoted three hymn stanzas, two of them corrupted versions of "Amazing Grace", and a third – not by Newton – beginning "When we've been there ten thousand years/Bright shining like the sun… ". Despite its weak link with the rest of the hymn, a form of this third stanza appeared as part of "Amazing Grace" in many early twentieth-century hymnals, thanks largely to the hymnodist and publisher Edwin O. Excell (1851–1921).[1]

"Amazing Grace" would originally have been chanted without accompaniment; the tune now popularly associated with Newton's words was unknown to him. Between 1779 and 1807 the hymn was published in four further collections – three American – an early indication that the hymn resonated strongly in the New World. As with other hymns of this period, the words were sung to a number of different tunes. In Britain the hymn was first sung to the tune "Hephzibah"; in the early 1800s in the eastern United States possibly to "Loving Lambs", an early American folk-melody first known as a plantation tune; while by the late nineteenth century as many as ten different tunes were in use. Two tunes similar to the familiar modern tune were published in the United States in *Columbian Harmony* (Cincinnati, 1829). Then in 1831 our tune, now called "Harmony Grove", appeared in *Virginia Harmony* (Winchester, Virginia), set to Isaac Watts's "There is a Land of Pure Delight". Finally in 1835 William "Singin' Billy" Walker of South Carolina "tidied up" the tune, gave it a new name – "New Britain" – set "Amazing Grace" to it for the first time, and published it in his *Southern Harmony* collection, which sold an estimated 600,000 copies, mainly in the Southern states.

In 1844 the compiler Benjamin Franklin White published "Amazing Grace" to the tune "New Britain" in the popular collection *The Sacred Harp* (Philadelphia), helping widen the hymn's popularity in the Northern states. By the American Civil War it had become loosely linked with the Union side, with its inclusion in two hymnals for the troops, *Hymns for the Camp* and *The Soldier's Hymn Book*. The familiar tune and words were reintroduced to Britain during the late nineteenth century, though "Amazing Grace" was not as yet the most popular of Newton's hymns there.

The standard modern setting is from *Make His Praise Glorious* (1900), edited by Edwin O. Excell.[2] Some claim "New Britain" is an old Scottish tune, others an Appalachian folk-song or American plantation song. It could of course be both: a Scottish melody taken to America by emigrants and later adapted.

"Amazing Grace" has also been sung to the so-called "Old Regular Baptist" tune, and the Blind Boys of Alabama helped popularize a long-standing link with the tune "House of the Rising Sun". During the Civil Rights campaign of the 1960s the hymn became associated with the struggle for equality in the Southern states of America. With the growth of the recording industry, the hymn's popularity spread internationally. Easily adapted by musicians – singers can add melismatic phrases or alter the melody to match their style of singing or musical genre – the song has been frequently recorded, with *Allmusic* listing more than 1,800 recordings. "Amazing Grace" was first recorded in 1922 by Brunswick Records in a series of *Sacred Harp* song recordings. Several early recordings feature African-American singing preachers, most popular of whom was the Revd J. M. Gates, as well as J. C. Burnett, with a fiery rendition. At the same time, folk-song collectors such as the Lomax Family, Herbert Halpert, Sydney Robertson, and John Henry Faulk made recordings that illustrate the hymn's wide geographical and social diffusion.

"Amazing Grace" continued its unusual career outside the church. Arlo Guthrie performed it at the opening of the Woodstock Festival, New York State, in 1969, while Judy Collins recorded it for her album *Whales and Nightingales* (1970), and within weeks it entered the pop charts of both the USA and UK. The best-selling instrumental single ever in the UK is an RCA recording of "Amazing Grace" (1972) by the Pipes and Drums and Military Band of the Royal Scots Dragoon Guards. This success led pipe bands all over the world to adopt the tune, and perhaps reinforced the notion of its Scottish origin. After the attack of 11 September 2001 on the World Trade Center, "Amazing Grace" was heard played poignantly on bagpipes at funeral and memorial services for members of the New York Fire Department and Police Department.

Left: John Newton, author of "Amazing Grace" and many other enduring hymns.
Below: "Amazing Grace" was taken up as an anthem in the United States by the Civil Rights campaign in the 1960s. Here black people are demonstrating against school segregation in St Louis, Missouri, USA.

10

Gloria in Excelsis Deo: The Making of Catholic Baroque

The end of all good music is to affect the soul.

Claudio Monteverdi

Above: Part of the original score by Antonio Vivaldi for one of his sacred choral works.
Right: Portrait of the Italian composer Claudio Monteverdi by contemporary painter Bernardo Strozzi (1581–1644).

♫ Into the Baroque

Until the Renaissance, a composer would choose a particular "mode" to write in – for example the Dorian or Ionian mode – and the resulting work would be known as a "mass in the Lydian mode" or "motet in the Dorian mode".[1] However, after the Renaissance, modes were gradually displaced by major and minor keys. In the modal system, no one note dominates; by contrast, in major and minor keys one note – the tonic, to which a melody naturally gravitates – is of greatest significance, often being called the "home note". In the key of C major, for instance, C is the tonic and G the dominant. From this period until the twentieth century the predominant key of a composition was usually included in its title, as for instance a "mass in C major".

In pre-Renaissance modal music, just as no note or tone was more important than another, no line or part dominated. The essence – and glory – of Renaissance polyphony lies in the intertwining of parts and the resulting resonances. This changed too, with momentous effect: from this period, most pieces possess a dominant line or part: what we know as the "melody". In Baroque style, of the four vocal lines – soprano, alto, tenor, and bass – the two outer parts (soprano and bass) tend to be the most important. The soprano often has the "tune" or melody, and the bass a vital role in counterpointing the melodic line and providing a solid, rhythmic base for it. The inner parts – alto and tenor – provide a complementary harmonic role. In Baroque music the voices are often accompanied chord-style on harpsichord, lute, or perhaps chamber organ.

Things also changed rhythmically. In place of the often irregular rhythms of the Middle Ages and Renaissance, by the period of the Baroque (broadly from the mid-seventeenth century) most compositions were written in three-time (3/4, 3/8, 6/8, etc.) or two-time (2/4, 4/4, etc.). Everything had become more regular, more regulated, and more systematized. In addition, composers began for the first time to specify the type of instrument or voice they required or intended for a particular line or section of their music; such requirements were notably missing from earlier music, which could have been played on almost any available instrument. From this period, a composer would specifically ask for – and expect – a violin, trumpet, or flute, for example.

Some of the greatest Baroque composers were Protestant – pre-eminently Bach and Handel, who are discussed in chapter 11 – but this should not obscure the fact that many great Catholic liturgical composers wrote in this powerful style, considered characteristic of the Catholic Reformation.

🎵 Italian Baroque

Born into this period when composers were beginning to explore monody and turn away from polyphony, Claudio Monteverdi (1567–1643), from Cremona in Italy, showed himself a master of both styles and often opted for the style – old or new (*antico* or *novo*) – he felt most suited the text or the work. The result is music of great exuberance and drama. Although best known for his pioneering opera, *Orfeo*, Monteverdi also wrote outstanding music for the church, including

three masses, the first a "parody" mass in the *stile antico*, and his *Vespro della Beata Vergine* ("Vespers of the Blessed Virgin",[2] 1610) in the *stilo moderno*, probably an unsuccessful job application to Pope Paul V for a position in Rome. Monteverdi's *Vespers* comprise a number of contrasting movements, including five psalms and the hymn *Ave Maris Stella*, not necessarily intended to be sung in sequence, or indeed all on the same occasion. They also include two great settings of the *Magnificat*, one in six parts solely for voices, the other in seven parts for voices and instruments. In the *Vespers*, Monteverdi employs full orchestra, organ, double-choir, and vocal soloists, resulting in a work as dramatic – with its opening fanfare and sumptuous instrumental writing – as his great opera.

After having served the ducal court of the Gonzaga family at Mantua, Monteverdi was appointed *maestro di cappella* at San Marco,

Possible portrait of composer and violin virtuoso Antonio Vivaldi, "The Red Priest", by François Morellon de La Cave, 1723, now in the Museo internazionale e Biblioteca della musica, Bologna, Italy.

Venice, in 1613, where he remained until his death. His reputation faded, and it was not until a new edition of his works was published between 1926 and 1942 that his music was reassessed.

Apart from the extraordinary Hildegard of Bingen, every composer named so far has been male. Another exception is Isabella Leonarda (1620–1704), who entered the Ursuline convent of Collegio di Sant' Orsola at Novara in Italy at the age of sixteen, became mother superior in 1686, and by 1693 was *madre vicaria*. Leonarda wrote more than 200 works, mainly solo motets, in a succinct, "tender" style, many probably to her own texts. She also composed masses and psalm settings, sometimes employing violins to support the voices.

Monteverdi was followed by other Italian composers in the sacred Baroque tradition, such as Francesco Cavalli (1602–76) and Antonio Lotti (c. 1666–1740). Perhaps most significant is Antonio Vivaldi (1678–1741), who wrote as many as sixty-eight pieces of sacred music with a clarity and directness that place his work among the most accessible of Baroque music. Vivaldi's popularity is relatively recent; although his operas were greatly in demand at the peak of his career, his fame soon waned and he died a pauper. Some of his works were published in his lifetime, but most were forgotten. The story of the discovery in 1926 by Professor Alberto Gentile of a large cache of Vivaldi manuscripts possesses all the intrigue of detective fiction. Now safe in the National Library, Turin, this huge collection includes five volumes of sacred works besides much else.

Vivaldi was born in Venice, where his father was a violinist at San Marco. A virtuoso violinist by the age of twenty-five, Antonio was then ordained – his flame-coloured hair gained him the nickname

"The Red Priest" (*il prete rosso*) – and started to teach music at the Ospedale della Pietà, an orphanage for foundlings which also boasted a conservatoire for women, the *figlie di choro*. Vivaldi composed for frequent concerts by the women, who apparently "[sang] like angels, play[ed] the violin, the flute, the organ, the cello, and bassoon". Until recently, who sang the tenor and bass parts for his compositions has been a mystery; now it is suggested – with manuscript evidence for such singers as "*Paulina dal Tenor*" and "*Anna dal Basso*" – that women of the Pietà sang all four parts.[3] At the Pietà, Vivaldi had to write music within the capabilities of its young performers, often in haste as demand was constant, so tended to rely on stock musical figures and proven methods. Probably best-known and most frequently performed is his joyful and deceptively easy-looking *Gloria in D* (RV 589), composed between 1713 and 1717, which has no male soloists. Vivaldi also wrote an oratorio, *Juditha Triumphans*, with subject matter from the Apocrypha.

Although he lived a very short life, Giovanni Battista Pergolesi (1710–36), named after the town of Pergola, composed a much-loved *Stabat Mater*. He became so admired that his name was attached to many other composers' works in their attempts to hijack his success: scholars are still trying to decide exactly which pieces Pergolesi did write.[4] Born at Jesi, near Ancona in Italy, Pergolesi was physically weak and had a persistent limp. His first known work, the cantata *O salutaris hostia*, is dated 1729, while his sacred drama, *La conversione e morte di San Guglielmo* ("The Conversion and Death of St William"), was first performed in 1731. In 1736 he joined the Franciscan Confraternitá dei Cavalieri di San Luigi di Palazzo at Pozzuoli, near Naples, and, while his health was rapidly deteriorating, wrote his two best-known works, the *Stabat Mater* for soprano, alto, strings, and organ, and the *Salve Regina in C Minor* for soprano, strings, and continuo. The *Stabat Mater* successfully blends the old and new styles of Baroque and Classical – religion as a rational and an emotional exercise. The chromatic sequences and understated operatic effects foreshadow Viennese Classicism, yet the music has a Baroque grounding in counterpoint.

♫ The Origins of Oratorio

Oratorio originated in the informal meetings, or "spiritual exercises", of the Congregazione dell' Oratorio in Rome, founded in the 1550s by the Catholic Reformer Filippo Neri (1515–95), the name deriving from the "oratory" (hence "oratorio") or prayer hall where these spiritual meetings, largely for the aristocracy, were held. Neri was striving to bring spirituality to the Catholic laity in a popular way as one response to the Lutheran Reformation. Music, particularly *laude* (hymns in the vernacular), helped attract people, and membership soon spread to other cities. The *laude* had straightforward

tunes and before long were developed into more dramatic form: the oratorio, an extended musical setting of a sacred, usually non-liturgical, text for chorus, orchestra, and vocal soloists, but with no acting or scenery. The form and style of oratorio are, for much of its history, similar to those of opera, apart from a greater use of the chorus.

An early sacred opera by Emilio de' Cavalieri (c. 1550–1602), *Rappresentatione di anima, et di corpo* ("The Representation of Soul and Body", 1600), applied the novel recitative style of Florentine opera to the Italian mystery play, or *sacra rappresentazione*, and was first performed at the Chiesa Nuova in Rome. However, the most significant early oratorio composer was Giacomo Carissimi (1605–74), *maestro di cappella* at the Jesuit Collegio Germanico, Rome, whose *Jephte* (Jephtha) is sometimes regarded as the earliest masterpiece of the genre. The story, taken from the Old Testament, is told mainly by a narrator in an unemotional style, while emotion is depicted dramatically by chorus and soloists, as in the closing chorus, "Lament, lament!" – which Handel later borrowed for the final chorus of his own oratorio *Samson*.

Besides being a notorious womanizer, eventually murdered for his sexual adventures, the Italian Alessandro Stradella (1639–82) was also a gifted composer of oratorios, most notably *San Giovanni Battista* (St John the Baptist), commissioned by the Confraternity of Florentines in Rome, and written to an Italian rather than Latin text. Stradella's music builds an atmosphere of degeneracy in the court of King Herod and gives Salome a suitably beguiling aria, *Queste lagrime*. After this period the main Italian oratorios we know of are fourteen by Carissimi's pupil Alessandro Scarlatti (1660–1725), in which Scarlatti included recitative with developed arias.

Carissimi also influenced such major German Protestant composers of oratorios as Schütz and Handel; but outside Italy, the

opposition to the setting by Reinhard Keiser (1674–1739) of C. F. Hunold's libretto *Der blutige und sterbende Jesus* ("The Bleeding and Dying Jesus", 1704). The oratorio libretto known as *Brockes Passion*,[5] set by Handel, Keiser, Telemann, Mattheson, and others, made more prominent use of the chorus than Italian composers did; and, like Bach, it introduced chorales. In Berlin, the Passion by Carl Heinrich Graun (1704–59), *Der Tod Jesu* ("The Death of Jesus", 1755), was performed almost annually.

♫ French Baroque

Marc-Antoine Charpentier (1643–1704), who studied with Carissimi in Rome, seems to have been the earliest French composer of oratorios, though he preferred terms such as *historia*, *canticum*, *dialogue*, or *motet* for his works, which were apparently performed as extended motets during festive masses, at church concerts, and private Lenten events. Charpentier used the chorus as narrator, as crowd, and to comment, and brought an

Italian oratorio mainly served as a Lenten substitute for opera at the Roman Catholic courts of central Europe, particularly Vienna, where oratorios were performed during services in a chapel. The leading oratorio composers in Vienna were Antonio Draghi (c. 1634–1700) and Antonio Caldara (1670/71–1736), who set oratorio texts by the court poets Apostolo Zeno and Metastasio.

Hamburg was the main centre for early eighteenth-century German oratorio, despite

Above: Portrait of the French composer Marc-Antoine Charpentier, from an engraving by Pierre Landry, 1682.
Below: The Château de Versailles, Île-de-France, France. Much of the music and architecture of Louis XIV's reign expressed grandeur and formality.

Italianate sensuousness and sensitivity to the rather formal and grandiose French style of word-setting. As *maître de musique* (director of music) at the Sainte-Chapelle, Paris, from 1698, Charpentier used the large choir in his many sacred works, which include, as well as oratorios, a major celebratory *Te Deum,* a fine *Missa Assumpta est Maria,* and a Christmas *Messe de minuit,* each movement of which is based on an old French carol.

Both Henri Dumont (originally Henry de Thier, 1610–84) and Jean-Baptiste Lully (1632–87), the latter an Italian by birth, wrote a number of motets for use during low mass for their patron, King Louis XIV, who preferred this shorter version. These works are in effect cantatas for solo, chorus, and orchestra. Lully also wrote a huge *Te Deum* with trumpets and drums, in celebration of the Sun King's recovery from illness, supplying the requisite ceremonial splendour. It was while conducting this work that Lully jabbed his toe, causing a fatal gangrenous abscess.

A contemporary of Lully, Michel-Richard Lalande (1657–1726) also wrote motets,

including a striking *De profundis* ("Out of the Depths", 1689). Lalande's pupil, François Couperin (1668–1733), "*dit le Grand*" (called "the great"), wrote little for the church, but what he did write was strikingly unpompous for France during the reign of the Sun King. Couperin synthesized the graceful lyric style of French contemporary music with the more energetic Italian approach. His *Quatre versets d'un motet composé de l'ordre du roy, chanté à Versailles* ("Four Verses of a Motet Composed by Command of the King, Sung at Versailles", 1703), and a setting of Psalm 119:129, *Mirabilia testimonia tua* ("Thy Testimonies are Wonderful"), were for two sopranos and a small instrumental ensemble; and his charming *Motet de Sainte Suzanne* in D major (c. 1698) for soprano, counter-tenor, baritone, and chorus. Between 1713 and 1715, Couperin wrote three moving *Leçons de ténèbres*[6] (from the *Lamentations of Jeremiah*) for a community of nuns, scored for just two sopranos, bass viol, and organ, for performance in gradually extinguished candlelight on the three days before Easter.

Christian Music in Latin America[1]: 1500–1800

♫ European Conquest and Colonization

The Christian "good news" entered the American continent in the 1500s hand in hand with the armies of the first two great European global imperial powers: Spain and Portugal. What some call an "encounter of cultures" was far from a meeting on equal terms of people respecting each other's ways of life. Yet out of this tragic scenario came some of the finest Christian music in the American continent.

Spanish territories in America stretched from Argentina in the south to California in the north,[2] while Portugal held the land which is today Brazil.

Cathedral Music

By the end of the 1500s Spaniards had raised splendid cathedrals in all the major urban centres of the continent, where Spanish polyphonic music – then at its height with Morales, Guerrero, and Victoria – was introduced. The most important American church music movement from the sixteenth to the eighteenth centuries flourished around these majestic sanctuaries.

Musically, the most active centres were in Guatemala (Antigua), Mexico (Mexico City, Puebla, and Oaxaca), Colombia (Cartagena de Indias and Bogotá), Ecuador (Quito), Peru (Lima and Cuzco), and Bolivia (La Plata, Sucre). At least six distinguished choirmaster/composers should be mentioned: Hernando Franco (1532–85), Juan Gutiérrez de Padilla

(1590–1664), Francisco López Capillas (1608–74), Antonio de Salazar (1650–1715), Gaspar Fernándes (1570–1629), and Manuel de Sumaya (1670–1740). Their works, rediscovered in the twentieth century, are on the same artistic and technical level as those of the European Golden Age of polyphony.[3]

In Brazil, the Portuguese established convents and churches in the north (Olinda, Recife, and Salvador), and further south in Rio de Janeiro and São Paulo. In the 1700s, the discovery of gold and precious stones prompted the development of the Minas Gerais area and the establishment there of various churches and fraternal orders. Contemporary European courts were under the influence of the Italian Baroque style. With understandable delay, this style also made itself felt in church and court music in Brazil, originating one of the most interesting periods of American colonial music, the Brazilian Baroque.[4] In Lima (Peru), on the Pacific coast, Baroque music also appeared with the Italian Roque (Rocco) Cerutti (1688–1760) and his accomplished Peruvian disciple, José de Orejón y Aparicio (c. 1706–65), ranked by some as the best native composer in this area of South America.

The discovery and publication of long-forgotten music from archives in Latin America has revolutionized our knowledge of musical culture in the urban and missionary centres between the sixteenth and eighteenth centuries. From Argentina in the south to the California missions in the north, European, native American, and *mestizo* composers created a Renaissance and Baroque repertoire that was uniquely Latin American and comparable in magnitude and originality to the musical innovations of the outstanding European music centres of the period.

Blend of Styles and Lives

The "uniqueness" of the works of these composers lies not so much in the standard Latin works they wrote for church rituals as in the pieces they provided for celebrations outside the sanctuaries. For such occasions they turned to the *villancico*, a Spanish genre with ancient popular roots, linked to Christmas music since the 1600s, and made a fusion of classical polyphonic music with local aboriginal and black African rhythms, set to texts in vernacular languages (including the broken Spanish spoken by blacks and aboriginals). The sum of these elements granted their music some of the unmistakable signs of originality: freshness, authenticity, and relevance.

What prompted these European-born composers to tread the unpredictable path of "hybrid" music is essential to understanding Latin American music in general and Christian music in particular. Beside the obvious fact that it gave them a chance to experiment (which cathedral music did not), it shows the composers' interest in local expressions of popular culture, which at that time and place were considered inferior,

Singet dem Herrn ("Sing Unto the Lord a New Song", BWV 225), with one of the happiest pieces of counterpoint ever written, is often considered his greatest. Bach's setting of the *Magnificat* in E major (BWV 243), first performed at Christmas 1723, later revised and transposed to D major (first performed in 1733), is another miniature masterpiece, exhibiting many of the characteristic strengths of Bach's music, and opening and closing with a triumphantly joyful Italianate section reminiscent of Vivaldi.

The Passions

Bach's *Johannes Passion* ("St John Passion", BWV 245, 1724) was performed on his first Good Friday in Leipzig, though some of its music dates back to his Weimar years. As we have seen, musical settings of the Passion story performed in church during Holy Week date back as far as the Middle Ages, when they were sung in Latin, originally just to plainchant. This type of Passion – but in the vernacular – took root in Germany from the mid-sixteenth century, and with the addition of chorales remained in use until the mid-seventeenth century. By then, a new form of "oratorio Passion" had evolved, with elements borrowed from oratorio: arias and choruses with specially written poetic texts; recitatives replacing plainchant; and instruments accompanying the voices. This type of Passion culminated in the great settings of J. S. Bach.

With its blending of devotional and dramatic elements, the oratorio Passion could present the Gospel accounts of Christ's passion more richly than either liturgical music or opera. It worked on three levels: the Gospel narrative (set as recitatives and crowd choruses); a contemporary, personal contemplation of the events (the arias); and a devotional congregational response (the chorales). The sayings of the crowd are sung succinctly, sometimes very intensely, by the chorus. In the *St John Passion*, the action stops during the eight arias and an emotional response is voiced.

According to Bach's obituary, he composed five Passions, but only the *St John* and *St Matthew* have survived intact. The larger and more elaborate *St Matthew Passion* has cast an unnecessary shadow over the earlier work; the *St John*, though smaller, is no less impressive, its peculiarly dramatic character partly due to the distinctive character of the Fourth Gospel itself.

Bach amended his *St John Passion* for Good Friday 1725, altered it again around 1730, then in the 1740s restored it to more or less its original form. The words of John are sung by a narrator ("The Evangelist", a tenor), while the words of Jesus (bass), Pilate, and Peter are given to separate soloists, and the response of the Jewish people is sung by the chorus. Into the narrative from John's Gospel (in Luther's German translation) Bach interpolated arias and congregational hymns (chorales) calling for music different from the narrative, their sustained melodies and stable rhythms providing a contrast to the looser, reciting (recitative) styles of the Evangelist and the characters in the drama. The Lutheran chorales, splendidly harmonized by Bach, throw light on each new step of the narrative. For instance, when Jesus asks, "If I spoke, why strike me?", this is followed by the chorale "O Lord, Who Dares Smite Thee?". The work ends with a lullaby, *Ruht wohl* ("Rest Well"), a consoling farewell to Christ's incarnation, and the chorale *Ach Herr, lass dein lieb' Engelein* ("May Angels Bear My Soul Away"), celebrating the hope in Christ's resurrection.

The *St Matthew Passion* (BWV 244) was first performed on Good Friday 1727, and is much more ambitious in conception than the *St John*. An old woman in the congregation objected, "God help us! It's an opera-comedy!" – bewildered by Bach's elaboration of the simple Lutheran chorales. Bach scored the work for two choirs of twenty voices plus two orchestras of at least twelve musicians. The work is not only much longer than the *St John*, it is also more contemplative. In the *St Matthew*, the Evangelist's chanted narration is broken only by short choruses sung to the biblical words. When Jesus sings, he is accompanied by softly played violins, sometimes known as the "halo effect". The final elegy is in C minor, a key unrelated to the tonality of the first part; there is no resolution to the major to confer a sense of finality. For Bach, this was not the end of the story but a pause before the triumph of the resurrection.

While continuing to direct cantatas and Passions in the Leipzig churches, Bach also composed great non-liturgical works such as the *Goldberg Variations* (BWV 988), as well as the *Mass in B Minor* (BWV 232) and his *Weinachts-Oratorium* ("Christmas Oratorio", BWV 248, 1734). The latter is not technically an oratorio, though today often performed as a unified work, but a series of six cantatas for performance at six separate services between Christmas Day and Epiphany (6 January).

Bach's final choral masterpiece, the *Mass in B Minor*, is too massive for liturgical use. In writing it, Bach was possibly striving to draw up a final statement of his belief and a summation of his creativity – a musical testament. The work has the normal sections of the Catholic mass – *Kyrie, Gloria, Credo, Sanctus, Benedictus,* and *Agnus Dei* – but most are subdivided and include contrapuntal or polyphonic choruses and operatic arias. Bach copied out the score between 1747 and 1748, but it was selected from materials drawn from various periods in his previous twenty-five years' composing, a "borrowing" not arising from lack of time but from his conviction that the selected settings were the most appropriate for the text.

The choruses of the *Mass in B Minor* range from the severely polyphonic "old style" (for instance the *Gratias* and *Credo*) to brilliant high Baroque concerto (the *Gloria in excelsis* and *Et resurrexit*) and the prelude and fugue (*Sanctus* with *Pleni*). The *Christe eleison* is the perfection of the Italian duet with a *ritornello*.

Above: Portrait of Carl Philipp Emanuel Bach, composer son of Johann Sebastian Bach.
Right: Portrait of Georg Frideric Handel by George Knapton (1698–1778).

The foundation of mass music is Gregorian chant, so Bach introduces plainsong for the statements *Credo in unum Deum* and *Confiteor unum baptisma*.[4] Yet, despite its diverse origins and various styles, the *Mass in B Minor* gives the overwhelming impression of an undivided work, comparable in scale and variety with a splendid Gothic cathedral.

Bach often marked his music manuscripts with Christian acronyms, such as JJ (*Jesu juva* – "Help me, Jesus") and INJ (*In Nomine Jesu* – "In the name of Jesus"), and usually finished them SDG (*Soli Deo Gloria* – "To God alone be glory"). A cynical age is tempted to see this as mere convention – even superstition. Yet, given the empathy Bach exhibits for the biblical texts he sets, and his close study of them, such a response would appear misplaced. When an inventory was drawn up after his death, Bach's library contained eighty-three religious works, including two editions of Luther's complete writings. In the margin of his Bible commentary he had written: "Where there is devotional music, God is always at hand with his gracious presence."

Bach – obscure enough in his lifetime – was forgotten almost as soon as he died, and many of his manuscripts lost. The Baroque style was already out of fashion and the public wanted something novel. Yet Bach's musical successors recognized his genius. On a visit to Leipzig in 1789, the young Mozart heard for the first time Bach's *Singet dem Herrn* at St Thomas's. A contemporary reported that Mozart's "soul seemed to be in his ears" and the composer copied out the music for himself. Possibly it helped inspire the grand fugues in Mozart's late choral works, such as his *Requiem*. Later Beethoven punned ponderously that *Bach* ("brook" in German) was the wrong term for him – rather his name should be Ocean.

Bach's sons continued the musical tradition of the family, composing in the briefly fashionable Rococo/early Classical style. C. P. E. Bach, W. F. Bach, and J. C. Bach all wrote some sacred music. Carl Philipp Emanuel Bach (1714–88) was probably the most musically gifted of Johann Sebastian's progeny, composing in a transitional style between the Baroque of his father and the Classical of Mozart and Haydn. While never lacking in respect for his father, Carl later turned his back on the complex polyphony of Johann Sebastian in favour of a more subjective, expressive approach (*empfindsamer Stil*). In 1767 C. P. E. Bach succeeded Telemann as musical director of Hamburg's five churches, hurriedly composing huge amounts of music. Before this he had, like his father, written an impressive *Magnificat* (1749). He also wrote the oratorio *Die Israeliten in der Wüste* ("The Israelites in the Wilderness", 1769).

♫ Georg Frideric Handel

Georg Frideric Handel (or Händel, 1685–1759) is the only musical figure of the era whose stature rivals that of Bach. Handel was born at Halle in Germany, but is best known for his English oratorios, particularly *Messiah*. From an unmusical family, he was apprenticed at the age of seven to the organist of the Marienkirche, Halle. In 1703, Handel moved to Hamburg, where he wrote a version of the *Brockes Passion* (1704).

Around 1706, Handel spent three years in Italy, travelling to Florence, Venice, Rome, and Naples, and meeting among others the Italian composer Domenico Scarlatti. In Rome Cardinal Carlo Colonna commissioned from him settings of two psalms, including Psalm 110 (*Dixit Dominus*, for five solo voices, five-part chorus, and orchestra), which was played there during Vespers. At Easter 1708, Handel's oratorio *La resurrezione* was first performed, though the woman who sang Mary Magdalene was forced to withdraw on the second night after papal complaints about the impropriety of a woman performing on stage, and was replaced by Pippo – a male castrato – to satisfy the pope's conscience. Such works reveal Handel's growing mastery of Italian style.

In 1710 Handel returned to Germany, but, responding to a London craze for Italian opera, moved to England in 1712. He wrote a *Te Deum* and *Jubilate* for Queen Anne, to celebrate the Treaty of Utrecht, ending the War of the Spanish Succession. In 1714 Handel's former employer, the Elector of Hanover, became King George I of Britain, bestowing favours on Handel, who now made London his permanent home and in 1727 became a British citizen.

Handel's earliest series of English works is the eleven *Chandos Anthems* (1717–20), written for the chapel of James Brydges, first duke of Chandos, at Cannons, Middlesex, where Handel became musical director in 1717. These anthems are sometimes (understandably) awkward in their setting of the English text, but – joyful, penitential, or ceremonial – include magnificent choral writing, as in *O Come Let Us Sing Unto the Lord*. Handel continued to compose in the Italian style, but also began to absorb some of the characteristics of English choral music. For the coronation of George II in 1727, he wrote four coronation anthems, of which the most well known is *Zadok the Priest*, performed at the coronation of every English sovereign since.

Handel was London's leading composer of Italian operas, yet today is better known as

the creator of oratorios. The English oratorio is essentially his invention – a synthesis of elements of the English masque, the English anthem, French classical drama, Italian *opera seria* and *oratorio volgare*, and the German Protestant oratorio. For Handel "oratorio" usually signified a three-act dramatic work on a biblical – normally Old Testament – subject, with prominent use of the chorus, performed as a concert in a theatre. Although libretti of his oratorios with "stage directions" were sold, any staging was purely imaginary. The Handelian chorus supplied "scenery" and action, mood, and message.

Handel's oratorios originated possibly almost by accident when the planned 1732 staging of a revised version of his *Esther* (first written in 1718) was banned by the bishop of London.[5] The work's success in a resulting concert version is said to have prompted Handel to compose two more "oratorios" in 1733, *Deborah* and *Athalia*. Many more English oratorios followed, of which *Messiah* (1742) is of course the best known. *Israel in Egypt* (1739) has been described as a "vastly extended anthem" and was written in just twenty-seven days. In its original form it was indifferently received and Handel re-presented it, introducing Italian-style solos between the choruses in an attempt to induce the audience to sit it out. *Israel in Egypt* is notable for its grand double-choruses, such as the "Hailstone" chorus and the fugal chorus "He Led Them Through the Deep".

Next came the oratorio *Saul* (1739) – arguably one of Handel's finest – from which the "Dead March" is often extracted as a funeral piece. In *Saul*, Handel evoked biblical instruments in an attempt to bring to life for his audience the Old Testament world. Besides David's own instrument, the harp,

Handel imitates the sounds of the "timbrells" (on kettledrums borrowed from the Tower of London), the *shalishim* used when the women of Jerusalem welcome the victorious Saul and David (on a specially built "tubalcain"), and the ram's horn *shophar*, which he suggested on the trombone. Yet this work met with little better initial reception than *Israel in Egypt*.

After 1740, Handel completely abandoned Italian opera and concentrated on English oratorio. *Messiah* was not heard in London until 1743, when George II is said to have leapt to his feet during the "Hallelujah Chorus", followed as protocol required by the entire audience, a custom that has continued ever since. When congratulated after the performance for his "noble entertainment", Handel protested (perhaps sensitive to churchmen's criticisms of the genre): "… I should be sorry if I have only succeeded in entertaining them; I wish to make them better."

Messiah, though the best known, is least typical of Handel's oratorios. Unlike his other biblical choral works, it has no plot and is a collection of texts drawn from both Old and New Testaments. It has no named characters, just solos for different voices;

Left: A performance of Handel's *Messiah* during the Handel Festival at London's Crystal Palace in 1865, featuring a vast orchestra, choir, and audience: colourized line drawing from contemporary *Illustrated London News*.
Right: The last page of the original score of *Messiah*, with Handel's signature, 1741.

it falls into three main parts – incarnation, passion, and resurrection – all interwoven with Old Testament prophecies. Asked by a contemporary how a non-native English speaker could so sympathetically have interpreted the text, Handel responded, "Madam, I thank God I have a little religion."

Even at its Dublin première in 1742, *Messiah* was hailed as a masterpiece. Since then, it has never fallen out of favour with the public or with amateur and professional performers. There have been countless different realizations of the work – a 1784 Handel Commemoration Festival at Westminster Abbey boasted an orchestra of 250 players and chorus of 275 singers, and a Victorian extravaganza at the Crystal Palace in London in 1859 involved 2,756 singers and 460 players – though "authentic" chamber performances are more favoured today. Handel so enhanced a British love of choral music-making that almost every amateur classical choir includes *Messiah* and other Handelian oratorios in its repertoire.

Among Handel's other outstanding oratorios of this period is *Samson* (1743), first performed (as a concert piece) at Covent Garden Theatre, London. Based distantly on Milton's *Samson Agonistes*, this oratorio is particularly dramatic, including such expressive airs as Samson's "Total Eclipse" and the soprano's triumphant "Let the Bright Seraphim". Handel followed this with the less well-known *Joseph and his Brethren* (1744) and *Belshazzar* (1745). *Judas Maccabaeus* (1747) was written opportunistically as a patriotic tribute to the bloody victor of the Battle of Culloden (1746), using a hastily written libretto by the Revd Thomas Morrell and borrowing sections from *Belshazzar* – yet it still emerges as one of Handel's best celebratory works, featuring the popular "See the Conquering Hero Comes", later conscripted as a hymn-tune. After *Joshua* (1748) and *Susanna* (1749) came *Solomon* (1749) – celebrating the end of the War of the Austrian Succession, and idealizing

Georgian England as God's chosen nation, and presumably George II as a latter-day Solomon.[6] In Handel's own favourite, *Theodora* (1750), unusual in being not biblical but based on the story of an early Christian martyr, the composer compelled attention with bold changes of tone, emotional swings from joy to rage, and passages of great sadness. His final oratorio was *Jephtha* (1752).

Few Englishmen attempted to emulate Handel's mastery of oratorio, though there were works by Maurice Greene (1696–1755), Thomas Arne (1710–78), and John Stanley (1712–86). Yet his oratorios were not received without controversy in England: many continued to attack the practice of performing musical dramas based on Scripture in the profane setting of the commercial theatre or concert hall. The hymn-writer John Newton preached for a full year against the performance of *Messiah* in a secular place of entertainment, while *The Universal Spectator* inveighed against it as the "Height of Impiety and Prophaneness".

Beethoven described Handel as "the greatest composer who ever lived". Yet for a long time most of his output seemed destined for oblivion, with *Messiah*, the *Water Music*, and a couple of other popular favourites standing in for the rest. However, today most of Handel's oratorios have crossed into the mainstream repertory.

CHAPTER 12

The Viennese Tradition: Liturgical and Non-Liturgical Sacred Music

I know that God is nearer to me than to other artists…
I have always recognized and understood him and have no fear for my music.

Ludwig van Beethoven

In eighteenth-century Catholic Europe, sacred choral music was generally confined to the cathedral, the great church, and to the private chapel of the aristocrat. Oratorios were occasionally performed during Lent at theatres, or on rare occasions a rich patron might stage one in his home. However, ordinary, rural parishes could not hope to reproduce the performance music of the court and cathedral, and had to make do with much humbler fare.

♫ The Classical Mass

The epicentre of the "Classical" style was the city of Vienna, where the Catholic church remained supreme and absolutism ruled. The church used three forms of the mass, all of which were set by such master composers of the Classical era as Mozart, Haydn, Beethoven, and Schubert. On regular Sundays a shorter form of the mass, the *Missa brevis* ("brief mass"), was used as preferred by Enlightenment rulers such as the Emperor Joseph II. The high mass (the complete text of the mass) was used at church festivals and was favoured by composers, as it normally afforded them both a larger orchestra and a longer extent. Finally, there was the requiem mass (for the departed).

Some Catholic writers have argued that many of these settings were unsuited to the liturgical needs of the church and were motivated more by composers' musical

Vue et Perspective de la Trinité a Vienne.
A Paris chez Chereau rue S.t Jacques au dessus de la Fontaine S.t Severin aux 2 Colonnes N.o 257.

The Graben, Vienna, one of the city's most famous streets, with the dome of St Peter's Church (*Peterskirche*).

ambitions than by any devotional impulse. Musicians are accused of having been more anxious to achieve dramatic effect than to express the symbolism of the mass, and of subordinating the text to the music.

These Viennese Classical composers were generally little influenced by the German Passions, cantatas of Bach, or oratorios of Handel (though there are exceptions), but took careful note of Alessandro Scarlatti's cantatas, which established the *da capo* aria and offered a fine model for vocal writing. Scarlatti's ten masses and twenty-four oratorios, though little known today, provided an important starting-point for the Viennese school of composers.

♪ Haydn

Franz Josef Haydn (1732–1809) was born at Rohrau, in Lower Austria, and spent nine years as a choirboy at St Stephen's Cathedral, Vienna, before being summarily ejected when his voice broke. Haydn lived precariously until 1761, when he entered the service of the Esterházys, one of Hungary's most influential aristocratic families, and moved to their estate at Eisenstadt. Prince Nikolaus "the Magnificent" remained Haydn's patron from 1762 until his death in 1790, when the court musicians were dismissed, although the Esterházys continued to pay Haydn's salary and allowed him to retain his title of kapellmeister.

In 1766 Haydn took over responsibility for composing at the Esterházy court, a task that included setting masses for chapel use, and wrote an early masterpiece, his *Stabat Mater* (1767). Haydn's *Missa Sancti Nicolai* (St Nicholas Mass, 1772), the fourth of the Esterházy masses, is also known as the "Mass in 6/4 time" for the unusual tempo of its opening *Kyrie*, with its rather pastoral lilt. This mass was possibly written by Haydn to thank his master for returning the household (and

Above: Portrait of Franz Josef Haydn by Christian Ludwig Seehas (1753–1802).
Right: St Stephen's Cathedral (*Stephansdom*), Vienna, by Rudolf von Alt (1812 1905). Beethoven realised just how deaf he was when he saw birds flying from the church tower because of the tolling bells but couldn't hear the bells.

musicians) from an over-extended summer residency in Esterházy, which the composer had earlier attempted to terminate by means of his celebrated "Farewell" Symphony. The eighth of Haydn's early masses, the *Mariazell Mass*, or *Missa Cellensis*, in C major (1782), was written for the Mariazell monastery in Styria, to which Haydn had made a pilgrimage as a young man. During this period too, Haydn wrote his first oratorio, *Il ritorno di Tobia* ("The Return of Tobias", 1775), based on a story from the Apocrypha.

Haydn rejected contemporary criticisms of excessive cheerfulness in his church music, claiming contemplation of God made his heart leap for joy. If experiencing composer's block, he said, "I try to find out if I have erred in some way… thereby forfeiting grace; and I pray for mercy until I feel I am forgiven"; and he once defended a joyful setting of *qui tollis peccata mundi* ("[he] who carries away the sins of the world"), saying he was thinking not so much of the sins as of their being taken away.

Between 1783 and 1792 no new Haydn masses appeared, largely because the Emperor Joseph II ordered the simplification of liturgical practice and banned orchestral accompaniment to music in church, in line with numerous papal decrees. However, in 1787, commissioned by Cadiz Cathedral, Spain, Haydn wrote an unusual sacred work with no text, *Die sieben letzten Worte unseres Erlösers am Kreuze* ("The Seven Last Words of Our Saviour on the Cross"), intended to provide an instrumental, contemplative interlude between the bishop's Good Friday commentaries on each of Jesus' seven sayings. The original orchestral version

became so popular that Haydn also arranged the work for string quartet, piano, and four solo voices and chorus, to a text supplied by Baron Gottfried van Swieten, the Viennese court librarian; of these, the version for string quartet is most often performed today.

Only after he completed the last of his 104 symphonies in 1795 did Haydn compose his choral masterworks – *The Creation*, *The Seasons*, and the last six great masses. After the death of his patron Prince Nikolaus in 1790, Haydn was allowed to visit England, where he gained fame and fortune with his final twelve symphonies and attended one of the great Handel festivals held in Westminster Abbey. At a performance of *Messiah* in 1791 he was so moved by the "Hallelujah Chorus" that he broke down in tears exclaiming: "He [Handel] is the

master of us all!" Much impressed by Handel's oratorios, and especially by their use of the Baroque chorus, Haydn's own choral writing blossomed between 1795 and 1802.

When the Emperor Francis II rescinded his predecessor's ban on orchestras in church, Haydn composed six masses for the Esterházy court, scored for full orchestra and in a musical idiom similar to the opera and symphony, setting the standard for the Classical mass. In these masses Haydn largely rejected the "cantata" approach, where choruses alternated with set arias, and instead treated the mass sections symphonically, with solo and ensemble passages growing out of the larger choral and orchestral textures. These masses exhibit a new musical unity more suited to the concert hall than the chapel, as it was difficult to interpolate the necessary prayers and responses of the liturgy into them.

First, in 1796, came the *Heiligmesse* in B flat and the *Missa in tempore belli* in C ("Mass in Time of War"), also known as the *Paukenmesse* ("Kettledrum Mass") from its use of timpani. Less well known among these six late masses is the *Missa Sancti Bernardi von Offida* – also known as the *Heiligmesse* since the *Sanctus* contains a phrase from the old hymn *Heilig, heilig* ("Holy, holy") – written to mark the recent canonization of a Capuchin monk. Composed at a time when Napoleon's armies were threatening Vienna, Haydn's *Paukenmesse* is memorable for its heart-rending choral cries of *Dona nobis pacem* ("Give us peace!") in the *Agnus Dei*; a timeless plea for respite from war – which may well have influenced Beethoven when writing the concluding section of his own *Missa Solemnis*.[1]

Nelson's victory at the Battle of the Nile, depicted in 1834 by Thomas Luny (1759–1837), was celebrated in Haydn's *Nelson Mass* (1798).

Probably the best known of Haydn's late masses is the setting known variously as the (*Lord*) *Nelson Mass*, *Missa in Angustiis* ("Mass for Straitened Times/Times of Trouble"), and *Imperial Mass*, in D minor (1798). A faithful servant of the old European aristocracy, Haydn shared their anxiety over the threat from Revolutionary France; this mass expresses relief after Nelson's victory over the French at the Battle of the Nile. (Trumpet calls at the end of the *Benedictus* are supposed to commemorate Nelson's naval triumph.) Haydn probably performed the work for Nelson himself two years later, when the much-fêted sailor visited Eisenstadt.

The *Theresienmesse* in B flat (1799, the "Theresa Mass", named after the Empress Maria Theresa, wife of Francis II) is the fourth of Haydn's final set of masses. In its *Gloria* and *Credo*, both constructed on a huge scale, Haydn fuses Handelian choral influences with brilliant classical orchestration, culminating in a final fugal section, *Et vitam venturi saeculi, Amen*, that contains some of the most boisterous music he wrote. Haydn's *Schöpfungsmesse* ("Creation Mass", 1801) is named after its musical quotations from his oratorio of the same name, and the *Harmoniemesse* ("Wind-Band Mass", 1802) for its elaborate writing for woodwind. Haydn also composed a late *Te Deum in C* (1799).

Returning from London to Vienna in 1795, Haydn took with him an English libretto based on the opening chapters of Genesis and on John Milton's *Paradise Lost*.[2] After having it rendered into German by Baron van Swieten, Haydn set to work on *Die Schöpfung* ("The Creation"), which he completed in 1798. "I was never so devout as when I was working on *The Creation*," he claimed. "I felt so impregnated with Divine certainty, that before sitting down to the piano, I would quietly and confidently pray to God to grant me the talent that was needed to praise him worthily." This work, with its dazzling orchestration, was an instant success.

Like most oratorios, *The Creation* has named characters, is divided into acts and scenes, and consists of choruses, recitatives, and arias, opening with an orchestral "Representation of Chaos" – a departure from the conventional overture. At the first performance, the Viennese audience was so excited by the sudden explosion of sound at the words "… and there was light" that "the orchestra could not proceed for some minutes". But *The Creation* represents a development upon its Handelian predecessors; Haydn's use of orchestral colour, adventurous harmony, and rhythmic and melodic inventiveness, and the work's overall unity, give it a quasi-operatic vividness. Within the work there are many instances of effective musical word-painting, such as the depiction of storms, sunrise, and a variety of animals and birds, while the great choruses, "The Heavens are Telling" and "Achieved is the Glorious Work", are the work of a musician who venerated Handel and contain fine multiple-voice part writing.

Haydn claimed that his second oratorio *Die Jahreszeiten* ("The Seasons", 1801) "broke [his] back", and had been forced upon him by van Swieten, whose text amounted to "vulgar Frenchified trash". Apart from the final stirring solo and chorus, which treat the meaning of life, the last trumpet, and the afterlife, it is concerned largely with the weather and essentially mundane matters. At its first performance it was possibly even more successful than *The Creation*, but has never been as well loved in Britain, despite being based on a poem by the Scottish writer, James Thomson (1700–48).

♫ Mozart

Not surprisingly, Wolfgang Amadeus Mozart (1756–91) – with a father, Leopold, who was deputy kapellmeister to the Salzburg court – produced many great works for the church. Yet for much of

Mozart's short adult life orchestras were banned from the church (as we have seen) and there was little call for church music, so most of his church music dates from his earlier years. Leopold recognized his son's musical gifts and pronounced him "a miracle". While visiting Rome in 1768, Mozart heard Allegri's *Miserere*, and wrote it out from memory when refused access to the score. The musicologist Alfred Einstein described Mozart as a mere "visitor on earth", while the theologian Karl Barth whimsically suggested that in heaven the angels play Mozart.

Of Mozart's more than 600 works, around sixty were written for the church – including fifteen complete masses, the incomplete *Mass in C Minor*, the *Requiem*, four litanies, two vespers, and many shorter pieces. Evidence from his letters suggests Mozart's church music was not the mere product of a hired hand, but arose from his own convictions: "God is ever before my eyes. I realize his omnipotence and I fear his anger; but I also recognize his love, his compassion and his tenderness towards his creatures." Several of his religious works – including *Davidde Penitente* ("The Repentant David") and the *Coronation Mass* – were the result of secret vows to the Almighty.

Between 1766 and 1781, when he finally left his native Salzburg, Mozart composed more than fifty liturgical works, drawing on the music of Venice, Rome, and Naples that he had studied earlier. From 1772 Mozart was employed as *Konzertmeister* and court and cathedral organist to the archbishop of Salzburg, Hieronymus Colloredo, who did not wish the mass to last longer than forty-five minutes – which limited Mozart's musical contribution to just twenty minutes. Mozart composed nine masses for the archbishop, who was not looking for innovation or a distinctive style. Living almost literally under the shadow of the palace of the prince-archbishop, Mozart wrote a *Regina Coeli* ("Queen of Heaven", K 108, 1771), *Litaniae Lauretanae de Beata Maria Virgine* (KV 109/74e, 1771; K 195, 1774), another *Regina Coeli* (K 127, 1772), and the *Litaniae de venerabili altaris sacramento* (K 125).

Left: Mozart possibly wrote his *Coronation Mass* to celebrate the miraculous image of the Virgin Mary on the ornate Baroque altar at the Maria am Plain pilgrimage church, near Salzburg, Austria.
Right: Lithograph portrait of Constanze Weber (1763–1842), Mozart's wife, by his brother-in-law Joseph Lange.

The brilliantly operatic solo cantata-motet *Exsultate, jubilate,* concluding with its celebrated "Alleluia" (K 165/158a, 1773), was written in Italy for the castrato singer Venanzio Rauzzini, who had appeared in Mozart's opera *Lucio Silla*. Mozart has sometimes indeed been criticized for the excessively operatic style of some of his liturgical works.

However, in his *Coronation Mass* (K 317, 1779), performed at the "coronation" of a miraculous image of the Virgin Mary, at the Church of Maria am Plain, near Salzburg, Mozart put his distinctive mark on the genre.[3] Here he adopted a simpler, less florid, style, still drawing on Italian influences, but tempering them with the expressiveness of *Sturm und Drang* ("storm and stress") from Germany and the musical craftsman's tradition of Salzburg, creating his own assured, noble style.[4] For its serenity, the *Coronation Mass* has been compared with the late Baroque architecture of the Austrian pilgrimage churches of Balthasar Neumann and Dominikus Zimmermann.

The *Vesperae solennes de confessore* (K 339, 1780), probably written for Salzburg Cathedral, was Mozart's second setting of the vespers, consisting of five psalms (*Dixit Dominus, Confitebor, Beatus Vir, Laudate Pueri, Laudate Dominum*) and the *Magnificat*. The best-known movement is the *Laudate Dominum*, a soprano aria with a long, floating line of great beauty, with four-part chorus.

In 1781 Mozart got himself dismissed by Archbishop Colloredo. Mozart detested both the archbishop and the city of Salzburg, though his *Exsultate, jubilate* and *Coronation Mass* do not betray it. He now moved to Vienna, where he held no official church position and, before his death ten years later, wrote only four further liturgical works: the *Kyrie* in D minor (K 341, 1781), the short motet, *Ave verum corpus* (K 618, 1791), and two great unfinished works, the *Mass in C Minor* and the *Requiem in D Minor*. Free of the controls imposed by Colloredo, Mozart

achieved in these works some of his most memorable music for the church.

Mozart's *Mass in C Minor* (K 427/417a, 1782–83), is, like Haydn's *St Cecilia Mass*, a "cantata" mass. He began work on it in 1782, probably shortly after marrying Constanze Weber, to keep a promise that he would perform it in her honour. Constanze claimed Mozart wrote it to fulfil a vow "on her safe recovery after the birth of their first child"; it represents his loving gift to her. According to Mozart's sister Nannerl, the work was first performed in St Peter's Church, Salzburg, on 26 October 1783, with Constanze singing one of the solo soprano parts, but not until 1901 did the mass achieve its first performance after Mozart's day.

Full of tenderness, humanity, and compassion, the *Mass in C Minor* is the most ambitious and elaborate of Mozart's liturgical works. Planned on a scale comparable to Bach's *Mass in B Minor*,[5] it is influenced by Mozart's knowledge of the music of Bach and Handel and coloured by the Italian operatic style. The mass is scored for four soloists and four-part chorus, with the *Gloria* subdivided into seven separate sections, including a florid *Laudamus te* for solo soprano, spanning two octaves; a massive *Gratias agimus tibi* for five-part chorus; a "soul-shuddering" *Qui tollis* double chorus; a contrapuntal *Quoniam tu solus* for two solo sopranos and tenor; and a *Cum Sancto Spiritu* as double fugue for chorus and full orchestra. The *Mass* was never completed, lacking an *Agnus Dei* and having only fragments of the *Credo*.

Equally pious and profound – though lasting only forty-six bars – is Mozart's motet *Ave verum corpus* (K 618, 1791), composed in a simple, homophonic style. Mozart wrote this jewel for Anton Stoll, choirmaster of the village of Baden bei Wien ("near Vienna"), when Constanze was convalescing there. Since the village church had limited resources, Mozart scored the work for just four-part chorus, strings, and organ. Like the *Hostias* in his *Requiem*, and some numbers in his opera *Die Zauberflöte* ("The Magic Flute"), Mozart's *Ave verum* expresses the simple grandeur he also employed in his Masonic music.

The origin of Mozart's final work, his *Requiem* (K 626), has become the stuff of speculation and romantic legend. Unfortunately the playwright Peter Shaffer magnified this "mystery" with his acclaimed play (then film) *Amadeus* (1979). According to Mozart's wife, during the summer of 1791 an "unknown messenger" delivered "a letter without a signature" asking if Mozart would write a requiem. Mozart agreed, but was warned that any attempt to discover who had commissioned the work would be in vain. Later, the messenger "appeared like a ghost", demanding impatiently: "What about the requiem?"Constanze also claimed that the "mysterious messenger" carried off the uncompleted manuscript after the composer's death.

However, the mystery has not defied detection. The patron was Count Franz Walsegg, who wanted a requiem for his

The romanticized *Mozart Composes His Requiem* (c. 1854) by William James Grant (1829–66) depicts the dying composer being comforted by his wife, Constanze.

wife, and insisted on anonymity because he wanted to pass off the work as his own. Mozart's fevered imagination seems to have added a doom-freighted mystery to this unromantic proposition.

Mozart became increasingly ill while working on his opera *La clemenza di Tito* and *Clarinet Concerto*, and on the production of *Die Zauberflöte*, rendering him unfit to continue with the requiem. Pathetically, he is supposed to have told his wife he was writing the *Requiem* for himself, and started to complain he was being poisoned – for which there is no evidence. Mozart's final illness set in and he died on 5 December 1791, receiving a simple interment, though not the "pauper's burial" of myth. Desperate for money, Constanze asked Mozart's pupil Franz Xaver Süssmayr (1766–1803) to finish the *Requiem*, and his version is still performed today – though alternative attempts have been made to complete and orchestrate the score, recently by Robert Levin of Harvard University.

How much of the work was composed by Süssmayr will never be clear, as we do not know how far he was working to Mozart's instructions. Mozart wrote down complete only the *Introit* and *Kyrie*, leaving voice parts, bass, and some indication of instrumentation for numbers 2–8 up to the eighth bar of the *Lacrymosa*, and the manuscript continues similarly up to the *Offertorium*; the rest is in Süssmayr's hand. When the music publishers Breitkopf and Härtel asked Süssmayr in 1800 how much of the work he composed, he replied that the *Sanctus*, *Benedictus*, and *Agnus Dei* were entirely original work of his own. However, we know Mozart sang parts of the *Requiem* to his wife and Süssmayr in his last days, so some scholars argue that even the three movements claimed by the latter are based on material by Mozart. Beethoven's typically exasperated verdict was: "If it wasn't all written by Mozart, then it must have been written by another Mozart!"

From the outset, the *Requiem* has been regarded as one of Mozart's greatest achievements, integrating Mozart's Viennese Classicism with Baroque techniques he acquired from Handel and Bach. In the two movements Mozart himself definitely completed, we find Gregorian chant (*Te decet hymnus*) and the Baroque fugue (*Kyrie*) combined with Mozart's personal expressiveness. The composer of the opera *Don Giovanni* is recognizable in the intense *Dies irae*, and equally unforgettable are the throbbingly painful *Lacrymosa* and finely counterpointed *Recordare*. "The personal tragedy surrounding the composition of the *Requiem* should not obscure Mozart's triumph as artist in this last flowering of his genius" (Basil Lam).

Luigi Cherubini (1760–1842) was still writing in an unmodified Classical style after the French Revolution, and his two requiem masses, in C minor and D minor, are liturgical in their purpose, the music subservient to the text. His *Missa Solemnis* (1811) is vicariously important in that it later influenced Beethoven's work of the same name. At the age of seventy-six Cherubini composed his *D Minor Requiem* for his own funeral, with an affecting setting of *Pie Jesu*.

♫ Beethoven

Beethoven was far from an orthodox Christian. Though born into a Roman Catholic family, he avoided church and distrusted priests. Beethoven seems to have envisaged the artist as challenged to strive through his or her art toward the transcendent world, the realm of God, materially visible as the "starry heavens". The declaration of Schiller's "Ode to Joy", unforgettably set to music in the final movement of Beethoven's *Ninth "Choral" Symphony*, expresses some of the composer's own deep-seated impulses.

Ludwig van Beethoven was born in 1770 in Bonn, Germany, where his father and grandfather were court musicians. Free himself of obligations to court or to church authorities, Beethoven wrote little music for the church. His first major work for chorus, soloists, and orchestra was his early oratorio *Christus am Ölberge* ("Christ on the Mount of Olives", op. 85), first heard in 1803 but only published, after revision, nearly ten years later. It seems a long way from Handel's *Messiah*, and is like an opera without costumes or set, with melodramatic choruses, orchestral interludes, and theatrical solos. Beethoven claimed to have composed it in just two weeks and the work exhibits variability consistent with such haste. Sometimes bombastic, sometimes formulaic, it is rarely performed today.

In 1807 Prince Nikolaus Esterházy (grandson of Haydn's patron) requested of Beethoven a mass for liturgical use. In accepting the commission, Beethoven praised Haydn's masses as "inimitable masterpieces": no empty words, since he clearly studied Haydn's work before

writing his own mass. Rejecting the quasi-operatic flavour of *Christus*, he composed his beautiful *Mass in C Major* in the Viennese Classical tradition, "treat[ing] the text as it has seldom been treated" (his own claim), and describing this work as "especially close to [his] heart". The contemporary critic E. T. A. Hoffmann, anticipating the tempestuousness of Beethoven's *Fifth Symphony*, was surprised to discover in it "childlike cheerful feelings… ". However, Esterházy himself took against it, putting down the composer with the words, "Well, Beethoven, what's this?", provoking rage in the composer and a long interval before his next mass.

In his final period, during which he wrote some of his most profound and complex works, including the *"Choral" Symphony*, Beethoven produced a Christian work that he himself considered his greatest: the *Mass in D*, or *Missa Solemnis*. At the top of the score he wrote: "From the heart – may it again – go to the heart."[6] A massive work by a master at the height of his powers, written in the symphonic rather than choral tradition, the *Missa Solemnis* drew on the complexities of Beethoven's late style. Though originally intended for the enthronement in 1820 of Beethoven's friend, pupil, and patron, Archduke Rudolf, as archbishop of Olmütz, in Moravia, the mass was not completed in time. It has occasionally been used in the Roman Catholic church, but is too long, calls on too large a musical force, and is possibly too subjective for regular liturgical use.

As with his earlier *Mass in C Major*, Beethoven started by exploring the Latin text of the mass, even commissioning a German translation the better to penetrate its meaning. He set each phrase of the text to reflect its particular liturgical and symbolic meaning, sometimes using ancient, traditional musical figures. He went back to the music of Palestrina, Handel, J. S. and C. P. E. Bach, believing that by studying

*that's all. Therefore let me sing your praises
and grant me your paradise.*

Less operatic than his *Stabat Mater*, it was
first performed in Passy, near Paris, in 1864.

Though referred to as the <u>little</u> *Messe
Solennelle*, the work lasts longer than eighty
minutes, and includes the full text of the high
mass, plus *O salutaris hostia*, normally reserved
for the feast of Corpus Christi. Rossini said it
was his final legacy, and that it offered a lesson
on writing for the voice. Far from "solemn"
emotionally, his mass is as quirky as his other
late works – Rossini described it as "the last
mortal sin of my old age". Musically eclectic,
he includes the Palestrina style (*Christe eleison*),
a bouncy march tune (*Domine Deus*), and
theatre music (solos such as *Domine Deus* and
Quoniam). Rossini's final major composition,
it was received enthusiastically by Meyerbeer
and other contemporary Parisian musical
opinion-shapers. Its composer later
orchestrated it, mainly to prevent another
musician from so doing.

Schubert

The piece many people immediately think
of when the sacred music of Franz Schubert
(1797–1828) is mentioned is "*Ave Maria*",
though it was originally a German *Lied*,
"*Ellens-Gesang Nr. III*", from Walter Scott's
poem "The Lady of the Lake". Long after
Schubert's death, the Latin words of "Hail
Mary" were fitted to the music, and "*Ave
Maria*" it has remained ever since.

But Schubert did write a number of
sacred works, including three early settings
of the *Kyrie* and six Latin masses. He
conducted his own first complete mass,
a grand festival *Mass in F Major*, at the
Vierzehnheiligenkirche, Vienna, in 1814.
His *Mass in G Major* is, by contrast, a small,
pastoral work, melodious and harmonically
undemanding, which has become his most
popular. He also wrote a *Mass in B Flat
Major* and one in C major between 1814 and
1816. Schubert's two later festival masses,
one in A flat major and one in E flat major,
are both long – the *Gloria* of the former
ending with 199 bars of *Amens*. Although the
Mass in A Flat Major (1822) was Schubert's
personal favourite, the *Mass in E Flat Major*
(1828), completed shortly before his death,
and which he never heard, is arguably his
greatest. With its innovative combination
of recitative and aria and experiments in
chromaticism and modulation, it is more
passionate and intense than its predecessors.

Schubert's *Deutsche Messe* ("German
Mass") is a simple setting of poetry by
Johann Philip Neumann (1774–1849) that
can be sung with a wind band or organ
accompaniment only – typical of the eight
German masses of Michael Haydn (1737–
1806) and of other contemporary composers.
Other sacred works by Schubert include five
settings of the *Tantum ergo* (formerly sung
at benediction); four offertory motets set to
various texts; a rather unsubtle Handelian
cantata, *Mirjams Siegesgesang* ("Miriam's
Song of Victory"); the 23rd Psalm; and
Lazarus, an unfinished Easter cantata set

to a German text by August Niemeyer. Schubert also wrote settings of the *Salve Regina* (the Latin antiphon for compline), a partial setting of the *Magnificat*, and two *Stabat Maters* – one a partial setting of the Latin text, the other of a German version by Friedrich Klopstock. Schubert demonstrated a certain ecumenism, composing an a cappella setting of the Hebrew text of Psalm 92 (*Tov Vhodos*, "It is good to give thanks to the Lord") for vocal quartet and baritone solo, at the request of Solomon Sulzer, chief cantor of the new synagogue in Vienna.

Outspoken in his agnosticism as in much else, Hector Berlioz (1803–69) nevertheless composed a much-loved, consciously archaic-sounding sacred work, *L'Enfance du Christ* ("The Childhood of Christ", 1850–54), an oratorio-style piece on the birth and boyhood of Jesus. Often performed at Christmas, the chorus of shepherds – its "Shepherds' Farewell" – is particularly satisfying. As a memorial to those who died in the French July Revolution of 1830, Berlioz wrote a massive *Grande Messe des Morts* (1837), or *Requiem*, scored for huge forces, including a chorus of at least 210 – and up to 900 – voices and five orchestras or bands, including sixteen timpani – but just a single tenor soloist. At the centre of the work is a five-section setting of the *Dies irae*, written to colossal dimensions. Wits have suggested this is a mass to waken the dead – not to comfort them – and it is another example of a sacred work that could never be performed within the Roman Catholic liturgy. Berlioz said that of all his works he would like this to survive. On a similarly large canvas, he also wrote a *Te Deum* (1849) which requires two choirs of 100 voices each, plus 600 children.

Another Frenchman, Charles Gounod (1818–93) – like Liszt – felt a calling to holy orders, though in his case it was never realized. He wrote a still-

Left: Statue of Hector Berlioz in La Place Vintimille, now Le Square Berlioz, Paris, France.
Right: Lithograph of Felix Mendelssohn by Friedrich Jentzen from a painting by Theodor Hildebrandt (1804–74).

popular setting of *Ave Maria*, based on J. S. Bach's *Prelude No. 1 in C Major* from *The Well-Tempered Clavier*, as well as masses, a requiem, hymns, and sacred songs, few of which are performed today. Gounod's two major oratorios, *The Redemption* (1882) and *Mors et Vita* ("Death and Life", 1885), dealing respectively with Jesus' life and death, and the risen Christ, were all the rage in their day but are now scarcely known.

An accomplished organist, the Belgian composer César Franck (1822–90) added considerably to the church organ repertoire. Of his organ-playing, the archbishop of Paris said: "He'll bring more souls to God than we ever can." Franck also wrote a cantata, *The Redemption*, rarely performed today, two masses, and two oratorios, *The Tower of Babel* and *The Beatitudes*, part of his planned setting of the entire Sermon on the Mount. He composed a popular setting of the motet *Panis Angelicus*, the penultimate stanza of Thomas Aquinas's *Sacris Solemniis* hymn for the feast of Corpus Christi, originally for tenor solo, organ, and strings.

Mendelssohn

Felix Mendelssohn (1809–47) was born in Hamburg, Germany, the grandson of the great Jewish philosopher Moses Mendelssohn, an influential advocate of Jewish assimilation. Felix's father, Abraham, acted on Moses' philosophy by having his children baptized into the Lutheran church in 1816 and adding the name Bartholdy to the family name Mendelssohn. Like Mozart, Mendelssohn was a child prodigy, composing more than 100 works between the ages of eleven and fourteen, and playing the organ, violin, viola, and piano as well as conducting. Mendelssohn visited Britain ten times, where he became widely recognized; Queen Victoria's consort Prince Albert dubbed him a "second Elijah", possibly referring to his Jewish roots.

Mendelssohn considered Bach's "the greatest Christian music in the world" and in 1829 conducted the first performance of his *St Matthew Passion* since the composer's death. This proved a turning-point in the revival of Bach's music, and brought the young Mendelssohn much acclaim. It also occasioned one of his few known references to his origins: "To think that it took an actor and a Jew's son [*Judensohn*] to revive the greatest Christian music for the world!"

Mendelssohn's well-known *Wedding March*, from the incidental music to *A Midsummer Night's Dream* (op. 61), written in 1843, was played at the wedding of Queen Victoria's daughter Victoria, and has remained popular at marriage ceremonies. He also wrote many smaller-scale sacred works – some with English texts – for

Above: Portrait of Giuseppe Verdi by Giovanni Boldini, 1886.
Right: Oil painting of the Piazza San Marco, Milan, Italy, in 1845.

unaccompanied choir and choir with organ, perhaps most famous of which is *Hear My Prayer*, with its second half "O for the Wings of a Dove", a favourite for choirboy soloists. The hymn-tune "Mendelssohn", adapted by W. H. Cummings from a melody in Mendelssohn's *Festgesang* cantata for the 400th anniversary of Gutenberg's invention of printing, is the standard setting for Charles Wesley's Christmas hymn "Hark! The Herald Angels Sing".

To celebrate the 300th anniversary of the Lutheran church, Mendelssohn wrote his *"Reformation" Symphony No. 5 in D Major* (1829–30); ten years later he wrote the *Lobgesang* ("Hymn of Praise"), the choral *Symphony No. 2 in B Flat Major* – essentially a Protestant cantata with biblical texts. Felix's sacred music is often redolent of the harmonies and rhythms of the Lutheran hymns of his Protestant upbringing. While his music displays familiarity with Baroque and early Classical music, it also bridges the Classical and Romantic eras, blending his structural and harmonic concepts with older musical conventions.

In the early nineteenth century there was a great upsurge of choral activity in Western Europe. Concert halls were built, large choral societies established, and composers exploited the new markets, turning the oratorio into one of the most popular forms of music for public performance. Mendelssohn wrote two large-scale biblical oratorios, *St Paul* (*Paulus*, 1836) and *Elijah* (*Elias*, 1846), both influenced by J. S. Bach and Handel. After completing *St Paul*, Felix was sent a libretto about the Jewish prophet Elijah, and opted for this subject for his new commission from the Birmingham Musical Festival. The resulting oratorio, *Elijah*, was an immediate success, even rivalling *Messiah* in its popularity.[1] *Elijah* is dramatic, memorable, reverent, and not too difficult, including tuneful tenor and bass arias such as "If with All Your Hearts" and "Lord God of Abraham"; rumbustious choruses such as "Thanks Be to God"; the three-part female chorus "Lift Thine Eyes" based on lines from Psalm 121; and the contralto aria "O Rest in the Lord" as the angel consoles Elijah. All these entered the church repertory, and over the last fifty years a new appreciation of Mendelssohn's work has helped remove the Victorian varnish from *Elijah*.

Among Mendelssohn's other choral works is the sacred cantata *Lauda Sion* (1846) and the chorus, "There Shall a Star Come Out of Jacob", from an uncompleted oratorio, *Christus* (not Mendelssohn's title). More Romantic is *Die erste Walpurgisnacht* ("The First Walpurgis Night"), a setting for chorus and orchestra of a ballad by Mendelssohn's aged admirer Goethe, describing Druid rituals in the early years of Christianity.

Mendelssohn's success irritated the composer Richard Wagner sufficiently for the latter to denigrate him, three years after his death, in an anti-Semitic pamphlet entitled *Das Judenthum in der Musik* ("Jewishness/Judaism in Music"), claiming Mendelssohn and other Jewish composers were inherently incapable of musical greatness. This marked the start of a tendency among some Germans to smear Mendelssohn's achievements, culminating in the Nazis' ban on the performance and publication of Mendelssohn's works in the 1930s, as part of their anti-Semitic policy.

There has been considerable recent debate concerning Mendelssohn's Jewish identity. A study by Jeffrey Sposato[2] argues that Mendelssohn's oratorios are the product of a staunchly Lutheran composer, who, by the time of *Elijah*, had established himself firmly enough as a Christian composer of sacred music to enable him to write a work that allowed both Jews and Christians to identify with, and take pride in, its protagonist. Sposato believes *Elijah* represented "an attempt to reconcile his Christian faith and his Jewish heritage".

The personal life of the composer Franz Liszt (1811–86) was, to say the least, conflicted. While passionately involved in Christianity, he was no less passionately involved with women – and of course with music. Liszt pleaded to enter a seminary in Paris at the age of seventeen, and finally achieved his desire in 1865 when, at the age of fifty-four, he entered the Third Order of St Francis of Assisi in Rome and became Abbé Liszt. A virtuoso pianist and composer, Liszt claimed: "I have taken a serious stand as a religious, Catholic composer." Elsewhere he said: "The church composer is also preacher and priest and where words are not enough to convey the feeling, music gives them wings and transfigures them." Liszt considered he "wept blood" in writing his *Psalm XIII*. In addition to piano music with religious titles, such as *Harmonies poétiques et religieuses*, two *Légendes*, and *Années de pèlerinage*, Liszt wrote settings for five psalms, a *Missa choralis* (1865), a *Hungarian Coronation Mass* (1867), and oratorios. In his huge and dramatic oratorio *Christus* (1855–67) he set his own libretto, drawn from the Latin text of the Bible. Toward the end of his career, Liszt became fascinated by Gregorian chant, which influenced such works as his 1879 oratorio *Via Crucis* ("The Way of the Cross").

Verdi

Giuseppe Verdi (1813–1901) was of course first and last an opera composer. He wrote little else, with the major exception of his massive *Requiem*, which the German critic Hans von Bülow cheaply dubbed Verdi's "latest opera, in church vestments". When his admired friend Rossini died in 1868, Verdi planned to commemorate him with a *Messa per Rossini* ("Mass for Rossini"), each of its thirteen sections to be written by a different Italian composer. Verdi wrote the final section, a *Libera me*, for soprano, chorus, and orchestra, but the organizing committee abandoned the entire project just nine days before its planned première.[3]

The death of the Italian nationalist writer Alessandro Manzoni, author of *I promessi sposi* ("The Betrothed"), in 1873 prompted Verdi to return to the idea of composing a requiem, in which he incorporated his contribution to the abortive joint work. His *Requiem* was first performed the following year at the Church of San Marco, Milan – the only church in that city where women were permitted to sing. Rebutting von Bülow's smart comment, Brahms commented of the *Requiem* that "only a genius could have written such a work".

Verdi was no conventional Christian – he professed agnosticism and distrusted organized religion – and the sacred text is indeed treated operatically, with the connotations of secularity and profanity this implies. God is portrayed as terrifying judge as well as benevolent saviour, and consolation, repeatedly offered, is repeatedly withdrawn. Unforgettable is the irruption of orchestra and chorus in the terrifying *Dies irae*, with the bass drum marking the unaccented beats. Only Berlioz's *Tuba mirum* in his *Grande messe des morts* rivals the power of this movement. Victorian London found the *Requiem* – which has been described as "a bunch of opera singers let loose in a cathedral" – too theatrical for its taste. However, the composer's wife defended him

fiercely: "The religious spirit and the way in which it is expressed must bear the stamp of its period and its author's personality."

Verdi's final work was also religious: his *Four Sacred Pieces* (*Quattro Pezzi Sacri*) for chorus and orchestra were written at various times in his later years and published in 1898, though not intended to be played together. They are difficult to categorize as liturgical or concert pieces. The earliest, dating from 1888, is the *Laudi alla Vergine Maria*, a setting for unaccompanied women's voices of part of the last canto of Dante's *Paradiso*, followed in 1889 by an *Ave Maria* for unaccompanied mixed chorus, composed on an "enigmatic" scale. The *Stabat Mater* (1896–97) is a brief setting for choir and orchestra, unusually with no word of the text repeated, while the fourth and final piece is a vast *Te Deum* (1895–96) for double chorus and orchestra, to which Verdi was so attached that he asked that a copy be placed in his coffin. The choral writing, unaccompanied for long stretches, is difficult to perform successfully. One critic has described these last works as "strange pieces that blend beauty with austere compression".[4]

Known almost exclusively for his great series of operas – particularly the *Ring* cycle – it is little known that Richard Wagner (1813–83) left a massive, unfinished work entitled *Jesus of Nazareth*, based on his own harmony of the Gospels, or that he completed another huge work, *The Love Feast of the Twelve Apostles*, for orchestra and no fewer than three choruses. Critics also discern Christian themes in operas such as *Tannhäuser* and *Lohengrin*, and particularly in Wagner's final work, *Parsifal*, which, some feel, uneasily fuses Christian and racist ideas.

Yet, while seeming to admire Jesus, Wagner rejected what he called the "Jewish tribal god, the god of punishment and war" and dismissed the Ten Commandments – views which cannot be divorced from his anti-Semitic opinions. He managed to hold contradictory views on Jews in general, and on Jesus the Jew in particular, claiming outrageously: "It is more than doubtful if Jesus himself was of Jewish extraction."[5]

The Cecilian Movement

In mid-nineteenth-century Germany a movement was initiated by Karl Proske (1794–1861) to restore what he believed to be the *vere musica ecclesiae* ("true music of the church"). By his definition, this music consisted solely of Gregorian chant and the polyphonic music of Palestrina and certain of his Renaissance contemporaries. Proske was appointed kapellmeister of Regensburg Cathedral, Germany, in 1830, and made unsparing efforts to trace and transcribe ancient music manuscripts in order to preserve this tradition.

Proske was supplanted by the composer Franz Xaver Witt (1834–88), who in 1867 founded the *Allgemeiner Deutscher Cäcelien-Verein* ("Cecilian" Movement), which exported the cause to other European countries, setting up a *Scuola Gregoriana* ("Gregorian school") in Rome itself. However, the movement's positive aim of resurrecting ancient styles was soon overtaken by a negative campaign to extirpate all non-liturgical and orchestral masses written in the intervening years, blacklisting reams of sacred music, and crusading against the use of any instrument other than the organ in church. By intervening in this dogmatic and reactionary way, the movement eventuated in the writing of many poor and unoriginal compositions. Witt himself composed what amounted to pastiches of sixteenth-century liturgical music, and was succeeded by Franz Haberl (1840–1910).

Of the nineteenth-century Austrian composers, Anton Bruckner (1824–96) was by far the most committed Catholic. Son of a village organist, and himself a fine organist, Bruckner grew up in the Austrian church music tradition of Haydn, Mozart, and Schubert, writing several early pieces for church use, including a small *Mass in C* (1842) at the age of seventeen, five versions of *Tantum ergo* (1846), a *Requiem* (1849), which he revised as late as 1894, and a *Missa Solemnis* (1854), yet it was some time before he found his own voice. After moving to Vienna, Bruckner discovered in Simon Sechter a teacher who immersed him in Bach and Beethoven and helped shape his mature style.

Bruckner now wrote a number of mainly unaccompanied simple and direct motets,

Portrait of Johannes Brahms by K. Rona, 1896.

such as his *Vexilla Regis* and *Os justi*, that contrast in scale and ambition with his vast symphonies. Of Bruckner's seven *Masses* only the last three, from the 1860s – confusingly numbered 1, 2, and 3 – are now regularly performed. *No. 1 in D Minor* and *No. 3 in F Minor* are concert masses, though their first performances took place in a liturgical setting. The *F Minor Mass* (1867–68) is his largest choral work and was first performed in Vienna in 1872. Bruckner's preoccupation with the symphony is obvious in these masses; conversely his symphonies can be viewed as non-verbal versions of his sacred works.

Bruckner's simpler *Mass No. 2 in E Minor* was liturgical, commissioned by the bishop of Linz in 1866 for open-air performance at the consecration of a chapel at Linz Cathedral, with only wind instruments accompanying and with no solo voices. Greatly influenced by Beethoven's *"Choral" Symphony* and by Wagner's *Tristan und Isolde*, the piece meant much to Bruckner. The *Kyrie* is in the style of Palestrina, while the *Sanctus* opens with a direct quotation from the equivalent passage in the same composer's *Missa Brevis*. Bruckner also wrote a *Te Deum* (1881–84), with which he was satisfied enough to write: "When God calls me to him and asks, 'Where is the talent I gave you?' I shall hold out the rolled-up score of my *Te Deum* and I know he will judge me mercifully."

Brahms

Johannes Brahms (1833–97) said of the title of his choral masterpiece, *Ein deutsches Requiem (A German Requiem*, op. 45), "I should like to leave out the word 'German' and refer instead to 'Humanity',"[6] his requiem remaining possibly the most consoling written. The traditional Roman Catholic liturgical text for the requiem mass is a prayer for the dead, filled with terrifying images of the Last Judgment; by contrast, Brahms's text, compiled by him

from Martin Luther's German translation of the Bible, aims to comfort the living who face death. Brahms was agnostic yet brought up to respect Lutheran traditions and the music of J. S. Bach. Introduced to the music of Samuel Scheidt and Heinrich Schütz by the German musicologist J. A. Philipp Spitta (1841–94), Brahms composed a number of unaccompanied motets.

Brahms was only thirty-three when he completed most of the *Requiem*, which had begun to gestate a decade earlier in response to the death of his friend, the composer Robert Schumann, and later to the death of Brahms's mother in 1865. Brahms's text does not mention Christ, and has only a passing reference to redemption, in the final movement; it offers comfort and endurance rather than salvation and resurrection. His *Requiem* introduced a new genre, the "requiem of consolation", contrasting with the grief of Mozart's *Requiem* and the operatic requiems of Verdi and Berlioz.

In musical structure Brahms's *Requiem* forms a seven-movement "arch", with the most comforting music at its centre. At the heart of the requiem is its shortest movement, the tranquil chorus "How Lovely are Thy Dwellings", often performed on its own. Brahms saves his most dramatic music for the sixth movement, where the baritone sings, "We shall all be changed… at the sound of the last trumpet," whereupon the music erupts in a blaze of sound.

A German Requiem is Johannes Brahms's longest work and, since its first performance in Vienna in 1867, it has been subjected to much critical debate, while enjoying continued popularity with audiences. The German critic Hanslick doubted it was suited to the concert hall, implying its religious nature called for a sacred venue, while other critics objected to its "mystical", contemplative tone, which they contrasted with the straightforward Protestantism of Schütz and Bach. Wagner abhorred the *Requiem*, and was outraged by Brahms's claim to have written a "German" work, as in the title *Ein deutsches Requiem*.[7] Arnold Schoenberg later rebutted Wagner's rejection of Brahms as a conservative;[8] following this re-evaluation, the work found new appreciation, as among Brahms's more modern compositions.

While Brahms was far from being a conventional Christian, Gustav Mahler, a convert to Catholicism, confessed he could not compose a mass because he could not affirm the *Credo*.

The critic Mosco Carner said of the Bohemian/Czech nationalist composer Antonín Dvořák (1841–1904): "Religious music was to him a means to express in the first place his feeling of devotion, his idea of the deity."[9] But Dvořák was essentially an instrumental composer, to whom religious music was a sideline. He wrote a beautiful *Stabat Mater* (1880) after losing three of his children in rapid succession; and also composed *Biblical Songs* (1894), based on ten of his favourite psalms, and described as "ten variations on the theme of God", as well as a large-scale *Requiem* (1891), and a dramatic oratorio, *Saint Ludmila*, to celebrate the conversion of the Czechs to Christianity. Just as Verdi's has been dismissed as excessively theatrical, Dvořák's *Requiem* displays a rather inappropriate cheerfulness, partly deriving from his frequent employing of Slavonic folk-melodies. Dvořák also wrote a *Te Deum* (1892) in the form of a miniature choral symphony, with orchestration that in places suggests birdsong.

The French composer Gabriel Fauré (1845–1924), a pupil of Camille Saint-Saëns (1835–1921) and organist at St Sulpice, Paris, though not a practising Catholic, wrote a simple, austere, and much-loved *Requiem* (1887–90), the ethos of which he defended:

It has been said my Requiem does not express the fear of death and someone has called it a lullaby of death. But it is thus that I see death: as a happy deliverance, an aspiration towards happiness above.

Scored for soprano and baritone solo, chorus, organ, and orchestra, Fauré's orchestral setting is very spare, while the chorus often evokes Gregorian chant. The most celebrated section is the ethereal *Pie Jesu*, written for female soprano, and often sung by a boy treble; but even the much-shortened *Dies irae* is contemplative rather than dramatic. The *Requiem* is Fauré's most performed work; though written for liturgical use, it soon entered the concert hall. The French composer Nadia Boulanger (1887–1979), who greatly admired it, claimed, "No disquiet or agitation disturbs its profound meditation, no doubt tarnishes its unassailable faith."

Fauré also wrote a short *Messe Basse* ("Low Mass") for high voices, originally in collaboration with André Messager (1853–1929), and known in that form as the *Messe des pêcheurs de Villerville*, but revised in 1906

Photograph of Gabriel Fauré taken around the turn of the nineteenth century.

officially not disapprove) the singing of hymns in worship until 1820, when the Diocese of York sided with Thomas Cotterill (1779–1823), curate of St Paul's Church, Sheffield, and James Montgomery (1771–1854), editor of a Sheffield newspaper, who had published a controversial new collection which became influential within Anglicanism, *A Selection of Psalms and Hymns for Public and Private Use, Adapted to the Services of the Church of England* (1819). Cotterill's congregation had rebelled when he tried to impose his hymn-book on them and took him before the diocesan consistory court. There, the chancellor of the diocese, with typical Anglican compromise, concluded that both hymns *and* metrical psalms were technically illegal, but, because their use had become widespread, he felt unable to enforce his ruling. The archbishop's permission to use hymns in Cotterill's church in Sheffield was subsequently taken to imply permission for the use of hymns throughout the established church.

The son of a Moravian minister, and originally from Ayrshire in Scotland, James Montgomery wrote about 400 hymns, as well as "adjusting" the texts of others' hymns. He left a quaint description of how inspiration came to him: "I lie in wait for my heart and when I can string it to the pitch of David's lyre, I will set a psalm 'to the chief Musician'." Best known of Montgomery's hymns are the Christmas "Angels from the Realms of Glory", "Hail to the Lord's Anointed", "Stand Up, and Bless the Lord", and the bereavement hymn "Forever with the Lord".

A number of verses by the seventeenth-century rector of Bemerton, Wiltshire, the metaphysical poet George Herbert (1593–1633), were set to music when the Church of England began to take up hymn-singing, such as "Let All the World in Every Corner Sing". Reginald Heber (1783–1826), bishop of Calcutta, wrote a number of memorable hymns, including a favourite missionary number of Victorian times, "From Greenland's Icy Mountains",

with its triumphal, imperialistic overtones.[1] Heber suggested a specific day in the church's calendar for each of his hymns, so becoming the first Anglican liturgical hymn-writer. He wrote "Brightest and Best of the Sons of the Morning" for Advent, the archaic-sounding "By Cool Siloam's Shady Rill", the militant "The Son of God Goes Forth to War", and for Trinity Sunday, "Holy, Holy, Holy! Lord God Almighty!" – a metrical paraphrase of Revelation 4:8–11, taking the ancient *Ter sanctus* as his starting-point. Queen Victoria's Poet Laureate Alfred, Lord Tennyson (1809–92), declared this to be the greatest hymn ever written.[2] "A good hymn," he stated, "is the most difficult thing in the world to write." Nevertheless, his contemporaries published some 400,000 original and translated hymns, dozens of whose words and tunes became familiar throughout the English-speaking world, as yet without the help of recordings, radio, or television.

♩ The Oxford Movement

The Oxford Movement, inaugurated in 1833 with the aim of reconnecting the Church of England with its Roman Catholic roots and of restoring "the beauty of holiness" to the Anglican communion, produced many new English hymns by such fluent poets as John Keble (1792–1866), William Walsham How (1823–97: "For All the Saints" and the Sunday School hymn "It is a Thing Most Wonderful"), Henry Lyte, and others. Keble's *The Christian Year* became a key text of the Tractarian Movement (another name for the Oxford Movement), consisting of poems for the feasts and fasts of the church year. It included a number of verses which became familiar hymns, such as "New Every Morning" and his paraphrase of the Beatitudes, "Blest are the Pure in Heart".

John Mason Neale (1818–66), a leading figure in the movement, translated the medieval Latin text *Veni Emmanuel* to create the English Advent hymn "Draw Nigh, Draw Nigh, Emmanuel" (later altered to "O Come, O Come, Emmanuel"), set to a fifteenth-century processional adapted by Thomas Helmore.[3] Neale was an inveterate collector and writer, specializing in translations not only from Latin but from Greek originals, and also wrote the hymn "Art Thou Weary, Art Thou Languid?" Well-known versions of Neale's include "Jerusalem the Golden", translated from selected stanzas of Bernard of Cluny's 3,000-line poem *Hora novissima* on the glories of the heavenly country,[4] "All Glory, Laud and Honour", originally by Theodulf of Orleans (750/60–821),[5] and the Christmas hymn "Good Christian Men, Rejoice". Neale's popular St Stephen's Day (26 December) carol "Good King Wenceslas" is neither a translation nor based on any known incident, though it features the historical Czech patron saint Vaclav (Wenceslas) the Good, who reigned in Bohemia between 922 and 929. The tune originated in Scandinavia, and was first published in *Piae Cantiones* in 1582 for the spring carol *Tempus adest floridum* ("Spring Has Now Unwrapped the Flowers").

Frederick William Faber (1814–63), brought up in a Calvinist-leaning family, converted to Roman Catholicism under the influence of John Henry Newman. An enthusiastic advocate of congregational hymn-singing at a time when the practice was not widespread in Catholic churches, Faber wrote a number of hymns to expand the Catholic repertoire: many were also taken up by Protestants, albeit sometimes in modified form. Still widely sung are "There's a Wideness in God's Mercy", "Faith of Our Fathers", "My God, How Wonderful Thou Art", and "Hark, Hark My Soul!" Other products of the Oxford Movement were the version by Frederick Oakeley (1802–80) of the eighteenth-century Latin hymn "*Adeste, fideles*" ("O Come All Ye Faithful")[6] and the carol by Edward Caswall (1814–78), "See, Amid the Winter's Snow", normally sung to "Humility" by Sir John Goss. Caswall published a collection of English versions of Latin hymns, *Lyra Catholica* (1849), best known of which is "Jesus, the Very Thought of Thee", a version of the twelfth-century "*Jesu dulcis memoria*".

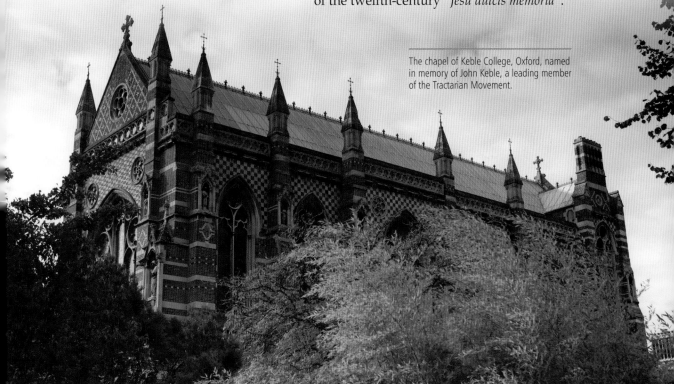

The chapel of Keble College, Oxford, named in memory of John Keble, a leading member of the Tractarian Movement.

♫ Ancient and Modern

The seminal Anglican collection, *Hymns Ancient and Modern*, the first hymnal specifically created for the Church of England, was published in 1861, apparently the result of a railway-carriage conversation between two clergymen who wanted to see standardization in hymnals. Another of this collection's aims was to provide hymns for the entire Christian year, including its seasonal festivals. Ruthlessly edited by the Anglo-Catholic Revd Sir Henry Williams Baker (1821–77), it accepted hymns from every shade of churchmanship – high and low – as well as from Dissenters such as Watts, Doddridge, Montgomery, and of course the Wesleys. Baker altered and edited the hymns high-handedly – though not necessarily deleteriously – to such an extent that Victorians joked that the popular acronym "HAM" actually stood for "Hymns Asked for and Mutilated"! One instance of Baker's gifted editor's eye is his transmutation of the plodding version by William Whiting (1825–78), "O Thou Who Bidd'st the Ocean Deep", into the popular "Eternal Father, Strong to Save".

The resulting new hymnal was astonishingly successful, selling 4.5 million copies in its first seven years, and over its first century going through a number of editions, the most recent entitled *Common Praise* (2000), overseen by Professor Henry Chadwick (1920–2008). The 1875 edition became the "standard" edition, used for more than a century. Its eclectic hymn selection, liturgical organization, and printed music made *Ancient and Modern* the first modern English hymnal, as well as the most successful. It was also the first influential hymn-book to print the tune on the same page as each hymn – and the first to attach "Amen" to every hymn.

To *Ancient and Modern* Baker himself contributed such hymns as "Lord, Thy Word Abideth" and "The King of Love My Shepherd is… ", a paraphrase of Psalm 23.

New hymn-tunes also appeared in the hymnal: John Bacchus Dykes (1823–76) contributed "*Melita*" for "Eternal Father, Strong to Save" and "Gerontius" for "Praise to the Holiest in the Height"; Sir Arthur Sullivan the march "St Gertrude" for "Onward Christian Soldiers" (by Sabine Baring-Gould) and *Lux in Tenebris* for "Lead, Kindly Light", written by Cardinal Newman when he feared he was dying. Other new tunes came from such composers as Sir John Stainer; Sir John Goss (1800–80), organist at St Paul's Cathedral, for such hymns as "Praise, My Soul, the King of Heaven"; and William Henry Monk (1823–89), the musical editor of *Hymns Ancient and Modern*, with "Eventide" for "Abide with Me".

The Anglican clergyman Henry Francis Lyte (1793–1847), author of *Poems Chiefly Religious* (1833) and *The Spirit of the Psalms*

Below: Portrait of Cardinal John Henry Newman, beatified in 2010, by John Everett Millais, 1881.
Right: A middle-class Victorian congregation stand to sing a hymn in an Anglican church. Everyone has a hymn book. The "cushions" on the floor are for kneeling to pray.

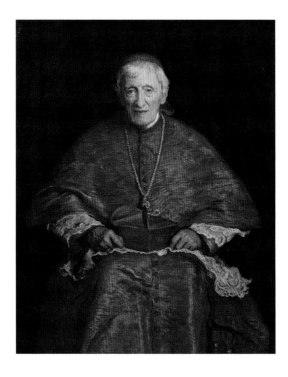

the Lord in the Beauty of Holiness!", as well as the militant "Fight the Good Fight", based on words of the apostle Paul.[7]

Adopted as a wartime and peacetime anthem in many countries and languages, "Eternal Father, Strong to Save" is variously called the "Royal Navy Hymn", the "United States Navy Hymn", or simply the "Navy Hymn", and normally sung to the tune "*Melita*". The US Episcopal Church introduced revised versions to accommodate other sections of the American armed forces, such as submariners and space personnel. Also popular with both military bands and church organists is the hymn "The Day Thou Gavest, Lord, is Ended" by John Ellerton (1826–93), co-editor of *Hymns Ancient and Modern*. Often labelled an "evening hymn", it was originally intended as a missionary hymn, with imperial echoes in its text. Its elegiac tune, "Ellerton", has – like that of "Abide with Me" – surely helped prolong its popularity. Ellerton wrote a number of other hymns – but unusually refused to copyright any of them. An architect from Hackney in London, James Edmeston (1791–1867), wrote "Lead Us, Heavenly Father, Lead Us", a hymn that often finds a place in wedding services, most often to the tune "Mannheim" by the German composer Friedrich Filitz (1804–76).

(1834), wrote among other well-known hymns a stirring version of Psalm 103, "Praise, My Soul, the King of Heaven", sung at the weddings of George VI and Elizabeth II, and "Abide with Me", much used at British funeral services, and since 1927 somewhat incongruously sung by the crowds attending the Football Association's Cup Final at Wembley Stadium in London. Lyte used as his source for this hymn, written shortly before his death, the disciples' words on the road to Emmaus: "Abide with us: for… the day is far spent" (Luke 24:29, KJV). John Monsell (1811–75), an Irishman who became a Church of England rector in Surrey, wrote what is sometimes regarded as the theme of the Oxford Movement, "O Worship

♫ The Church of Scotland

In the mid-nineteenth century, psalmody and a few Scripture paraphrases remained the sole texts permitted to be sung in the Church of Scotland until a slim collection of eighty-nine hymns was officially approved in 1861. By contrast, the Free Church of Scotland minister Horatius Bonar (1808–89) was responsible for more than 600 hymns, of which "I Heard the Voice of Jesus Say… ", "Fill Thou My Life…", and the missionary hymn "Go, Labour on, Spend and Be Spent" are probably best known today. To commissions from Ira D. Sankey, the evangelist D. L. Moody's vocalist, Bonar also wrote the gospel songs titled "A Pilgrim's Song" – opening "A few more years shall roll… " – and "Yet There is Room".

♫ Some Women Hymn-Writers

Quintessentially Victorian was the children's hymn "All Things Bright and Beautiful", written by Cecil Frances ("Fanny") Alexander (1818–95) – possibly inspired by lines from S. T. Coleridge's *The Rime of the Ancient Mariner*, "He prayeth best, who loveth best/ All things great and small… ". Its third verse, setting out a rigid, God-ordered class system, is invariably omitted today:

> *The rich man in his castle,*
> *The poor man at his gate*
> *God made them, high or lowly,*
> *And order'd their estate.*

Influenced by the Oxford Movement, Mrs Alexander, wife of the Anglican archbishop of Armagh, now in Northern Ireland, published her hugely successful didactic *Hymns for Little Children* (1848) after hearing her godchildren complain how dreary they found the catechism. Her collection also included "There is a Green Hill Far Away" and "Once in Royal David's City", though it is difficult to imagine any modern child singing another of her hymns, "We are but

Little Children Weak". Since 1919, "Once in Royal David's City", sung to the simple tune by Henry John Gauntlett[8] (1805–76), has opened the annual *Service of Nine Lessons and Carols* broadcast annually from King's College Chapel, Cambridge, on Christmas Eve, by tradition with a boy treble singing the first verse unaccompanied.[9] In Britain the usual tune for "There is a Green Hill" is "Horsley", by William Horsley, a friend of Mendelssohn.[10]

Frances Ridley Havergal (1836–79), born in Worcestershire, in the English Midlands, also belongs to the band of Victorian women hymn-writers. Probably best known is her devotional prayer, "Take My Life, and Let it be… ". Other hymns by Havergal include "In Full and Glad Surrender" – possibly drawing on the Holiness teachings of the contemporary Keswick Convention movement – "Like a River Glorious… ", and the militant "Who is on the Lord's Side?" In similar vein, the sickly Charlotte Elliott (1789–1871), one of whose poetry collections was titled simply *The Invalid's Hymn Book* (1835), wrote "Just as I Am… ", which in the mid-twentieth century became associated with Billy Graham's evangelistic crusades, which often used this piece during the "altar call" for seekers to walk forward. Another notable hymn by a Victorian lady is "At the Name of Jesus", by Caroline Noel (1817–77).

Robbing the Devil of his Choicest Tunes: Music and The Salvation Army

Music has always been important to The Salvation Army. William Booth's East London Christian Mission, launched in 1865, used musical methods that continued into The Salvation Army, formed to combat the influence of alcohol, improve the social conditions in which many people lived, and bring the Christian message to the urban poor. By the early 1870s Booth and his wife Catherine had compiled several hymn-books: *The Christian Mission Hymn Book*, *Hymns for Special Services*, *The Penny Revival Hymn Book*, and *The Children's Mission Hymn Book*. In 1876 *The Christian Mission Hymn Book* contained 531 hymns, spirituals, and songs set to popular and national tunes.

The Salvation Army's first band was recognized by William Booth in 1879, consisting of Charles Fry, a

Portrait of William Booth, founder of the Salvation Army, by Sir Hubert von Herkomer (1849–1914).

Salisbury builder, and his three sons. Soon brass bands had sprung up all over the country, yet Booth remained suspicious of music groups and solo singing. While he allowed bands in outdoor evangelism, he only grudgingly permitted them in indoor services and did not allow "songster brigades" (choirs) until 1898, although he featured "musical specials" on his itinerant missions and his own children were gifted performers.

Yet music became Booth's strongest tool in developing his movement. One secret of the Army's musical success was taking well-known music-hall and popular songs and marrying them to Christian lyrics. Booth famously said: "I rather enjoy robbing the devil of his choicest tunes… It is like taking the enemy's guns and turning them against him" (1877).

Booth's priority was soul-saving, whatever the means:

> Whereas… we have proved the great utility of musical instruments in attracting crowds to our open-air and indoor meetings, we do here express our desire that as many of our Officers and Soldiers generally, male or female, as have the ability for so doing, learn to play on some suitable instrument… This includes violins, bass viols, concertinas, cornets or any brass instruments or anything that will make a pleasant sound for the Lord.[1]

In 1885 Booth restricted Army bands to using only music from sacred vocal works published by the Army, and not until 1901 did he permit "original" music for brass bands – and even then it had to refer to "salvation" songs. The *raison d'être* of the Salvationist musician remains as defined by Booth: "All his beating and blowing is to get people first into the barracks [the Salvation Army hall] and then to the Penitent Form."

At its Fourth International Congress (1914), just two years after the founder's death, The Salvation Army boasted 1,674 brass bands (26,000 players) and 13,000 songsters in 56 countries. The music of The Salvation Army became a vast resource, unmatched in the twentieth century by any Protestant denomination. Music is inseparable from the Army: across the world its brass bands are an immediately recognized symbol and many musicians have entered their profession through playing in Salvation Army brass bands.

The Salvation Army today has roughly 2,500 brass bands worldwide, consisting of such instruments as cornets, flugelhorns, alto horns, baritones, euphoniums, trombones, tubas, and percussion. The standard of playing is high and bands such as the International Staff Band are the equal of professional ensembles.

The Army tradition in music is to use the popular idiom of the day. The Army's Joystrings, led by Major (then Captain) Joy

Webb, a hit pop group in the 1960s and early 1970s in the UK and beyond, reached the charts and were featured on British television, making the hit single "It's an Open Secret" in 1964. Another popular band was The Insyderz, an American ska-core group of the 1990s and early 2000s. Other bands such as New Zealand's Vatic, Chamberlin, Hypemusic, and The Lads, Britain's Electralyte, Australia's Soteria Music Ministries and Escape, and the USA's transMission, The Singing Company, HAB, and BurN carried on this Salvation Army tradition.

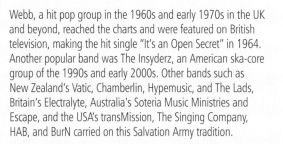

Above: The Salvation Army is identified worldwide with its distinctive band music.
Opposite: A traditional Christmas carol book, the cover illustrated with an idealized English Victorian carol-singing scene.

In the Deep Midwinter: The Story of Carols

Carols seem to fall into that category of things which people either love or loathe. Many warm to their traditional imagery and association with Christmas: others strive to avoid them, associating carols with sentimentality and mawkish music.

Carols are normally narrative, contemplative, or celebratory in content, often with a simple, straightforward sentiment and in strophic form. Most surviving medieval carols were written for professional cathedral singers, with a few exceptions such as *"Nova! Nova!"* that may have been more widely performed.[1] Among the oldest is *"Puer natus in Bethlehem"* ("A Boy is Born in Bethlehem"), dating from the thirteenth century. Though the majority of carols were for Christmas Eve and Christmas Day, others were for Holy Innocents' Day, Epiphany, and Twelfth Night (for instance "The Twelve Days of Christmas", which appears in "broadsides" from the eighteenth century onwards). The carol "The Seven Joys of Mary", which appears with many variants in Britain and the USA, grew out of pre-Reformation devotion to the Virgin, and has survived for centuries in vernacular devotional verses in the folk tradition. The carol "I Saw Three Ships Come Sailing In", for which the earliest known printed text dates from 1666, probably derives from the European folk memory of the supposed journeyings of relics of the Magi, the "Three Kings of Cologne".

♪ The German Tradition

In Germany, carols were more frequently sung in Catholic churches than in Lutheran, where Christmas hymns predominated. Some carols were sung antiphonally (*in Wechsel*), for instance *"Quem pastores laudavere"* ("Shepherds Sang Their Praises"), which was divided between four groups, each group taking a line in turn. *"Maria durch ein' Dornwald ging"* ("Blest Mary Wanders Through the Thorn") is characteristic of German fifteenth-century folk carols, and features the flowering rose, a popular emblem. The traditional Bohemian carol *"Kommet, ihr Hirten"*, in German, or *"Nesem vám noviny"*, in Czech ("Come, All Ye Shepherds") has been claimed by both language groups.

Many perennially popular carols date from the seventeenth century, and were often linked with "shepherd dramas" or with the tradition of cradle-rocking practised at midnight mass and are normally in a fitting triple-time *Wiegenlied* ("cradle-song") beat, while other carols probably accompanied the blessing of the crib. One of the most popular German carols, *"Resonet in laudibus"* ("Let the Praises Resound"), sung both to the tune of the same name and to the possibly older tune, *"Joseph, lieber, Joseph mein"*, is linked with cradle-rocking. Another "rocking" carol is *"Ein Kindlein in der Wiegen"* ("He Smiles Within His Cradle").[2] The traditional Czech cradle-song *"Hajej, nynej, Jezísku"* ("Jesu, Jesu, Baby Dear"[3]) has similar origins. Some carols are found in several versions and, like many folk-songs, seem to have grown through a process of accretion. A good example of this is *"Es ist ein Ros' entsprungen"* ("Of Jesse's Line Descended" or "A Great and Mighty Wonder"), found in many different forms and with up to twenty-three different verses.

The Lutherans also sang more formal chorales to celebrate Christmas. Luther wrote *"Vom Himmel hoch, da komm' ich her"* ("From Highest Heaven I Come to Tell…") for his own family to celebrate Christmas Eve, and set it to the riddling folk-song/dance *"Ich komm' aus fremden Landen her"* ("I Come Here from Foreign Lands"). Early in the nineteenth century a traditional German tune was linked to the words *"O Tannenbaum"* to celebrate the Christmas tree, which some Lutherans erroneously believe was invented by Martin Luther, but is in fact rooted in pre-Christian European traditions.

MUSIC-LOVERS LIBRARY

CAROLS FOR CHRISTMASTIDE BOOK 2

1/6 NET CASH

♪ The English Tradition

The earliest authorized English Christmas hymn was Nahum Tate's ever-popular and much parodied "While Shepherds Watched Their Flocks by Night" (1700), paraphrasing Luke's account of the Nativity (Luke 2:8–14). For the next eighty years it remained the sole Christmas hymn "permitted to be used in [Anglican] churches", and was sung to any tune in common metre (CM – 8.6.8.6.). Only with the publication of *Hymns Ancient and Modern* in 1861 did the now-familiar "Winchester Old" begin to oust the other melodies then in use.[4]

Some English carols, such as some of those collected by Davies Gilbert and William Sandys in the early nineteenth century, were performed by village "waits" as they visited houses of the parish on Christmas night. Such peripatetic carollers often sang for gifts of money, food, and drink ("luck visits"), while others carried Advent images. On luck visits known as "wassails", they toasted the householders from a common bowl. Best known of the luck-visit carols is "God Rest You Merry, Gentlemen", which probably came originally from France and boasts many versions throughout Europe.

Two important Victorian collections helped preserve the English carol: *Carols for Christmas-tide* (1853), by J. M. Neale and Thomas Helmore (owing much to *Piae Cantiones*), and *Christmas Carols New and Old* (1871) by H. R. Bramley

and John Stainer. Other carols, traditional in the folk-music sense, have been carefully preserved. For instance, the collector Cecil Sharp transcribed the text and tune of "The Holly and the Ivy" from a singer in Gloucestershire, while Ralph Vaughan Williams collected "On Christmas Night, All Christians Sing" (the "Sussex Carol") in West Sussex.

♪ French and European Traditional Carols

Medieval French carols were based on the processionals sung as clergy and choir left the chancel, and derive from the "line dance" or *carole* which the French clergy are said to have performed in Gothic cathedrals. Like Germany and Britain, France has a strong tradition of carols, such as the traditional Breton *"Entre le boeuf et l'âne gris"* ("Between the ox and the grey ass"). *"Guillô, pran ton tamborin"* ("Guillo, come, and Robin too") is a dance-like noël from Provence that forms part of a local repertory of pipe-and-tabor dances and noëls played during midnight mass.[5] *"Noël nouvelet"* can be traced back to a late-fifteenth-century manuscript, and is a *chanson d'aventure*, a form of medieval French verse where the singer wanders in a rural setting and has a chance encounter. The seventeenth-century French carol *"Quelle est cette odeur agréable"* is based on the annunciation to the shepherds; *"Quittez, pasteurs"* ("O Leave Your Sheep") has a traditional melody from Besançon; while the popular *"Il est né, le*

Glade jul ("Merry Christmas", also known as "Silent Night", 1891) by the Danish artist Viggo Johansen (1851–1935).

divin Enfant" is sung to a tune similar to an old Normandy hunting-tune, *"Tête bizarde"*.

The Basque traditional carol *"Birjina gaztettobat zegoen"* ("The Angel Gabriel from Heaven Came" – "Gabriel's Message") was first collected in 1895, and translated into English by the folklorist Sabine Baring-Gould (1834–1924), as was the popular *"Oi Betleem!"* ("Sing Lullaby!"), though in this case the English is a virtually new text rather than a translation.

The carol "Cold December's Winds Were Stilled", popular in the United States, is translated from a Catalan original, *"El Desembre congelat"*, and sung to a melody derived from an old drinking-song, *"C'est notre grand-pèr Noé"*. Probably the most popular Spanish carol in English-speaking countries is the traditional *"Veinticinco de Diciembre"* ("Twenty-fifth Day of December"), with its recurrent *"Fum, fum, fum!"*, imitating a drum or guitar.

The Neapolitan carol *"Quanno nascette Ninno"* ("When Christ, the Son of Mary/in Bethlehem was Born") is typical of the carols customarily sung by mountain shepherds in Italy. By tradition, they came down into the cities of southern Italy and Sicily at Christmas, playing and singing pastoral music on the *ciaramella* (small shawm) and *zampogna* (bagpipe). Some eighteenth-century composers took up this pastoral *siciliana* rhythm to suggest Christmas: Handel's aria "He shall feed his flock" in *Messiah* is similar to the traditional tune to *"Quanno nascette Ninno"*, which he possibly heard during his stay in Italy between 1707 and 1709.

🎵 America

The tune to the carol "Ye Nations All, On You I Call", attributed to "Singin' Billy" Walker in his *Southern Harmony* (New Haven, Connecticut, 1835), was probably notated from oral tradition, as was the tune to "Hail the Blest Morn!" from unwritten music of American Baptists and Methodists. Christmas songs and carols also figure among spirituals, as discussed on p. 193. The folk-song collector Edric Connor stated that the only West Indian carol he could locate was "The Virgin Mary Had a Baby Boy", which he heard performed by a ninety-four-year-old Trinidadian in 1942. The music of the verse is in calypso idiom, but the refrain has a strongly African echo. The American folk-song collector and performer John Jacob Niles (1892–1980) later owned up to writing a number of so-called "folk carols". Among his own compositions are "Sing We the Virgin Mary", written in a *faux*-medieval style, and "I Wonder as I Wander", which he claimed to have based on an Appalachian fragment.

The evergreen carol "O Little Town of Bethlehem" was written by Phillips Brooks (1835–93), Episcopalian rector of the Church of the Holy Trinity, Philadelphia, Pennsylvania, following a visit to the "Shepherds' Fields" outside Bethlehem. The carol's plea for peace reflects the fact that Brooks's ministry in Philadelphia was during the American Civil War. The musical setting invariably used in the United States was written by the organist at Holy Trinity, purportedly after waking from deep sleep on Christmas Day – though in Britain it is usually sung to "Forest Green", Vaughan Williams' arrangement of the traditional English tune "The Ploughboy's Dream".

The New Englander Edmund Hamilton Sears (1810–76) expressed a similar longing for peace in "It Came Upon the Midnight Clear", the last stanza looking to the day "when peace shall over all the earth/its ancient splendours fling". Another American clergyman remembered for just a single Christmas carol is John Henry Hopkins (1820–91), who first published "We Three Kings of Orient Are" in *Carols, Hymns, and Songs* in 1865. "O Holy Night" is a version by John Sullivan Dwight of the French poem *"Minuit, chrétiens"* by Placide Cappeau, the music by Adolphe-Charles Adam, who also wrote the ballet *Giselle*.

The opening two verses of "Away in a Manger" originally appeared anonymously in 1885 in a Lutheran Sunday School book, *Little Children's Book for Schools and Families* by J. C. File, while verse three was added by John Thomas McFarland (1851–1913). It is frequently alleged that the text is by Martin Luther, a baseless claim possibly originating from the carol's first appearance in a Lutheran publication.[6]

🎵 Modern Carols

Many modern composers have added to this popular genre. The essentially secular carol "Ding! Dong! Merrily on High" was set by G. R. Woodward (1848–1934) to a vigorous dance, *"Branle de l'officiel"*, by the French composer "Thoinot Arbeau", the anagrammatical name of Jehan Tabourot (1519–95). As in his carol "Past Three O'Clock", set to a tune with a refrain used by the London Waits,[7] Woodward employed an archaic style for his text. A popular modern English carol is Gustav Holst's setting ("Cranham") of Christina Rossetti's poem "In the Bleak Midwinter".[8]

The Legendary Story of "Silent Night"

Translated into any number of languages, "Silent Night" is today sung by millions every Christmas. Possibly as a result of this carol's peculiarly moving simplicity, a plethora of legends has accumulated to explain its origins.

Stille Nacht! ("Silent Night") was probably performed for the first time on Christmas Eve 1818 at St Nicholas's Church, Oberndorf, in Austria, near Salzburg, during midnight mass.[1] The priest, Joseph Mohr (1792–1848), and choirmaster, Franz Xaver Gruber (1787–1863), apparently sang a duet, accompanied by Mohr's guitar, with the choir repeating the last two lines of each verse in harmony. Mohr's setting – a lullaby – has the lilting sound of an Austrian folk-melody.

One enticing tale has it that mice destroyed the church organ's bellows, necessitating a new hymn that could be accompanied by guitar alone.[2] Another has Mohr writing the lyrics at the last moment, having just discovered the organ was out of action.[3] An Austrian television version shifts Oberndorf to the more filmogenic Alps and adds to the mix villainous railway speculators and a two-faced priest; while a German author endows Gruber with a zither instead of a guitar and links Mohr with a conflagration in Salzburg. As for the melody, proposed composers include Haydn, Mozart, and Beethoven. Yet another legend claims that "Silent Night" was promptly forgotten after its first performance in 1818.

The facts are more prosaic. Joseph Mohr, a young priest attached to the pilgrimage church in Mariapfarr, Austria, wrote the six-stanza *Stille Nacht!* in 1816. Two years later, after moving to Oberndorf, he visited his friend Gruber, a schoolteacher in nearby Arnsdorf, on Christmas Eve. Gruber looked at Mohr's words and came up with a melody they could sing together later that evening.

As for the carol vanishing after this "première": the organ-repairer Karl Mauracher apparently found a copy of it at St Nicholas's Church soon after the first performance and took it back to his native Ziller Valley. This was just the start of the travels of this deceptively simple carol, sometimes known as the "Tyrolean Folk-Song". Two families of itinerant folk-singers from the Ziller Valley (not dissimilar to the Trapp Family Singers of *The Sound of Music* fame) added the song to their repertoire and trekked it around German-speaking countries as a "folk-song". In 1839 the Rainer Family took "Stille Nacht!" to the USA, performing it there at the Alexander Hamilton Monument, in the graveyard of New York's Trinity Church. John Freeman Young, the rector at Trinity, translated the now-familiar English version, "Silent Night".

A piano arrangement of "Silent Night", published in the German collection, *Weihnacht's Sang und Klang.*

Although written by two Roman Catholics, "Silent Night" has become particularly popular with Lutheran Protestants. It was poignantly sung in their respective languages by British and German soldiers in the First World War during the Christmas Eve truce of 1914, being one of their few shared carols. "Silent Night" has been recorded by more than 300 artists, notably by Bing Crosby and Mahalia Jackson.

After Joseph Mohr died and the song had become well known throughout Europe, Franz Gruber tried in vain to put straight the record regarding its composition. As recently as 1995 a manuscript in Mohr's hand, with the inscription *Melodie von Fr. Xav. Gruber*, was discovered, bestowing belated authenticity on the Gruber–Mohr authorship. This manuscript, dated 1818, is for guitar accompaniment and probably approximates to the first performed arrangement. Several notes in the melody were later altered to create the tune known today.

CHAPTER 15

Camp Meetings and Revivals: The Making of the American Gospel Tradition

People come to hear Sankey sing and then I catch them in the gospel net.

D. L. Moody

Worshippers in New England sing from hymnals as they process to church during the Great Awakening of the mid-eighteenth century.

♪ Music of the Camp Meetings

In the late eighteenth century a new religious phenomenon appeared in the eastern states of America: the "camp meeting", a religious meeting organized at a set place and attracting an audience from miles around. Since transport was poor, families often left home temporarily and set up camp at the venue – hence the name. Camp meetings often continued for days and featured both revivalist preaching and vigorous, enthusiastic singing, sometimes accompanied by extraordinary phenomena such as people falling prostrate to the ground, dancing uncontrollably, and on occasion even croaking like frogs.[1] These camp meetings often had mixed white and black participation. The camp meeting movement continued through the nineteenth and into the twentieth century: the American composer Charles Ives (1874–1954) remembered attending with his father, who led the singing on his cornet.[2]

Camp meetings engendered their own characteristic music – popular, with simple harmonies, easy to sing and to remember. The crowds were largely illiterate and there were no hymn-books, so the songs or hymns often had a rousing, memorable chorus, the opening words of which frequently served as the piece's title. The leader would often yell the verses and the audience would respond with the chorus; singing could be accompanied with other physical responses such as clapping, shouting, and even dancing. Sometimes the black participants continued singing for hours "short songs of disjointed affirmations, pledges or prayers, lengthened out with long repetitious choruses… ", some of which features are also typical of spirituals and were later emulated in white gospel music. Typical camp-meeting gospel songs included "Where are the Hebrew Children?", "Come to Jesus", and "I Do Believe". These simple but memorable hymns soon stimulated renewed hymn-writing in both the eastern USA and Britain.

The American Presbyterian Charles Grandison Finney (1792–1875), "father of modern revivalism", selected from camp meetings features he thought "worked" – including the new singing style – and carried them back into the church to manufacture "revivals", so introducing customs that have exercised a lasting effect on American worship practice. For instance, at the front of the church, in addition to a place for the minister, a position was allocated for the song-leader. Finney was fully aware of the potential of music to create a suitable atmosphere, so also provided space for a choir or vocal quartet beside the minister.

Gospel Hymns

Fuelled by Finney's methods, American "revivalist" meetings used congregational hymn-singing modelled on the camp meeting to create an emotional situation in which listeners would be open to gospel appeals. Written for this purpose were rousing gospel songs such as Robert Lowry's "Shall We Gather at the River?", its lyrics referring both to the River Jordan of the Gospels and to the rural venue of the camp meeting.[3] These gospel songs were more easily accessible to the non-churched than more theologically complex and musically sophisticated hymns, though some regular church-goers repudiated them as "vulgar choruses".

In Cincinnati, Ohio, in 1874, Philip P. Bliss (1838–76) published a small collection entitled *Gospel Songs*,[4] his title shortly becoming the generic label for songs of this type. Converted at a revival meeting and inspired by the music publisher William Bradbury, Bliss worked as a peripatetic musical educationalist, using a melodeon (button-key accordion) to accompany his songs, and editing and publishing numerous songbooks. Bliss wrote both text and melody for such popular gospel songs as "Wonderful Words of Life", "Hallelujah, What a Saviour", "Whosoever Will", and "Almost Persuaded", and also the music for "It is Well with My Soul". Bliss's "Hold the Fort", which used the imagery of the American frontier to illustrate the doctrine of the perseverance of the saints, became one of the singer Ira D. Sankey's signature pieces.

Other writers who helped lay the foundations of the American gospel hymn tradition include W. J. Kirkpatrick (1838–1921), H. R. Palmer (1834–1907), T. C. O'Kane (1830–1912), J. R. Sweeney (1837–99), W. H. Doane (1832–1915, who wrote the memorable but simple tune to

Arabella Hankey's hymn "Tell Me the Old, Old Story"), Edwin O. Excell, and Charles H. Gabriel (1856–1932). Philip Phillips (1834–95) was probably the first solo gospel singer to set up an international concert tour, taking in some twenty countries, subsequently recorded in his illustrated book *Song Pilgrimage Round the World* (1880). His example was followed many times over by vocalists of the twentieth century.

The Sacred Harp

We noticed previously that the 1698 edition of the "Bay Psalm Book" included shape notes to help those who could not read conventional music. The shape of the note-head in this notation indicated the degree of the scale to be sung. Andrew Law (1749–1821) systematized shape notes, using a different pattern for each of the steps "*fa-mi-sol-la*", creating a method that became very popular, particularly in the rural South. The shape-note tradition favoured three-part writing (treble, tenor, and bass) and stark, simple harmonies, often using fifths and octaves. Shape-note music is usually sung at a steady "jog-trot" speed, ignoring rest beats, and in a deadpan style.

In 1844 Benjamin Franklin White published the hugely influential shape-note hymnal *The Sacred Harp*, endlessly reprinted in subsequent decades, its title being

adopted as the name of a singing movement particularly strong in the American South. "Sacred Harp" singers would gather to perform hymns from this collection, often sitting in a circle, first learning the notes by singing the pitch indicated by the shape notes, then adding the words. Their task was made easier by reusing the same tune for a number of different hymn texts. Sacred Harp singing sessions became common in rural churches, community groups, and family homes. The tradition never died out and was revived later in the twentieth century. The Sacred Harp is widely regarded as a "white ethnic" tradition, largely due to George Pullen Jackson's *White Spirituals in the Southern Uplands* (1932), in which the author erroneously calls Sacred Harp "indigenous American folksong", but it also has deep roots in African-American church traditions.

Shaker Music

The Shakers – "The United Society of Believers in Christ's Second Appearing" – began as a sect in Manchester, England, in 1758, but by the early nineteenth century had

Left: Charles Grandison Finney, "father of modern revivalism".
Right: A nineteenth-century hand-coloured woodcut illustrating Shakers singing at a meeting in Lebanon, New York State, USA, in the 1870s. The men and women are segregated, and sit to sing.

spread to North America. Best known today for their distinctive crafts and furniture, in the early years their music was equally unusual: spontaneous, improvised, and passed on by oral tradition. Music was central to Shaker culture, and their tunes were simple and singable. The earliest known Shaker song is "In Yonder Valley" by Father James Whittaker (1787). Most early Shaker songs have a folk-like quality, being written for dancing, and were sung without words, using syllables such as "*lo-lodle-lo-lum*".

The most famous Shaker song, Elder Joseph Brackett's "Simple Gifts", has only one verse and refers to related dance movements – "to turn, turn will be our delight". By contrast, Shaker hymns have at least two verses, and sometimes more than

a dozen. The best-known early ballad hymn, titled "Mother", is about Mother Ann Lee (1736–84) and her mission from England to America; it was written by Elder Richard McNemar (1770–1839) with a tune by Brother Joel Turner (1772–1855).

Since the Shakers were pacifists, they did not fight in the American Civil War, but expressed concern about the conflict. Sister Cecilia DeVere (1836–1912) reportedly sang the pacifist hymn "A Prayer for the Captive" three times in her sleep, after which it was copied down. After 1870, the Shakers turned to more traditional forms of songs and hymns, many in four-part harmony and with more sentimental texts, for example "Prayer Universal" (1890s). Shaker music survives today in the last Shaker community, at Sabbathday Lake, Maine.

Moody and Sankey

The most celebrated American revivalists of the second half of the nineteenth century were the Chicago preacher D. L. Moody (1837–99) and his song-leader Ira D. Sankey (1840–1908). Dwight L. Moody, apparently tone-deaf, still set great store by music at his revival meetings and invited the travelling singer/song-writers Phillips and Bliss to become his "music men". When they turned him down, Moody recruited Ira David Sankey, sometimes known as "The Sweet Singer of Methodism", who had been influenced by the Sunday School songs of William Bradbury.

Shortly after Sankey and Moody joined forces, they made a successful trip to Britain, Sankey taking a "musical scrap book" of songs with him to use in their revival meetings. Sankey's songs had an immediate impact: he reported people sang them in the Tyneside shipyards, on the streets, and in trains. Revivalist hymns provided comfort for the dispossessed of industrialized Britain and North America; the British hymnologist

The Chicagoan evangelist D. L. Moody (left) and his song-leader Ira D. Sankey.

Eric Routley (1917–82) claimed that Moody and Sankey "brought religion to people... untouched by the established forms of churchmanship". While designed for evangelism, gospel music also provided a form of popular entertainment in towns that offered little else.

Over his career, Sankey wrote around 1,200 gospel songs and hymns, often in a characteristic storytelling form, usually accompanying himself in performance on a little reed organ or harmonium. With such heart-tugging numbers as "There Were Ninety and Nine" (by the Scotswoman Elizabeth Clephane [1830–69][5]), "A Shelter in the Time of Storm", and "Under His Wings", Sankey stirred the audience with his music as Moody did with his sermons.[6] Moody was probably the first evangelist to have a full-time soloist travel with him, although Charles Finney had used the musician Thomas Hastings in a similar manner in New York.

The success of Moody's revival meetings in Britain prompted Sankey to publish his own first songbook, consisting of twenty-three songs from his "scrap-book", entitled *Sacred Songs and Solos, Sung by Ira D. Sankey at the Meetings of Moody of Chicago*, a souvenir pamphlet for those attending the revival meetings. On his return to America, Sankey noted that the revivalist duo P. P. Bliss and Daniel W. Whittle (1840–1901) had published a collection entitled *Gospel Songs*. The three now pooled resources, adding numbers by Philip Phillips, George C. Stebbins, James McGranahan, and Fanny Crosby, to create the enormously popular and influential *Sacred Songs and Solos and Gospel Hymns*, first published in 1875, with further editions following in swift order, eventually growing to comprise more than 1,200 numbers, including Sunday School songs. It was the growth of Sunday Schools, Bible classes, and evangelism in the American West that created a market for such cheap hymnals, with their simple music and texts.

The gospel song is distinct from the traditional hymn. Instead of treating theological topics such as the incarnation, atonement, and resurrection, gospel songs typically address more personal themes and are intended to touch hearts. The first person singular tends to predominate, as for instance in such numbers as "Each Step I Take, the Saviour Goes Before Me" and "I Think When I Read That Sweet Story of Old". The gospel song also frequently uses solos, repeats, burdens, and climacteric catchwords, with a generous use of the refrain; it is a conventional style of music with wide appeal. The melodic line of the gospel song is typically supported by a simple harmonic structure, with few changes; it can be quickly learned and easily remembered. Nineteenth-century critics noticed the similarity of some gospel tunes to music-hall songs: "Determine the pleasure you get from a circus quickstep, a negro minstrel sentimental ballad, a college chorus, and a hymn all in one...".

Hymns and Writers

In general, we have discussed the authors rather than the composers of hymns, though unarguably it is the tunes of such favourites as "Amazing Grace", "Dear Lord and Father of Mankind", and "Silent Night" that have disproportionately contributed to their memorability. One exception to the "author first" test is the American musician Lowell Mason (1792–1872), who was primarily an arranger – sometimes composer – of hymns. Mason, born in Medfield, Massachusetts, was concerned with musical education, publishing such books as *The Juvenile Psalmist* and *The Child's Introduction to Sacred Music*. Although he wrote a few enduring hymn-tunes of his own, such as "Olivet" and "Bethany", Lowell Mason excelled at arranging and reharmonizing hymns by the great writers – Isaac Watts, the Wesleys, and others. Among his memorable settings are those for "Nearer, My God, to Thee",

"My Faith Looks Up to Thee", and the Wesleyan classic "A Charge to Keep I Have".

Another composer and arranger particularly interested in musical education was William B. Bradbury (1816–68), who as a child sang in a choir conducted by Lowell Mason at Bowdoin Street Church, Boston. Appointed organist at the Baptist Tabernacle, New York City, in 1841, in the heyday of the Sunday School movement, Bradbury set about organizing children's choirs, free music classes, and young people's music festivals. He also wrote numerous hymn settings, including the irritatingly memorable tune to "Jesus Loves Me", the lyrics for which first appeared in a novel published in 1860 entitled *Say and Seal*, by Anna B. Warner (1827–1915)[7] and her sister Susan. Bradbury wrote other catchy gospel tunes to such texts as "He Leadeth Me", "Just as I Am", "Saviour, Like a Shepherd Lead Us", "My Hope is Built on Nothing Less", and "Sweet Hour of Prayer". Hymns such as these over time became "standards" of gospel music.

Eventually Bradbury resigned as an organist and devoted himself to composing, arranging, collecting, and publishing hymns, compiling more than fifty collections and forming the successful Bradbury Piano Company with his brother Edward. As a publisher, he encouraged other composers, such as Thomas Hastings (1784–1872), who wrote a much-used setting of "Rock of Ages" ("Toplady"). Bradbury was also associated with George Frederick Root (1820–95), who wrote a setting of Watts's "There is a Land of Pure Delight" ("Varina"), as well as popular martial songs of the American Civil War, such as "Tramp! Tramp! Tramp!".

Bradbury notably cultivated the indefatigable hymn-writer Fanny (Frances Jane) Crosby (1820–1915), blind from the age of two months, and author of possibly more than 8,000 hymns. Born in South East (now part of Brewster), Putnam County, New York, Crosby started writing as a child.

In adulthood, moved by Watts's hymn "Alas! And Did My Saviour Bleed", she discovered she had a facility for writing verse, to tunes supplied by William Bradbury. An agreement with his publishing company resulted in her supplying him with at least three new hymn texts per week for years. So productive did Crosby become that Bradbury credited her hymns to around 100 different pseudonyms, including Jenny Glenn, Kate Grinley, and Ella Dale, together with a number of men's names.

Although written in the nineteenth century, Crosby's hymn "To God Be the Glory!" did not rise to prominence until Billy Graham featured it in his earliest British evangelistic crusade, at Harringay, London, in 1954. Quickly recognizing its popularity, Graham reimported the hymn to the United States, where Nashville soon saw its potential too. Among other lastingly popular gospel hymns by Crosby are "Blessed Assurance", "All the Way My Saviour Leads Me", "Tell Me the Story of Jesus", "Jesus is Tenderly Calling", "Jesus Keep Me Near the Cross", and "Safe in the Arms of Jesus", which she played at the funeral of US President Ulysses Grant in 1885.

"What a Friend We Have in Jesus", by the Irishman Joseph M. Scriven (1819–86), was not originally intended for publication. Learning of his mother's serious illness, the author wrote to her enclosing the poem, which he entitled "Pray without Ceasing". Later Sankey commissioned for it the simple tune "Erie" (1868) from Charles C. Converse (1834–1918), a professional musician, and added the hymn to his collection. "The last hymn which went into the book became one of the first in favour," Sankey commented. This hymn acquired many versions, and is well known in Japan as *Itsukushimi Fukaki*.[8] Thomas Chisholm of Louisville, Kentucky, editor of the *Pentecostal Herald*, wrote the standard gospel hymn "Great is Thy Faithfulness" (1923), to which a stirring tune was supplied by the Revd William M.

Runyan (1870–1957), associated with the Moody Bible Institute, Chicago.

The hymn "Dear Lord and Father of Mankind", by the American Quaker poet John Greenleaf Whittier, comes oddly from the end of his poem "The Brewing of Soma", about creating this intoxicant for ecstatic Vedic rites two centuries before Christ. One of the most popular hymns in Britain, it owes much of its success to its regular tune, "Repton", by Sir C. Hubert H. Parry (1848–1918), originally written for his now-forgotten oratorio *Judith* (1888), and adapted to fit Whittier's text by the director of music at Repton School in 1924.

Many of the American evangelists who followed Moody felt they too needed their own songbooks, partly because strict copyright restrictions began to be imposed on gospel hymns. The commodity quickly spawned a booming publishing industry. Evangelistic and revival song-leaders such as Charles McCallon Alexander (1876–1920) and Homer Alvan Rodeheaver (1880–1955) were "more like masters of ceremonies [*sic*] or leaders of community songfests", and published linked and copyrighted hymn collections. Rodeheaver, who set up his own music publishing company (later to become part of the giant Word Music Inc.), sang, and sometimes played the trombone, at the mass meetings of the histrionic revivalist preacher Billy Sunday (1862–1935). Other sacred song soloists similarly played a signature instrument or had an orchestra play along with them. From early in his career, while working in the 1940s for the evangelistic organization Youth for Christ, Billy Graham used music at his "rallies", including on one occasion "smooth melodies from a consecrated saxophone".

In 1893 the African-American William Henry Sherwood published the first hymnal to include gospel hymns by black writers, the *Harp of Zion*, which included his own "Happy Hosts of Zion" and "Take it to the Lord".

Choir director Tom Bledsoe conducts a volunteer choir of more than 6,000 voices during a Billy Graham Crusade in St Louis, Missouri, USA, in 1999.

Christian Music in Africa

The story of Christian music in Africa stretches from the birth of Christianity to the globalization of the twenty-first century. Along the way, African Christians adopted, adapted, and originated musical expressions of faith in well over 1,000 languages and many musical styles. This discussion is limited to sub-Saharan Africa, includes Ethiopia with its unique musical history, but excludes the Indian Ocean islands.[1]

At least 45 per cent of the second largest continent's one billion people profess to be Christian. Many different Western "denominational" churches were introduced before, during, and after the colonial period, but today the fastest-growing segment consists of the African Independent churches. Growing from conflicts with Western missionaries, these churches sprang up during the colonial period between 1880 and 1960. Of these, the Kimbanguists of former Zaire, the Vapastori of Zimbabwe, the Aladura churches of Nigeria, and the Zionists of South Africa are probably best known.

Unlike many parts of the world where Christian missions introduced a "foreign" faith, Africa, at least in the north and Ethiopia, was Christian from very early on. Christian music in Africa includes congregational worship music such as chants, psalms, translated Western hymns and choruses, African hymns, and traditional choir music, but also music that has made its way into African life and the wider world through such means as YouTube and immigrant populations.

♫ The Early Period

African music was born among the cooking-pots and hunting-bows of the forests, savannahs, and coastlands thousands of years ago, centred on the annual rituals of planting and harvest, and on birth, marriage, death, hunting, and war. Cooking-fires and village centres were places of storytelling and celebration, infused with an oral tradition of song and dance. Call-and-response singing, complex rhythms, and spontaneous expression mark this lively music as unique to Africa, with the drum undergirding the participatory nature of singing. Little value is placed on the private ownership of music, which belongs to the community.

Christianity was first introduced into the African continent through Egypt and the Nubian regions soon after the first century AD, and the Egyptian (Coptic) Church and Ethiopian Orthodox Church are two of the largest remaining churches of North Africa. We know little about what music sounded like

Above: Ethiopian Orthodox priests sing at Bete Giyorgis (St George's) Church, Lalibela, the second holiest city in Ethiopia and an important pilgrimage centre.
Right: Domes at the east end of the Coptic Orthodox White Monastery, or Monastery of St Shenouda, Sohag, Egypt, founded in AD 442.

in the early churches of North Africa, although the Egyptian and Ethiopian Orthodox churches preserve a music tradition based upon sacred liturgies.[2]

The Ethiopian Orthodox Church began in the fourth century, when the Ethiopian royal court accepted Christianity, and has a highly developed liturgy, in form not unlike the high mass of the Roman Catholic church. The Ethiopian church teaches that its music is a direct gift of God. According to *The Lives of the Saints*, three birds visited the legendary sixth-century saint Yared and took him to heaven, where he was taught sacred music – *Zema* – and its notation. *Zema* became the church's liturgical music, and is still sung or chanted in the sacred worship language, Ge'ez. Yared is credited with writing and collecting a huge number of hymns and chants for the Christian year.[3] *Zema*, sung by male liturgists called Dabtaroc,[4] is taught primarily by oral tradition. The Dabtaroc first learn the Ge'ez language and the melodies written in special modes or scales, then go on to study liturgical dance and musical instruments.[5]

During the colonial period, Western missionaries entered Ethiopia, and mission churches grew alongside the Ethiopian Orthodox Church (EOC). Following the 1974 Communist revolution, evangelical missions were banned and evangelical Christians persecuted. During this time, some Christians began to sing "Pente"[6] music, an adapted form of the modern chorus, sung in Amharic, the national language.

♫ The Missionary Period

South of the Sahara, the first Christian missionaries were Roman Catholic priests who accompanied Portuguese explorers in the fifteenth century, and the first recorded mass was celebrated in 1482 in Guinea. But Christianity did not take hold at this time because most Europeans remained on the coast in fortified trading settlements.

Not until the nineteenth century did many Western missionaries begin to arrive in Africa and African people start to accept Christianity. Along with the Christian gospel the missionaries also brought Western culture and its music, particularly the hymn. African polyrhythms were complex and African tonal languages varied from region to region, making it difficult for early missionaries to learn them. Missionaries often believed their Western music expressed a reverence they could not hear in African sounds, and many also felt African music encapsulated African religious belief and that its associations with traditional practices could not be avoided. For such reasons, missionaries taught Western hymns, usually in translation. However, when translated into tonal African languages, these hymns sometimes did not carry an intelligible meaning.

Upon acceptance of Christianity, missionaries and new converts often burned the traditional African drums, thereby implying that African culture was inherently bad and African music evil beyond redemption. Hence African music was rarely used in Christian worship by the first missionaries.

Hymns were often taught by rote, although early missionaries also published text-only hymn-books. Missionaries also began to employ the tonic sol-fa notation system, developed as an

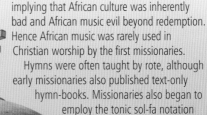

educational tool by the English Congregationalist minister John Curwen (1816–80), to teach Western melodies and harmonies. Often called "people of the book", Western Christians in Africa promoted a "book" music,[7] which tended to reflect the denominational hymnody and musical styles of their particular mission.

Tonic sol-fa became very important, especially for training choirs. Roman Catholic and Anglican missions, who brought with them developed liturgies, started choirs to lead the singing of the liturgy, and choirs were also formed in many mission schools. A strong choral tradition still holds in sub-Saharan Africa, where in many countries today choirs participate in school and church music festivals, singing both Western and African anthems.

In Africa, transplanted music is not necessarily assimilated in its original form; small adaptations often expand into alterations. Western musical scales did not fit with African scales, and African Christians often adjusted Western melodies to suit their own musical frame of reference. For instance, since the 1960s Africans have frequently adapted the simple hymns of the European and American Great Awakening into "town music",[8] adding syncopated rhythms and guitars, with texts written in the context of African urban life and spirituality.

Some missionaries attempted to incorporate African music into Christian liturgy. The earliest of these were Scottish Presbyterians, who around the beginning of the twentieth century started to set Christian words to traditional African melodies. Generally such innovations did not take hold until Africans themselves began to express the Christian message in their own melodies. With the Second Vatican Council (1962–64), the Roman Catholic church began to incorporate local languages and music into the liturgy, and a number of African masses appeared. In the Belgian Congo in 1954, the Belgian Franciscan Father Guido Haazen founded the "Troubadours", a choir of boys and teachers from Central School in Kamina for whom he wrote the *Missa Luba*, based on traditional song-forms in Kiluba. *Missa Luba* has since been recorded many times.[9]

Around 1960, when many African countries were wresting independence from colonial rule, Christians began to search for authentic African forms of worship. Especially in former mission churches, this often accompanied the introduction of Pentecostalism, with its choruses, handclapping, and a variety of African and Western musical instruments. Similar expressions spread into more conservative denominations, such as the Baptists and Presbyterians, and today there is a veritable harvest of new music.

With the rise of their discipline, ethnomusicologists began to research new and authentic African Christian music. The Swede Henry Weman (1897–1992), the South African Hugh Tracy (1903–77),[10] the Ghanaian J. H. Kwabena Nketia (b. 1921), and the British John Blacking (1928–90) all influenced those interested in African music.

In rural villages of Africa a new form of indigenous and spontaneous Christian music also appeared. Many Africans, far from the influence of foreign missionaries, first heard the Christian message in their own language as a result of the preaching of African evangelists. Having experienced healing and other miracles, believers often began to sing spontaneously of Jesus and his healing power. Ignorant of Western musical language, they used traditional forms. Their songs were shared in worship and began to spread from church to church by oral means, particularly via "church musicians", valued for their ability to memorize songs and lead congregations in exciting worship. Such Christian "heart music" is found in many African communities.

🎵 African Independent Christianity

There are probably more than 6,000 independent Christian movements in Africa. Beginning as early as 1819 in Sierra Leone, most of them started as a result of a "failure of love" by missionaries, who tended unilaterally to determine the meaning of Christ for African people. African Independent Churches (AICs) sprang up, as black prophets proclaimed a vision of Christ in African culture which included African music and a belief that the Holy Spirit is directly involved in the lives of believers.

In the early nineteenth century, for instance, John Masowe withdrew from his local mission church in what is now Zimbabwe and proclaimed himself the Black Christ for Black Africa, developing a strong following among the Shona people, who now call themselves Vapastori, or "Apostles of John". Music is central to Vapastori worship, featuring "Hallelujah" songs performed by men and women separated on opposite sides of the worship area. A unique feature of Vapastori music is a group of singers who appear to imitate the pipe organ.

Opposite: French missionary priests from the Sacred Heart of Jesus mission in Cameroon, where the mission first started work in 1910.
Left: Wakamba beat traditional *Ngoma* drums for dance, Kenya, East Africa.

"Promised Land" of freedom.[11] African-influenced musical styles also developed in the Caribbean.

♫ Music Technology and Synthesis

Following the Second World War, the British Broadcasting Corporation (BBC) and Voice of America started to broadcast African radio services; for the first time, rural African people heard the music of the world. With the introduction of vinyl records, cassette tapes and CDs, satellite TV, the Internet, and mobile phones, Africa joined the global communication village. Church and mission media centres were established in the 1950s and 1960s to broadcast the Christian message over the radio and increasingly recorded Christian musicians, gradually moving from hymns to African-styled gospel and contemporary sounds.[12]

Rhythm, a core element of African music, was reintroduced into Africa through the music of Elvis Presley and popular Western artists of the following decades, such as Michael Jackson.[13] Cuban railway workers brought African-influenced rumba to Zaire. Missionaries began to import electronic synthesizers and African musicians took up old and new instruments, "baptizing" them for Christian use. The vibrant continent of Africa makes use of a wide range of resources – from mouth bows and gourd-resonated xylophones to MIDI keyboards and guitars – to "make music to the Lord".

Today, some of the most exciting music comes from the slums of Africa's cities. Affordable video cameras and computer technology spawned a generation of musicians who communicate a gospel of social justice, hope, and godly living through rap, hip-hop, reggae, and the like in local languages, in styles still influenced by the American media.

J. Nathan Corbitt

In the 1950s in Kenya, the Kikuyu people's anti-colonial movement, the Mau Mau, wrote new resistance songs to familiar tunes from *Hymns Ancient and Modern*. Meetings that seemed to be swaying to "Abide with Me" or "Onward Christian Soldiers" were in reality being exhorted to fight for independence or regain stolen land. Similarly, *"Nkosi Sikelel' iAfrica"*, now the national anthem of South Africa, exhibits a typically African mix of politics and religion.

Christian Music and Freedom

It has been estimated that between 1450 and 1900 more than 11.5 million Africans were sold into slavery across the Atlantic, a dispersion known as the "African Diaspora". As Africans were transported to the New World, music helped maintain their solidarity and communication. Songs both sacred and secular – primarily a Western dichotomy – were sung in the fields to lighten work, at times of death, and in new forms of worship. Much of this music takes deliverance themes from the Bible, particularly Exodus, where God brought the Israelites out of slavery in Egypt into the

CHAPTER 16

"I Got a Home in Dat Rock": Spirituals and the Blues

O Canaan, sweet Canaan,
I am bound for the land of
*   Canaan.*

Spiritual, anon.

An African-American congregation at worship in Washington DC, USA, in the 1870s; coloured illustration from the *Illustrated London News*.

♫ Black Churches

As early as 1755 the American hymn-writer Samuel Davies wrote, "I cannot but observe that the Negroes, above all the Human species that I ever knew, have an Ear for Musicke, and a kind of extatic [*sic*] Delight in Psalmody… ". Eighteenth-century American churches were segregated, and not until the 1770s were blacks allowed to form their own churches. By the turn of the century many free urban blacks in the North had formed separate congregations. In 1794 Richard Allen, founding bishop of the African Methodist Episcopal Church in America, published a hymnal for his Philadelphia congregation, *A Collection of Spiritual Songs and Hymns*, consisting of fifty-four hymns (without tunes), largely by Isaac Watts, the Wesleys, and other writers favoured by Methodists. Allen's *Collection* was the first for a black congregation and the first to use wandering refrains – verses or short choruses attached at random to hymn stanzas – a form of improvisation. Since improvisation is also intrinsic to spirituals, this may connect the musical practice of enslaved blacks with free blacks, such as Allen and his Philadelphia church.

Observers of black congregations in the early nineteenth century noted distinctive performance styles, movements, and experiences of singing and shouting, with links to revivals and camp meetings. We noticed earlier that blacks often numbered among the participants at camp meetings.

Contemporary writers referred patronizingly to "the merry chorus manner of the Southern harvest field" as well as to "the alternating call-and-response style of the slave song, and indeed, of African music".

🎵 "Negro" Spirituals

The 1790 United States census reported more than 750,000 blacks. The music of these blacks, most of whom were enslaved in the South, hugely influenced American religious (and secular) musical forms. Slaves who had been cruelly transported from Africa and forced to work in the Southern plantations of America also had to adopt the faith of their masters, who believed Christian teaching would help instil in them both obedience and contentment. Until the 1770s, African-Americans were banned from forming churches, but in their "praise houses", away from the eyes of their owners, slaves could express their deep longings and anxieties in their own way. The "spirituals" sung in these meetings drew variously on hymns, the Scriptures, and African styles of singing, their language using rich imagery, often from Old Testament narratives, to express secret yearnings for freedom and veiled critiques of slavery.

The distinctive music of the spirituals melded the rhythms and melodic inflections of African music and the folk-songs of the early North American colonies – many imported from the British Isles or other parts of Europe – with the intensity of an oppressed people expressing deep-felt desires and needs. Some of the music derives from hymns by Watts, Newton, and the Wesleys heard in the Baptist and Methodist churches where slaves were typically taken by their owners. Such hymns' use of freedom from captivity as a metaphor for Christian salvation resonated strongly with black slaves' aspirations for political and economic – as well as spiritual – freedom.

Since most slaves were kept illiterate and had no formal musical training, we have little written evidence for the earliest history of the spiritual. Most spirituals are labelled "anonymous" since we now have no knowledge as to their original composers or writers, and most were modified and elaborated as they were passed on from slave group to slave group over decades. Nor do we know exactly when spirituals first appeared: early reports of distinctive black slave music date to the 1820s, although some claim that spirituals appeared before this in the Caribbean. By 1860 the first collection had been created, and the term "spiritual" referring to black religious folk-songs seems to have entered common usage.

Black slaves, where allowed to attend camp meetings, discovered legitimacy there for practices that were frowned on in orderly white churches and imported some of these features into their own music. The style and performance of camp-meeting music encouraged improvisation – shouted responses, riffs on favourite phrases, stretching and bending the sounds – all features that African-Americans used in spirituals, as they did later in gospel, blues, and jazz.

Improvisation played a significant part in the creation of the spiritual, combining Bible verses and hymn stanzas with words from sermons and from prayers used in worship, often adding repetitive refrains. Like the songs of the camp meeting, the structure of the spiritual was generally simple, typically opening with a chorus where the first line was repeated, followed by a new line, following which the first line was repeated again. Such a structure was well suited to a call-and-response type of performance, which required no written text or printed music. The verses would often use similar repetition, making the songs easy to memorize. For example:

I got a home in dat Rock, don't you see?
I got a home in dat Rock, don't you see?
Between de earth an' sky,
Thought I heard my Saviour cry,
I got a home in dat Rock, don't you see?

> *Poor man Lazarus, poor as I, don't you see?*
> *Poor man Lazarus, poor as I, don't you see?*
> *Poor man Lazarus, poor as I,*
> *When he died he foun' a home on high*
> *He had a home in-a dat Rock, Don't you see?*

I got a home in dat Rock, etc.

Spirituals tended to favour stories rather than doctrines, and narratives rather than dogma; to the story was then added a meaning, moral, or teaching ("don't you see?"). Spirituals were also adaptable: there was no definitive text; verses could be added, versions personalized, and words and ideas imported from other remembered songs and hymns. Spirituals would "mix and match" characters from the Old and New Testaments – for instance, Noah, Moses, David, Jonah, Jesus, and Peter – and draw promiscuously on biblical images – crowns, chariots, flaming swords, stars, and trumpets – as well as utilize contemporary imagery such as railway trains. Metaphors of escape could be taken as both spiritual and political – journeys from earth to heaven, from sin to salvation, and from slavery to freedom. The black ex-slave Frederick Douglass explained in his autobiography:

> *A keen observer might have detected in*
> *our repeated singing of 'O Canaan, sweet*
> *Canaan, I am bound for the land of Canaan'*

Above: Portrait of Abraham Lincoln (1809–65), President of the United States during the American Civil War, by George Henry (1853–1923).
Opposite: Chris Thomas King plays Blind Willie Johnson in Wim Wenders's film *The Soul of a Man* (Germany, 2003).
Below: Nineteenth-century plantation slaves load rice on a barge on the Savannah River, near the border between Georgia and South Carolina, USA.

> *something more than a hope of reaching*
> *heaven. We meant to reach the north – and*
> *the north was our Canaan.*[1]

The spiritual "My Lord, What a Morning!" seems to have evolved from the hymn "Behold the Awful Trumpet Sounds" (published in Richard Allen's 1801 hymnal)

and "Were You There When They Crucified My Lord?" may have evolved from the white hymn "Have You Heard How They Crucified Our Lord?" (the closer personal identification with the crucifixion is significant). Recurrent themes appear in spirituals, including faith, hope, patience, weariness, and the struggle to be free – all apt to the condition of slavery. But spirituals also included seasonal songs and carols, such as "O Mary and the Baby, Sweet Lamb!",[2] "Rise Up, Shepherd, and Follow!",[3] and "Mary Had a Baby".

After the American Civil War and the emancipation of the slaves, spirituals experienced a temporary challenge. Many freed blacks wanted to forget these songs as they represented a relic of a terrible past. The old plantation songs fell into disuse and the hymns and chanted psalms of the Northern states took their place as many African-Americans attempted to embrace European culture and hymnody. However, groups such as the Fisk Jubilee Singers preserved the heritage of the spiritual and handed it on to the next generation, as we shall see later.

A century after, in the 1950s and 1960s, the American Civil Rights Movement picked up and adapted spirituals such as "This Little Light of Mine" and "We Shall Not Be Moved", using them as political anthems in their struggle against segregation. Songs that had moulded the imagination and aspirations of African-Americans for generations became vehicles for expressing the political wishes and aims of the Civil Rights Movement. For instance, the plea for equality was vividly expressed in "I got a robe, you got a robe/All God's chillun got robes…".

The Blues

The black novelist Richard Wright has suggested that, in contrast to the spirituals – created by slaves living and working in and around the plantation homes and close to their masters' white

culture – the blues were created by slaves working the more remote fields, freer to develop their own musical culture, less influenced by, and more independent of, their white masters. So the blues probably grew out of the work-songs, "field hollers", and ballads of African-American slaves as they worked the soil, picked cotton, and cut cane. Slaves were prohibited from talking to each other while working in the field, but work-songs and "field hollers" were permitted, and by these means the slaves could communicate in a way that could not easily be understood by their white overseers. Singing also helped relieve the monotony of their toil and kept workers energized by rhythmically synchronizing their movements, though work-songs were also sung for entertainment and self-expression.

In contrast to the sacred content of spirituals, the blues tend to deal with downbeat experiential themes such as betrayal, rejection, addiction, exhaustion, and depression, though still sometimes call rhetorically on the "Lord".

Whereas after emancipation the spiritual was sung in churches, the blues were typically heard in taverns, bars, honky-tonks, and brothels; spirituals were the music of church, blues of those outside the church and so "the devil's music", with the guitar becoming "the devil's instrument". The lines were clearly drawn, and performers found it very difficult to cross.

A few – often blind – performers bridged the gap. "Blind" Willie Johnson (1897–1945) from Brenham, Texas, straddled the divide between spirituals and blues, and performed exclusively spiritual songs on his guitar, using a masterly slide or "bottleneck" technique. Johnson recorded a number of such songs between 1927 and 1930, including "Nobody's Fault but Mine" and "Dark Was the Night, Cold Was the Ground", about the crucifixion, influencing a host of later artists, including Led Zeppelin, Bob Dylan, and Eric Burdon of The Animals. Other significant spiritual/blues gospel singers included Washington Phillips (1880–1954), whose best-known song was "Denomination Blues"; "Blind" Joe Taggart; the Revd Edward W. Clayborn; and the blind woman evangelist Arizona Drane(s) (c. 1891 – c. 1963), who introduced piano accompaniment to previously mainly unaccompanied Holiness church music.

"Nkosi Sikelel' iAfrika"

"Nkosi Sikelel' iAfrika" – the stirring South African national anthem – had inauspicious beginnings, written by an assistant teacher and choirmaster at the newly founded Methodist Church in Nancefield, Enoch Mankayi Sontonga (c. 1872–1905). Born in Uitenhage, Sontonga trained as a teacher at Lovedale, Alice, and at the time of his death was choirmaster of a church in Johannesburg.[1]

Sontonga wrote in tonic sol-fa and collected his songs in an exercise book. He composed "Nkosi Sikelel' iAfrika" in 1897; two years later it was sung at the ordination of a Tsonga Methodist minister. Sontonga wrote only the first verse; the Xhosa poet, S. E. K. Mqhayi (1875–1945), wrote seven additional verses. In 1927 the Lovedale Press in Eastern Cape published all the verses in a pamphlet, and it was also included in the Presbyterian Xhosa hymn-book, Ingwade Yama-culo Ase-rabe (1929).

The Ohlange Zulu Choir, founded by the Revd J. L. Dube, performed Sontonga's moving hymn in Johannesburg, further popularizing it. In 1912, at the first meeting of the South African Native National Congress (SANNC) – forerunner of the African National Congress – "Nkosi Sikelel' iAfrika" was sung after the closing prayer. It was first recorded in 1923 by Solomon T. Plaatje, a founding member of the ANC, accompanied on the piano by Sylvia Colenso. In 1925 the ANC officially adopted "Nkosi Sikelel' iAfrika" as a closing anthem for its meetings.

The song soon spread beyond South Africa and has been translated into a number of different languages. For decades "Nkosi Sikelel' iAfrika" was regarded by the oppressed as the national anthem of South Africa and sung as an act of defiance against the apartheid regime. It has come to symbolize the struggle for African unity and liberation in South Africa, and is also the national anthem of Tanzania and Zambia. In 1994 it became part of South Africa's official national anthem.

There are no standard versions or translations of "Nkosi Sikelel' iAfrika" so the words vary from place to place and from occasion to occasion. Generally the first stanza is sung in Xhosa or Zulu, followed by the Sesotho version.

Nkosi, sikelel' iAfrika;
Malupakam' upondo lwayo;
Yiva imitandazo yetu
Usisikelele.
Chorus
Yihla Moya, Yihla Moya,
Yihla Moya Oyingcwele.

(The first verse and chorus as composed by Sontonga in 1897.)

CHAPTER 17

Apocalypse Now! Sacred Music and the Concert Hall in the Twentieth Century

Music is as well or better able to praise [God] than the building of the church and all its decorations; it is the church's greatest ornament.

Igor Stravinsky

Charles Ives, the maverick American composer.

In the twentieth century, despite a massive falling away of the faithful from Western churches, many composers inheriting the symphonic tradition continued to write Christian-themed music, though more often for the concert hall than for liturgical use.

Like his compatriot Dvořák, Leos Janáček (1854–1928), born near Brno and educated at a monastery school, was much interested in his native Moravian folk-music. Janáček's oratorio-like late work, the *Glagolitic Mass* (sometimes also called the *Slavonic Mass*), incompatible with liturgical use, sets the Old Church Slavonic text and was first performed in Prague in 1926. The term "Glagolitic" refers to the first Slavonic alphabet and celebrates the pan-Slavism which Janáček supported. The composer wrote the work in just a month, following a woodland walk, and explained its genesis:

I felt a cathedral grow out of the vast expanse of the woods. A flock of sheep were ringing their bells. Now I hear the voice of an arch-priest in the tenor solo, a maiden angel in the soprano and in the choir – the people… I see the vision of St Wenceslas and I hear the language of the missionaries Cyril and Methodius.

Three movements are purely instrumental, since in Bohemia the mass commonly began and ended with music to mark the entrance and exit of the clergy.[1]

The Hungarian composer Zoltan Kodály (1882–1967) similarly explored folk-music, using it, along with Gregorian chant, Bachian polyphony, and Renaissance harmonies, in his blazing *Psalmus Hungaricus* (1923) for tenor, chorus, and orchestra, written for performance by amateur choirs upon the fiftieth anniversary of the uniting of the towns of Buda and Pest. The text is a paraphrase of Psalm 55

("Give ear to my prayer, O Lord") by the sixteenth-century Hungarian poet Mihály Vég. Kodály also wrote a *Te Deum* and *Missa Brevis*, with organ accompaniment.

Charles Ives (1874–1954) is almost the definition of American eccentricity. A successful insurance executive, he composed extraordinarily unconventional music, often with strongly Christian themes, and was an advocate of the hymn-singing of "that old-time religion". Born in Danbury, Connecticut, USA, Ives was the son of another idiosyncratic musician,[2] who for instance required young Charles to play "Swanee River" in C major on the piano while simultaneously singing it in E flat – a tonal complexity later reflected in Charles' own compositions.[3] Ives' works were notorious for their polyrhythms, free dissonance, collage effects, and use of chance. The composer Bernard Herrmann commented: "In 1890 Ives was writing poly-tonality, in 1902 polyrhythms, atonality and tone-clusters that Stravinsky, Schoenberg and Ornstein received credit for originating years later." Ives made a number of ground-breaking psalm settings for Center Church on-the-Green, New Haven, Connecticut (1894), and his fondness for gospel songs is illustrated by the fifty or more hymn-tunes – such as "Jesus, Lover of My Soul", "Just as I Am", and "What a Friend We Have in Jesus" – that he quotes in various compositions.

Ives attended revival meetings, enjoying the music and the "power and exaltation in these great concaves of sound", noticing that the excitement engendered by the singing crowd sometimes pushed the key higher by as much as a whole tone. The titles of some of Ives's works reflect his interests – *A Revival Service* and *General William Booth Enters into Heaven* – and his *Symphony No. 3*, subtitled *"The Camp Meeting"* (1901–04, first performed 1946), uses hymns in its outer movements. The first movement of Ives' *Symphony No. 4* introduces the Epiphany hymn "Watchman" ("Watchman, Tell Us of

the Night"), while its "Comedy" movement features an epic chorus of individual voices marching toward the transcendent, each in its own way, own style, own tempo, and own key. In the mystical finale, the murmuring voices coalesce, and a chorus starts to sing wordlessly the tune of "Nearer, My God, to Thee".

Ives also found inspiration in the writings of the American transcendentalists Whittier, Emerson, and David Henry Thoreau – far removed from fundamentalist revivalism – somehow managing to hold both worlds in creative tension. Ives was a church-goer with an unbounded faith in the redemptive power of art; "Music," he wrote, "is life."

Despite his international life-style and musical approaches deriving from

Above: The Russian composer Sergei Rachmaninov was also a virtuoso pianist.
Right: Igor Stravinsky at a rehearsal of his *Canticum Sacrum ad Honorem Sancti Marci Nominis*, 1955, written in tribute to the city of Venice and its patron St Mark.

contemporary German, French, and Italian traditions, the Russian Orthodox Church was yet considered important by the pianist and composer Sergei Rachmaninov (1873–1943), who wrote significant music for that church, including a *Liturgy of St John Chrysostom* (1910) and several oratorios and cantatas. The *Liturgy*, for unaccompanied voices, is often regarded as insufficiently dramatic for the concert hall but too operatic for the Orthodox Church: "with such music it would be difficult to pray". Rachmaninov also set the Orthodox vespers (1915), in a "combined prayer service" known as the *All-Night Vigil* or *Vespers*, just before abandoning his native Russia for the USA.

Before developing his "twelve-tone technique" in the 1920s, the Jewish composer Arnold Schoenberg (1874–1951) wrote an a cappella choral piece entitled *Friede auf Erden* ("Peace on Earth", 1907) to a Christmas text by the Swiss poet Conrad F. Meyer, pleading for war to cease.

Stravinsky

Born in St Petersburg in Russia, Igor Stravinsky (1882–1971) soon abandoned the Orthodox faith of his childhood. Yet in the 1920s he confessed conversion to Christianity after an apparent miracle and "a reading of the Gospels and… other religious literature",[4] – with a resultant powerful impact on his life. In 1925 he had been scheduled to perform his own *Piano Sonata* – a work that marked a turning-point from his early works to a new neo-classical style – in the presence of such pillars of the avant-garde as Diaghilev, Honegger, and Schoenberg – an occasion that caused him great anxiety. Stravinsky developed an abscess on his right hand that would have limited his piano-playing, but, having prayed for help, discovered the abscess had vanished. The following year Stravinsky started to take communion again and around the same time set the Lord's Prayer in Old Slavonic (*Otche Nash'* – "Our Father" or *Pater Noster*) for unaccompanied voices, drawing on the Orthodox Church music he knew as a child. "The more one separates oneself from the canons of the Christian church, the further one distances oneself from the truth…" he wrote. "Art is made of itself, and one cannot create upon a creation, even though we are ourselves graftings of Jesus Christ."[5]

Stravinsky's *Symphony of Psalms* (1930) was a setting of the Latin *Vulgate* version of Psalm 39:13–14, Psalm 40:2–4, and most of Psalm 150. "It is not

a symphony in which I have included Psalms to be sung," he explained. "On the contrary, it is the singing of the Psalms that I am symphonizing." Stravinsky stated that the first movement was "written in a state of religious and musical ebullience"; the second movement he described as "a prayer that the new canticle may be put into our mouths. The Alleluia [the third movement] is that canticle."[6] The *Symphony of Psalms* retains traces of Stravinsky's earlier rhythmic style, with an insistent syncopation of the chorus phrase *Laudate Dominum* in the third movement, but in this work he abandons self-expression for the devotion of a new convert.

Having rediscovered faith, Stravinsky expressed powerful opinions about it. "Religious music without religion is almost always vulgar,"[7] he said. He also claimed it was essential for the composer of church music to be a believer "… not merely… in 'symbolic figures', but in the person of the Lord, the person of the Devil, and the miracles of the church."[8] Stravinsky summed up his achievement modestly: "Only God can create. I can make music from music."[9] At the same time, he was far from uncritical of the church and its music. He wrote *Three Sacred Choruses* (including *Otche Nash'*) for use in the Orthodox liturgy, claiming they were inspired by "the bad music and worse singing in the Russian Church".[10] Stravinsky also wrote a Catholic mass and sombre, atonal settings of such sacred texts as *The Flood*; *The Tower of Babel*; *Abraham and Isaac*; *A Sermon, a Narrative and a Prayer*; *Threni* (full title, *Threni, id est Lamentationes Jeremiae prophetae* [Lamentations of Jeremiah], 1957–58); and *Canticum Sacrum* ("Sacred Canticle", 1955). His mass, while a liturgical work, has all the musical challenges of his concert-hall works. Stravinsky's late work, *Requiem Canticles*, written after returning to visit his Russian homeland in 1962 following fifty years' absence, brought together and attempted to synthesize sounds from

Above: Samuel Barber in Spoleto, Italy, 1973.
Right: The American Jewish composer and conductor Leonard Bernstein.

various periods of his career – the Russian/ primitive, the modern American, and the neo-classical styles – in what has been described as a requiem for himself.

Some Americans

Samuel Barber (1910–81) wrote in an unashamedly neo-romantic style at a time when modernism was all the rage. His *Adagio for Strings*, originally the slow movement of a string quartet, has become well known and loved as an elegiac piece, now irrevocably linked with the events of 11 September 2001, since it was performed at a ceremony in New York and at the Last Night of the Proms in London in September 2001 to commemorate those killed in the attack on the World Trade Center.[11] Barber later transcribed this piece for unaccompanied eight-part chorus, as a setting of the *Agnus Dei* (1967). He also set medieval Irish sacred verse in *Hermit Songs* and composed *Prayers of Kierkegaard* for soprano, chorus, and orchestra.

In 1947, Aaron Copland (1900–90) – an American Jewish agnostic – uncharacteristically wrote a setting of Genesis 1:1–2:7 in the Authorized (King James) Version, entitled *In the Beginning*, as a single-movement motet for mezzo-soprano "storyteller" and a cappella chorus, employing a gentle narrative style, though jazz rhythms are heard at various points.

Virgil Thomson (1896–1989) loved the hymns of early America and incorporated two of them into his *Symphony on a Hymn Tune* (1928); he also wrote small choral works such as a *Missa Brevis* (1925) for unaccompanied men's voices, and another for women's voices plus percussion (1936). Similarly the US composer William Schuman (1910–92) pays tribute to early American hymnody and the "fug[e]ing tunes" of the eighteenth century in his *William Billings Overture* (1943), later revised as *New England Triptych* (1956).

The son of an Armenian, Alan Hovhaness (1911–2000) studied the ancient chants of the Armenian church and often used Eastern modes and patterns in his music. In his *Magnificat* (1959) he scored some parts as free rhythm (*senza misura*) to add to the sense of mystery. Hovhaness

also wrote a *Thirtieth Ode of Solomon* (1949), with cantillations for baritone soloist and accompanying instruments.

Before he commenced his starry career as a conductor, the Jewish composer Leonard Bernstein (1918–90) completed his *First Symphony*, subtitled "*Jeremiah*", in 1943, following programmatically the life of the Old Testament prophet. Its three movements are: "Prophecy"– Jeremiah's foretelling of the destruction of the Temple in Jerusalem and the Babylonian exile of the Jews; "Profanation" – the Jews' rejection of his prophetic message; and "Lamentation" – bewailing their fate. Bernstein utilized traditional Ashkenazi Jewish motifs in the work, and in the third movement quotes directly from the Jewish chant for the biblical book of Lamentations. Bernstein followed this Jewish theme in 1961 in his *Third Symphony*,

the "*Kaddish*" (the mourner's prayer in Jewish liturgy), with a part for a female speaker.

Commissioned for Chichester Cathedral, England, in 1965, Bernstein's *Chichester Psalms* are a setting of parts of the Hebrew text of several psalms (the composer banned performance in any other language). Bernstein also ruled out performance by a woman of the counter-tenor part – possibly to emphasize that the words of Psalm 23, "The Lord is my shepherd", are regarded as being by the shepherd-boy David.[12] Although intended for cathedral and amateur performance, sections of the *Chichester Psalms* are notoriously difficult to sing: the opening section of Part 1 is sometimes said to be one of the most taxing for choral tenors.

For the 1971 opening of the Kennedy Center in Washington, DC, Bernstein wrote a very non-Jewish *Mass*, "a theater piece for singers, players and dancers", with lyrics by Stephen Schwartz, who also wrote the Broadway musical and box-office success *Godspell*. Based on the liturgy of the Roman Catholic mass, Schwartz's book showed how Christian belief can be perverted, and attacked those who use Christianity to their own ends. Only Bernstein could have written it – and only in the 1960s. Up to the minute as ever, he included pre-recorded choral and percussion music played over loudspeakers. Perhaps wanting to point to the continuity of the Catholic liturgy with parts of Jewish tradition, Bernstein has the boys' choir sing the *Benedictus* in Hebrew – *Barukh haba be-shem Adonai* ("Blessed is he who comes in the name of the Lord"). At its première Bernstein's *Mass* was almost universally condemned as being in bad taste, the *New York Times* critic describing it as the greatest mélange of styles since the recipe for steak fried in peanut butter and marshmallow sauce. With strokes of brilliance and passages of kitsch, it attempted to synthesize pop, show business, and modern classical idioms.[13]

The opera *Amahl and the Night Visitors* (1951) by Gian-Carlo Menotti (1911–93), a setting of a miracle story about a crippled boy who meets the Magi, is unusual in having been commissioned for television. It achieved sustained popularity, with NBC broadcasting it in the USA every Christmas between 1951 and 1966.

Younger sister of the better-known Nadia, the French composer Lili Boulanger (1893–1918) died young, yet created impressive sacred music that has been virtually forgotten. Her settings of Psalm 24 for tenor, choir, organ, and orchestra (1916), Psalms 129 and 130 (*Du fond de l'abîme* [*De profundis*]) for alto, tenor, choir, organ, and orchestra (1910–17), and *Pie Jesu* owe something to her mentor Gabriel Fauré.

The French composer Francis Poulenc (1899–1963) returned to the Catholicism of his childhood in the 1930s, after which he wrote much choral liturgical music, striving to bring "peasant devotion" to his music, and modelling his practice on Stravinsky's *Symphony of Psalms*. Poulenc's sacred pieces include *Litanies à la Vierge Noire* ("Litanies to the Black Virgin"; a visit to the shrine of the Black Virgin of Rocamadour in the Dordogne helped the composer recover his Catholic faith); a *Gloria* (1959); the solemn, penitential *Quatre motets pour un temps de pénitence* ("Four Motets for a Time of Penitence", 1939) for unaccompanied choir; a mystical *Mass in G Major*; a *Stabat Mater*; and *Dialogues des Carmélites*, an opera about Carmelite nuns during the French Revolution. Poulenc said that when writing his *Gloria* he "had in mind those frescoes by Gozzoli where the angels stick out their tongues. And also some serious Benedictine monks I had once seen revelling in a game of football."

The Swiss composer Arthur Honegger (1892–1955), one of Poulenc's comrades in the group known as "*Les Six*", spent most of his life in France. He wrote the oratorio *Le Roi David* ("King David") in 1921 in straightforward style, for narrator, chorus,

The English composer Sir John Tavener, 2001.

Krzysztof Penderecki (b. 1933), a compatriot of Górecki, is most celebrated for his *Passion According to Saint Luke* (1966), where he uses huge tone-clusters, string ornamentation, and microtones to achieve his distinctive sounds. Penderecki reverted to a more melodious, less experimental, style in his *Polish Requiem* (1980–84), written during the struggles of the Solidarity movement in Poland – with a structure not dissimilar to Bach's *Passions*.

Born in Estonia, Arvo Pärt (b. 1935) left the Soviet Union for West Germany in 1980. Having earlier experimented with avant-garde serialism (music based on the twelve-tone system) and aleatoricism (music based on randomness), Pärt wrote nothing for a time and then in the 1960s, after immersing himself in medieval Burgundian choral music, found a new voice concerned with Christian ritual and the numinous, owing something to the early Renaissance composers Ockeghem and Obrecht. His style, like that of Górecki, has been dubbed "holy minimalism". Pärt, who has roots in Orthodoxy, says, "I have discovered that it is enough when a single note is beautifully played." Even his largest work, *Passio Domini Nostri Jesu Christi secundum Joannem* ("St John Passion", 1982/88), is minimalist. He has also set the ordinary of the mass of the Roman Catholic church in *Missa Syllabica* (1977), where the music is governed by the number of syllables in a phrase – not by the meaning.

The American composer Charles Wuorinen (b. 1938) has written a number of sacred pieces, such as his *An Anthem for Epiphany* (1974), *Genesis* (1989), and *Missa Renovata* (1992), often combining traditional instruments with electronic sounds.

Christian Music in Latin America since 1800

♫ Independence and Protestant Evangelization: 1800–1950

By 1830 all the Latin American Spanish and Portuguese colonies were undergoing the political reorganization that led to their present status as independent nations. British economic expansion in the 1800s was paralleled by the expansion of the modern Protestant missionary movement, also born in the British Isles.

Nineteenth-century British missionaries brought with them the hymnody described in chapters 9 and 14. But in the second half of the century, United States missionaries arrived and the story changed, for the missionary movement in the USA was closely connected to the birth of the "gospel song" (see chapter 15). Many missionaries received the "call" from a gospel song; the association with such powerful emotional experiences made the missionaries consider the gospel song a privileged instrument for communicating the Christian message, and gospel songs became for them almost the exclusive sacred music style. Consequently, local expressions were ignored and gospel songs and hymns reigned supreme in Latin American Protestant churches from the beginning of the nineteenth century until the middle of the twentieth.[1]

The propagation of gospel hymns and songs from the USA to the rest of the world via the modern Protestant missionary movement is an extraordinary intercultural event that has not been properly evaluated, perhaps due to the disregard — even contempt — of classical church musicians and scholars for "popular" music. At a time when sound recording systems and radio had not been invented, and music printing was still a precarious activity in many parts of the world, these songs — translated and taught by missionaries all around the world — were adopted by local converts as their own and eventually esteemed, in places such as Latin America, as the true Protestant (or *evangélico*) style of music and hymnology.

North American missionaries made such effective use of music that their converts became a "singing people" in Latin American societies where community singing was traditionally not considered a cultural feature. Protestants were both admired and seen as a strange people for the abundance and enthusiasm of their singing, which often included the organization of the first choirs in an area. Singing became an integral element of Protestant identity, contributing to their "different" nature as against Roman Catholic culture.

However, this sacralization of a particular music style resulted in the alienation from local culture of new converts. Most immigrants – cut off from their home culture and not yet having assimilated local ways of life – readily accepted "Christian" music and rejected everything pertaining to their existence before "meeting the Lord". As a result there is little original in Protestant Latin American church music in the 1800s and the first half of the 1900s. Even those few who did write new hymns felt constrained to follow the North American model.[2] A possible exception is the Mexican Vicente Mendoza (1875–1955), who besides translating many gospel songs wrote some original texts, a few of which he set to tunes with a slightly Mexican flavour. Some missionaries – especially when coming in contact with aboriginal people – declared local music inappropriate for Christian worship due to its pagan, sinful, and even satanic nature, and forbade the faithful to sing or play it. More recently, some Christian ethnomusicologists, regretting this, have successfully rescued and reconstructed original indigenous forms by helping aboriginal Christians to overcome the identification of Christian faith with Western (mainly US) culture.[3]

Another important stream of church music – mainly Lutheran and Reformed – came to Latin America in the 1800s with immigrants from Europe. But although some, such as the German immigrants, brought their traditional Protestant hymnology, many of their hymns were already strongly influenced by the gospel song.

🎵 Inculturation of the Gospel and Vernacular Music since 1950

Only well into the twentieth century did Christians around the world – Catholic and Protestant – start to produce original new music for the church in the language of their own cultures. The beginning of the Pentecostal movement in the USA in 1906 was followed by related religious movements in Latin America which initially flourished mainly among the lower social classes. Social and political revolutionary movements appeared, making strong claims for justice and

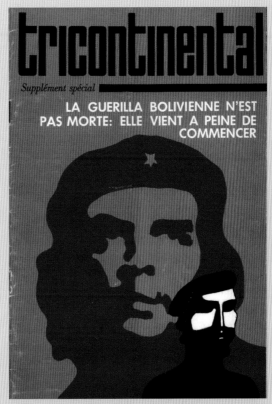

Left: Eighteenth-century Brazilian musicians depicted in "King and his Suite", a water colour by Carlos Juliao, now in the Biblioteca Nacional, Rio de Janeiro, Brazil.
Above: Cover illustration based on a famous photograph of the Bolivian revolutionary Ernesto "Che" Guevara (1928–67). The Cuban Revolution had a strong impact on Latin American theology and praxis.

equality for all people, the Cuban Revolution (1959) being the most influential on Latin America; the *Nueva Canción* ("New Song") movement, in various denominations across the continent, provided lyrics for these revolutionary ideals.

The Second Vatican Council established important liturgical reforms updating Roman Catholic worship, including the acceptance of vernacular languages and music styles. Liberation theology emphasized God's siding with the poor and oppressed, and promoted a new social order based on socialist principles: the base communities movement is its most solid embodiment in Latin America. There was also a new awareness of aboriginal peoples and cultures, especially through the increase in new artistic and musical expressions based on indigenous folk-music and dance.

These movements and events account for characteristic features of contemporary Latin American Christian music: texts calling for an awareness of social issues, and the

in the faithful a desire to *sing* biblical texts, especially the Psalms. With folk-music enjoying its heyday in the continent, numerous church songs on Bible texts were set to folk rhythms and melodies. These songs were usually not annotated, but transmitted orally and spontaneously in a worship context, and their authors not identified – either out of respect for the biblical text (authors would consider it wrong to put their names next to the Word of God) or because the song was a collective creation or a melody already familiar to the community. Hundreds of these anonymous psalms and other biblical songs are sung today all over Latin America.

Global Song

In 1954, Daniel T. Niles (Sri Lanka, 1908–70), one of the presidents of the World Council of Churches, and editor of the first hymnal of the Christian Conference of Asia, visited Argentina and introduced Sri Lankan church folk-songs to a group of theology students and teachers. These songs were among the first fruits of the Asian movement of inculturation of the gospel (the gospel in Asian terms), which Niles vividly explained with an image: "The Gospel came to us like a potted plant. We have to break the pot and set the plant in our own soil." Four years later, the author of this article wrote the first original Latin American church song in folk style in the twentieth century: "*El cielo canta alegría*" ("Heaven is Singing for Joy").

This was the modest beginning of a stream of Protestant songs which have run through Latin America in countless mainly home-made songbooks, booklets, recordings, and the like. These include the influential *Cancionero Abierto* ("Open Songbook"), a periodical collection edited in Buenos Aires (1974–90) which gathered and published a variety of new songs (many transcribed from oral versions) from Latin America and other parts of the world.[6] The hymn-writer Bishop Federico Pagura and the Uruguayan composer Homero Perera, among many others, contributed a number of songs, including the first Argentine tangos sung in church.

Twentieth-century Protestant missionaries encouraged the production of hymns and songs in local styles, and even contributed to it themselves,[7] and in the second half of the century found a positive response in the works of João Wilson Faustini (Presbyterian), Jaci Corréia Maraschin (Anglican), and Simei de Barros Monteiro (Methodist), the most important among many contributing to Brazilian Protestant church music. The World Council of Churches gathered and translated these Latin American songs, making them widely available to other regions of the world.

Catholic Song

In 1964, the previously mentioned *Misa Criolla* by Ariel Ramírez (1921–2010), the first in Spanish, using Argentinian

gospel's announcement of peace and justice; an emphasis on community; a concept of the sacredness of all human life, with no division between sacred and secular (making *sacred* music obsolete in favour of a more pragmatic definition as *church* music); music that is festive;[4] folk and popular tunes, with strong rhythmic patterns, inviting bodily expression – movement and dance; a variety of styles, surmounting divisions between classic and popular, serious and light, sacred and secular music.

Pentecostal Choruses and Psalms

The first stream of original Latin American church music was the creation among Pentecostal churches of short choruses (or *coritos*), which had as their immediate antecedent the gospel hymn, with its recurrent chorus. These *coritos* had more interesting local folk and pop rhythms, and texts stating facts of faith and life simply and clearly, but with grace and humour.

Pentecostalism, with its emphasis on the Bible and love for the words of its most popular Spanish version,[5] planted

and Bolivian folk rhythms, was recorded in Europe, to become a world best-seller. It is intended for concert rather than congregational use. A few years later, in Central America and the Caribbean, the first congregational masses appeared, especially as a result of the encouragement given to folk-musicians by people such as Bishop Romero, committed to the cause of the poor and the inculturation of the gospel.[8]

The decision of Vatican II to allow vernacular music styles in worship stimulated a tremendous response of singers and songs in Latin America, going beyond liturgical pieces to create an important new corpus of Christian song. At first, new songs from Spain, with progressive texts and enticing melodies, had a strong influence in Latin America. But soon local church musicians, some influenced by the robust sound of the secular *Nueva Canción*, burst out in a vigorous stream of folk-music. Among them were: in Argentina, Father Osvaldo Catena (1920–86), and his group of poets and musicians, *Pueblo de Dios* ("The People of God"), Alejandro Mayol, and Father Néstor Gallego, writing especially for children, and Julián Zini; in Peru, Gilmer Torres Ruiz and the *Siembra* group; and in Puerto Rico, Father William Loperena (d. 1996). Latin American (mostly Cuban and Mexican) and some US musicians also wrote Spanish and bilingual songs for the numerous Spanish-speaking communities in the USA.

Meanwhile, the popularity of solo singers and the appearance of the *cantautor* (singer/author/composer) on the secular scene, rapidly incorporated into church music practice, gave rise to the "evangelistic" singer. Using various popular styles (mostly within the range of US ballads), they are addressed mainly to youth. This new type of church music almost totally killed off the traditional parish choir, suddenly bereft of an attractive repertory.

Brazil, a world of its own within Latin America, with one of the richest folk-song reservoirs on the continent, saw the flourishing of popular song in church through the base communities movement. The knowledge of these songs outside Brazil has been limited by its being the only Portuguese-speaking country in Latin America, but where they have been translated into Spanish or English, they have become widely appreciated. As with Pentecostal songs, the authors are almost never mentioned.

Brazilian folk-singer and composer Milton Nascimento (b. 1942) wrote an exceptional work, the *Missa dos Quilombos*,[9] "to celebrate the death and resurrection of the black people in the death and resurrection of Christ", which was banned by the Vatican. In a very different vein, Father Zezinho (José Fernandes de Oliveira, b. 1941) began composing church songs in a pop style in 1964 and has since written around 1,500, some extremely popular in Latin American churches.

PABLO SOSA

Left: Latin American street musicians playing the harp, *charango*, and pipe.
Above: Brazilian guitarist and composer Milton Nascimento performs in 2001.

CHAPTER 18

"Surely Goodness and Mercy Shall Follow Me": Popular Church Music in the Twentieth Century

... When we stop to count our blessings, we realize we are truly blessed and can't help but praise him.

Bill Gaither

The styles, audiences, purpose, and performers of popular Christian music were already beginning to diversify during the nineteenth century. This process accelerated greatly during the next century, powered by the invention and widespread ownership of the gramophone, hi-fi, and most recently digital devices. Radio and television also helped alter the audience for Christian (and other) music, and led to a turning away from local music-making – in the church, the Sunday School or Christian organization, and home – to the more consumerist practice of listening to the latest professional performance, whether live, on vinyl, or digitally. This revolution also meant that music that was once regionally based – for example camp meeting and country music in the southern USA – could now be heard worldwide.

Additionally, diversification within the churches and the growth of more extempore and spontaneous worship in reaction to set patterns of worship – for example with the rapid growth of Pentecostalism both as a denomination and within many other denominations – brought radical changes of style and expectations.

♫ British Hymns and Christian Music

Conventional hymn-writing tended to be less prolific in twentieth-century Britain than in the preceding century. The popular "Jerusalem", composed by Sir C. Hubert H. Parry to William Blake's mystical and ambiguous poem of the same name, has become something of a reserve English national anthem. Parry's other great contribution to church music is his popular church anthem, *I Was Glad*, written for the coronation of Edward VII in 1902. He also wrote six unaccompanied motets, *Songs of Farewell* (1916–18), and fine settings of English religious verse, including Milton's

Blest Pair of Sirens (1887) and *Ode on the Nativity* (1912).

Although John Bunyan included the song "Who Would True Valour See" in *The Pilgrim's Progress* Part II (1684), where it is spoken by Mr Valiant-for-Truth, it was not used as a hymn until it appeared in *Hymns Ancient and Modern*. The hymnographer Percy Dearmer (1867–1936) later revised the text to begin: "He who would valiant be". The accompanying tune "Monk's Gate" first appeared in *The English Hymnal* (1906, edited by Dearmer and Vaughan Williams),[1] arranged by the latter from a Sussex folk-song entitled variously *Our Captain cried "All Hands"*, *Valiant*, and *Welcome Sailor*. Vaughan Williams objected to "the false sentimentality of many of our modern hymns" and wrote several new tunes, such as "*Sine nomine*" (to the hymn "For All the Saints"), and arranged many other English folk-tunes for church use.[2] British church-goers enjoy his resounding arrangement of the "Old Hundredth", written for the coronation of Elizabeth II in 1953. Vaughan Williams also co-edited *Songs of Praise* (1925), widely used in British schools, and the influential *Oxford Book of Carols* (1928).

Frank Houghton, the British missionary bishop of East Szechwan (in China), added several mission hymns to the canon, notably "Facing a Task Unfinished", as well as the Christmas hymn "Thou Who Wast Rich Beyond All Splendour", based on 2 Corinthians 8:9.

In the 1950s, a group of Anglicans formed the 20th Century Church Light Music Group and added a number of new hymn texts and tunes with eclectic roots, claiming that "the ordinary and transient music of today… has a rightful place in our worship". Prominent among this group were the Australian Malcolm Williamson (1931–2003),

later to become a notably unproductive Master of the Queen's Music, Geoffrey Beaumont (1903–70), and Patrick Appleford. Beaumont also wrote a *Folk Mass* that was controversially broadcast on BBC television in 1957, and dismissed as a "disturbing racket" by one newspaper.

A similar attempt was made in the 1960s by a group of Evangelical clergymen, led by the Revd Michael Baughen (b. 1930, later bishop of Chester). Their collection, *Youth Praise* (1966), which proceeded to sell more than a million copies, was also intended to reflect current musical tastes – though it probably better expressed the formative music of its compilers' youth. The collection was inevitably followed by *Youth Praise II* (1969) and by *Psalm Praise* (1970).

Of late twentieth-century British hymns, probably the most popular has been "Tell Out, My Soul… " by Bishop Timothy Dudley-Smith (b. 1926), a paraphrase of the *Magnificat* inspired by the opening words of the *New English Bible* (1961) version of Mary's song. Dudley-Smith was a significant contributor to *Psalm Praise* whose hymn "Lord, for the Years" also gained widespread popularity. Other enduring hymns from the *Psalm Praise* group include "Lord of the Cross and Shame" by Michael Saward (b. 1932), and "Go Forth and Tell" by James Seddon (1915–83).

In the United Kingdom, the BBC television Sunday evening broadcast of traditional hymn-singing, *Songs of Praise*, has remained popular since its initial broadcast in 1961, regularly attracting around 3 million viewers.

♫ Music Ministry in the USA

During the twentieth century it became the norm for denominations to publish their own hymnals, with hymns and sacred songs reflecting their respective liturgical patterns and theological nuances. Some hymnals

Left: The charismatic movement introduced the practice of raising the arms during praise. A late twentieth-century worship service, using projected text for the lyrics.

still straddled denominational lines, such as *Sankey's Sacred Songs and Solos*, which found a place in many evangelistically-orientated churches and chapels. Toward the end of the century, many churches replaced hymnbooks with overhead projectors, and in the 1990s with big-screen video projectors.

In America, especially after the Second World War, increasing numbers of churches in mainline denominations became prosperous enough to employ a full-time professional music director or minister of music, responsible for training the choir, planning the worship service, and other areas of music and worship, such as instrumental ensembles. Many churches now boasted a choir capable of tackling moderately difficult four-part vocal works, which encouraged the growth of a music publishing industry producing countless popular pieces for such choirs.

Some modern composers have written for these forces. Randall Thompson (1899–1984), in addition to symphonic works, wrote *The Peaceable Kingdom* (1936) for voices, taking both name and inspiration from the well-known painting by Edward Hicks and the text from the biblical book of Isaiah. Thompson's best-known choral work is *Alleluia*, an anthem written in 1940; later works include *A Feast of Praise* (1963) and *The Twelve Canticles* (1983), based on the composer's eleven favourite Bible passages. In similar vein, Leo Sowerby (1895–1968), winner of the Pulitzer Prize for music for *The Canticle of the Sun* in 1946, and sometimes referred to as the "dean of American church music", wrote for both concert hall and church. Born in Grand Rapids, Michigan, Sowerby was organist-choirmaster of St James's Episcopalian Cathedral, Chicago, and wrote numerous cantatas and anthems, as well as works for the organ.

♫ New Hymns

The twentieth century saw some abatement of the flow of new hymns, yet instant classics still appeared. Some were in the gospel song style of Sankey and Crosby: for instance "The Old Rugged Cross", with words and music by the Midwest evangelist and song-leader George Bennard (1873–1958), first performed at revival meetings at Pokagon, Michigan, in 1913. Sentimental and simple, it is widely loved and has been recorded by legions of artists including Elvis Presley, Jim Reeves, Johnny Cash and June Carter, Mahalia Jackson, Loretta Lynn, and George Beverley Shea. Similarly, James M. Black (1856–1938) was responsible for both words and music of the popular gospel hymn "When the Roll is Called Up Yonder".

Other instant classics and "standards" from the early twentieth century include "Count Your Blessings" by Johnson Oatman Jr (1856–1922), published by the prolific hymnographer Edwin O. Excell (1851–1921), which became particularly popular in

Engraving of a surpliced boys' choir in New York City, 1888.

Britain after performances by the evangelist Rodney "Gypsy" Smith (1860–1947).[3] Also from this period is the consoling "In the Garden" (1912), with text and tune by C. Austin Miles (1868–1946), who wrote hymns for the Hall-Mack Company, of which he later became manager.[4] Miles claimed he wrote this hymn after experiencing a vision of Mary Magdalene and the risen Christ in the Garden of Gethsemane. With classical music training and a theological education, Alfred H. Ackley (1887–1960) – linked to Rodeheaver, another of the great American sacred music corporations – was also a fecund producer of sacred songs, his best known probably being "He Lives". The story of hymns and hymn-writing in twentieth-century America cannot be divorced from the fortunes of a number of ambitious and enterprising music publishing companies, such as Hall-Mack, Bigelow, Manna, Hope, and Rodeheaver.

The "Praise" Chorus

Not far removed from these popular sacred songs was a new form appearing in the 1930s: the reprise or "praise" chorus. Dispensing with the six- or eight-stanza hymn, composers and writers opted for short, simple melodic songs, often just four lines long, and frequently reliant on Scripture for their lyrics. Some are redolent of nineteenth-century camp-meeting hymns and some indeed sprang from revival meetings and youth camps.[5]

Well-known "praise" choruses include "Surely Goodness and Mercy" by Dr Alfred B. Smith (1916–2001; "Dean of Gospel" or "Mr Singspiration"[6]) and "So Send I You" by the Canadian author E. Margaret Clarkson (1915–2008), who also wrote a number of "regular" hymns, including the much-used missionary number "We Come, O Christ, to Thee". The music for numerous praise choruses, including many for which he also wrote the words, was provided by John W. Peterson (1921–2006), who

eventually wrote more than 1,000 songs and thirty-five cantatas, including the well-known "Heaven Came Down", "It Took a Miracle", and "Jesus is Coming Again". Peterson, a major influence in American evangelical music in the 1950s, became Editor-in-Chief at Singspiration sacred music publishing company.

Probably the best-known practitioners of the easy-listening praise chorus are the Americans Bill (b. 1936) and Gloria (b. 1942) Gaither, with such numbers as "Because He Lives" (1969), "The King is Coming", "Jesus, We Just Want to Thank You", and "He Touched Me". In the majority of cases, Gloria wrote the lyrics and Bill the music, though on occasion they collaborated as composers. Bill Gaither also founded the Gaither Music Company. Other composers and writers soon followed the Gaithers' path. Of hundreds of praise choruses, among the best known are: "He's Everything to Me" by Ralph Carmichael (b. 1927); "Majesty" by Jack Hayford (b. 1934), founding pastor of The Church on the Way, Van Nuys, California; and "Jesus, Name Above all Names" by Naida Hearn (1944–2001).

Some praise choruses were "one-offs": "Seek Ye First", a setting of words from the Beatitudes,[7] was written by Karen Lafferty in the late 1960s "Jesus People" era, when attending Calvary Chapel, Costa Mesa, California. Her song travelled rapidly across America and then worldwide, ubiquitously accompanied on folk guitar. Chuck Smith, pastor at Calvary Chapel, in 1971 produced the album *The Everlastin' Living Jesus Music Concert* (later renamed *Maranatha!*[8]) featuring favourite music from his church, and subsequently set up Maranatha! Music Inc., producing further albums with artists and songs from the chapel.

While the Jesus People movement had faded by the late 1970s, its music continued to reverberate in evangelical churches as professional song-writers and "worship leaders" started to appear. The influential charismatic "Vineyard Movement", which sprang up in Beverly Hills, California, in 1975, like many other sacred music producers soon formed its own publishing corporation, Vineyard Music. New "standards" also continued to be created, notably "He is Exalted" by Twila Paris and "Shout to the Lord" (1993) by singer/song-writer Darlene Zschech (pronounced "check"), published by Hillsong Music Australia.

♪ Instrumental Changes

In the days before the piano, church music was essentially voice-centred – not just in the "golden age" of sixteenth-century polyphonic music, but in all vocal music up to the time of Bach and his contemporaries. The tunes of the "Old Version", for instance, were written primarily to be performed in unison and unaccompanied, although harmonizations were later added by such composers as Bourgeois and Goudimel in France, and Dowland and Kirbye in England.

By the nineteenth century, hymns were generally written for accompaniment on the organ, in four-voice harmony, a tradition that can be traced back to the four-part chorales of Luther's first hymnals. Where the organ proved too expensive – in some chapels and mission halls – the harmonium was used, offering a cheap imitation of the pipe organ.

However, by the mid-nineteenth century many tunes were being written for performance on the piano, with harmonizations, repeated sustained chords, and melodies that were not dependent on the power of the human lungs. The large number of hymn-tunes using repeated chords are a result of this relatively recent ubiquitous use of the piano, manufactured in thousands during the factory age. Over the course of the twentieth century, the pipe organ – sometimes unconsciously regarded as a prerequisite of a "proper" church – was supplanted in many churches by the electronic organ or piano. Along with the organ or piano, there was often also a church choir, trained to sing in four-part harmony, and sometimes vocal soloists.

With the emergence of "pop" music in the 1950s, it was not long before the guitar – and sometimes the drum-set too – began to invade the churches. The martial verb is not accidental: this arrival often provoked "worship wars" – typically inter-generational conflicts over the style and content, even the purpose, of Christian worship. Where guitars won the day, synthesizers and sequencers often followed, and many churches soon boasted their own "worship group", "praise band", or orchestra, accompanying both praise songs and hymns. In the 1980s, new non-church or mega-church organizations,

Left: The Chorale, by the English painter John Atkinson Grimshaw (1836–93), depicts a middle-class Victorian drawing-room complete with harmonium, on which the woman is presumably playing a sacred work.
Right: Black believers worship at a twenty-first century Elim Pentecostal church service.

such as the Willow Creek Community Church in Barrington, Illinois, and Rick Warren's Saddleback Community Church in Orange County, California, attempted to jettison anything musical that smacked of traditional "church", replacing it with praise bands and rock groups performing praise and worship music. In Britain the orchestra of All Souls, Langham Place, London, features at popular "Prom Praise" concerts at the Royal Albert Hall, with a worship and evangelism agenda.

In other churches, the struggles concerned taste: Lutherans fought for Bach rather than Handel, Catholics for Palestrina rather than Gounod. Parish choirs preferred the operatic-style arias of César Franck and Camille Saint-Saëns to the unaccompanied motets of Anton Bruckner. Some pastors discouraged the use at weddings of Wagner's "Bridal Chorus" from *Lohengrin*, or Mendelssohn's "Wedding March" from *A Midsummer Night's Dream*, citing their inappropriate secular origins, while others tried to dissuade mourners from using popular, if sentimental, gospel songs such as "I Go to the Garden Alone" at funerals rather than more orthodox Christian hymns celebrating the resurrection.

♫ Charismatic Practice

Among the strongest influences on churches worldwide during the twentieth century was the Pentecostal movement, which started its own denominations, and from the 1960s the Charismatic movement, which influenced almost all churches and denominations from Calvinist to Orthodox. In their services Pentecostal churches such as the Assemblies of God often featured gospel songs, sung in a lively manner, with handclapping, body-swinging, stomping, and *ex tempore* "amens". By the late twentieth century, singing was often accompanied not solely by a piano but also on electronic organ and an ensemble of guitars, keyboard, and drums – sometimes

with brass instruments too. In smaller and more informal Pentecostal churches, the congregation sometimes broke spontaneously into song, and was followed, rather than led, by the instrumentalists.

One of the strongest growth areas of the charismatic movement was in worship, where it encouraged more spontaneity and more physical involvement. Typical manifestations included not only speaking in tongues and "singing in the Spirit" (singing in tongues) but also the practice of lifting the arms during singing, as a visual and physical response to the presence of the Spirit. The charismatic movement is believed to have first entered the liturgical church in the late 1960s, when the Episcopal Church of the Redeemer in Houston, Texas,

experienced renewal. The Iona Community, on the island of Iona, off western Scotland, founded in 1938 by George Macleod, similarly experienced charismatic renewal in the 1970s, and its musical director John Bell built up its own, often folk-based, collection of songs. "Musicals" such as *If My People* by Carol and Jimmy Owens also sprang from this movement.

Charismatic churches have been hungry for the new worship-songs of such writer/ composers as (Dr) Graham Kendrick (b. 1950), challenging old hymn-singing traditions. Kendrick toured Britain in the late 1970s with the evangelistic organization Youth for Christ, out of which developed the Spring Harvest series of annual Christian music and teaching festivals.[9] These in turn spawned popular songbooks such as *Mission Praise* (1983) and the *Songs of Fellowship* series, which started to appear in 1985 and helped reshape evangelical worship. A new generation of song-writers such as Martin Smith and Paul Oakley provided "disposable" worship-songs promising ecstatic spirituality and passionate devotion to Christ through exuberant singing.

In complete contrast to this new informality, the Church of Christ in the United States (which arose from the Stone-Campbell Restorationist movement in the early nineteenth century and strives to recreate its understanding of the New Testament church) still practises only unaccompanied congregational singing, citing Ephesians 5:19 as its authority. As in the Orthodox Church, no instrumental music is employed in its worship services.

Despite all these changes within Protestant worship, some foresee a return to more traditional worship: "Maybe we will sing them to a different beat, accompanied by different instruments… But I am convinced that hymn singing will eventually loom large again… ".[10]

🎵 After Vatican II

The Second Vatican Council (1962–65) enacted liturgical reforms requiring that the regular services of the Roman Catholic church be performed in the vernacular, and removing the necessity for churches to use liturgical chant or other ancient musical forms. There resulted a period of rapid – even cataclysmic – change and innovation in musical practice and composition within Catholicism, comparable to the revolutionary changes at the time of the Protestant Reformation. Plainsong and a whole tradition of Catholic music was sidelined in favour of often rather amateurish guitar-playing and unsophisticated new liturgical compositions.

An early result of these changes was the introduction of "folk masses" – simple, vernacular liturgies, often accompanied by guitars. Particularly innovative was a group of Jesuits from the seminary at St Louis University – the "St Louis Jesuits" – who composed and recorded a contemporary style of liturgical music using pop-style melodies and acoustic guitars. Some of their compositions entered the mainstream repertoire of Catholic hymnody in collections such as *Glory and Praise* (1987), and were subsequently adopted by English-speaking Roman Catholic churches worldwide – and in time by some Protestants too. The St Louis Jesuits included Dan Schutte (b. 1947) – best known for "Here I Am, Lord" (1981) – and John Foley, both of whom went on to write individually. Closely basing his texts on the Bible, Schutte is one of the most popular and prolific Catholic worship-song composers of his generation. Among his other successful liturgical compositions are "Sing a New Song" (1972), "City of God" (1981), and "Table of Plenty" (1982).

Vatican II's loosening of restrictions precipitated the creation of many other folk masses. Bob Hurd wrote *Misa de las Américas* in Spanish; Peter Scholtes from Chicago the *Missa Bossa Nova*, as well as the song "They'll Know We are Christians by Our Love", an anthem for the Jesus Movement in the 1970s. Other popular masses included the *Mass of Light* by David Haas, the *Bread of Life Mass* by Jeremy Young, and the *Heritage Mass* by Owen Alstott. Although its composer was raised a Lutheran and subsequently joined the United Church of Christ, the *Mass of Creation* by Marty Haugen (b. 1950) is one of the most frequently used musical settings of the ordinary among English-speaking Roman Catholics. He has also written songs, such as "We Remember" and "Gather Us In".

Opposite: The Second Vatican Council meets in St Peter's Basilica, Rome, in 1963. Vatican II marked a watershed in Roman Catholic liturgical practice.

"How Great Thou Art"

The hymn "How Great Thou Art" had a circuitous odyssey before emerging in the late twentieth century as one of the world's favourite hymns. After walking through a spectacular thunderstorm in 1885, Carl Gustaf Boberg (1859–1940), Swedish poet, member of parliament, and editor of the Christian paper *Sanningsvittnet* ("Witness of the Truth"), was filled with awe at the grandeur of nature, and a poem, with the opening words *"O Store Gud"* ("O Great God… "), apparently started to come to him. He wrote nine stanzas, based on Psalm 145:3, "Great is the Lord, and most worthy of praise…". Two years later, visiting a church in Varmland, Sweden, Boberg was surprised to hear the congregation sing his verses to an old Swedish folk-melody. Boberg now published his poem in his newspaper, with the tune sometimes also known as *"Sanningsvittnet"*.[1]

After hearing Boberg's hymn in Estonia, Manfred von Glehn (1867–1924) translated the lyrics into German in 1907, starting *"Wie gross bist Du"* ("How Great You Are"), and it quickly became popular among German-speaking Christians. In 1925, a Chicagoan, E. Gustav Johnson, made a literal English translation from the German, starting, "O Mighty God, When I Behold the Wonder" – very different from the familiar modern version. It failed to catch on.

The Russian Baptist Ivan Prokhanov (1869–1935) also encountered von Glehn's German version and translated it into his native language in 1912, a translation that subsequently appeared in *Kimvali* ("Cymbals") and *The Songs of a Christian* (1922, reprinted 1927). Stuart K. Hine (1899–1989), a British missionary, heard this Russian version in Ukraine in 1933, and started to sing it as a duet with his wife at evangelistic meetings. Caught in a storm in the Carpathian Mountains, Hine translated Prokhanov's Russian into two English verses. He later added a third verse of his own – about the atonement – and subsequently a fourth – about the Second Coming. In 1949 Hine published both his English and Prokhanov's Russian versions in *Grace and Peace*, an evangelistic paper that circulated in at least fifteen countries, ensuring its wider diffusion. British missionaries also took the hymn to Africa and Asia. In Deolali,[2] India, Dr J. Edwin Orr of Fuller Theological Seminary, California, heard a choir of Naga people sing "How Great Thou Art" and took the hymn back

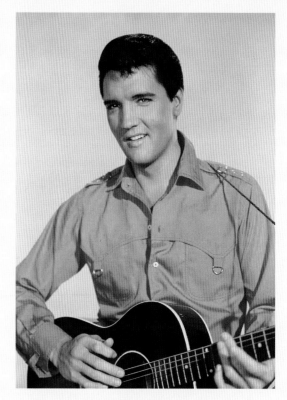

to America, where James Caldwell performed it at Stoney Brook Bible Conference, Long Island, in 1951.

The Canadian bass-baritone George Beverly Shea (b. 1909) memorably sang "How Great Thou Art" at Billy Graham's 1954 London Crusade, and Shea and Graham's song-leader Cliff Barrows further popularized it at subsequent Crusades, attracting renewed attention for the hymn in both Europe and the USA, where it soon appeared in numerous Christian songbooks and hymnals, and also became Shea's signature tune.

Elvis Presley's second gospel album, recorded in 1966, was entitled *How Great Thou Art*, and marked a milestone in his career, winning him the first of three Grammies, for the "Best Sacred Performance". In 1974 he won "Best Inspirational Performance" for his version of "How Great Thou Art" on the album *Elvis Recorded Live on Stage in Memphis*.

"How Great Thou Art" was voted the United Kingdom's favourite hymn by viewers of BBC television's perennially popular *Songs of Praise*, and a survey in the magazine *Christianity Today* in 2001 ranked it second only to "Amazing Grace" as the all-time favourite hymn.

Above: Elvis Presley's recording of "How Great Thou Art" won him a Grammy for "Best Sacred Performance".
Right: Javanese Gamelan instruments, including xylophones, drums, gongs, and metallophones.

Music Among Christians in South-East Asia

South-East Asia comprises thousands of linguistic, ethnic, and cultural groups across the mainland – Myanmar, Thailand, Laos, Cambodia, Vietnam, West Malaysia, and Singapore – and in the archipelagos – East Malaysia, Indonesia, Brunei, and the Philippines. The major world religions and historically dominant imperial powers – American, British, Chinese, Dutch, Portuguese, and Spanish – have all left their imprint among the peoples at this crossroads.

Physical geography played an important role in shaping the music of the area. Most musical instruments are made of bamboo, wood, or bronze, and include the free-reed mouth-organ (*khaen*) among Lao and north-eastern Thai; tuned bamboo rattle (*angklung*) and rattan flute (*suling*) in Java; tube zither (*ding goong*) among the Bahnars in Vietnam; the Jew's harp (Maguindanao and Maranao *kubing*) in Luzon; and sets of tuned bamboo tubes (*togunggak*) in Borneo. Musical instruments often come in ensembles, such as the *gamelan* among the Balinese and Javanese and the *talempong* bronze gong-chime ensemble in Sumatra.

Peoples of South-East Asia traditionally associate music and musical instruments with political and spiritual powers, with gongs and drums often regarded as the spiritual centre of the ensemble. Music is imbued with religious significance, believed to connect people to the spiritual world. For example, ritual chanting (known as *timang*) is widely practised among Ibans in Sarawak and West Kalimantan: a bard intones a stanza, followed by choral refrain; an assistant bard then chants a responsive stanza, again followed by the refrain. Such a pattern of statement and response with interjected refrain continues all night until the intended object is achieved. This pattern is carried over to hymn-singing among Christianized peoples in South-East Asia, where singing in the form of exchange between choir or soloist and the congregation is practised.

♫ Early Christian Encounters

Colonial policies helped shape the early development of Christian music. The Philippines underwent thorough Christianization under Spanish rule, except for Muslim communities in the south and tribal peoples in the highlands: pre-Christian traditions were eradicated and Friar schools instilled Spanish religious music traditions. In the East Indies, the Protestant Dutch were more interested in pursuing

economic interests than in establishing Christianity, and became patrons of indigenous music and art. As a result, Christian communities in Indonesia have struggled to relate their beliefs to indigenous ceremonial music and rites, an issue which did not normally arise among the Roman Catholics in the Philippines. For instance, the Toba Batak Protestant Church in Sumatra wrestled with the role of Toba ceremonial music and dance (*gondang sabanguran* and *tortor*) in Christian practice, from an outright prohibition by nineteenth-century German missionaries to greater recognition today.

Two Hymnals

After the Second World War, the ecumenical movement became important in developing distinctive South-East Asian Christian music. *The East Asia Christian Hymnal* (1963) and *Sound the Bamboo: The Christian Conference of Asia (CCA) Hymnal* (1990, 2000) marked a transition. The 1963 *Hymnal* contained 200 hymns, of which ninety-eight were attributed to Asian composers and sources, mainly from North-East Asia. This *Hymnal* westernized Asian Christian music, harmonizing it for piano and organ. Instead of translating the Asian songs, new words were written to accompany Asian tunes.

During the "Worship and Music in the Asian Churches Today" conference in Hong Kong in 1965 – the first East Asian gathering of musicians and composers after the Second World War – the 1963 *Hymnal* came under severe criticism. From the 1970s, compositions showed a more sensitive integration of lyrics and music. I-to Loh of Tainan Theological College, Taiwan, and Francisco Feliciano of the Asian Institute for Liturgy and Music in Manila led the contextualization of Asian Christian music, with Loh setting texts from one Asian country to musical languages of an Asian neighbour, for instance in his *Hunger Carol,* composed in the Indonesian *gamelan* style. Loh and Feliciano's partnership is evident in *Sound the Bamboo: The CCA Hymnal*, in which new compositions reflected on issues of justice, oppression, and suffering. The 2000 *Hymnal* contained selections from thirty-eight languages. Of its 315 hymns, 122 originated in South-East Asia, with forty from Cambodia, thirty-five from Indonesia, and forty-one from the Philippines. Access to previously more restricted areas widened the horizons of South-East Asian music and created new opportunities for cross-fertilization. The editors stated: "Our policy was not to impose Western harmonization on any hymns... The use of piano or organ should be sparing, with reliance on unaccompanied singing or more appropriate instruments."

Many other new hymnals appeared among Christian communities. The *Fen xing duan ge ji* ("Revival Choruses") published by Chin Lien Bible Seminary, Singapore, in 1974 testified to the impact of the revivalist John Sung among ethnic Chinese churches; the bilingual Indonesian-Chinese *Sheng jiao shi ge (Puji Pujian Kristen)* was published in Malang, Indonesia, in 1976; and Vietnamese and Khmer hymnals were published by the United Methodist Church in 1994 and 2001.

Yet Western music and hymns continue to be popular in South-East Asia, especially in urban centres such as Singapore and Manila, as a result not merely of missionary legacies but also of the role Western Christian music has assumed in the globalizing age, allowing Christians in isolated and threatened societies to see themselves as belonging to a larger, transnational community. In addition, locally composed Western-style Christian music is popular among young people. *Pop rohani* ("spiritual pop") represents a fresh initiative in reaching out to younger generations in South-East Asia.

MICHAEL NAI-CHIU POON

Above: Catholic Mass in a Vietnamese church, Ho Chi Minh City, Vietnam, South-East Asia.

CHAPTER 19

"(Give Me That) Old Time Religion": Gospel Music in the Twentieth Century

I'd rather sing about "old man Jesus" than about some old man some woman has lost.

Mahalia Jackson

During the nineteenth and twentieth centuries, gospel songs and hymns became an increasingly important part of church and chapel worship, and from early in the twentieth century the role of the professional gospel music performer evolved and grew, both at evangelistic events and at concerts. In this chapter we look at the development of gospel music as a professional and increasingly commercial product. Records, radio stations, and music festivals all helped popularize gospel and market its songs and performers.

In discussing gospel music, we are concerned not solely with composers, writers, and arrangers, but also and increasingly with the performers and artists. With the move into secular performance arenas – and particularly into radio, television, and the recording media – the role of the vocalist or instrumentalist became more and more central to popular music.

Gospel singers in Paris, France.

Gospel Light Jubilee Singers. Other groups included the Roberta Martin Singers, formed by the eponymous Roberta Martin (1907–69) with the aid of Thomas Dorsey, with the theme hit-song "Only a Look". Among many songs composed by Martin are "God is Still on the Throne" (1959), "Just Jesus and Me", and "Let it Be" (1962).

The first professional black gospel choir in the USA was Wings Over Jordan, founded in 1935 in Cleveland, Ohio, by Glenn T. Settle, starting out singing spirituals and achieving a regular national radio spot. In the 1940s "Wings" were overtaken by the St Paul Baptist Church Choir of Los Angeles (also known as the Echoes of Eden Choir), directed by James Earl Hines. This group displayed most of the features now associated with the gospel choir – handclapping, solo spots, polyphonic arrangements, and antiphonal styles – and performed not only spirituals but also traditional hymns and contemporary gospel. Hines was skilled at raising his audiences to a state of hysteria and "slaying" them in the aisles (as he termed it).

By the end of the twentieth century, most major American cities could boast their own large gospel choir, notable among which was the New Life Community Choir formed by John P. Kee, "Prince of Gospel", from Durham, North Carolina. Also successful was Britain's London Community Gospel Choir, founded in 1982 by the Revd Bazil Meade, which rapidly built up its repertoire, recruiting members from a number of different London churches.

US gospel group the Dixie Hummingbirds.

♪ Gospel Quartets

Significant influence on gospel music was exercised by the barber-shop male-voice quartets that flourished informally around barbers' shops in African-American neighbourhoods. The division of these quartets into lead, soprano, tenor, and bass was copied by gospel quartets. In 1902, the Dinwiddie Colored Quartet (also known as the Dinwiddie Quartet and the Dinwiddie Quartette) was the first black vocal quartet to record on disc, with songs such as "Down on the Old Camp Ground" and "Gabriel's

Trumpet". (The Unique Quartette had recorded on wax cylinder ten years earlier.)

In addition to quartets, gospel music also inspired singing quintets, sextets, and so forth, many of them based in southern states such as Mississippi. To the familiar spirituals and gospel hymns these groups started to add original numbers by the likes of Dorsey, Lucie Campbell, and Kenneth Morris. Black groups often matched fancy names with flamboyant styles, such as the Sensational Nightingales, the Mighty Clouds of Joy, or the Dixie Hummingbirds. These groups often appeared on the same bills and competed with one another, utilizing various performance gimmicks – for example "bending" notes or altering tempi. In 1939 the Dixie Hummingbirds recorded sixteen songs for Decca, still in the slow style of the Jubilee Singers; but gradually groups such as the Kings of Harmony, from Birmingham, Alabama, introduced a harder style.

Southern Gospel

At the same time, a white "southern gospel" genre was also forming. Convention-style singing was pioneered in the American South by the charismatic schoolteacher, James D. Vaughan (1864–1941), founder of the Vaughan School of Music (1911), where many gospel performers learned their trade, and owner of one of the first Tennessee radio stations, WOAN, from which he broadcast southern gospel music. Vaughan, from the Nazarene Church and with a Holiness and Wesleyan background, wrote hundreds of songs, such as "I Feel Like Travelling On". His first published songbook, *Gospel Chimes*, used shaped notes.

In 1903 Vaughan set up the James D. Vaughan Music Publishing Company, at Lawrenceburg, Tennessee, which was to become one of the biggest gospel publishers in the USA. In 1910 he sponsored a travelling quartet to sell his songbooks, claimed to be the origin of the southern gospel music business. The quartet's first concert alone

resulted in the sale of 5,000 copies of his book, and before long sixteen quartets were travelling as far afield as Illinois. Vaughan eventually sold more than 6 million gospel songbooks, and founded Vaughan Phonographic Records, the first record company in the American South.

White gospel groups, such as the Happy Goodman Family, the Thrasher Brothers, and the Speer Family, were often drawn from a single family. Other significant white gospel quartets included that of V. O. Stamps (1892–1940), who started out working for Vaughan, but in 1924 set up his own music company. In 1926 J. R. Baxter (1887–1960) bought a stake in Stamps's company, and the resulting Stamps-Baxter Quartet performed frequently on radio, though their quartet-style music was slow in gaining acceptance among mainstream, denominational churches, even in the South. Yet such groups influenced Elvis Presley while he was evolving his style in the 1950s.

By the early 1950s, gospel performers started to add instrumentation to their vocal performances. Guitarist Howard Carroll joined the Dixie Hummingbirds in 1952, and from 1953 their recordings featured guitar and drums. Often, the lead singer gained prominence over the rest of the performers. Sam Cooke (1931–64) became the lead vocalist of the Soul Stirrers, taking over from R. H. Harris, who felt that gospel music had become excessively dependent on gimmicks.

♫ Black Soloists

Son of a slave father, the African-American Revd Dr Charles Albert Tindley (1851–1933) was among the first to write gospel *songs* – a new phenomenon, neither hymn nor spiritual, but a "merger of black folk-tunes and sentiments with the music of shabby white evangelism [that] is one of the greatest chapters in American popular music" (Anthony Heilbut). Tindley, minister of a huge African-American Methodist church in Philadelphia, published a collection of his songs – he was responsible for both lyrics and melody – in 1901, and a further popular and frequently reprinted collection, *New Songs of Paradise*, in 1916; six years later he created the Tindley Gospel Singers. He was the first hymn-writer to claim copyright on a hymn. Among Tindley's notable numbers are "We'll Understand It Better By and By", "Leave It There" (or "Take Your Burdens to the Lord"), recorded by many gospel vocalists, and "Lord, I've Tried". Some have argued that his 1901 song "I'll Overcome Some Day"[3] forms the basis of the 1960s Civil Rights anthem, "We Shall Overcome". Tindley's songs have a camp-meeting fervour that evolved naturally into the gospel style.

Another early gospel song-writer was Lucie (Lucy) E. Campbell (1885–1963) from Memphis, Tennessee, both of whose parents were ex-slaves. For forty-seven years Campbell was musical director of the National Baptist Convention and showcased gospel choirs. Among her own celebrated songs are "He Understands; He'll Say 'Well done'", "In the Upper Room", and "Jesus Gave Me Water", a hit for the Soul Stirrers. In 1921 Campbell's National Baptist Convention published a significant collection, including some songs by Tindley, entitled *Gospel Pearls*.

♫ The "Father" of Black Gospel Music

Just one generation on from slavery, black artists were making best-selling recordings and touring major cities. But Thomas A. Dorsey (1899–1993) – the so-called "father of gospel" – was the "breakthrough" artist of the genre: a one-man industry, writing, composing, performing, organizing, publishing, and directing gospel music. Gospel music historian Anthony Heilbut

Thomas A. Dorsey, "father of gospel", c. 1970.

claims Dorsey welded "gospel, blues, jazz and country music into a distinctive musical style", adding to these his familiarity with ragtime, vaudeville, and circus music. Dorsey (not to be confused with trombonist and dance-band leader *Tommy* Dorsey) started playing ragtime and blues while a teenager in Georgia, listening to the likes of the legendary "mother of the blues" "Ma" Rainey (with whom he later performed) and Bessie Smith, and playing the piano at brothels and dance-halls. A performance of Tindley's song "I Know a Great Saviour, I Do, Don't You?" moved young Dorsey and pulled him toward gospel music. But the churches did not at first welcome his jazz/blues style; he was told: "You can't sing no gospel. You can only preach it." The blues were frowned on by black churches because of their provenance, as we have seen.

Dorsey lived through this initial discouragement and devoted his career to gospel music. He spent the next twenty years touring the USA, performing his gospel blues songs with a team of vocalists and gradually finding both acceptance and imitators. Soon gospel choirs had been set up in many churches, and annual conventions offered a platform to upcoming artists. Among Dorsey's best-known songs are "Precious Lord, Take My Hand"[4] (written after the death in childbirth of his first wife and their infant son) and "There'll Be Peace in the Valley for Me". Many in the church continued to regard him as a renegade for joining Christian lyrics with "the devil's music" – jazz and the blues – though he took black gospel to new levels by melding it with the complex harmonies and intense emotions of the blues.

One of Dorsey's singers, Sallie Martin (1895–1988), "the mother of gospel music", helped market his songs and later, with the song-writer Kenneth Morris – author of "Dig a Little Deeper" and "Jesus Steps Right In" – set up Martin and Morris Music Company, the biggest black-owned gospel publisher. Morris achieved fame by arranging and adding verses to "Just a Closer Walk with Thee", a song he allegedly heard a railroad porter sing. He is also credited with introducing the Hammond electronic organ to gospel music – a marriage that was to endure.

Known as the "crown prince of gospel" (the epithets are not inventive), the Revd James Cleveland (1931–91) first heard gospel music at Pilgrim Baptist Church, Chicago, directed by Dorsey. A Baptist pastor, Cleveland has been described as the creator of the modern gospel sound, bringing together gospel, jazz, and pop in arrangements for large choirs. He recorded fifty-four albums of gospel and in 1968 founded the Gospel Music Workshop of America, which spread gospel singing across the United States in an age more used to rock and soul. Having strained his vocal cords as a teenage member of the Thorne Crusaders, Cleveland was left with a rough-edged

voice that he made his signature sound, and which led him to concentrate on playing the piano, arranging, and composing. His arrangements of standards such as "(Give Me That) Old Time Religion" and "It's Me, O Lord" transformed them into driving new numbers for the Gospelaires trio.[5]

Edwin K. Hawkins (b. 1943), one of the creators of the urban contemporary gospel sound, is best known, with his Edwin Hawkins Singers (originally the Northern California State Choir), for his arrangement of Doddridge's eighteenth-century hymn "Oh Happy Day" (1968/69), which sold seven million copies and became the best-selling black gospel single.

♫ Gospel Goes Commercial

Gospel music steadily expanded from its church roots to become a medium of entertainment. The musicians did not restrict themselves to churches, but were increasingly performing in big secular venues and forging successful recording careers. In 1938 came the first record by the gospel star Rosetta Tharpe (1915–73).[6] Tharpe (the surname is a misspelling of her husband's surname Thorpe) was born Rosetta Nubbin in Cotton Plant, Arkansas, and raised in a Holiness church – the Church of God in Christ. Known as the "original soul sister" of recorded music, Tharpe mixed sacred lyrics with an early form of rock accompaniment and was happy to perform as "Sister Rosetta Tharpe" in night-clubs and with big bands in secular concert halls – shocking many church-goers, not least by her reputation for bisexuality. Tharpe provoked many of the old questions about what "sacred" music was – and wasn't.

Probably the greatest gospel singer of this period was Mahalia Jackson (1911–72), from New Orleans, Louisiana, who moved to Chicago and joined the Greater Salem Baptist Church Choir. With a powerful contralto voice, Jackson recorded four songs for Decca in 1937 that failed to make an impression; yet she went on to make eight records with million-plus sales. Regarding her music as an act of worship – "I promised the Lord that I'd dedicate my life to him in song" – Mahalia refused to sing the blues: "blues are the songs of despair, gospel songs are the songs of hope". She is remembered for such numbers as "When I Wake Up in Glory", "I Can Put My Trust in Jesus", and "Move On Up a Little Higher" by W. Herbert Brewster,[7] recorded in 1947 and eventually selling eight million copies. From 1956, Mahalia became involved with the Southern Christian Leadership Conference (SCLC) campaign against segregation and racism in America. At the Prayer Pilgrimage for Freedom in 1957 she sang "I Been 'Buked and I Been Scorned" at the Lincoln Memorial in Washington, DC, and on the same spot in 1963 she sang before Dr Martin Luther King Jr made his celebrated speech, "I have a dream… ".

Like Jackson, gospel singer Clara Ward (1924–73) became a powerful contralto soloist. But Ward was also a prolific writer and arranger, adding to the repertory such gospel numbers as "How I Got Over", "Prince of Peace", and "Come in the Prayer Room". However, with her group the Ward Singers she attracted criticism from Christians for performing sacred music in night-clubs, decked in jewellery, sequinned gowns, and preposterous wigs, and for a performing style mocked as "clowning" but loved by devotees.[8] During the 1950s the Wards toured regularly with the gifted singer and preacher the Revd C. L. Franklin, father of Aretha – later "queen of soul".[9]

C. L. (Clarence LaVaughn) Franklin, born in rural Mississippi, became an acclaimed preacher, as master of "the whoop" – the rhythmic and ecstatic style of African-American sermon delivery. As he preached he would "tune" a word, giving it a musical intonation, gradually transforming his sermon into a rhythmic, chanted presentation. "[The minister] says one thing and the congregation says it back, back and forth, back and forth, until we're rocking together in a rhythm that won't stop."[10] Franklin gained a national reputation with radio broadcasts of his church services (which included Aretha's church singing debut when she was fourteen) and through records of his sermons, which led to extensive touring.

Following in the path of Jackson and Ward is the "queen" (or "first lady") of gospel music, Pastor Shirley Caesar (b. 1938), who started singing at the age of ten as Baby Shirley. Between 1958 and 1966, Caesar toured with The Caravans – a female gospel group – but subsequently pursued a solo career.[11]

Left: Mahalia Jackson, an African American gospel singer who refused to sing the blues.
Right: Kirk Franklin performing in Chicago, Illinois, USA.

Most influential in the late twentieth century was Andraé Crouch (b. 1942), son of a Los Angeles street preacher. Crouch wrote and performed gospel songs with his band the Disciples before pursuing a solo career. An African-American, Crouch appeals to both black and white audiences, bringing together black gospel and southern gospel traditions. Like Crouch, Jessy Dixon is a black gospel singer who found a new audience among whites, after having been spotted by Paul Simon. Dixon later joined white gospel singers Bill and Gloria Gaither in their big Homecoming events that started in 1991, bringing together Contemporary Christian Music and southern gospel music.

Current gospel performers include Helen Baylor, Yolanda Adams (b. 1961), and BeBe (b. 1962) and CeCe (Priscilla, b. 1964)

Winans. The Winans are African-American siblings who first appeared in 1982 on the television show *Praise the Lord* as part of the "PTL Singers". They left in 1987 to form a duo, drawing on gospel and rhythm and blues. BeBe and CeCe ("Christian music's Whitney Houston") were among the first African-American artists played frequently on CCM radio stations, achieving their greatest success with their album *Different Lifestyles* (1991), featuring "Addictive Love" and "I'll Take You There".

British record companies took note of the success of gospel music in the USA and attempted to emulate it with home-grown artists such as Paul Johnson, The Escofferys, Lavine Hudson, and Bryan Powell. British gospel covers a spectrum from funk bands such as Four Kornerz, the traditional praise and worship sound of Noel Robinson and Nu Image, from the African-influenced Muyiwa and Riversongz to the urban style of groups such as Raymond and Co. and Siani, and solo performers such as Priscilla Jones and Roger Samuels.

In the United States, Kirk Franklin (b. 1970) with his choir, The Family, released his first album with relatively traditional gospel music in 1993, but then started successfully to experiment with a more modern sound. A similar path was followed by sisters Erica and Tina Atkins, *née* Campbell, who perform as Mary Mary, and by Yolanda Adams.

Music Among Christians in the Indian Subcontinent

The apostle Thomas probably first brought Christianity to India. Later, Nestorian and other Christian groups from the Middle East settled in India, bringing Syriac liturgy and music. The Portuguese came to India in the late fifteenth century, carrying with them the Latin liturgy. Subsequently different rites, Latin and Syrian, evolved, with chanting of the liturgy as the normal form of music.

With Dutch, German, British, and other European involvement in Asia from the early eighteenth century, there came Protestant missionaries, emphasizing vernacular translation of the Bible and worship in India's regional languages. This led to the singing of indigenous melodies, and the incorporation of local cultural traditions into Christian song. With low literacy rates and the lengthy process of Bible translation, Christian songs were widely used to propagate the Christian gospel as well as in worship.

Many individuals contributed to Christian music in the nineteenth century. In Kerala, Moses Walsalm wrote tonic sol-fa music in the local folk tradition for street theatre, with songs based on biblical incidents and Christian and moral themes. In *Christheeya Gana Manjari* he collected 115 tunes and 220 Christian song-texts, still found in the most widely used Protestant hymn-book in Kerala, the state with the highest percentage of Christians. Walsalm drew on melodies from different Indian musical traditions, even systematizing Carnatic music (elaborate south Indian "classical" music) so it could be sung in corporate worship. This paved the way for the Syrian churches to emulate some of the Protestant liturgical reforms, for instance starting to use the vernacular – Malayalam – for singing, while retaining their ancient chant tunes.

English imports

In the garrison towns and cities of nineteenth-century India the English-speaking community sang imported hymns. By the beginning of the twentieth century, the Tractarian Movement and Evangelical Revival led by Moody and Sankey began to influence churches in India. Hymns translated into various south Indian languages were forced into the same metre as their English-language originals and were used widely in worship, paving the way for revival convention songs. This type of Christian song, with its easy tunes and rhythms, is still very popular. At the peak of the nationalist movement in India, with an increased emphasis on Indian theology, attempts were made to popularize Carnatic music and Indian dance forms.

Vatican II (1962–64) and the Eucharistic Congress in India in 1964 had a major impact on the Indian church. Churches using the Latin, Romo-Syrian, and Malankara-Syrian rites translated their liturgies into Malayalam and other local languages and began to use vernacular translations of the Bible. The Roman Catholic church adapted secular tunes and accepted influences from other Christian denominations, though chant is still widely used.

Instruments

Percussion instruments are very important in the music of India, and a far wider variety of these instruments is used than in the West. Various types of percussion orchestras take part in Indian Christian festivals. Electronic keyboards and rhythm sets are widely utilized today, and contemporary pop music, propagated through cinema and television, has influenced Christian music, although the Christian hymns, convention songs, and contemporary songs and chanting first developed in the nineteenth century are still widely used. The rapid development of electronic media has made passive listening to music more popular than participation. As a result far more Christian music CDs than books are being sold, paving the way for the rise of new Christian groups, fellowships, and house churches both in urban and rural areas which sing contemporary Christian music both in English and in vernacular languages.

Sugu J. M. Chandy

CHAPTER **20**

"I Wish We'd All Been Ready": The Making of the Contemporary Christian Music Industry

We need a whole lot more of Jesus, and a lot less rock'n'roll.

Larry Norman

Contemporary Christian Music (CCM) is a new phenomenon, arising since the 1960s from the boom in pop and rock and the rise and rise of the recording industry. Big enough by the 1990s to attract the attention of major recording companies, CCM is sometimes cynically regarded as a Christian subculture "cover" for the secular rock industry, a parallel universe to the secular entertainment business. CCM – also known as "inspirational music" – is essentially popular music whose lyrics focus on the Christian faith: the term usually refers specifically to the Nashville-based Christian pop, rock, and worship music industry – a blending (sometimes blurring) of Christian-based content with secular pop music style – and is often music released by overtly Christian recording companies.

Many artists in the Christian rock scene tend to copy the styles of successful mainstream performers, providing "godly" alternatives to what is popular. Critics often question how interesting, creative, and original CCM is, and whether "Christian music" connects and communicates with anybody outside the Christian community. Many artists who work under the CCM banner have difficulty in defining "Christian music" – and often believe, rightly or wrongly, that they are the object of unfair and biased treatment by the secular media.

A distinction is normally drawn between Contemporary Christian Music and modern worship music. Most CCM artists do not expect their music to be used in church, but listened to at home, in cars or on iPods, like regular pop music. One Christian rock star

Larry Norman, pioneer of "Jesus Music", c. 1970.

explained, "I'm not trying to change what goes on in church… I just want to make entertainment more worshipful."

♪ Jesus Rock

The roots of CCM lie in the American Jesus Movement of the 1960s and the more or less contemporaneous rise of the secular rock industry. The "Jesus Rock" scene was originally the haunt of anti-establishment Jesus radicals, whose lively faith sometimes covered a multitude of theological and musical sins. Jesus Rock was intended to serve Christian evangelism, apologetics, and entertainment and owed its musical ethos largely to Memphis, Liverpool, and rock'n'roll. From the 1970s, specifically Christian record labels and recording companies started to appear. By the 1980s, CCM had become an identifiable industry – and by the 1990s a veritable empire.

CCM is far from uncontroversial. Many conventional and conservative Christians have never accepted it, seeing rock'n'roll as at best secular and at worst "of the devil" – corrupting the young and intrinsically unfit for Christian participation. John Lennon's headline-catching claim that the Beatles were "more popular than Jesus" did little to endear rock to conservative church-goers in the 1960s.

It was possibly the radical, disinhibiting, and shocking essence of rock music that first linked it with fundamentalist Christianity – itself a "radical" movement of change, revival, conversion, and inspiration. "Christian rock" seemed to offer a suitable means of expressing the born-again experience. The extraordinary scenes of fervour and passion experienced at American camp meetings and revivals from the early nineteenth century onwards are not so far removed from the mass hysteria and breakdown of inhibitions witnessed at rock concerts in the 1960s. Geographically, too,

American fundamentalism and rock'n'roll shared common roots in the southern USA's culture, as well as a search for authenticity, and a rejection of consumerist conformity.

In the early years, however good their material, Christian artists faced a distribution problem: secular stores had no interest in their records, and Christian bookshops were unwilling to stock them either. Things started to change as interest in CCM grew and opposition diminished. Christian summer music festivals such as Explo '72 in Dallas, Texas – featuring Larry Norman and Barry McGuire, as well as Johnny Cash and Kris Kristofferson – helped raise the profile of the new genre. In addition, Christian conversion testimonies by prominent rock figures such as Peter Green of Fleetwood Mac, Richie Furay of Buffalo Springfield, and disco queen Donna Summer garnered further publicity for CCM.

By the late 1970s the rawness and radical style of the "Jesus Music" era was evolving into greater musical sophistication and a less apocalyptic message. Mainstream companies began to recruit Christian artists and acquire Christian labels. Word Records was bought by ABC in 1974; Sparrow made a distribution deal with MCA in 1981; Elektra/Asylum agreed to distribute Light Records in the secular market in 1982; and CBS Records even launched its own (short-lived) Christian label, Priority. However, these initial efforts at co-operation between mainstream companies and Christian artists were largely unsuccessful, partly because the Christian performers did not have the "star" quality the corporations were looking for.

Beginnings
Sometimes dubbed the "father" of Contemporary Christian Music, Billy Ray Hearn, a Baptist from Georgia, created the musical *Good News* in 1967, modelled on a successful secular touring show, *Up with People*. Written in a folk idiom, *Good News* was adopted by the Southern Baptists, and

Hearn signed up with Word Inc. to create further projects. Christian-themed musicals were in the air: *Godspell*, by Stephen Schwartz and John-Michael Tebelak, opened off-Broadway in 1971, and Andrew Lloyd-Webber's *Jesus Christ Superstar* had its première on Broadway the same year. Hearn encouraged the composers Ralph Carmichael and Kurt Kaiser to create a Christian youth musical, *Tell It Like It Is*, released on LP in 1970. Though far removed from heavy rock, anything that smacked of secular pop raised the hackles of many conservative Christians, whose fears were heightened by writers such as Bob Larson, whose book *The Day Music Died* (1972) attacked the pop-star idolatry, "sinful" lyrics, and "demon-invoking" beat of rock music. Hearn next launched Myrrh Records at Word, one of the first labels dedicated to

CCM, and four years later founded his own label, Sparrow Records, for which he signed up such major artists as 2nd Chapter of Acts, Barry McGuire, Keith Green, and John Michael Talbot. Hearn sold Sparrow to EMI in 1992, where it continued to thrive, with acts such as Steven Curtis Chapman and BeBe and CeCe Winans.

In the later 1960s and 1970s in the UK, many pop and beat groups were formed by younger Christians outside the commercial music world. While their music was partly evangelistic, designed to present the Christian message in a form accessible to a generation brought up on Mersey Beat, folk rock, and psychedelic rock sounds, it

Gospel artists Richard Smallwood (b. 1948) and Shirley Caesar (b. 1938) with Billy Ray Hearn, founder of EMI Christian Music Group, and Bill Hearn, also of EMI Christian Music Group.

also reflected their desire to make Christian music in styles they themselves enjoyed.

Jesus Music

A far cry from Hearn's light-hearted musical, "Jesus Music" first appeared early in the 1970s. The artists looked like psychedelic rockers, and both musicians and fans resembled the stereotypical "hippie". One of the earliest groups was the All Saved Freak Band (initially Preacher and the Witness), formed around 1968 in Cleveland, Ohio, by the former Assemblies of God evangelist Larry Hill, who set up his own Church of the Risen Christ (CRC). Hill and the CRC became increasingly cult-like, moving to a communal farm and stockpiling arms for an anticipated "last battle". Less controversial groups included Agape, a southern California hard-rock band, founded in 1968 and disbanded in 1974, and The Exkursions, who played at some Billy Graham rallies – though Agape proved too much for Christian radio stations.

A pioneer of "Jesus Music" who trod an individual path, Larry Norman (1947–2008) has been described as the "father of Christian rock music"; Norman regarded himself as "too secular for the Christians and too Christian for the secularists". His first album, *Upon This Rock* – often seen as the first Contemporary Christian Music album – was released in 1969 by Capitol, gambling that Jesus Rock might be worth investing in. Norman's music gained a following in the emerging counter-cultural movement, simultaneously eliciting vituperation from the conservative religious establishment. By 1972 Norman had moved to MGM, where he created three albums – "The Trilogy" – *Only Visiting This Planet*, which legendary Beatles' producer (Sir) George Martin helped record in London, *So Long Ago the Garden*, and *In Another Land*.

Contemporaries of Norman included the archetypal "hippie for Jesus", Randy Stonehill (b. 1952), with a folk-rock style not

dissimilar to that of James Taylor, Dallas Holm (b. 1948), and Randy Matthews (b. 1950). A number of CCM artists enjoyed secular musical careers before converting and pursuing Christian music: this was true of Barry McGuire (b. 1935), who made a "Jesus Music" album entitled *Lighten Up* in 1974; Phil Keaggy (b. 1951), one of Christian rock's early innovators, who converted to Christianity in 1970; and Keith Green (1953–82), whom Decca Records had planned to make a teen idol, but who later wrote popular worship standards such as "O Lord, You're Beautiful" and "There is a Redeemer".

One of the early successes was 2nd Chapter of Acts, founded in Los Angeles in 1971 – deriving their name from the chapter in the Bible describing the descent of the Holy Spirit in tongues of fire – who sang an unusual hybrid of old hymns, hard rock, and American theatre music. Another significant early group was Resurrection Band (or Rez Band), formed in Milwaukee, Wisconsin, in 1973 and led by Glenn Kaiser.

The folk-rock singer/song-writer (John) Mark Heard (1951–92) died prematurely but attracted a posthumous cult following. Rich (Richard Wayne) Mullins (1955–97), a singer/song-writer from Indiana, is remembered for his worship-songs "Sing Your Praise to the Lord" – recorded by Amy Grant – "Step by Step", and "Awesome God". In 1993, he formed A Ragamuffin Band and recorded *A Liturgy, A Legacy, & A Ragamuffin Band* (1993), a concept album drawing inspiration from Catholic liturgy.

Among the most successful Christian singer/song-writers are Steven Curtis Chapman (b. 1962) and Michael W. Smith (b. 1957), who wrote gospel numbers such as "Great is the Lord" and crossed over into the mainstream in the 1990s. Sandi Patty (b. 1956), too, had a "cross-over" career, achieving success with Christian audiences, but also making albums that achieved wider success. Sometimes known as "The Voice", she attracted criticism for being the highest-

CCM pioneer Amy Grant performs at the Grand Ole Opry House, Nashville, Tennessee, USA.

included the hit signature track *"El Shaddai"* by Michael Card, "Sing Your Praise" by Rich Mullins, and "In a Little While" by Grant and Gary Chapman. With *Unguarded* (1985) Grant attempted to become the first Christian artist to achieve success as a mainstream pop singer, some regarding this move as a "sell-out".

"Evangelical rock's court jester", Steve Taylor (b. 1957) brought much-needed satire to Christian music. Equally controversial is singer/song-writer Michael Knott, whose album *Rocket and a Bomb* (1994) had a title track addressed to "Mrs God", and a cover portraying Jesus as a barman. By contrast, Steve Camp (b. 1935) abandoned the music business for a pastorate, believing CCM had built an "unholy" alliance with the mainstream music business. In his opinion: "We are flooded today with what I refer to as 'God-is-my-girlfriend' songs…". Another individualistic singer/song-writer/producer/ author is Charlie Peacock, who disowns the concept of Contemporary Christian Music, believing Christian artists should work directly in the mainstream, without the mediation of the Christian ghetto.

♫ Christian Rock

A controversial subgenre of CCM is "Christian rock", with bands who stir intense feelings for and against – just like secular rock bands. The Christian entertainment world seems to engender similar controversies to the secular world, but with a time-delay. Just like secular rock, Christian rock too has numerous subdivisions: metal, punk, grunge, ska, progressive, alternative, and so forth.

Christian rock bands form and break up continually. One of the oldest enduring acts, Petra, founded by Bob Hartman (b. 1949) in 1972, was among the best-selling Christian bands of the 1980s and 1990s. Another enduring group is The

paid singer in the American Christian music industry and like many other artists reverted to covering classic hymns. Twila Paris (b. 1958) made a successful career as a singer/song-writer; her praise-songs are found in the newer hymnals, notably "He is Exalted", "How Beautiful", and "We Bow Down". Australian singer/song-writer Rebecca St James Smallbone (b. 1977), who records as Rebecca St James – dismissed by some as "the Christian Alanis Morissette" for mimicking mainstream music trends – describes herself as "a minister first".

Amy Grant (b. 1960), often regarded as one of the pioneers of gospel and CCM, in 2007 became the best-selling CCM artist, having sold more than 30 million units worldwide. Her breakthrough album *Age to Age* (1982)

77s (originally the Scratch Band) founded in 1979, centred on song-writer/vocalist Michael Roe. In the 1980s "Pastor" Bob Beeman created a notorious thrash-metal band named Vengeance (later Vengeance Rising); the cover of their first album showed a human hand, with blood oozing from a spike wound.

Another musical form with its Christian exponents is rap, with dc Talk – formed in 1988 in Lynchburg, Virginia – probably its best-known performers. Successful, too, have been the loud, aggressive four-man band P.O.D. ("Payable On Death"), formed in 1992. However, the music writer Steve Turner doubts the validity of "Christian" rap: "Rap is a way of life, rooted in the shared hardships of the ghetto, and a credible Christian contribution would have to come from inside."[1]

The Australian group Mortification, formed in 1990, became a leading Christian heavy metal band, while Audio Adrenaline's first album melded contemporary pop genre pastiches with evangelical lyrics. Sixpence None the Richer (the name derived from a phrase in C. S. Lewis's *Mere Christianity*) topped the secular charts in 1999 with their single "Kiss Me", which was barred from

nomination for a CCM music award because it lacked explicitly Christian lyrics. Soon after forming in Australia in 1986, the Newsboys (originally "The News") moved to the United States, satirizing American kitsch culture. Like other Christian artists, they later turned to making praise and worship albums.

Taking their name from the Anglo-Saxon poet who died in 680, Caedmon's Call, formed in 1992, is a folk/rock band with an acoustic-based sound. Jars of Clay,[2] formed in the early 1990s, boasted an alternative rock folk/pop sound, with successful standards such as "I Need Thee Every Hour" and "God Will Lift Up Your Head". Lead singer Dan Haseltine said, "our songs… [are] not really there to explain our faith… ", claiming art can "make people feel what's true rather than telling them".

♪ Outside the CCM Tent

Apart from these artists, several megastars have created and performed Christian music without sheltering under the CCM umbrella. The British pop musician Cliff Richard (Harry Webb), who in 1966 publicly announced he was a born-again

Christian, abandoned his earlier rock'n'roll for pop. Never abrasive, and possibly the most successful artist in British pop music history, Cliff Richard showed great staying power in an industry renowned for short careers. He evolved from an Elvis Presley-like rocker, to a teen idol, and finally to a mellow rock singer of songs that sometimes carry a Christian theme. Although Cliff Richard has never achieved recognition in the USA, over his career he has sold more than 250 million records.

Between 1979 and 1981, Bob Dylan devoted his career to evangelical Christianity, polarizing his fans as greatly as had his "conversion" from acoustic guitar to electric rock in the mid-1960s. Dylan made three overtly Christian albums: *Slow Train Coming* (1979), with its chart single "Gotta Serve Somebody", *Saved*, and *Shot of Love*, but abandoned the explicitly Christian worldview in subsequent albums. A thread of religious interest had been clear in his lyrics since the biblical language of early songs such as "The Times They are a-Changin'".[3]

The other major artists to have displayed a Christian stance outside CCM are U2, the rock band from Dublin. U2's musical vision was in part shaped when three members of the band became involved in a Pentecostal-influenced group in Dublin in the late 1970s and early 1980s. Though they are not a "Christian band", U2 espouse a holistic vision of Christianity, most publicly represented by Bono. U2's 1987 *The Joshua Tree* became the fastest-selling album in British chart history, and the rhythmic gospel single "I Still Haven't Found What I'm Looking For", with U2's most overtly Christian lyrics, reached No. 1 in the USA.

The Future

The recession and financial crises of 2008/10 brought to the forefront the question whether the Christian music industry, which faced major difficulties, would survive. Illegal downloads haemorrhaged money from record companies, many Christian bookshops closed, radio stations and record companies shed jobs, and music trade show attendance plummeted. Band tours and festivals fought for audiences and artists and cut back on gigs. Although music *consumption* increased after 2004, album sales were about half what they were in 1999. Copying (that is, pirating) CDs is a major problem, as is the widespread availability of music on the Internet, television, radio, and portable devices. Record labels are in dire straits, many restructuring and some disappearing.

Left: Singer Leigh Nash performs with Matt Slocum and Justin Cary, who form Sixpence None the Richer, on *The Tonight Show with Jay Leno* on NBC, USA.
Above: Bob Dylan plays the piano at a recording session for "Like a Rolling Stone", 1965.

Christian Music in Australia and New Zealand

Christian hymn-singing first came to Australia and New Zealand from the ships of explorers from north-west Europe in the seventeenth and eighteenth centuries,[1] and Christian hymnody became firmly entrenched in the religious culture after European settlement. During colonial settlement in Australia, church music became a marker of identity of European heritage and denoted denominational differences. The early colony was dominated by traditional churches, evangelical Protestantism, and Catholicism. Hymns were sung from printed hymnals brought with the settlers: Presbyterians sang metrical psalms, Methodists the hymns of the Wesleys and their followers, and Anglicans used *Hymns Ancient and Modern*. As the church developed in the early nineteenth century, the organ was introduced to corporate worship, but not without controversy and opposition. Not until the middle of the century did alternative patterns of worship establish themselves, heralding a new era of denominationalism.

During this time, centred around St Mary's Cathedral, Sydney, the Catholic church featured regular public performances, specializing in religious music from the "fine music" tradition. Presbyterian worship, by contrast, had neither choirs nor instruments, consisting of metrical psalms and paraphrases led by a precentor. Presbyterians, like Anglicans, remained highly suspicious of congregational hymnody, with its potential to invoke "irrational emotionalism". The other prevailing denomination at this time, the Wesleyan Methodists, revelled in their reputation as a singing people, devoted to the works of John and Charles Wesley.

A number of original hymns and hymn melodies were produced from the start of European settlement in New Zealand. Among the earliest are a surviving hymn in a manuscript by a Free Church Presbyterian settler actually written aboard an immigrant vessel in 1847, and Bishop Pompallier's six hymns written in the Maori language for his Catholic converts (published in Paris in 1859). Though Australian hymn-writers became more prolific and influential in later decades, they too existed from early times.

As the twentieth century approached, churches continued to make major changes to their musical culture. Presbyterians saw the introduction of the choir, then hymns, and finally the organ, each change commonly meeting some resistance.

Anglican and Catholic churches were characterized by dignified, restrained worship, with congregational singing subordinate to more formal musical involvement. However, the Anglicans finally adopted hymns as a regular feature of congregational worship and established St Andrew's Cathedral Choir School, Sydney, in 1885.

Another prominent change, which first took hold in the Methodist and Presbyterian churches, was the ending of precentor leadership, resulting in increased involvement of congregations in corporate worship and the introduction of new musical styles. Evangelistic songs – American spirituals, revival songs, and gospel hymns – found increasing popularity in New Zealand and Australia in the later nineteenth century. The Salvation Army, established in Australia from 1880, used such songs powerfully with the non-church community. Enhancing the popularity of these new songs were the missions of (largely) North American evangelists, with Ira D. Sankey's *Sacred Songs and Solos* becoming a revered songbook throughout Australia and New Zealand.

♫ Pentecostalism

One of the strongest influences on the musical culture of evangelical churches in Australia and New Zealand during the twentieth century was the development and ascendancy of the Pentecostal church – the only religious group to have developed in the last two centuries not brought to Australia by immigrants. Since its recognized inception in 1909 – at Melbourne's Good News Hall under the direction of Mrs Janet Lancaster – it has become the fastest-growing Christian movement in Australia.

The rise of Pentecostalism helped pave the way for the Christian music that arrived as part of the charismatic renewal in the mid-1960s and early 1970s in the form of new hymns, praise songs, and other forms of congregational song in popular music styles. Although most were imported from the USA and UK, it was not long before local composers turned their attention to the new sound, and ultimately influenced congregational music worldwide. Most successful of these was husband-and-wife team, David and Dale Garrett from New Zealand, who wrote and compiled the *Scripture in Song* (1979–88) songbooks that became popular worldwide. While drawing on material from the USA and UK, they also promoted local song-writers and exposed their work to the global Christian audience, paving the way for the wealth of material produced in this region at the end of the twentieth century. Unlike the early hymns, there were now attempts to

infuse local spiritual understanding and references into the songs, of which the works of the Australian Geoff Bullock ("The Great Southland") and the New Zealander Colin Gibson are strong examples.

By 1987 contemporary Australian Christian music was dominated by David and Rosanna Palmer, operating from Harvard Christian Life Centre, Melbourne; the pioneer Australian Christian rock band Rosanna's Raiders; and the "Power Praise" music emerging from Melbourne. In Sydney, the major player was the newly developing Christian City Church, founded in 1980 by the New Zealander Phil Pringle, who released their (and Australia's) first live congregational album in 1990.

During the 1990s and 2000s Pentecostal churches became the dominant producers of congregational music, often also sung in mainstream Protestant churches despite differences in theology. Pentecostal churches often have larger congregation sizes and ideologically-aligned networks that support flourishing production centres. The most significant producers of contemporary congregational song in Australia and New Zealand have been Christian City Church, Planet Shakers, Parachute, and Hillsong Church, all of which release music to the global Christian music market. Of these, Hillsong has been the most successful and largely represents the sound of Australian Christianity.

Hillsong Church is Australia's largest church, with a Sydney-based congregation in excess of 18,000 people. From humble beginnings in 1983, they expanded the Hillsong "brand" to churches in London, Paris, Kiev, and Stockholm. A significant part of Hillsong Church, especially since 1992, has been its music production and publishing arm, Hillsong Music Australia. Hillsong Church (as Hills CLC) recorded their first album of congregational song in 1988 (*Spirit and Truth*). Hillsong Music Australia claim annual worldwide sales in excess of 2 million albums; much of their success has been focused around their song-writers and worship leaders, initially revolving around the songs of Geoff Bullock. Darlene Zschech became the face and voice of Hillsong Music from 1995, with her international smash hit "Shout to the Lord", a song which became synonymous with Hillsong Church.

MARK EVANS

Left: The nave of St Mary's Catholic Cathedral, Sydney, Australia.

21

"Ain't Nobody Nowhere Nothin' without God": Christians do Country, Folk, and Jazz

Shall we gather at the river?

Below: Cumberland River, downtown "Music City, USA" Nashville, Tennessee.
Right: The Carter Family – "first family of country music" – Maybelle, A. P., and Sara Carter (left–right).

Country music, like gospel, has its roots in the music of the camp meetings and revivals of early and mid-nineteenth century North America. Christian folk similarly draws on sources in early country and gospel music, as well as on the folk traditions of Europe and of early New England settlers. Christian jazz and rhythm and blues too draw strongly on early nineteenth-century Christian sources, as well as on African-American music genres. Boundaries and categories between these types of sacred music are essentially porous and flexible: artists and groups move between styles and typically draw on traditions from more than one of these genres. While the Nashville music industry sometimes seems set on defining genres, it is more important to focus on the quality of the material and the performer than to attempt to analyse its exact definition.

♩ Country Music

This distinctive style, associated with the southern states of the USA, has always included a strongly Christian segment. Many of its performers have sung Christian hymns, sacred songs, and choruses derived from camp meetings and revivals, often launching their careers singing in small local churches and chapels, particularly in the South, and only later venturing on professional tours, and singing and playing at venues in major industrialized cities. Today the centre and capital of country music is "Music City, USA", Nashville, Tennessee, where until 1974 the "Grand Ole Opry" country music show was staged at a large downtown venue named the Ryman Auditorium, a nineteenth-century church building. The show is now held at the huge, purpose-built Grand Ole Opry House, nine miles east of downtown Nashville.

Between 1927 and 1956, the biggest stars of country music were the Carter Family – "the first family of country music" – originally consisting of A. P. Carter (1891–1960), his wife Sara (1898–1979), and his sister-in-law Maybelle Carter (1909–78), all originating from Virginia. In 1939/40 Maybelle Carter's daughter June also joined the group. They did not perform exclusively – or even mainly – Christian material, but sacred songs fitted comfortably into their repertoire. The Carters had a wide impact on the development of country music, and also on southern gospel, the 1960s folk revival, and on numerous pop and rock musicians, and were important not only for their repertoire and numerous recordings, but also for Maybelle's distinctive guitar style, known as the "Carter scratch". Using thumb and one or two fingers, she picked the melody on the lower strings while maintaining the rhythm, brushing her fingers across the upper strings; this "Carter style" was adopted by many later guitarists.

Other major stars made country-and-western-style recordings of sacred songs. The "king of the cowboys", Roy Rogers (Leonard Franklin Slye, 1911–98), entered the charts with "Little White Cross on the Hill", and with his wife Dale Evans (1912–2001) later made a number of albums featuring country-style sacred songs.

A subgenre of country, blue grass, spawned by Bill Monroe (1911–96),

was named after his band, the Blue Grass Boys. In 1945 the banjo virtuoso Earl Scruggs joined the band and "blue grass" reached its defining point, with breakneck tempos and instrumental virtuosity that included solo "breaks" on banjo, fiddle, and mandolin, and sophisticated vocal harmonies. Among the Blue Grass Boys' sacred numbers were "Wicked Path of Sin" and the album *I'll Meet You in Church Sunday Morning* (1964). Others soon followed the blue grass style, including the "first family of blue grass gospel music", the Lewis Family, who recorded almost sixty albums, including *Singing in My Soul* and *Shall We Gather at the River?* A similar family blue grass band was formed by the Easter Brothers, who also recorded a number of Christian albums.

Country has its solo stars as well as its groups and family bands. Stuart Hamblen (1908–89), like Roy Rogers a movie cowboy, experienced evangelical conversion in 1949 at an early Billy Graham Crusade in Los Angeles, and started a radio

"Cowboy Church of the Air". His signature composition, "It is No Secret (What God Can Do)", was subsequently taken up by Pat Boone, Elvis Presley, and Johnny Cash among others. Other Hamblen songs uneasily combined hell-fire warnings with upbeat renditions. Another icon of country music, Hank Williams (1923–53), included gospel in his repertory and regularly performed at Grand Ole Opry until banned for persistent drunkenness in 1952. Some of his religious recordings – often recited rather than crooned – were marketed under the pseudonym "Luke the Drifter".

Probably the biggest name in country music, which developed its peculiar myths and costumes, was Johnny Cash (1932–2003), who also performed rock and roll, folk, gospel, and blues. Habitually in dark clothing, Cash became known as "The Man in Black". Strongly influenced by gospel music in childhood, in 1968 Cash married June Carter, of the Carter Family, and around the same time rediscovered his Christian faith. With his distinctive bass-baritone voice, Cash's music often dealt with sadness and redemption. Sacred albums include *The Holy Land* (1968), *The Gospel Road* (1973), and *My Mother's Hymn Book* (2004).

> *[Cash] never became a great guitarist, his voice had a limited range, and his lyrics veered between poetry and doggerel. But the combination of that voice, those words and that guitar far exceeded the greatness of any one element.*[1]

♫ Folk

"Singin' Billy" Walker (1809–75) compiled three shape-note tune-books, *The Southern Harmony* (1835), *The Southern and Western Pocket Harmonist* (1846), and *Christian*

Harmony (1866). Although he lists himself as composer of many of their tunes, a number were "borrowed" from folk-music (not the term he used). A number of his tunes were subsequently picked up by Sacred Harp singers and his hymnal became the handbook for the singing schools he set up throughout the south-eastern states of the USA.

One of the earliest American folk-singers to record Christian material was Ernest Stoneman (1893–1968) from Virginia, who played banjo, guitar, autoharp, and harmonica. Struggling with poverty during the Great Depression, he formed the Stoneman Family, a family group that recorded albums such as *Old Rugged Cross* and *Family Bible* (1988).

Johnny Cash (John Ray Cash, 1932–2003) – American country music and rock music singer, guitarist, and songwriter – performs on stage.

The folk revival of the 1950s and 1960s, closely allied to the Civil Rights Movement, saw folk collectors and singers such as Pete Seeger ("Down by the Riverside") and John and Alan Lomax, as well as artists such as Bob Dylan ("Gospel Plough"), Joan Baez ("All My Trials"), and Peter, Paul, and Mary ("Children, Go Where I Send Thee"), pick up and adapt spirituals for their own repertoire. As early as 1946 the Golden Gate Quartet released the song "No Restricted Signs in Heaven", pointing out Christianity had no room for segregation. The CNCC and Congress for Racial Equality (CORE) sponsored gospel-type groups such as the Freedom Singers, who adopted spirituals and gospel songs with lyrics modified for their political purpose: for instance "Woke Up This Morning with My Mind on Jesus" became "Woke Up This Morning with My Mind on Freedom". Other favourites taken up by the movement included "We Shall Not Be Moved" and "Ain't Gonna Let Nobody Turn Me 'Round".

In mid-twentieth-century Britain the revival of folk-music was emulated by Christian writers such as Sydney Carter, most famously in "Lord of the Dance", based on the Shaker hymn "Simple Gifts". He was following in the tradition of the nineteenth-century British Chartist Ebenezer Elliott, who wrote a hymn in folk style, "When Wilt Thou Save the People?". As we have seen elsewhere, folk-singers also appropriated such church songs as "Amazing Grace".

In the 1960s, "Jesus folk-singers" appeared too. The British duo Jonathan and Charles made a pioneering album called *Another Week to Go* (Inter-Varsity, 1967), which might be described as "Christianized" Simon and Garfunkel, with tracks such as "Mrs Chisholm's Weekend".[2] John Fischer (b. 1947) released his first album, *The Cold Cathedral* (1969), around the same time on the American Catholic label F.E.L. Publications, and followed this with *Have You Seen Jesus My Lord?* (1970).

Starting his career in the folk-rock genre, Don Francisco (b. 1946), from Kentucky, changed direction to perform Christian ballad-type songs solely on acoustic instruments. His album *Forgiven* (1977) featured the popular number "He's Alive". Francisco frequently based his songs on Bible stories or passages, sometimes critiquing "churchianity", as in his country-flavoured "Steeple Song". Similarly Noel "Paul" Stookey, best known as a member of the 1960s trio Peter, Paul, and Mary, which broke up in 1970, became part of the Jesus Movement. His "The Wedding Song (There is Love)" was written as a wedding present for Peter (Yarrow) of Peter, Paul, and Mary.[3] Canadian singer/song-writer Bruce Cockburn (b. 1945), who started recording in the 1970s, espouses an overtly political stance, criticizing aspects of US foreign policy and leaders of the Moral Majority in such songs as "If I Had a Rocket Launcher". A skilled guitarist, he brings together Anglo-Celtic folk and Third World sounds.

Popular with both Protestant and Catholic audiences, John Michael Talbot (b. 1954) discovered resonances with the writings of Catholic mystics, especially Francis of Assisi, and became a Franciscan friar in 1978. *The Lord's Supper* (1979) is a quiet musical adaptation of the Catholic eucharist; *The Painter* was recorded with the London Chamber Orchestra in 1980, followed by *Troubadour of the Great King* (1981), commemorating St Francis's 800th birthday. Talbot's *Come to the Quiet* (1980) is a contemplative instrumental album, often used by religious groups in periods of silence.

Though often described as a CCM artist, Michael Card (b. 1957), a Baptist from Madison, Tennessee, writes soft, reflective folk-style pieces, informed by theological and liturgical study. Among his best-known numbers is "*El Shaddai*" (Hebrew for Almighty God), which Amy Grant made her speciality.

🎵 Jazz

Of the modern music genres, jazz is probably the least explored by Christian composers and performers, partly because jazz is often mainly or solely instrumental, and in part due to its popular association with night-clubs, alcohol, and drugs.

An exception is the three "Sacred Concerts" created by Duke Ellington (1899–1974). Ellington had previously written sacred songs such as "Come Sunday" and "David Danced Before the Lord", but his first Sacred Concert, in September 1965, marked a new departure, opening with "In the Beginning, God". Three years later he gave a second series of Sacred Concerts, which included "Something 'Bout Believin'" and "Supreme Being". Ellington's third and final Sacred Concert, in October 1973, came shortly before his death and included his own rendition of "Ain't Nobody Nowhere Nothin' without God".

John Coltrane (1926–67), another of the jazz greats, was raised a Christian but went on to explore Islam, Sufism, Hinduism, Jewish Kabbalah, Buddhism, astrology, theosophy, and philosophy. Many see his modal, improvised music as a metaphor for his personal religious search. In the notes to *A Love Supreme* (1964), Coltrane stated:

...during the year 1957, I experienced, by the grace of God, a spiritual awakening which was to lead me to a richer, fuller, more productive life… in gratitude, I humbly asked to be given the means and privilege to make others happy through music.

The work included a word-based recitation, "*Psalm*", with the refrain "Thank you, God". For many, Coltrane's music reflects both West African music and American gospel.[4]

Jazz composer and pianist Dave Brubeck (b. 1920) joined the Roman Catholic church in 1980, after writing a mass, *To Hope!* He had previously written an oratorio on Christ, *The Light in the Wilderness* (1968), which contains a jazzy setting of the Sermon on the Mount, and a cantata, *The Gates of Justice* (1969), using words of Scripture with quotations from Dr Martin Luther King Jr.

Above: Duke Ellington, creator of three "Sacred Concerts", c. 1960.
Left: Jazz musician Dave Brubeck at the piano.

Christian Music in China

Robert Morrison (1782–1834), the first Protestant missionary to China, created not only the first Chinese translation of the Bible but also the earliest Chinese versions of a number of English hymns and Anglican psalms, put into poetic form for singing by Chinese writers.[1] In the 1860s another early missionary, William Chalmers Burns (1815–68), created collections of well-known British hymns in the Fu Zhou, Shan Tou, and Xia Men dialects, while the Congregationalist, Presbyterian, and Baptist denominations, as well as Chinese evangelists, soon created further text-only Chinese hymnals.

All these denominational collections included some original indigenous hymns. *The Union Hymn Book* (1916) was a joint venture by missionaries from different denominations, for which a full music version appeared in 1922. This was a forerunner of *Hymns of Universal Praise* (1936), the result of unprecedented co-operation by six denominations. This hymnal contained more than 512 items, selected from thirty-one previous Chinese hymnals, and was highly regarded for its contents, literary achievement, careful translations, and well-fitting tunes. It included sixty-two hymns by Chinese authors and seventy-two tunes that were either Chinese originals or based on Chinese folk-tunes. This hymnal became the most widely circulated in China, with more than 400,000 copies in print by 1949. Yang Yinliu and Lew Tingfang, its chief editors and translators (of 210 translations, 150 were by Yang), set new standards in translation. Around this time, Wang Shenyin published the first known Chinese history of hymns,[2] an invaluable companion to the hymnal.

Chinese Christians came under great pressure and persecution during the first three decades of the new Communist China formed in 1949, and churches were closed down or taken over by the government. After the Cultural Revolution, churches were allowed to reopen and resume Sunday worship in 1979, under the supervision of the Three-Self Patriotic Movement. The church now had no denominational affiliation, and worship was unified under a single structure and pattern, using a single hymnal in the sole official language, Mandarin.

In less than three years *The New Hymnal* (1983) was created, containing 400 hymns, more than a quarter of which were written and/or composed by Chinese Christians, and fifty-six published for the first time. This hymnal was edited by a committee of pastors and church musicians, including Cao Shengjie, Lin Shengben, Shi Qigui, Hong Luming, supervised by Bishop Shen Zhikao, Yang Yinliu, and Ma Geshun, and became the official and most influential Chinese hymnal of the second half of the twentieth century. It helped shape Chinese Christian spirituality, reusing well-known old hymns and introducing new ones to the rapidly growing church. In 1999 a translation was published by the Chinese Christian Literature Council that made more Chinese hymns known to the English-speaking world. A *Hymnal Supplement* of about 200 additional hymns, collected under the supervision of Cao Shenjie and covering a wider theological agenda, was published in 2009.

In the 1980s, church choirs started up again in China and gathered momentum as conductors trained under Ma Geshun, a professor of the Shanghai Music Conservatory who specialized in choral conducting.[3] Some of the hymns in *The New Hymnal* were recorded on cassette in the early 1990s and enjoyed unprecedented circulation, setting standards of performance for the next generation of choir leaders, and exemplifying Ma's pioneering approach to Mandarin choral diction.

Meanwhile, Chen Zhemin, President of Nanjing Jinling Seminary, was teaching hymnology to all seminarians, the first Chinese theologian to promote church music at seminary level. Anthems translated into Chinese were published in the Jinling Choral Series, followed by new Chinese anthems by Ma Geshun, Lin Shengben, Shi Qigui, and others, in response to requests from church choirs throughout the country.

The contributions of Wang Shenyin and He Shoucheng to hymnology and of Ma Geshun and Wu Lingfen to choral conducting, and numerous new anthems, hymns, and spiritual songs[4] are creating a lively musical heritage in the Christian church in China.

Angela Tam

Robert Morrison (right), first Protestant missionary to China, working on a translation project.

Christian Music of the Pacific Islands

Christianity was brought to the Pacific islands first through explorers in the eighteenth century, and then more systematically by missionaries during the nineteenth century. In early mission work, hymnody was one of the main evangelistic tools, with heavy reliance on Wesleyan hymns from the English "canon", along with German hymns. Where previous ancestral music had often been chant-based, these hymns facilitated the development of Western musical fundamentals and notational literacy. Protestant missionaries also encouraged group and choral singing, with three- and four-part harmony common. This choral tradition, still strongly apparent throughout the Pacific, was easily adopted by locals, who had often used communal music-making as part of indigenous religious ceremonies.

Although missionaries in some areas, for example East Polynesia, did not tolerate the translation of hymns, for the most part hymns were quickly translated into local dialects. Evidence of this local translation can be found from 1871 in Papua New Guinea, and even earlier in Tonga and other parts of Polynesia, and hymn traditions soon began to meld with local musical cultures. Christian music in the Pacific has undergone constant reinvention, as traditional styles meet indigenous styles, new instruments are introduced, and more global trends become assimilated into island culture.

One of the ways this blending occurs is through the instrumentation used to accompany Christian song. One of the most extraordinary examples came from Heinrich Zahn (1880–1944), a German Lutheran missionary who lived among the Jabem and Bukawac peoples of Papua New Guinea (PNG) from 1902 until 1932. Zahn formed bands of local conch-shell players to accompany singing, believing the "compilation" of native traditions and imported styles would allow the continued development of church song in PNG. Throughout the islands the instruments used in worship continued to adapt, evolve, and change, with the introduction first of guitars, ukuleles, mandolins, and harmonicas, and later of electronic synthesizers, drum machines, and electric guitars.

Early hymn-writers, especially foreign missionaries, were often influenced by the landscapes they encountered in the Pacific, and worked such imagery into their theology. Indigenous composers often incorporated local intonations and styles into their music, with each mission area or village developing separate musical signatures, particularly rhythmic ones.

Christian music is today part of the social fabric of many Pacific islands, with Christian songs not restricted to the churches. One of the dominant musical styles in Vanuatu in recent decades has been Christian music (both congregational and Contemporary Christian Music [CCM]), often performed and heard outside the church. On Yap, as elsewhere throughout the Pacific, communal singing of Christian song can occur at various social celebrations. Church choirs also perform outside the church in festivals and regional, national, and international competitions. One of the biggest such festivals is Zion Fest, held annually in Vanuatu. Much of the locally produced Christian music commercially available in the Pacific is by church-based choirs. While gospel song is enduringly popular throughout the Pacific, and more prevalent than traditional hymnody, it is also not uncommon for local composers to create Christian songs from popular international hits, facilitated by the absence of copyright regulation in many of the Pacific islands.

MARK EVANS

An inhabitant of Tanna Island, Vanuatu, South Pacific, blows a conch-shell horn. The German Christian missionary Heinrich Zahn formed conch-shell bands.

Further Reading

Foley, Edward B., *Worship Music: A Concise Dictionary*, Collegeville, Minn.: Michael Glazier, 2000.

Braun, Joachim, transl. Douglas W. Stott, *Music in Ancient Israel/Palestine*, Grand Rapids, Mich.: Eerdmans, 2002.

Martin, Ralph P., *Worship in the Early Church* (2nd ed.), Grand Rapids, Mich.: Eerdmans, 1974.

Foley, Edward, *Foundations of Christian Music: The Music of Pre-Constantinian Christianity*, Nottingham: Grove Books, 1992.

Apel, Willi, *Gregorian Chant*, Bloomington: Indiana University Press, 1958.

Mellers, Wilfrid, *Celestial Music?*, Woodbridge: Boydell Press, 2002.

Werner, Eric, *The Sacred Bridge*, vols 1, 2, New York: Columbia University Press/Ktav, 1959, 1984.

Leaver, Robin A., "British Hymnody from the Sixteenth through the Eighteenth Centuries", in Raymond F. Glover, ed., *The Church Hymnal Companion*, New York: Church Hymnal Corp., 1990.

Burrows, Donald, *Handel*, Oxford: Oxford University Press, 1995.

Boyd, Malcolm, *Bach*, Oxford: Oxford University Press, 2000.

Robbins Landon, Howard Chandler, *Haydn: Chronicle and Works*, Bloomington: Indiana University Press, 1977.

Barth, Karl, *Wolfgang Amadeus Mozart*, Grand Rapids, Mich.: Eerdmans, 1986.

Hildesheimer, Wolfgang, *Mozart*, New York: Vintage, 1983.

Küng, Hans, *Mozart: Traces of Transcendence* (Grand Rapids, Mich.: Eerdmans, 1991).

Steinberg, Michael P., "Mendelssohn and Judaism" in Peter Mercer-Taylor, ed., *Cambridge Companion to Mendelssohn*, Cambridge: Cambridge University Press, 2004.

Todd, R. Larry, *Mendelssohn: A Life in Music*, Oxford: Oxford University Press, 2003.

Robertson, Alec, *Requiem: Music of Mourning and Consolation*, London: Cassell, 1967.

Blumhofer, Edith W., and Noll, Mark A., *Singing the Lord's Song in a Strange Land: Hymnody in the History of North American Protestantism*, Tuscaloosa: University of Alabama Press, 2004.

Bradley, Ian C., *Abide with Me: The World of Victorian Hymns*, London: SCM Press, 1997.

Watson, J. R., *The English Hymn: A Critical and Historical Study*, Oxford: Oxford University Press, 1999.

Cone, James H., *The Spirituals and the Blues*, New York: Orbis Books, 1972.

Elliott, Graham, *Benjamin Britten: The Spiritual Dimension*, Oxford Studies in British Church Music, New York: Oxford University Press, 2006.

Heilbut, Anthony, *The Gospel Sound: Good News and Bad Times*, New York: Limelight Editions, 1985.

Powell, Mark Allan, *Encyclopaedia of Contemporary Christian Music*, Peabody, Mass.: Hendrickson, 2002.

Thompson, John J., *Raised By Wolves*, Chicago: ECW Press, 2000.

King, Roberta, *et al.*, *Music in the Life of the African Church*, Waco, Tex.: Baylor University Press, 2008.

Evans, Mark, *Open Up the Doors: Music in the Modern Church*, London: Equinox Publishing, 2006.

Zahn, Heinrich, *Mission and Music: Jabêm Traditional Music and the Development of Lutheran Hymnody*, Boroko, Papua New Guinea: Institute of Papua New Guinea Studies, 1996.

Thistlethwaite, Nicholas, and Webber, Geoffrey, eds, *The Cambridge Companion to the Organ*, Cambridge: Cambridge University Press, 1998.

Wills, Arthur, *Organ* (2nd ed.), London: Kahn and Averill, 1993.

🎵 Some Essential Recordings

European Sacred Music, 12th and 13th Centuries: Theatre of Voices, cond. Paul Hillier, Harmonia Mundi HMX 28907356.57.

Gregorian Chant: Salve Regina: Benedictine Monks of the Abbey of St Maurice and St Maur, Philips 420879-2.

A Feather on the Breath of God: Sequences and Hymns by Abbess Hildegard of Bingen: Gothic Voices with Emma Kirkby, dir. Christopher Page, Hyperion CDA 66039.

Pérotin: The Hilliard Ensemble, Hillier, ECM 837 752-2.

Guillaume Dufay, *Sacred Works*: Huelgas-Ensemble, cond. Paul van Nevel, Harmonia Mundi HMC 90 1700.

Ockeghem, *Missa Ecce ancilla, Ave Maria, Intemerata Dei Mater*: The Clerks' Group, Wickham, Proudsound PROU CD 133.

Josquin, *Josquin and his contemporaries*, Hyperion CDA 67183.

William Byrd, *The Great Service*: Choir of Westminster Abbey, cond. James O'Donnell, Hyperion CDA 67533.

Palestrina, *Missa Papae Marcelli*: Choir of Westminster Cathedral, cond. David Hill, Hyperion CDA 66266.

Thomas Tallis, *Spem in alium*: The Sixteen, cond. Harry Christophers, CORO Corsacd 16016.

Schütz, *Musikalische Exequien, Motetten und Konzerte*: The Monteverdi Choir, English Baroque Soloists, His Majesties Sagbutts and Cornetts, cond. Gardiner, Deutsche Grammophon Archiv 423 405-2.

Hymns Through the Centuries: Cathedral Choir Society of Washington, DC, J. Reilly Lewis, Aeolian Recordings, ADR6J002D.

Monteverdi, *Vespers*: Figueras, Fiehr, La Capella Real, Coro del Centro Musica Antica di Padova, cond. Savall, Astree E 8719: 2CDs.

Vivaldi, *Gloria*: Nelson, Kirkby, Choir of Christ Church Oxford, Academy of Ancient Music, cond. Preston, L'Oiseau-Lyre 414 678-2.

Pergolesi, *Stabat Mater; Salve Regina in C Minor*: Kirkby, Bowman, The Academy of Ancient Music, cond. Hogwood, L'Oiseau-Lyre 425 692–2.

Handel, *Messiah*: English Concert Choir, The English Concert, cond. Trevor Pinnock, Deutsche Grammophon Archiv 423 630-2.

Handel, *Solomon*: Watkinson, Argenta, Hendricks, Rodgers, Rolfe Johnson, Varcoe, Monteverdi Choir and English Baroque Soloists, cond. Gardiner, Philips 412 612–2: 2 CDs.

Bach, *St Matthew Passion*: Arnold Schoenberg Choir, Vienna Concentus Musicus, cond. Harnoncourt, Teldec 8573-81036-2.

Bach, *St John Passion*: Argenta, Holton, Rolfe Johnson, Varcoe, Hauptmann, Chance, Monteverdi Choir, cond. Gardiner, Deutsche Grammophon Archiv 419 324-2: 2 CDs.

Haydn, *Die Schöpfung* ("Creation"): Janowitz, Wunderlich, Krenn, Fischer-Dieskau, Berry, Vienna Singers, Berlin Philharmonic Orchestra, cond. Karajan, Deutsche Grammophon DG 435 077-2: 2 CDs.

Mozart, *Mass in C Minor*: McNair, Montague, Rolfe Johnson, Hauptmann, Monteverdi Choir, English Baroque Soloists, cond. Gardiner, Philips 420 21-2PH.

Mozart, *Requiem*: Bonney, von Otter, Blochwitz, White, Monteverdi Choir, English Baroque Soloists, cond. Gardiner, Philips 420 21-2PH.

Beethoven, *Missa Solemnis*: Janowitz, Ludwig, Wunderlich, Berry, Vienna Singverein, Berlin Philharmonic Orchestra, cond. Karajan, Deutsche Grammophon DG 423 913-2: 2 CDs.

Rossini, *Stabat Mater*: Lorengar, Minton, Pavarotti, Sotin, London Symphony Orchestra and Chorus, cond. Kertesz, Decca 417 766 2DM.

Verdi, *Requiem*: Dunn, Curry, Hadley, Plishka, Atlanta Symphony Chorus and Orchestra, cond. Shaw, Teldec CD80152.

Janáček, *Glagolitic Mass*: Söderström, Drobková, Livora, Novák, Czech Philharmonic, cond. Mackerras, Supraphon C37-7448.

Stravinsky, *Symphony of Psalms*: Suisse Romande Chamber Choir and Orchestra, cond. Järvi, Chandos CHAN 9239.

Britten, *War Requiem*: Harper, Langridge, Shirley-Quirk, London Symphony Orchestra and Chorus, cond. Hickox, Chandos CHAN 8983/4: 2 CDs.

Messiaen, *Quatuor pour la fin du Temps*: Chamber Music Northwest, Delos CD 3043.

Penderecki, *Polish Requiem*: Haubold, Winogradska, Terzakis, Smith; Polish Radio Symphony Orchestra, cond. Penderecki, Deutsche Grammophon DG 429 720-2: 2 CDs.

Because He Lives: Bill and Gloria Gaither, Spring House SPCN 7-474-05299-7.

The Art of Field Recording, Vol. 1: *Goodbye Babylon*, a 5-CD compilation of folk religious music from the early 1900s to the 1940s, Dust to Digital, Atlanta.

The Lost Music of Early America: Music of the Moravians by the Boston Baroque, Telarc CD-80482, issued 1998.

♫ Internet

Kassa, Jossi, http://www.youtube.com/watch?v=Cve6yEW1OFQ# One of the best worship videos from Ethiopia in Amharic.

Mission Driven, Save me Saviour (Forgive), http://www.youtube.com/watch?v=lTLzG1FH0xQ

Mission Driven Youtube Channel, http://www.youtube.com/user/missiondriven

Haazen, Father Guido, Missa Luba: Work Song, http://www.youtube.com/watch?v=fBfN3FX0BUQ

Notes

Chapter 1 Before the Church

1. See 1 Samuel 10:5, 1 Kings 1:40, Isaiah 5:12, 30:29, Jeremiah 48:36.

2. Also in 2 Kings 11:14, 12:13, and 2 Chronicles 5:12.

3. 1QM.

4. Tutankhamun's tomb was discovered in 1922. Among the treasures found in the tomb were two trumpets, one of silver and the other of copper. In 1939 a recording was made of a military bandsman playing the silver trumpet, which unfortunately shattered the instrument. You can hear part of this recording at: www.philharmonia.co.uk/thesoundexchange/the_orchestra/world_instruments/africa/trumpet.html

5. See also "the Sea of Kinnereth", Numbers 34:11, an alternative name for the Sea of Galilee.

6. Ivor Jones suggests that 1 Samuel 10:5 lists the regular instruments of the "Canaanite orchestra": namely, round-frame drum, double-reed V-shaped pipe (*aulos*), and lyre with an asymmetrical frame.

7. The harp has the neck attached directly to the body, but the lyre has a crossbar attached indirectly by means of two arms.

8. James Bennett Pritchard, *Ancient Near Eastern Texts Relating to the Old Testament*, Princeton: Princeton University Press, 1950, p. 288.

9. *Antiquities*, vii.12.3.

10. The Second Temple was built after the Babylonian captivity of the Jews and stood from 516 BC to AD 70.

11. For the obscure word *sumponyah* in Daniel 3, the scholar Ivor Jones prefers the translation "kettledrum" (some early translators suggested bagpipes, hurdy-gurdy, or dulcimer).

12. For a detailed discussion see T. C. Mitchell and R. Joyce, "The Musical Instruments in Nebuchadnezzar's Orchestra" in D. J. Wiseman, ed., *Notes on Some Problems in the Book of Daniel*, London: Tyndale Press, 1965, pp. 19–27.

13. Edward Foley, *Foundations of Christian Music: The Music of Pre-Constantinian Christianity*, Nottingham: Grove Books, 1992, p. 30.

14. Mishnah, *Tamid*, 5.

15. Exodus 15:1–19, 21.

16. John Arthur Smith, "Musical Aspects of Old Testament Canticles in Their Biblical Setting", in Iain Fenlon, ed., *Early Music*, vol. 17, Cambridge: Cambridge University Press, 1998, pp. 232–35.

17. Alexander Maclaren, *The Book of Psalms*, vol. 1, London and New York: Hodder and Stoughton, 1893.

18. *Tamid*, 7.4.

19. As General William Booth of The Salvation Army famously asked, on hearing a Salvationist sing "Bless His Name, He Set Me Free" to the tune of the Victorian music-hall ditty "Champagne Charlie is My Name": "Why should the devil have all the best tunes?"

20. Mishnah, *Tamid*, 7.3.

21. Johanan in *b. Megillah* 32a.

Chapter 2 Psalms and Hymns and Spiritual Songs

1. *b. Berak.* 32a.

2. Alexander Buchanan Macdonald, *Christian Worship in the Primitive Church*, Edinburgh: T. & T. Clark, 1934, p. 112.

3. Philo, *De Vita Contemplativa*, chapters 80ff.

4. The Rule of the Community, 1QS X, Florentino García Martínez, *The Dead Sea Scrolls Translated: The Qumran Texts in English*, Grand Rapids, Mich.: Eerdmans, 1994, p. 95.

5. Quoting, among other passages, Psalms 65:5, 139:14, 145:17, 86:9, 22:27.

6. Wilhelm Schubart and Carl Schmidt, eds and transl., *Acta Pauli*, Hamburg: J. J. Augustin, 1936, pp. 50–51.

7. Hanoch Avenary, "Jewish Music", *New Oxford Companion to Music*, Oxford: Oxford University Press, 1983, vol. 1, p. 955.

8. Ramsey MacMullen, *Christianity and Paganism in the Fourth to Eighth Centuries*, New Haven: Yale University Press, 1997, pp. 103ff.

9. *The New Oxford History of Music*, vol. 2, London: Oxford University Press, 1954, p. 2.

10. From earliest times Christians have sung as well as recited their theological convictions, a tradition that continued through succeeding centuries. For a full discussion of this hymn, see Robert H. Gundry, "The Form, Meaning and Background of the Hymn Quoted in 1 Timothy 3:16", in W. Ward Gasque and Ralph P. Martin, eds, *Apostolic History and the Gospel. Biblical and Historical Essays Presented to F. F. Bruce*, Exeter: Paternoster Press, 1970, pp. 203–22.

11. Ralph P. Martin, "Aspects of Worship in the New Testament Church", *Vox Evangelica*, 2, London, 1963, pp. 6–32.

12. Gordon D. Fee argues this passage is *not* a hymn in "Philippians 2:5–11: Hymn or Exalted Pauline Prose?", *Bulletin for Biblical Research*, 2, 1992, pp. 29–46.

13. Scholars have suggested the following additional passages as fragmentary Christian hymns: John 1:1–4; 1 Peter 1:18–21; 2:21–25; Revelation 5:9–10; 12:10–12; 19:1ff. For a full discussion of Colossians 1:15–20 see Ralph P. Martin, "An Early Christian Hymn – (Col. 1:15–20)", in *The Evangelical Quarterly*, 36, 1964, pp. 195–205.

14. W. S. Smith, *Musical Aspects of the New Testament*, Amsterdam: W. ten Have, 1962, pp. 43ff.

15. Gerald Abraham, *The Concise Oxford History of Music*, London: Oxford University Press, 1979, p. 54.

16. Known as "Pliny the Younger" to distinguish him from his more famous uncle, a noted Roman naturalist.

17. Betty Radice, transl., *The Letters of the Younger Pliny*, Harmondsworth: Penguin, 1963, p. 294; Ralph P. Martin, "A Footnote to Pliny's Account of Christian Worship", *Vox Evangelica*, 3, 1964, pp. 51–57.

18. Tertullian, *Apology*, 39:17–18, transl. S. Thelwall, in Alexander Roberts, James Donaldson, and A. Cleveland Coxe, eds, *Ante-Nicene Fathers*, vol. 3, Edinburgh: T. & T. Clark, 1885.

19. *Clement of Alexandria*, transl. William Wilson, in Alexander Roberts, James Donaldson, and A. Cleveland Coxe, eds, *Ante-Nicene Fathers*, vol. 2, Edinburgh: T. & T. Clark, 1885. Some scholars suggest this hymn is not by Clement but dates from earlier.

20. B. P. Grenfell and A. S. Hunt, eds, *The Oxyrhynchus Papyri*, part 15, London: Egypt Exploration Fund, 1922, pp. 21–25; Egon Wellesz, *Byzantine Music and Hymnography*, Oxford: Oxford University Press, 1949, pp. 125ff.

Chapter 3 The Church Goes Public

1. Robert A. Skeris, Χρομα Θεου, *Musicae Sacrae Melethmata*, vol. 1, Altötting: Coppenrath, 1976, p. 78.

2. John Chrysostom, *Discourses Against Judaizing Christians*, transl. Paul W. Harkins, Washington, DC: Catholic University Press, 1979, pp. 26–27.

3. Yet the same Basil condemned all stringed instruments except the psaltery, on the tortuous ground that their sound emanates from below the strings, making an analogy between the body of an instrument and the "passions of the flesh".

4. Ambrose, *On Psalm 1, Exposition 9*, transl. Erik Routley, *The Church and Music*, London: Duckworth, 1950, p. 129.

5. See page 33.

6. *The Pilgrimage of Etheria* (*Peregrinatio Etheriae*), rediscovered in Arezzo in Italy in the nineteenth century and first published in 1887 in an inadequate version. Now see John Wilkinson, *Egeria's Travels: Newly Translated*, Warminster: Aris and Phillips, 1999 (3rd edn.).

7. Egon Wellesz, *New Oxford History of Music*, vol. 2, Oxford: Oxford University Press, 1954, p. 1. Cf. E. Werner, "Preliminary Notes for a Comparative Study of Catholic and Jewish Musical Punctuation", *Hebrew Union College Annual*, 15, Cincinnati, 1940, p. 351.

8. Migne, *Patrologia Graeca*, 16:1017.

9. The term "Ambrosian" is used both for later hymns modelled on those of Ambrose – eight four-line strophes, with four iambic feet per line – and for other types of chant used in Milan.

10. Alexander Roberts and James Donaldson, eds, *Nicene and Post-Nicene Fathers*, vol. 1, Edinburgh: T. & T. Clark, 1885.

Music in the Orthodox Church

1. As with the Western modal system, the Byzantine modes exist in both authentic and plagal forms.

Chapter 4 Christian Chant

1. A. Z. Idelsohn, *Jewish Music and its Historical Development*, New York: Schocken Books, 1967, p. 47.

2. "*Laudes, hoc est Alleluja canere, canticum est Hebraeorum*": *ibid*, p. 61.

3. This continuing pattern of clergy versus laity, from pre-Christian Jewish psalm-chanting to modern priest-led worship, became a major issue of contention at various points in church history.

4. The catechumens – those being prepared for membership of the church – were dismissed with the Latin words *Ite, missa est*. The same words were used at the close of the service to dismiss the members. Hence the word "mass", a corruption of *missa*.

5. Ambrosian chant was still sung in the diocese of Milan in the mid-twentieth century.

6. The *Cento antiphonarius* attributed to Gregory consisted of 23 tracts (verses of Scripture to be sung direct), 110 graduals, 100 alleluias to be sung responsorially, 150 introits (sung at the beginning of the mass), 150 offertories (sung when the bread and wine are offered to God), and 150 communions (sung during the distribution of the eucharist).

7. Egon Wellesz defined the trope as an amplification, embellishment, or intercalation added in either words or music to Gregorian chant used in the authorized liturgy, and the sequence as a special kind of trope consisting of words only, or of words and music, or of music only, in the melismas attached to the melody of an alleluia.

"Sybil of the Rhine"

1. It has been suggested Hildegard suffered from migraines which stimulated these visions. Descriptions of her visions include classic migraine symptoms, such as seeing points of intense light, sickness, paralysis, and blindness.

Chapter 5 Medieval Polyphony

1. A plainchant hymn to John the Baptist, written by the Benedictine monk Paulus Diaconus (c. 720 – c. 799).

2. Once attributed to Hucbald of St Amand, and sometimes to Odo of Cluny (879–942).

3. See H. Davey, *History of English Music* (2nd ed., 1921) pp. 16–17 and P. Weiss and R. Taruskin, *Music in the Western World*, London, 1984, p. 69.

4. Léonin is said to have introduced this form: see p 67.

5. An English monk, possibly from Bury St Edmunds, studying at the University of Paris, and known to posterity – like some twentieth-century spy – as "Anonymous IV", said of Léonin: "He wrote the Great Book of Organa, for the Mass and the Office, to enlarge the divine service. This book was used until the time of the great Pérotin, who shortened it and rewrote many sections in a better way. Pérotin was the best composer of descant – he was even better than Léonin – and he wrote the best four-part organa, such as *Viderunt* and *Sederunt*, with the most ample embellishments of harmonic art."

6. See p. 72.

7. Alec Robertson, *Music of the Catholic Church*, London: Burns & Oates, 1961, p. 83. The reactionary bishop Cirillo Franco asked with a rhetorical flourish: "What the devil has music to do with the armed man or with the nightingale or with the duke of Ferrara?" (1549: *ibid*, p. 96.)

Chapter 6 The Music of the Renaissance

1. The melodic idea that began a new section of music was known as a *punctus* (point); the composer often set

these "points" against each other for different voice parts, *punctus contra punctum* ("point against point"), hence "counterpoint".

2. It is unclear where the epithet *"non Papa"* derives from, but it is possibly a joke.

3. The Flemish polyphonic composer Tielman (or Tylman) Susato (c.1510/15–70) set up the first music printing house in the Netherlands and published the enormously popular *Souterliedekens*.

4. The nineteenth-century scholar Giuseppe Baini published a monograph on Palestrina in 1828 that reinforced the legend of the "saviour of church music".

5. An often-repeated story, apparently originating from the Protestant martyrologist John Foxe, that Taverner at one point converted to Protestantism and did "repent him very much that he had made songs to popish ditties in the time of his blindness" (or that he became a fanatical persecutor of Catholics) has no evidential grounding.

6. The Latin text comes from the Sarum rite, and is adapted from the apocryphal book of Judith. The English translation begins: "I have never put my hope in any other but in you, O God of Israel…".

7. "Jerusalem, Jerusalem, convert to the Lord thy God."

Chapter 7 A Safe Stronghold

1. Luther's insistence on liturgical freedom helped to allow his own *Deutsche Messe* to fall into disuse in succeeding centuries.

2. A German translation was published by Michael Weiss in Moravia in 1531.

3. The hymn-book was printed in Nuremberg, though the title page states Wittenberg (centre of Luther's Protestant movement – now "Lutherstadt Wittenberg"), probably to gain greater acceptance.

4. While Petri had Catholic sympathies, Finno was a Lutheran Protestant.

5. There is some debate whether the collection should be attributed to Sweden or Finland. At the time of its first publication, Finland formed part of Sweden. The Finns see *Piae Cantiones* as the remnant of pre-seventeenth-century national music.

6. "Latin Songs of the Ancient Finnish Bishops and Church Superiors".

7. Grundtvig is also considered the father of Danish folk-schools.

Chapter 8 "In Quires and Places Where They Sing…"

1. P. Le Huray, *Music and the Reformation in England*, Cambridge: Cambridge University Press, 1978, p. 13.

2. Merbeck (also known as Marbeck) was convicted of heresy in 1543, but obtained a royal reprieve.

3. "Hymn" here means a metrical psalm.

4. His epitaph delightfully states he has "gone to that blessed place where only his harmony can be exceeded".

5. Full title: *Cathedral Music, Being a Collection in Score of the Most Valuable and Useful Compositions for That Service, by Several English Masters of the Last 200 Years.*

6. Wesley wrote a scathing exposé of contemporary English cathedral music, with proposals for its improvement: *A Few Words on Cathedral Music and the Musical System of the Church, with a Plan of Reform* (1849).

Oranges and Lemons

1. In England the "passing bell" and the "Nine Tailors" developed during the Middle Ages. The passing bell was rung when someone was *in extremis*, while the "Nine Tailors", made famous by Dorothy Sayers' detective novel of the same name, was played on a death. ("Tailor" is a corruption of "teller".) It involved sounding a large bell – nine times for a man, six for a woman, and three for a child – followed by one strike for each year of their age. In this way deaths were immediately announced to everyone within hearing.

Chapter 9 Psalms, Canticles, and Hymns

1. Epistle to the reader, in *La Forme des prières et chantz ecclésiastiques* ("The Form of Church Prayers and Hymns"), Geneva, 1542.

2. Calvin's first collection of psalm versions, *Aulcuns pseaulmes et cantiques mys en chant*, was published in 1539 during his exile in Strasbourg.

3. The name comes from its numbered position in Sternhold and Hopkins' collection (see below p.114).

4. Sternhold had already published his first collection of psalms, dedicated to Edward VI, in 1549; after Sternhold's death, Hopkins, a Suffolk minister, published another collection with thirty-seven of Sternhold's versions and seven of his own, in 1551, and further editions in the succeeding years, culminating in the influential 1562 edition.

5. The majority of hymns are written in a small number of metres, or syllable patterns. Most frequently encountered are: "common metre" (CM), 8.6.8.6 – a quatrain (four-line stanza) with alternate lines of iambic tetrameter and iambic trimeter, rhyming in the second and fourth lines and sometimes in the first and third; "long metre" (LM), 8.8.8.8 – a quatrain in iambic tetrameter, rhyming in the second and fourth lines and often in the first and third; and "short metre" (SM), 6.6.8.6 – with iambic lines in the first, second, and fourth in trimeter, and the third in tetrameter, rhyming in the second and fourth lines and sometimes in the first and third. Hymns written in a particular metre can be sung to any tune in that metre, providing the poetic foot (e.g. iambic or trochaic) also conforms. Most modern hymnals include a metrical index of tunes.

6. His unfortunate epithet derives from his skills in racking Catholics in the Tower of London.

7. It has been suggested this style of singing stretches back a long way, and a similar style predominated throughout Europe and in the early American colonies, before it was replaced by the regular beat and four-part harmony.

8. From a supplement first published in 1700.

9. Erik Routley suggested the alternative title "liberator of the English hymn".

10. See for instance part of the "Old Version" Psalm 102:

"By reason of my groaning voice/My bones cleave to my skin,/As pelican in wilderness/Such case now am I in…".

11. The collection included an improving poem, "Against Idleness and Mischief", with the opening lines, "How doth the little busy bee/improve each shining hour…", parodied by Lewis Carroll as "How doth the little crocodile/Improve his shining tail…" in *Alice's Adventures in Wonderland*.

12. Watts's original second line was "…where the young Prince of Glory died"; this was later altered to "…on which the Prince of Glory…".

13. Altered to the now familiar "O God, Our Help" by John Wesley. This hymn has become canonic, and is sung or played at times of British national crisis and remembrance.

14. Charles's and John's father, Samuel, rector of Epworth, Lincolnshire, spent years attempting to create a verse transposition of the book of Job.

15. The lyrics originally began: "Hark, How All the Welkin Rings".

16. The tunes in *The Beggar's Opera* were themselves borrowed from various sources.

17. Every line but two is found in *The Oxford Dictionary of Quotations*, Oxford: Oxford University Press, 1995.

18. This is not the only hymn that has gained popularity from its association with a Welsh tune: others include "What a Friend We Have in Jesus" ("Blaenwern"), "I Will Sing the Wondrous Story" ("Hyfrydol"), "Immortal, Invisible, God Only Wise" ("St Denio"), "Judge Eternal, Throned in Splendour" ("Rhuddlan"), and "Jesu, Lover of My Soul" ("Aberystwyth").

19. John Field and Thomas Wilcox, *Admonition to Parliament for the Reformation of Church Discipline*, London, 1571.

20. A tune which starts with all four voices singing in rhythmic and harmonic unity, but later has each voice enter successively and imitatively: a good example is the tune "Northfield" by the American hymn-writer Jeremiah Ingalls (1764–1828).

"Amazing Grace"

1. This stanza has often been credited to John P. Rees (1828–1900), but it was already in print by 1790, added to an old hymn, "Jerusalem, My Happy Home", in *A Collection of Sacred Ballads*, compiled by Richard and Andrew Broaddus.

2. Edwin O. Excell travelled the USA as a song-leader with the evangelist Sam P. Jones. Excell wrote more than 2,000 gospel songs and edited ninety song books, publishing hymn-books in Chicago with his company, the Bigelow–Main–Excell Company, which eventually merged with Hope Publishing Company of Wheaton, Illinois.

Chapter 10 *Gloria in Excelsis Deo*

1. Modal scales provided the musical material for plainsong and all other music until the present scales emerged toward the end of the seventeenth century. If you play the white notes from middle D for an octave on the piano, this is probably the oldest scale in Western music: the Dorian mode, the most popular scale of the medieval period. Similarly E to E on the white notes is the Phrygian mode, F to F the Lydian, and G to G the Mixolydian. Each of these scales contains a different arrangement of semitones and so sounds distinctive, even when transposed in pitch, as they frequently are.

2. Full title in English: "A mass of the most holy Virgin for six voices for church choirs and Vespers to be sung by more voices, with a few sacred songs suitable for the chapels and chambers of princes; a work by Claudio Monteverde[i] recently composed and dedicated to the most holy Pope Paul V".

3. A recent recording by the King's Consort revives this practice, with tenor and "pseudo-bass" sung by female soloists: Vivaldi, *Sacred Music*, vol. 6, 2001, Hyperion B000050X9O.

4. A fine *Magnificat in B flat* often attributed to Pergolesi is probably by Francesco Durante (1684–1755).

5. *Der für die Sünde der Welt gemarterte und sterbende Jesus* ("Jesus Tortured and Dying for the Sins of the World") by Berthold Heinrich Brockes (1680–1747).

6. Only three sections survive.

Christian Music in Latin America

1. The term "Latin" America is misleading since it designates only the European component in this region's population, ignoring the aboriginal ethnic groups.

2. The Spanish dominion was divided into two viceroyalties. New Spain (*Nueva España*), with Mexico City as its capital, included Mexico, Central America (except Panama), the Caribbean, portions of the present-day United States (California, New Mexico, Arizona, Texas, and Florida), and the Philippines. The viceroyalty of Peru, on the Pacific coast, with Lima as its capital, comprised the whole of South America (except Brazil and the Guianas), namely modern Venezuela, Colombia, Ecuador, Peru, Bolivia, Chile, Argentina, Uruguay, and Paraguay.

3. Steven Barwick, the American musicologist (d. 2006), pioneered the study of Mexican sacred polyphony with his 1949 doctoral dissertation at Harvard University. Three years later, Robert M. Stevenson wrote *Music in Mexico: A Historical Survey*, New York: Thomas Y. Crowell, 1952, the first book on the subject in English, and the first in a long series of books and articles essential for the study of Latin American music.

4. Although designated Baroque, the works show some of the traits of early Classical European music. Among its main composers were José Joaquim Emerico Lobo de Mesquita (1746–1805) and the Afro-Brazilian José Mauricio Nuñes García (1767–1830), the first to introduce secular music (*modinha*) in his church works.

5. The first complete mass in the twentieth century to use Latin American folk-music, written by the Argentinian composer Ariel Ramírez in 1963, bears the title *Misa Criolla* (*criollo* being the Spanish term for the French *créole*).

6. As Oscar Romero (1917–80), the Salvadorean bishop and martyr, put it 400 years later.

7. It is possible to listen to various versions of this *villancico* on YouTube.

8. Alice Corbin Henderson, *Southwest Crossroads, Cultures and Histories of the American Southwest.* (http://southwestcrossroads.org.record)

9. The award-winning film *The Mission* (Roland Joffé, 1986) depicts daily life in one of these *reducciones*, and highlights the conflicts between the Guarany people, the Spanish and Portuguese colonial governments, the Roman Catholic church, and the Jesuit missionaries.

10. So drastic was his transformation that only in 1941 was the Uruguayan musicologist Lauro Ayestarán able to show that "Brother" Domenico, in Córdoba, and "Maestro" Zipoli, in Italy, were one and the same person.

11. In 1959 Robert Stevenson was the first to find at Sucre in Bolivia copies of a mass attributed to Zipoli. Other works were found in 1968 by the Chilean Samuel Claro. The most important find was by a Swiss Jesuit, Hans Roth, in 1972, in Chiquitos, Bolivia: 2,500 pages that include the bulk of Zipoli's work in South America.

Chapter 11 Bach and Handel

1. When ordered by the church authorities to stop over-embellishing the hymns, he responded by stopping dead on the final chord.

2. Bach was only the third choice from a number of candidates, who included Telemann. One town councillor commented notoriously: "As the best are not available, I suppose we must take one of the second-rate men."

3. Also particularly well-known is "Jesu, Joy of Man's Desiring", the last movement of Cantata 147, *Herz und Mund* ("Heart and Mouth"), often performed today in an arrangement for piano solo.

4. The musicologist Wilfrid Mellers suggested Bach applied theological numerology to parts of the mass, for instance in the *Credo*, where he repeats a plainsong motif forty-three times, forty-three being the figure alphabet equivalent of the word *Credo*, and in the concluding *Gloria*, which consists of 129 bars: 3 (i.e. Trinity) x 43.

5. This has been questioned as of dubious authority, with the alternative suggestion that Handel was acting on grounds of economy and practicality. Handel never gave any hint after 1732 that he would have preferred a stage production of any of his oratorios.

6. *Solomon* includes the frequently excerpted "Arrival of the Queen of Sheba".

Chapter 12 The Viennese Tradition

1. The American composer Leonard Bernstein staged Haydn's work as a musical protest against the Vietnam War.

2. Wilfrid Mellers calls the libretto "a German translation of a rhymed rehash by Thomas Linley of bits of Milton's *Paradise Lost*, with addenda from the Old Testament": *Celestial Music*, Woodbridge: Boydell, 2002, p. 99.

3. It is alternatively suggested the epithet derives from the performance of this mass at the coronation of Emperor Leopold II in Prague in 1791.

4. The *Agnus Dei* in this mass is the prototype of the aria "*Dove sono*" in Mozart's opera *The Marriage of Figaro* (1786).

5. In extending the work well beyond the maximum duration of forty-five minutes required in Salzburg, Mozart was defying the Emperor Joseph II's restrictions on church music.

6. "*Von Herzen – möge es wieder – zu Herzen gehen*!" However, the scholar Lewis Lockwood has suggested that this inscription, rather than being addressed universally as has generally been understood, was a private message to the original patron, Archduke Rudolf (in *Beethoven: The Music and The Life*, London: W. W. Norton, 2003, p. 407).

Music in the Orthodox Church in Russia

1. Some scholars have proposed the transposition of some segments of the voices in order to arrive at a smoother sonority, but the question is far from settled.

Chapter 13 Heights of Intensity

1. It has been suggested that the success of *Elijah* deterred other composers from attempting similar oratorios; it was some time before a major composer wrote another work in this genre.

2. Jeffrey S. Sposato, *The Price of Assimilation: Felix Mendelssohn and the Nineteenth-Century Anti-Semitic Tradition*, Oxford: Oxford University Press, 2006.

3. The Rossini *Mass* was reassembled and performed in Stuttgart in 1988, and proved to be uneven in quality.

4. Tim Ashley, *The Guardian*, London, 25 August 2001.

5. Wagner elsewhere claimed that Jesus came from "the silent vegetarian communities founded by Pythagoras" (Derek Watson, *Richard Wagner, A Biography*, London: Dent & Sons, 1979, p. 302).

6. The work is not liturgical and not a *missa pro defunctis*; the critic Eric Blom suggested it might better be called "A *Protestant* Requiem".

7. Its title has been connected to the completion of German unification in 1871: Edwin Evans, *Handbook to the Vocal Works of Brahms*, New York: B. Franklin, 1970, p. 167.

8. In his 1950 essay "Brahms the Progressive".

9. "The Church Music", in Viktor Fischl, ed., *Antonín Dvořák: His Achievement*, Westport, Conn.: Greenwood Press, 1970, pp. 167–68.

10. The great Elgarian conductor Sir Adrian Boult considered *The Kingdom* Elgar's best religious work.

Chapter 14 Hymns Ancient and Modern

1. The hymn became notorious for its lines: "Though every prospect pleases/and only man is vile".

2. Like many hymns, it owes much to its habitual tune, in this case "Nicaea" by J. B. Dykes.

3. Suspicions that the tune was a Victorian invention (or "forgery") were disproved when a manuscript version was discovered by Dr Mary Berry in the 1960s.

4. The English hymns "The World is Very Evil", "Brief Life is Here Our Portion", and "O Sweet and Blessed Country" all derive from the same Latin source.

5. Neale wrote one verse which is today universally omitted: "Be Thou, O Lord, the rider,/and we the little ass,/That to God's holy city/Together we may pass."

6. Professor Bennett Zon of Durham University, England, claims that "*Adeste, fideles*", collected by John Francis Wade

NOTES

in his *Cantus diversi* (1751), refers to the desired restoration to the British throne of Charles Edward Stuart – "Bonnie Prince Charlie". In its earliest forms, from the 1740s to 1770s, "*Adeste, fideles*" is often found in Roman Catholic liturgical books next to, or near, prayers for the exiled prince; and in Wade's books it and other liturgical texts are often "strewn" with Jacobite imagery. Zon believes the poem was written to mark the pretender's birth on 20 December 1720, and *Adeste, fideles* actually means "Come, faithful Catholics"; *laeti triumphantes, venite, venite in Bethlehem* ("Joyful and triumphant, O come ye… to Bethlehem") means "Joyful and triumphant Jacobites, come to England", and "Born the king of angels" means "Born king of the English"! The poem lost its Jacobite meaning soon after 1773, as Jacobitism rapidly ebbed in popular consciousness.

7. The latter hymn is often sung to the tune "Shepton Beauchamp" – a more respectable name for the Somerset folk-tune "Tarry Trousers", collected by Cecil Sharp at the end of the nineteenth century.

8. Gauntlett is said to have written 10,000 hymn-tunes!

9. For many in the English-speaking world, Christmas commences with the Christmas Eve *Service of Nine Lessons and Carols* at King's College, Cambridge, broadcast to the world by the BBC. This service was devised by Archbishop Benson when Bishop of Truro, and later simplified and modified for use at Cambridge in 1918 by the then Dean of King's College, the Very Reverend Eric Milner-White.

10. Mrs Alexander also wrote the hymn for adults, "Jesus Calls Us O'er the Tumult".

Robbing the Devil of his Choicest Tunes

1. From the first *Order for Bands*, 1880.

In the Deep Midwinter

1. The refrain "*Nova! Nova! 'Ave' fit ex 'Eva'*" celebrates Mary as the "new Eve", as others celebrate Christ as the second Adam.

2. From *Geistliche Nachtigall der catholischen Teutschen* ("Spiritual Nightingale of the Catholic Germans") by David Gregor Corner (1585–1648), published in Vienna in 1649.

3. In an earlier, more sentimental, English version, "Little Jesus, sweetly sleep, do not stir/we will lend a coat of fur".

4. Today in parts of Yorkshire the tune "Cranbrook" (better known with the local words, "On Ilkla Moor baht 'at") is still invariably used.

5. Guillô and Robin are stock characters of Provençal carols who bring food to the manger.

6. For an over-enthusiastic and over-long refutation of the Luther claimants, see Richard S. Hill: "Not So Far Away In A Manger: Forty-One Settings of an American Carol", *Music Library Association Notes*, series 2, 3/1, December 1945. An apparently non-existent "R. Mueller" is also occasionally credited with the carol's authorship.

7. Printed by John Playford in *The English Dancing Master*, 1665.

8. The carol has also been set evocatively by the English composer Harold Darke (1888–1976).

The Legendary Story of "Silent Night"

1. Today Oberndorf boasts a Silent Night Memorial Chapel (*Stille-Nacht-Gedächtniskapelle*), built on the site of St Nicholas's Church, and a museum devoted to the carol.

2. *Silent Mouse*, a 1988 television drama-documentary narrated by Lynn Redgrave, tells the story of the carol from the mouse's viewpoint.

3. The first reference to a broken organ is apparently in a book published in the USA in 1909. One version of this story goes that the organ could not be mended before the snows melted and spring arrived.

Chapter 15 Camp Meetings and Revivals

1. Primitive Methodists in Britain held similar camps.

2. Ives entitled his own *Symphony No. 3 "The Camp Meeting"*, and its three movements "Old Folks Gatherin'", "Children's Day", and "Communion".

3. Lowry (1826–99) was a Baptist minister and editor at the influential Bigelow Publishing Company.

4. Full title: *Gospel Songs, A Choice Collection of Hymns and Tunes, New and Old, for Gospel Meetings, Prayer Meetings, Sunday Schools etc.* It was soon amalgamated with Sankey's collection: see p. 193.

5. Clephane's other well-known hymn is "Beneath the Cross of Jesus".

6. Brown wax cylinder recordings of Sankey singing some of his classic songs are available from www.tinfoil.com. It has been suggested that the melody of "There Were Ninety and Nine" may derive from an old Southern plantation song, "A Wonderful Stream is the River of Time".

7. Anna Warner also used the pen-name Amy Lothrop.

8. A parody version, "When This Bloody War is Over", was sung in the Allied trenches in the First World War, and featured in the stage show (1963) and film (1969) *Oh! What A Lovely War*.

Christian Music in Africa

1. Egypt is more related to the Arab world, though physically attached to Africa, and North Africa is predominantly Muslim.

2. This music is also related to the worship music of the Falasha Jews of the Ethiopian region.

3. Kay Kaufman Shelemay, "Zema: A Concept of Sacred Music in Ethiopia", *The World of Music*, 24/3, 1982, pp. 52–66; "The Great Ethiopian Composer: St Yared", Ayele Bekerie, http://www.erkohet.com/index. php?option=com_content&view=article&id=113:styared&c atid=47:smnuindexoffathers&Itemid=17

4. Plural; alternatively spelt "Debteroc".

5. To hear a traditional *Zema*, see http://www.youtube. com/watch?v=uzbRtnEJGk8

6. "Pente" is derived from the word "Pentecostal".

7. While many missionaries published their own hymnals, the Anglican Society for the Promotion of Christian Knowledge (SPCK), founded in 1698, was the most prolific in providing hymnals in many different African languages that widely became the staple of worship, regardless of

denomination. Other denominations followed with their own versions, including translated Western choruses.

8. Joyce Scott, *Tuning in to a Different Song: Using a Music Bridge to Cross Cultural Barriers*, Pretoria: University of Pretoria Institute for Missiological and Ecumenical Research, 2000.

9. To hear a selection from *Missa Luba*, cf. http://www.youtube.com/watch?v=fBfN3FX0BUQ

10. Tracy also developed a new instrument called the "kalimba".

11. See following chapter.

12. Trans-World Radio began Christian broadcasting in Tangier, Morocco, in 1954. The Far East Broadcasting Associates, based in the UK, broadcast regularly in Africa in the 1970s.

13. Earlier, African musical elements had returned to the continent with the South African tour of the American Fisk University Singers (singing black gospel music) in the late nineteenth century, and with touring jazz musicians.

Chapter 16 "I Got a Home in Dat Rock… "

1. *My Bondage and My Freedom*, New York, 1855, p. 87.

2. Transcribed by Elizabeth Poston from a field recording of Ella Mitchell and Velma Wright in Texas, 1937.

3. First published in William Francis Allen, Charles Pickard Ware, and Lucy McKim Garrison, eds, *Slave Songs of the United States*, New York: A. Simpson, 1867.

"Nkosi Sikelel' iAfrika"

1. In 1996, Sontonga's grave, in Braamfontein cemetery, Johannesburg, was declared a national monument and a memorial was unveiled on the site by Nelson Mandela.

Chapter 17 Apocalypse Now!

1. Wilfrid Mellers offers a lengthy analysis of this work in *Celestial Music*, Woodbridge: Boydell Press, 2002, pp. 223–29.

2. Charles Ives' father, George, was the youngest bandmaster in the Union Army during the American Civil War.

3. Ives' *Sixty-Seventh Psalm* (1898) was written in C for the sopranos and altos, and in B flat for the tenors and basses.

4. Vera Stravinsky and Robert Craft, *Dialogues and a Diary*, Garden City: Doubleday, 1962, p. 64.

5. *Ibid*, p. 295.

6. *Ibid*, pp. 77–78.

7. *Ibid*, pp. 123–24.

8. *Ibid*, p. 125.

9. Robert Craft, "1949, Stravinsky's *Mass*, a Notebook", from Edwin Cole, ed., *Igor Stravinsky*, New York: Duell, Sloan, and Pearce, 1949, p. 206.

10. Stravinsky and Craft, *op. cit.*, p. 31.

11. In 2004, BBC 4 viewers in the UK voted it the "saddest classical work".

12. Bernstein recycled some material in this work from early sketches for his musical *West Side Story*.

13. Conductors such as Kent Nagano and Marin Alsop have worked hard to restore serious consideration of this work.

14. Messiaen managed to take with him copies of Bach's *Brandenburg Concertos* together with scores by Ravel, Beethoven, Berg, and Stravinsky. The camp commandant gave him manuscript paper.

15. Wilfrid Mellers offers a lengthy analysis of this work: *op. cit.*, pp. 204–17.

Christian Music in Latin America Since 1800

1. A similar situation is occurring today in relation to the "Praise Music" movement in Latin America, as in other parts of the world.

2. The first American Protestant hymnal in Spanish was edited in Mexico (1875) by a British Baptist missionary, Thomas Westrup (1837–1909), closely followed by one published in Buenos Aires, Argentina, (1876) by a Methodist missionary from the USA, Henry Jackson (1838–1914). From then on the production of hymnals was centralized by missionary societies in the USA and distributed from there to the rest of the continent.

3. The Instituto Universitario ISEDET (Protestant Institute for Higher Theological Studies), at Buenos Aires, Argentina, has been the centre of important work among the Qom (Toba) people in the north-eastern province of Chaco.

4. "*Pueblo que no celebra no se libera*" ("People who do not celebrate do not liberate themselves") is a popular saying among leftist Latin American Christians.

5. Translated by Casiodoro de Reina (1569) and Cipriano de Valera (1602).

6. *Cancionero Abierto*, vols 1–6, Buenos Aires: School of Music, Instituto Universitario ISEDET, 1974–90.

7. Evelyn Harper (1899–1989), Albert Ream (b. 1912?), and Norah Buyers (b. 1921) should be mentioned among those in Brazil.

8. The three main masses are: *Misa Popular Nicaragüense*, collective work, Nicaragua, 1968; *Misa Campesina Nicaragüense*, Carlos Mejía Godoy, Nicaragua, 1975; and *Misa Popular Salvadoreña*, Donna Peña and Guillermo Cuéllar, El Salvador, 1980. Despite being one of the most accomplished masses, the *Misa Campesina* has never been authorized for public worship by the Roman Catholic authorities.

9. *Quilombos* were settlements established by runaway slaves during the Portuguese colonial period.

Chapter 18 "Surely Goodness and Mercy Shall Follow Me"

1. Other significant hymnals published in this period include *Songs of Syon* (1904), edited by the Tractarian priest George W. Woodward, and the *Yattendon Hymnal* (1899), edited by the Poet Laureate Robert Bridges.

2. Ralph Vaughan Williams, Cecil Sharp, and others collected many English folk-songs from around the country to preserve an oral tradition that all but died out in the twentieth century.

3. Formerly a singer in William Booth's fledgling Salvation Army, Smith was summarily ejected after his wife accepted a small gift.

4. Miles also wrote under the pen-name A. A. Payn.

5. Similar "choruses" appeared in Britain in the 1920s and 1930s, often associated with the Keswick Convention Christian growth movement. Three books of Children's Special Service Mission (CSSM) and Scripture Union *Choruses* appeared between 1921 and 1939, with music owing much to the Victorian music-hall.

6. Singspiration, a movement started by Smith, grew to become another major US music corporation, owned for a time by Zondervan Inc., and subsequently part of Brentwood-Benson – "the world's no. 1 Christian music catalog".

7. Matthew 6:3.

8. From the Greek meaning "Our Lord, come!" (1 Corinthians 16:22).

9. Kendrick's signature song, "Shine, Jesus, Shine", is among the most frequently sung worldwide.

10. Richard J. Mouw, in Richard J. Mouw and Mark A. Noll, eds, *Wonderful Words of Life* (Grand Rapids, Mich.: Eerdmans, 2004), p. xiii.

"How Great Thou Art"

1. English-language hymn-books entitle the tune "*O Store/Sture Gud*".

2. A British army camp in India, and source of the British slang term "doolally" or "doolally tap" (corruption of Deolali), meaning camp fever, and hence eccentric or mad.

Chapter 19 "(Give Me That) Old Time Religion"

1. Fisk Free Colored School, set up in 1866; it was incorporated as Fisk University the following year. The epithet "jubilee" is from Leviticus 25, the year of jubilee representing restoration and the cancellation of debts.

2. Or sometimes "Walking in Jerusalem (Just Like John)". In the 1960s this song, like "Didn't My Lord Deliver Daniel?", was adopted by the Civil Rights Movement.

3. A. R. Shockly is sometimes jointly credited with writing this hymn, which first appeared in *New Songs of the Gospel* (1901). Others argue the Civil Rights song derives from an eighteenth-century melody, "Prayer of the Sicilian Mariners", published as "*O Sanctissima*" (1794), and yet others that its lyrics derive from a slave song, "I'll Be All Right". "We Shall Overcome" is copyrighted jointly by Zilphia Horton, Pete Seeger, Frank Hamilton, and Guy Carawan.

4. Also known as "Take My Hand, Precious Lord".

5. http://www.youtube.com/watch?v=Nz3gc55-mJQ, http://www.youtube.com/watch?v=fQGfY73bAdI&feature=related

6. http://www.youtube.com/watch?v=4xzr_GBa8qk

7. Brewster (1897–1987) wrote more than 200 songs, generally more theologically complex than Dorsey's, a number of them gospel standards.

8. An urban legend has it that on occasion their wigs touched the ceiling.

9. Interview with Nick Salvatore, author of *Singing in a Strange Land: C. L. Franklin, the Black Church, and the Transformation of America*, (Little, Brown & Co, New York,

2005) Jerry Jazz Musician, 2005.

10. http://www.youtube.com/watch?v=JixcK3w9bHY&feature=related, http://www.youtube.com/watch?v=3BBPDMVWAhM&feature=related

11. http://www.youtube.com/watch?v=EBB4-_mo2Dw

Chapter 20 "I Wish We'd All Been Ready"

1. Steve Turner, *Hungry for Heaven*, London: Hodder and Stoughton, 1995, pp. 216–17.

2. "But we have this treasure in jars of clay to show that this all-surpassing power is from God and not from us" (2 Corinthians 4:7, NIV).

3. The poet Allen Ginsberg spoke in 1975 of Dylan's "songs of redemption".

Christian Music in Australia and New Zealand

1. There is evidence that Tasman (1642) and Cook (1768) regularly conducted religious services aboard their ships, and sounds from these would have drifted across the sea toward land. The Dutch explored the area before the landing of Cook and his successors, who brought strong hymn traditions with them.

Chapter 21 "Ain't Nobody Nowhere Nothin' without God"

1. Steve Turner, *The Man Called Cash*, London: Bloomsbury, 2006, p. 294.

2. "Jonathan", originally from Oxford in England, also formed a 1960s group called the Excursions. He went on to become an Anglican minister in the USA, the Revd Dr John Guest.

3. Stookey assigned the copyright for this song to the Public Domain Foundation, which has donated more than $1.5 million to charitable causes: http://www.youtube.com/watch?v=T4_x24cVHr8

4. A church in Coltrane's name – initially named the One Mind Temple Evolutionary Transitional Church of Christ, then the St John Will-I-Am African Orthodox Church, and finally the Church of St John Coltrane, was set up in San Francisco (where else?) in 1971 by Bishop Franzo King.

Christian Music in China

1. The first collection of hymns was published in 1818 and contained thirty items, with a poetic Chinese title meaning "Godly Hymns That Nourish the Heart". All were English hymns translated into Chinese.

2. Reprinted as *Great Hymns and Hymn Writers*, Hong Kong: Council on Christian Literature for Overseas Chinese, 1955.

3. He was trained at Westminster Choir College, New Jersey, USA.

4. *The Songs of Canaan,* more than 1,000 of them by a single author, Xiao Min: a number of these songs were orchestrated by the well-known composer Huang Anlun and recorded to circulate beyond China.

Index

Acknowledgments

Alamy: pp. 13, 16 www.BibleLandPictures.com;
p. 25 The Art Archive; pp. 28, 47 The Art Gallery
Collection; pp. 34, 38 Classic Image; pp. 48, 148
imagebroker; pp. 52, 171 Mary Evans Picture Library;
p. 57 Alex Ramsay; p. 59 WoodyStock; p. 62 LianeM;
pp. 65, 99 Interfoto; p. 81 Tim Moore; p. 87 Wolfgang
Kaehler; p. 93 bilwissedition Ltd. & Co. KG;
p. 95 Mike Booth; p. 100 Paul S. Bartholomew;
p. 106 The Print Collector; p. 109 Rod McLean;
p. 115 World History Archive; p. 116 Rolf
Richardson; pp. 153 Lebrecht Music and Arts Photo
Library; p. 167 Martin Pick; p. 169 Stock Connection
Blue; pp. 179, 192 North Wind Picture Archives;
p. 187 B. O'Kane; p. 193 Photos 12; p. 210 Stuart
Corlett; p. 212 Frymire Archive; p. 215 Art Directors
& TRIP; p. 224 Pictorial Press Ltd

Art Archive: p. 12 Museo del Prado Madrid/Gianni
Dagli Orti; pp. 30, 139, 143, 155 Bibliothèque des Arts
Décoratifs Paris/Gianni Dagli Orti; p. 36 Byzantine
Museum Athens/Alfredo Dagli Orti; p. 50 Rossini
Conservatoire Bologna/Gianni Dagli Orti;
p. 54 British Library; p. 58 Nicolas Sapieha;
p. 78 San Pietro Maiella Conservatoire Naples/
Gianni Dagli Orti; p. 112 Stei am Rein Switzerland;
p. 145 Osterreichisches Galerie, Vienna/Harper
Collins Publishers; p. 150 Carolino Augusteo
Museum Salzburg/Gianni Dagli Orti; pp. 152, 163
Society Of The Friends Of Music Vienna/Alfredo
Dagli Orti; p. 156 Museo Bibliografico Musicale
Bologna/Alfredo Dagli Orti; p. 157 Schubert
Museum Vienna/Alfredo Dagli Orti; p. 160 Galleria
d'Arte Moderna Rome/Alfredo Dagli Orti;
p. 161 Museo di Milano Italy/Alfredo Dagli Orti;
p. 173 Salvation Army/Eileen Tweedy;
p. 189 W. Robert Moore/NGS Image Collection;
p. 192 Superstock; p. 196 Culver Pictures;
p. 207 Kharbine-Tapabor; p. 218 The Kobal Collection

Bridgeman: pp. 62, 92, 104, 159, 216; p. 27
Cryptoportico (photo),/Catacombs of Priscilla, Rome,
Italy; p. 29 Vatican Museums and Galleries, Vatican
City, Italy; p. 33 Boltin Picture Library; p. 41 The
Barnes Foundation, Merion, Pennsylvania, USA;
pp. 42, 69, 85, 206 Giraudon; pp. 53, 158 Roger-
Viollet, Paris; p. 70 Notre-Dame de Valere, Sion,
Switzerland; p. 72 Galleria degli Uffizi, Florence, Italy;
pp. 76, 146 Bonhams, London, UK; p. 80 Private
Collection; p. 91 Swann Auction Galleries; p. 96 The
Cobbe Collection Trust, UK; p. 103 O'Shea Gallery,
London, UK; p. 107 Forbes Magazine Collection, New

York, USA; p. 125 Peter Newark American Pictures;
p. 128 Alinari; p. 170 National Portrait Gallery,
London, UK; p. 174 Look and Learn;
p. 176 DACS; p. 214 Mallett Gallery, London, UK;
p. 245 Ken Welsh

Corbis: pp. 9, 75, 238 Atlantide Phototravel; pp. 10, 67,
85, 102 The Gallery Collection; p. 18 Hanan Isachar;
p. 24 Mimmo Jodice; p. 26 Brooklyn Museum;
pp. 27, 39 Alinari Archives; pp. 34, 121, 244 Bettmann;
p. 35 Abir Sultan/epa; p. 37 Jon Hicks; p. 46 Jose
Fuste Raga; p. 49 Shai Ginott; pp. 56, 79 David
Clapp/Arcaid; p. 68 Pascal Deloche /Godong;
p. 84 Dave Bartruff; p. 86 Fine Art Photographic
Library; p. 97 Dallas and John Heaton/Free Agents
Limited; p. 101 Barrett & MacKay/All Canada
Photos; p. 110 Christopher Cormack; p. 111 H. P.
Merten/Robert Harding World Imagery;
p. 113 Salvatore di Nolfi/epa; p. 117 Lebrecht
Authors/Lebrecht Music & Arts; p. 120 Burstein
Collection; p. 123 Rick Friedman; p. 130 Alain
Lecocq/Sygma; p. 132 Peter Adams; p. 133 Bojan
Brecelj; p. 136 Svenja-Foto; p. 165 Michael Nicholson;
p. 182 Chris Hellier; p. 186 Euan Denholm/X01999/
Reuters; p. 197 Marvin Koner; p. 221 Phillipe Lissac/
Godong; p. 223 Hulton-Deutsch Collection;
p. 235 Aaron Crisler/Retna Ltd; pp. 240, 246 Walter
Bibikow/JAI; p. 241 Michael Ochs Archives

David Alexander: p. 15

Getty Images: pp. 100, 185, 229, 236; p. 15 Alistair
Duncan; p. 220 Godong; pp. 226, 231 Michael Ochs
Archives; p. 228 Time & Life Pictures;
p. 233 WireImage

Lebrecht: pp. 11, 53, 73, 82, 89, 90, 95, 105, 127, 130,
135, 140, 141, 144, 155, 175, 178, 195; p. 17 Z. Radovan;
pp. 31, 134, 149, 154 Interfoto; pp. 45, 55, 188
Leemage; pp. 64, 124, 244 NYPL Performing Arts;
pp. 83, 138 ColouriserAL; p. 126 TL; pp. 180, 181,
190 North Wind; p. 198 Horst Tappe;
p. 199 S. Lauterwasser; p. 201 Neil Libbert;
p. 205 Richard Haughton; p. 208 F. Henderson;
p. 209 JazzSign; p. 219 Chris Stock;
p. 237 D. Hunstein; p. 242 Laurie Lewis

Tim Dowley: pp. 20, 99, 123